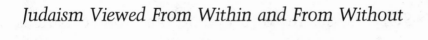

Judaism Viewed From Within and From Without

SUNY Series in Anthropology and Judaic Studies

Walter P. Zenner, Editor

Judaism Viewed from Within and From Without

Anthropological Studies

Edited and with introductions by
HARVEY E. GOLDBERG

State University of New York Press

Chapter 4 of the present work appeared in a slightly different version in *The Anthropology of Experience*, edited by James W. Turner and Edward Bruner, copyright 1986 by the Board of Trustees of the University of Illinois.

Parts of chapter 9 of the present work appeared in *Studies in Judaism and Islam*, edited by Shlomoh Morag, Issachar Ben-Ami, and Norman Stillman, Jerusalem, Magnes Press, 1981, pp. 293–345.

Published by
State University of New York Press, Albany

For information, address State University of New York
Press, State University Plaza, Albany, N.Y., 12246

Library of Congress Cataloging-in-Publication Data
Judaism viewed from within and from without.

  (SUNY series in anthropology and Judaic studies)
  Includes index.
  1. Jewish law—Interpretation and construction. 2. Judaism—United States. 3. Jews—United States—Social conditions. 4. Judaism—Israel. 5. Anthropology. I. Goldberg, Harvey E. II. Series.
BM520.2.J83   1986   306'.6   86-5877
ISBN 0-88706-354-3
ISBN 0-88706-356-X (pbk.)

To the memories of
Vietor Turner
and
Barbara Myerhoff—
colleagues, teachers, and friends

Contents

Preface

The idea for this book was first suggested by Victor Turner during his visit to Jerusalem in 1980 as guest of the Israel Anthropological Association. Some of the papers presented at that occasion form the kernel of the present work. The project was given impetus by Barbara Myerhoff's visit a year later, and began to take final shape during a second visit to Israel by Vic and Edie Turner during the first half of 1983.

The completion of this volume has been inspired by the extraordinary combination of warmth and incisiveness that these scholars shared. Vic, bringing an extensive exposure to, and sensitivity toward, many of the world's religions was to have written the epilogue to this volume, but his untimely death left that task undone. Barbara, whose commitment to the study of Jews and Judaism followed a penetrating involvement in a Native American culture, continued to encourage this project throughout her own illness. Each, in a characteristic manner, showed the importance of viewing a tradition from without and from within, and it is to the memories of Vic and of Barbara that this work is dedicated.

In the initial stages of the project I was assisted by a selection committee consisting of Shlomo Deshen, Don Handelman, and Haim Hazan. The introduction, at different stages of its development, was read by various colleagues and teachers, including Virginia Dominguez, Moshe Greenberg, David Weiss Halivini, Don Handelman, and Ismar Schorsch. Gershon Bacon was kind enough to go over the section introductions with a historian's eye. The final product also benefited considerably from the comments of several anonymous reviewers, and from the editorial skills of Haim Goldgraber which were combined with a keen appreciation of the subject. I am grateful for all the advice

ix

received: that which was incorporated into the work and that which I am still considering.

Edgar Siskin of the Jerusalem Center for Anthropological Studies made a grant available for translation, editing, and the final preparation of the manuscript. It is my hope that the volume will serve as a tribute to his concern for, and support of, the fields of anthropology and Jewish studies.

Judy, my wife, helped me in more ways than I can tell. Her participation has taught me that the phrase *'ezer k'negdo* (Genesis 2:20), which the rabbis knew could be understood in different ways, has yet to exhaust its plenitude of meanings.

The field created by the intersection of Judaic studies and anthropology has grown since this project was initiated, and the volume in no way pretends to be representative of the present state of work underway, except insofar as it points to manifold possibilities of future research. The focus on contemporary Jewish communities in the United States and Israel reflects the limitations of space, and the fact that these are the largest extant concentrations of Jews today. Anthropologically informed studies of Jewish topics appear to be developing in France, and one hears of clandestine attempts to document Jewish life in the Soviet Union.

The papers presented herein vary in the extent to which they refer to Judaic texts, not all of which are available in translation. References to a number of these works, which have their own traditional system of citation, have been confined to the notes, while publications which can be fit into standard citation formats may be found in the references sections. A glossary of some of the Judaic concepts mentioned has been provided, but this, of necessity, meets a limited purpose. Fuller information is available in many of the English-language studies cited, as well as in reference sources such as the *Encylopedia Judaica* (New York: MacMillan, 1971). This work has been abbreviated as EJ, while BT refers to the Babylonian Talmud.

In transcribing words from Hebrew (or Yiddish, or Arabic), there has been an attempt to steer a course between conventional English-language forms and linguistic precision, and to present standard terms or dialectical forms, as required by the situation. Arbitrary choices have been made which will not please the purist, but the newcomer may find some guidance in the glossary.

Introduction: Reflections on the Mutual Relevance of Anthropology and Judaic Studies

HARVEY E. GOLDBERG

In recent years a growing number of anthropologists have turned their attention to the study of Jewish life and have widened, thereby, the scope of Jewish studies. To those unfamiliar with these disciplines in their modern forms, this combination of perspectives may seem surprising. Classically, anthropology has dealt with remote tribal cultures having no written language. Investigation of these cultures has therefore involved the prolonged exposure of a researcher to the way of life of natives far from the researcher's own familiar society. Judaism, on the other hand, has meant the study of a traditional civilization, whose hallmark is the sacred scriptures and writings based on them, and is normally researched by scholars pouring over texts in libraries and archives. An appreciation of contemporary concerns within both realms of scholarship, however, will reveal areas of mutual relevance in which anthropology may enrich Judaic studies and where anthropological understanding can benefit from a consideration of Jewish history and culture.

A brief glance at the history of anthropology shows a consistent expansion in the sphere of its concerns. While early researchers in American anthropology were mainly oriented toward documenting the vanishing way of life of indigenous North American societies, it was formally decided, in the 1930s, that the acculturation of these groups into the wider society was a legitimate and important area of study

1

(Redfield, Linton, and Herskovits 1935). After World War II, anthropology became squarely involved with many of the countries of the
third world, including some which boasted written traditions that were
centuries, or even millennia, old. Anthropologists still continued to
carry out most of their work in villages and small towns, but it became
apparent that in order to understand these communities in their wider
context, an appreciation of a society's past and its major cultural con-
tours was imperative. The challenge of relating simultaneously to a
great tradition such as Islam or Buddhism, embodied in historical texts,
and to a little tradition, manifested in daily village life, thus became part
of the anthropological program (Redfield 1956, Chap. 3). This challenge
is particularly sharp in the case of Judaism.

It is by no means a new development that social scientists have
trained their attention to Jewish topics. Central figures in the history of
social thought have attempted to incorporate Judaism within the purview of their theories. Frazer (1918) labored to show how the cross-
cultural study of folklore could illuminate books of the Old Testament,
and Durkheim (1912) made systematic reference to biblical material in
his discussion of the division of labor in society. Max Weber's (1952)
analysis of ancient Judaism placed it within the framework of the comparative study of religion and civilizations that he was developing. Yet,
despite these important efforts on the part of scholars who helped
shape contemporary anthropology, the study of Judaism has remained
relatively isolated from advances in that discipline.

A number of reasons may be advanced for this isolation. Stated
rather directly, the new approaches were often not complimentary to
Jewish religion and culture. Anthropological theory, when it first
developed in the nineteenth century, concentrated on what it called
"primitive culture," "primitive thought," and so forth, with the implicit
notion that certain methods of analysis were especially fitted to those
types of society. Accepting these methods as relevant therefore meant
acquiescing to the evaluation of Judaism as primitive. Even when
Judaism was placed in a broader historical or developmental framework, as was characteristic of most social theorizing in the nineteenth
century, it was often portrayed as representing an early stage of
religious evolution, implicitly ignoring its development over the centuries or denying its possible appropriateness as a contemporary religion. In addition, broad conceptual schemes were often put forth by
scholars who did not have the necessary linguistic tools to examine
Jewish textual and historical materials first hand, so that specialists in

the field, particularly those with an attachment to Judaism, had ample reason to studiously ignore them.[1] It is therefore not difficult to see why various approaches to comparative religion at first evoked a hardened uninterest on the part of students of Jewish tradition.

The lack of attention to advances within anthropology on the part of Judaic scholars had another, more subtle source, this being the difficulty inherent in dealing with the topic of religion. One of the main contributions of the modern study of Judaism was to show that classic texts, which had been viewed over the centuries as sacred, could be seen as social, political, or economic documents and placed in historical perspective. At the same time that this enabled a more sophisticated understanding of the growth (and decline) of different strands of Jewish civilization, it simultaneously permitted researchers to ignore religious questions per se. The concentration on topics, such as the dating of texts, determining their authorship, or understanding them in their social-historical contexts, often allowed scholars to skirt around the *content* of religious life because this was difficult to discuss objectively. There was a hesitancy to attempt the direct interpretation of ritual and other symbolic systems because they were considered to be intractable to disciplined study.

The study of symbolic systems, however, has become central in the theoretical effort of anthropology during the past generation. While terminology varies among scholars and schools of thought, the word "symbol" is used by many to mean any representation that is important in human life whether the object represented derives from the natural world, intrapsychic dynamics, social processes, or experiences and conceptions of the numinous. In sharpening its tools for the analysis of systems, including, of course, religious systems, anthropology has borrowed from fields such as linguistics, literary criticism, drama, and so forth, thereby contributing to new approaches known variously as "structuralist," "semiotic," "hermeneutic," and the like. Insofar as this new theoretical thrust does not ignore the more solid concepts that anthropology shares with other social sciences, and links the realm of symbols and meaning to economic trends, social stratification, or political struggle, the way is paved for a deepened understanding of the historical experiences of all societies, whether tribal, traditional, or modern.

Bolstered by these new theoretical perspectives, an attempt will be made to explore fruitful linkages between Jewish studies and anthropology using the following format. First, trends will be indicated within

Jewish studies which appear compatible with contemporary emphases
in anthropological inquiry. The discussion will be illustrated by reference to biblical studies, highlighting convergences between textual interpretation and theoretical approaches, such as the research metaphor
which sees cultures as texts. It will be argued, among other points, that
it is now possible to surmount some of the barriers that kept Judaic
scholars from attending to the contributions of comparative religion.
This will lead to a discussion of religion and the study of symbols in
contemporary anthropological thought which makes such integration
possible. Examples of anthropologically inspired contributions to
Jewish studies will be cited, and it shall be claimed that Jewish studies
can benefit from anthropological insights, while also arguing that the
science of man may be enriched by the consideration of Jewish civilization. Here, the prominence of text in social life, and the linkage between text and ritual, or other kinds of performance, are salient. This
study will conclude with an appeal for greater interchange between
scholars whose forte is textual/historical analysis and text-sensitive
researchers in the social sciences.

Biblical Studies and Anthropological Theory

The Study of the Bible and Anthropological Concepts

An attempt will be made to expose some common ground of interest to both students of anthropology and Judaica by citing examples
concerning the Bible. The biblical text represents that product of Jewish
civilization which has received tremendous attention, both from Jews
and non-Jews. The very referral to the Bible as part of *Jewish* civilization
hints at an ideological problem (which may effect scholarship), as to
where the true continuation of biblical society and religion is to be
found. The Christians' assertion that they were the true Israel was
rebutted by most Jews, and both Christians and Jews rejected Moham-
mad's claim to be the "seal of the prophets." Needless to say, one's
overall orientation to the biblical text affects the way specific verses
and chapters[2] are understood, and this holds true with regard to modern
literary/historical research as it did in the case of religiously motivated
scholarship over the centuries.

In a useful volume by Hahn (1966), some of the major modern approaches to the study of the Bible are outlined and evaluated. One chap-

ter deals with the influence of anthropology on biblical studies, referring to the impact of scholars such as Frazer, W. R. Smith (1914), and Hubert and Mauss (1964). In addition to specific instances where anthropological concepts have been applied to biblical material, one can point to similar formulations of general method that have appeared in the study of culture and the study of Judaism. In both instances there was a shift from the major paradigm of the nineteenth century, which stressed development and evolution, to the more particularistic and in-depth appreciation of particular cases with their own specific patterning, which characterizes contemporary work.

Evolutionary thinking was embedded in the higher criticism of the biblical text, associated most prominently with the name of Wellhausen (1885). Wellhausen showed how the text may be separated into sources, and also suggested ways for the dating of the different sources. A basic assumption in the process of dating was that biblical religion underwent a clear process of evolution in which literary prophecy (such as that of Isaiah and Jeremiah) stood at the pinnacle. Almost by definition, no literature from before that date could exhibit this most advanced stage of ethical monotheism. This caused Wellhausen to conclude that much of the legal and ritual material in the Pentateuch, which reflected a monotheistic view, must have been written *after* the period of classic literary prophecy (a theory which stood in opposition to the time-honored notion of Mosaic authorship of the whole Pentateuch). It thus became a "basic tenet of the critical view of the history of Israelite religion that no monotheistic literature dates to the pre-prophetic period" (Kaufmann 1960, 153).

Challenges to Wellhausen's theory, formulated during the present century, dovetail with the arguments developed against nineteenth-century evolutionism and diffusionism[3] in anthropology, although there does not seem to have been any direct influence between these scholarly trends. Kaufmann (1960, 60ff.) argued that the monotheistic outlook, which pervades the biblical text, was an original Israelite creation, a world view which characterized this religion from the outset. In a manner that appears familiar to the readers of *Patterns of Culture* (Benedict 1934), he shows that individual passages and episodes in the Bible must be comprehended within the *gestalt* that informs biblical literature as a whole, in spite of its individual similarities to non-Israelite materials discovered by archeologists. The different literary strands (the Priestly Code, Deuteronomy, and so on) within the Bible do not reflect more or less advanced monotheism,[4] but all reflect the same basic religious values. Just as Boas (1896) demonstrated that one could not know a priori, on the basis of an evolutionary theory, which cultural traits appeared first in actual historical sequence, so Kaufmann argued that evolutionary assumptions are not valid in sorting out which elements of a text must have been earlier and which must have come later.

A similar intellectual stance is found in the writings of Cassuto (1973), but this time working with a detailed knowledge of comparative Semitic linguistics. As Boas argued in the case of American Indian languages (1940, 206-207), it was a mistake to analyze Semitic languages with grammatical categories based on classical Greek and Latin. Many of the puzzling and "corrupted" sentences of the text, which modern critics interpreted by emendation were shown to be intact when viewed as belonging to widespread Semitic linguistic and literary forms. Moving from the strictly linguistic sphere, Cassuto directly takes to task the documentary hypothesis (1961). While the present text may reflect different literary sources, the first task of understanding is not the disassembling of the books of the Bible to their elements, but the discovery of how they hold together in their present version.

This method does not accept the view that the extant text stems from a not-too-thoughtful cut-and-paste job of a redactor, but that the present text, which indeed brings together varying literary traditions,[5] has an integrity of its own which is incumbent on the researcher to reveal. Stated succinctly (Cassuto 1973, 1):

> We must not forget that the conception of order may vary among people and in different periods, and that there are systems of arrangement that appeared natural and correct to the peoples of the ancient East, yet would never occur to a person accustomed to ways of Western thinking, which is the offspring of Greek civilization. When we bear this in mind, many seemingly bizarre features in the compilation of the Biblical books become easily and clearly intelligible of their own accord.

This approach toward text parallels up-to-date anthropological views of culture. Culture is composed of disparate historical elements, but always contains a coherence of its own, although there is much debate about the nature and tightness of that coherence. In any event, a separation and classification of the historical sources of a given way of life, or its division into more primitive and more advanced components, are seen by few contemporary anthropologists as the end-point of cultural understanding.

It is found that in several respects, similar formulations of method have appeared in the study of culture and the study of Judaism. These convergences cannot be considered completely independent, of course, because they reflect more general intellectual positions. It is equally true, however, that the two disciplines have usually not had a direct influence on one another, particularly in regard to the parallels suggested.[6] With the assumption that these parallels are significant, it shall be argued, in the following section, that there are good reasons for Judaica scholars to attend to developments in the anthropological study of religion.

We have attempted to show that recent approaches to the study of the biblical text demand an appreciative stance, seeking to reveal the premises of the biblical literature rather than impose conceptual frameworks and evaluations from the outside. It is no wonder that students espousing this perspective recoiled from earlier approaches to comparative religion when the Bible was viewed as an example of "savage philosophy" (Frazer 1918, II:424) or discussed as a "society of a very inferior type" (Durkheim 1964, 138). The heritage of modern Jewish studies, which had developed in the nineteenth century, and "had displaced Christian scholarship from its once unchallenged domination of the study of Judaism" (Schorsch 1983, see p. 15), was unlikely to be receptive to concepts imported from a potpourri of the world's cultures.

As has been indicated, however, anthropological theory itself no longer accepts these simple designations, but has become the standard bearer for the claim that every culture is to be understood in its own terms. In addition it has supported the view, which has more recently become explicit, that a culture should be able to speak for itself, that is, that Western science does not necessarily monopolize the road to disciplined historical understanding. Some aspects of these developments will now be explored in an attempt to pave the way for greater interchange between anthropology and students of Judaica.

The Bible is Not Alone: Anthropology, the Greeks, and Orientalism

It would clearly be a mistake to claim that the critical eye cast at early and tribal religions focused on the Bible or Judaism as its only target. Leach and Aycock (1983, 13) have shown that Frazer was at first prepared to apply his analysis to the central myths of Christianity, but drew back in the face of negative reaction on the part of offended colleagues. The issues which created a barrier between Judaic and comparative scholarship were by no means confined to Jewish studies alone. Modern historical criticism, as it developed in Europe, also hit close to home, debunking, if you wish, certain aspects of classical antiquity which had been seen as the ideological basis of much of modern civilization. In addition, Judaism was not the only non-Western civilization to be subjected to study in a manner which appeared to detract from its full humanness. This was true of most of the civilizations studied under the general rubric of "orientalism" (Said 1978).

With regard to Greece and Rome, it began to be realized that there was much in ancient society that in fact differed from contemporary enlightened life. This was put forth clearly by Fustel de Coulange (1874, 10):

> To understand the truth about the Greeks and the Romans, it is wise to study them without thinking of ourselves, as if they were entirely foreign to us; with the same disinterestedness and with the mind as free, as if we were studying ancient India or Arabia.

As discussed by Humphreys (1978), classicists debated among themselves whether the comparisons with primitive religions constantly suggested by Frazer were relevant to ancient Greece, particularly after the processes of demythologizing which preceded the Periclean age. Thus the issue as to whether theoretical and methodological issues raised by the anthropological study of religion can deepen the understanding of classical civilizations, in itself, can be viewed in a comparative perspective, and is not necessarily seen as a confrontation with one particular group or tradition.

In Humphreys's (1978, 12) view, Frazer's mistake was to "confuse inspiration and classification. If Bongo Bongo rainmaking rites illuminate one aspect of Greek ritual, that does not imply any general affinity between the Bongo-Bongo and the Greeks." She goes on to say: "Fruitful interpretations of Greek institutions have been inspired by the Iroquois confederacy, Zulu age regiments, the Kwakiutl potlatch" without implying any general affinity between these societies and the Greeks. With this distinction in mind, it is not unreasonable to assume that inspiration for understanding the biblical text might also come from the study of diverse exotic societies. Futhermore, if this is accepted as a possibility, it may be argued on an *a fortiori* basis that one might seek inspiration from rabbinic scholars who have extensive familiarity with the text. This is a point which will be returned to shortly.

It is also useful to place unsympathetic scholarly views of Judaism in the context of a recent critique of orientalism (Said 1978). This critique has shown that the underlying attitude of much of Western scholarship concerning Eastern civilizations indicates the otherness of these civilizations, and their implied devaluation in relation to the West. Several themes run throughout this work, and by considering the implied opposite of the criticisms, perhaps some alternate constructions may come into view.

One theme is that orientalists "orientalized" the Orient, by developing modes of analysis which were seen as specific to the societies that they were studying, and which were predicated on the assumption of otherness which separated those societies from the West (see the passage quoted from Fustal de Coulange). This, among other things, had the effect of setting orientalism apart from intellectual efforts aimed at a genuinely comparative science of human society, and based on assumptions of the unity of the human condition. A second claim is that Western scholars writing about the East assumed that it was their task to represent the Orient, as the orientals were unable to represent themselves. These issues have become of growing concern to anthropologists involved in the study of non-European societies generally, and it is useful to consider the implied antithesis of these criticisms (study in terms of general theory, and study by non-Westerners) in relation to one another.

It is clearly a desideratum to have societies (all societies) studied by a variety of scholars who bring to bear a number of different perspectives, whether in terms of specific disciplines, or in terms of the general cultural background of the researchers. What such a program of study would and should look like is, however, still a question of debate. A recent conference on "Indigenous Anthropology in Non-Western Countries," gave expression to a range of views (Fahim, Helmer, et al., 1980). Some argued, for example, that "Africans return to their own cultural 'roots,' in search of a new epistemology that . . . might provide a 'better fit' between social reality—as perceived by a member of that society—and anthropological paradigms." Some others argued that the product would not be a better fit, merely a different perspective (1980, 645).

Bahloul (1983, 42) has rendered a personal account, as a Jew from Algeria, of the complexities of studying her own culture:

> In sum, anthropology, which imposed upon me the necessary distance
> to carry out analysis, aided my self-reconciliation with the stubborn

savage in my culture. Having extirpated myself from that universe because of its widespread devaluation, I was equipped with the analytic apparatus of anthropology to rediscover the *other* in my culture, this time by the prestigious path of science. The five years of work had become a permanant going-and-coming, from outside to in. The anthropological discourse which I had attempted to elaborate did not begin as a curious approach to the *other*, but as a laying-bare of the *other* in my own culture, of my own difference, too long (and still) experienced poorly by those of whom I speak, and who I am. Upon becoming an anthropologist I, the savage, reversed the roles; by casting an anthropological gaze upon my own group, I posed a challenge to that belittling glance by making it my own, breaking that anthropological relationship which solicits and elicits speech; to appropriate that speech and thereby transform the savage to an anthropologist of his own "savageness."

She does not advocate an indigenous form of analysis, but implies that a thorough appropriation of the tools of anthropology can bring an indigenous culture to the liberating experience of self-criticism and self-understanding.

This statement may be contrasted with the attitude of the nineteenth-century scholars who, in the name of Judaism, sought to apply the standards of Western scholarship to Jewish studies. The Science of Judaism movement (*Wissenschaft des Judentums*),[7] in the words of Schorsch (1975, 9), "became the medium through which Judaism would come to know itself." With a dominant note being sounded by Hegel, these scholars viewed their work as "the chance to link Judaism with the unfolding of the universal World Spirit," and tended to downplay aspects of Judaism which did not fit in with an enlightened age.[8] Bahloul's account (with its sensitivity to personal ramifications of scholarly work), moves beyond the vision of the *Wissenschaft* quest for self-consciousness, for now, a century and a half after that program was enunciated, it has been acknowledged that no human group can claim to be fully released from its own primitivity.

The issue of the contribution of non-Western intellectual traditions to social science inevitably leads to a discussion of the *literatures* of the civilizations in question. Thus Zunz, one of the founders of the Jewish *Wissenschaft* movement, issued his call for modern Judaic research in terms of *Etwas ueber die rabbinische Literatur* (1818), which amounted to an outline for the study of Jewish civilization. Said (1978, 291) has noted that modern social science experts on the Middle East usually ignore the realm of literature. It is therefore significant that a session at a conference of the Association of Social Anthropologists, which was explicitly designed to stress the point of view of indigenous scholars, was formulated as "The Anthropology of Literary and Oral Sources" (Jain 1977). It thus appears that anthropologists who take seriously the attempt to establish indigenous anthropology as central to the study of man will have to take texts into account, more than in the past, and to find ways of building bridges between the study of text and context. Indigenous exegesis of classical texts is clearly one important element to be included in such an endeavor.

The Rabbinic Interpretation of the Biblical Text:
Its Relevance to Anthropology

One example of an indigenous literature is the encyclopedic compendium of rabbinic biblical interpretation dating from talmudic times until the present. This literature may be viewed in many ways, as reflections of varying periods, as an example of how the meaning of biblical passages are modified according to the needs of different situations, or as insightful excursions into the subtleties of the text itself. Written in postbiblical Hebrew (as well as in Aramaic, Greek, and Arabic), these commentaries are closed to many modern biblical scholars whose education did not include training in the special languages and styles of these writers. While it is true that many of these commentaries are homiletic in purpose, and take great liberties with the plain meaning of the text, it is also the case that they reflect the work of men who had thorough familiarity with text, often knew it by heart, and were very much in tune with its rhythms and its tensions. Greenberg (1969, 6–7) discusses why the contemporary scholar should consult these commentaries, not as an authoritative source, but as a repository of sensitive interpretations which frequently are justifiable by contemporary criteria. To quote briefly from one of his arguments:

> The flood of verbiage to which we are subjected has so impaired our sensitivity to the use of words that we have trouble reading the works of a less voluble age and clime, when talk was briefer and more charged with meaning, when culture was more homogeneous and speech could therefore be more allusive. Premoderns cherished word plays and heard them everywhere, they were more familiar with symbolically numbered repetitions and did not have to be nudged, as does the modern reader, to find them in the sacred text. In these respects, premodern exegetes were closer to the ancient modes of expression than we; hence reading them is a freshening experience.[9]

Traditional rabbinic exegesis is thus often able to provide insights into the text that do not immediately seem apparent to the modern reader. Anthropology, of course, has had extended exposure to thought and communication in premodern and even nonliterate societies, so anthropologists should be in a position to appreciate some of the insights of traditional hermeneutics. What follows are two (of many possible) examples of traditional interpretation which show great similarity to standard notions in social anthropology.

One instance comes from the 11th century exegete, Rashi, who, basing himself on the *Bereshit Rabba* midrash, made the following observation about Joseph's brothers when they are about to embark on their first trip to Egypt to purchase supplies (Genesis 42:3): "So far as their feeling of brotherhood (toward Joseph) was concerned they were divided into ten, because the love and hatred that all of them bore him were not alike, whereas in regard to buying corn, they were at one and united." Taking into account the fact that the midrash sometimes refers to the brothers as "the tribes," a keen appreciation can be seen of what anthropologists call "segmentary opposition," whereby the unity of lineages is defined by virtue of opposition to outsiders, while in other contexts the same lineages exhibit marked internal differences.[10]

A second example is also from Rashi. In commenting on the verse (Leviticus 19:14) "You shall not insult the deaf, or place a stumbling block before the blind, You shall fear your God: I am the Lord," Rashi observed, concerning the phrase "You shall fear your God": "In all actions where it is given only to the heart of him who does it [to know the motive that prompts him], and where other people have no insight to it, Scripture states: "You shall fear your God." This textual interpretation shows an understanding of the anthropological principle that supernatural sanctions become crucial in those areas where social or human sanctions are ineffective.

Instead of different perspectives emerging from the study of text and context, there are here two (and many could be added) instances of convergence where textual analysis and social analysis stress similar points. There are several reasons why this may not be uncommon in rabbinic exegesis, reasons which may apply to a greater or lesser extent to other literary traditions. First of all, the rabbinic tradition is one which is structured by *halakhah*, a concern with following the rules and laws laid down in the Torah and elaborated over the generations by scholars. The texture and integrity of Jewish life are provided by what people *do* in this regard, and much less by their stated or implied beliefs. The biblical text is thus scrutinized for the rules of living, for concrete directives for action in specific situations. The verse in Leviticus is thus viewed as a binding commandment, entailing legal sanction, and not as a generalized moral axiom "not to put a stumbling block before the blind." Given this standpoint, it is not surprising that Rashi's legalistic view of the matter brings him to an interpretation quite compatible with the social anthropological tradition, which also was shaped in large measure by juridical thinking (Lowie 1937, 39-54). A sociological-legal component is thus automatically built into a great deal of traditional interpretation. The rabbis also assumed that the law was of concern to the biblical characters, even those, such as Abraham or David, who in fact predated its emergence as a coherent legal system in talmudic times, and that these individuals followed the rules that in fact evolved later.

A second (and corollary) reason why the study of text does not necessarily diverge from the study of context is that the rabbis and the audiences of their homiletic lessons saw in the lives of the biblical heroes models for their own lives. Not only were they sensitive to the use of words in a premodern setting, as suggested by Greenberg, but the kinds of situations presupposed by such speech were seen as similar to their own situations. It of course can be greatly misleading to assume that the social background of the Israelite kingdoms in the first millennium B.C.E. was similar to that of eleventh century France (the time of Rashi). On the other hand, there may be aspects of preindustrial society in the realms of family life, or in the relations of the ordinary members of a society to a ruler, which are widespread and which are easily comprehensible to individuals in many premodern settings. Moreover, the suggestion can be made that some social patterns of the Jews in medieval society were subtly *shaped*, or at least given meaning, by the text they studied, their lives being, as it were, the playing out of a script which was read and heard again and again.[11] It is thus prefectly reasonable that, as a method of discovery, the ways that the rabbis related the texts to social situations should be scrutinized for clues as to plausible social contexts for the biblical period itself.

In this section two examples of rabbinic exegesis have been presented with reference to the biblical text. Here is a literary genre which can be said both to represent itself, depicting a society which is, at once, tribal and scribal (Boon 1982), and to do so in terms that merit universal appreciation. Thus, the rabbinic interpretations offered easily fit into a framework of contemporary anthropological understanding. The examples cited relate to the areas of concern of social anthropology, or the comparative study of social forms. With the growing interest in cultural theory, viewed in a semiotic framework, a hermeneutic perspective in which culture is seen as text, suggests even further possibilities for a comparison between traditional and modern forms of interpretive understanding. This, in a sense, brings us to a full circle. A discipline which at its outset attempted to see through religion eventually finds that an important method by which to understand religion, and certain aspects of culture in general, may be adopted from religion itself.[12] Before considering the interpretive approach further, some discussion is warranted about the place of religion in the context of *Wissenschaft* studies, and in anthropology.

Problems in the Study of Religion

As discussed already, the study of world civilizations inevitably brings the anthropologist into intellectual confrontation with classic texts, which very often are religious in content. Moreover, it has been suggested that these texts might be related to not only as *objects* of study, but as sources of insight, that is, as *contemporaries.* This clearly is a problematic stance for any discipline viewing itself as a positive science, in the narrow sense of that term. It does not seem clearly differentiated from a commitment to these texts, which sees them as a source of truths that span time and place, and smacks of an intellectual orthodoxy which claims that the early greats already knew the truths which sometimes are rediscovered by the moderns who are, by definition, of diminished stature. In other words, it raises, or reraises, the problematic questions involved in the disciplined study of religion.

Both anthropology, and the modern study of Judaism, have shown complex, ambivalent, and sometimes contradictory attitudes toward the topic of religion. The problematics of religion in modern Jewish studies will be mentioned briefly, after which some of the developments and conceptions in contemporary anthropology and related disciplines, with regard to religion, will be sketched. It is thereby hoped that the potentiality of a constructive dialogue between students of comparative religion and experts in specific traditions will be seen.

Religion in the Science of Judaism

In attempting to establish a modern approach to the study of Jewish civilization, many of the nineteenth-century scholars of the *Wissenschaft* movement saw themselves as doing work which was different from studying religion in a traditional sense. In Zunz's words, "since religious thought lacks an objective foundation and makes for divisiveness, it is better left with the theologians and sermonizers, and should not become a subject of scholarship" (quoted in Glatzer 1964, 35). Instead, the science of Judaism claimed, scholarship was to deal with history. Schorsch (1975, 10) phrases the *Wissenschaft* view as: "History alone transcended the passions and partisanship of a turbulent age, and it alone had access to the truth that would accord a revamped Judaism its rightful place in the century of self-cognition."

It was common for these scientific pioneers to be involved in the contemporary issues of religious reform within Judaism, but precisely for that reason, perhaps, they avoided intense intellectual involvement with the religious forms of the past. Advances were made in various realms of historical study, and in the latter part of the nineteenth century there emerged the conception of Jewish *social* history, of which Dubnow (1925–1929) is a prominent example. In the present century this approach developed further and is represented by the major works of Baron (1942) and Katz (1961). These authors certainly see themselves as contributing to an understanding of the religious history of the Jews, but the thrust of their work is to elucidate the social implications of religious practices and values, rather than explore religious notions and symbols *sui generis*. It is fair to claim that many scholars of Jewish history feel that they are on safer ground in dealing with demography, communal structure, or the relations between Jews and Gentiles than directly seeking an understanding of the religious beliefs and practices of the past.

The most notable exception to this generalization is to be found in the work of Scholem (see Biale 1979). In clear reaction to an overly rationalistic position, Scholem set out to examine the Kabbalah, that aspect of preenlightenment Judaism which, in the eyes of nineteenth-century savants, had come to stand for the obscurantism of the past. Scholem said that "men like Graetz, Zunz, Geiger, Luzzatto and Steinscheider had little sympathy—to put it mildly—for the Kabbalah. At once strange and repellent, it epitomized everything that was opposed to their own ideas and to the outlook which they hoped to make predominant in modern Judaism" (Scholem 1941, 1).

Through his landmark researches, which involved the unraveling of complex symbolic systems of myth and ritual, Scholem succeeded in restoring an understanding and appreciation of this side of Jewish life running from talmudic times through the Hasidic movement in the eighteenth century (and which appears to have some appeal to post-moderns). Always exhibiting some degree of dialectical tension with the other more established expressions of Judaism, the mystic tradition is now recognized as a major feature of Jewish religious life, and Judaism thereby conceived in a more internally diverse, pluralistic, and dynamic manner than before.

Scholem conceives his work as the study of *religious* phenomena. He places the Kabbalah within the framework of a general theory of mystical experience, while focusing on the specific nature of Jewish mysticism and its various historical developments. His work appears to be held in high regard by anthropologists,[13] but his explicit concern with religion is not matched in other fields of contemporary Jewish studies. Thus the move toward greater historical contextualism has led most other Jewish scholars to shy away from speaking of Judaism and the Jewish religion (for a recent exception see Halivni 1986). Cautious not to let their history become subservient to an overall ideological position, the subject of religion, which is involved with Jewish history, the biblical text, rabbinic responsa, and so forth, but not identical with nor exhausted by any of these, is somehow ignored.

In this regard Goshen-Gottstein (1980) has pointed out that in the realm of biblical studies on the part of Christian (mostly Protestant) scholars, there is a range of positions, from those who relate to the text in strictly philological, historical, or literary terms to those who see themselves simultaneously as biblical exegetes and theologians. No such range exists among Jewish scholars, where the view is that either one point of view *or* the other is taken. Again, the topic of religion, as susceptible to disciplined analysis, seems to disappear. There is no doubt that this caution is admirable and that great intellectual and emotional effort may be required to avoid the pitfalls of merging the two approaches. It is also the case that one would not expect a fruitful outcome from the attempt to study the Jewish religion alone, disembodied from any of its concrete contexts. On the other hand, as the comparative study of religion becomes more mature, it points to certain questions that might enrich and be enriched by the detailed study of

Judaism. It would therefore be unfortunate if significant questions in the realm of religion are simply being overlooked by Judaic scholars equipped to relate to them (see Neusner 1982, Chap. 1).

Anthropological Approaches to Religion

Anthropology, too, has exhibited different phases with regard to the study of religion. With great simplification, three such phases may be highlighted. The first, roughly corresponding to the heyday of evolutionary theory (Lowie 1937), often was individual in emphasis and assumed a qualitative difference between the spiritual life of primitive man and that of more advanced societies. The individualism usually focused on cognitive capacities (see, for example, Tylor (1871) and Frazer (1890)),[14] seeing primitive belief systems as taking the place of more advanced forms of understanding. Religion was thus studied in terms of preconceived notions of what religion must have meant to early man, based on the fitting of ethnographic data from many parts of the world into an overarching definition or theory. Little attention was accorded to the diverse social and cultural contexts that contributed to the meaningfulness of rites and myths in specific circumstances.

A second phase resulted from both theoretical advance and methodological refinement. Durkheim's theory (1912) of religion and social life in general was an attempt to establish a unified and comparative science of society in which all societies, evolutionary advance notwithstanding, were to be seen as expressions of the same basic social process. Freud's theories, despite his use of outmoded anthropology in *Totem and Taboo* (1913), is significant in that it attempted to bring all psychic life (pathological and normal) into one analytical framework (Lévi-Strauss 1963, 1), and the same applies to his ideas on religion. In the realm of methodology, Malinowski (1922) showed once and for all that the forms of thought and the institutions of exotic cultures cannot be viewed from an intellectual distance, but become meaningful in daily and seasonal life in precisely the same ways as do parallel forms in complex societies. These studies accepted religion as an integral aspect of human social life, and not as a deficient mode of thinking or feeling that would ultimately disappear.

The Recognition of Religion

This point of view, which came to be known as the *functional* (or *structural-functional*)[15] approach to society and religion dominated anthropology for several decades, and still forms the basis of much contemporary anthropological work. Numerous studies showed the intricate links between cultural forms, such as worship at ancestral shrines (or the practice of sacrifice), and specific social structures, while, within the culture-and-personality school of American anthropology, researchers highlighted associations between the content of myths and psychoanalytically conceived personality processes (Wallace 1966, 13ff.). Religion was thus accepted as a natural feature of human society, but normally understood to be an expression of something else more basic. By the 1950s, a number of anthropologists began to look past the functional perspective in an attempt to penetrate more deeply the nature of religious life itself. The problem was posed by Lévi-Strauss (1955), in connection with the "structural study of myth":

> If a given mythology confers prominence on a certain figure, let us say an evil grandmother, it will be claimed that in such a society grandmothers are actually evil and that mythology reflects the social structure and social relations; but should the actual data be conflicting, it would be as readily claimed that the purpose of mythology is to provide an outlet for repressed feelings.

He then goes on with his early attempt to develop an approach to myth which first and foremost unravels the structure and meaning of the myth itself, before jumping to the link with social or personality processes.

A similar development appears in the work of Turner on the *Chihamba* ritual among the Ndembu in central Africa. In his initial analysis of this curing ritual, Turner showed how the ritual reduced tensions inherent in the matrilineal social structure, attempted to close the breaches developing between village factions, and aimed to reestablish friendly relations with other villagers. Later, Turner (1962) began to move beyond his earlier analysis focusing on *kavula*, the central spiritual being of the *Chihamba* ritual. This analysis explores aspects of religion not encompassed by the social-structural perspective.

> One might argue with some point that Kavula represents the ultimate unity of Ndembu society, transcending all its contradictions of principle and value. He is, for example, "grandfather" of his cult members, he is a "chief," he is a "slaveowner," he is the "husband" of the afflicting ancestress, he clearly typifies virility and huntsmanship. But such a sociological explanation would not adequately account for many of his

characteristics; his connection with meteorological phenomena, such as thunder, lightning and the rains. It would not cover his patronage of the fertility of crops and game. It would not explain his power over human health and other biological processes. Nor would it account for his intensely personal relationship with his worshippers, nor for his mystical death and rebirth. The ethical and spiritual values he represents and sanctions are no mere product of the social process. Indeed Ndembu religion has its own set of ends, which clearly transcends the social category. There is here no necessary casual nexus between the social and ritual structures. The latter is certainly not monocausally determined by the former (1975, 181–82).

Both these writers thus helped move the anthropological study of religion to its third phase, still very much in evidence (with its own diverse emphases and internal debates), and which, while not neglecting social and cultural context, attempts to discover the intricacies and significance of religious behavior, without reducing it to an epiphenomenon of other facts. This development within anthropology is closely linked to an understanding of man as constantly interpreting the world, which requires methods of inquiry capable of comprehending the process of interpretation. In the next section, an attempt will be made to indicate some features of this line of thought, and present, in part, its theoretical justification.

The Interpreting Animal

The latest phase of the anthropological study of religion, while decidedly an advance, may be seen, in a limited sense, as a return to the concerns of the first period of theorizing and research. The early period is epitomized in the work of Frazer (1890), who established categories of primitive thought, such as sympathetic magic, and then sought to show how ethnographic phenomena the world over fit into those categories. He thus treated the primitive world as a unity, as if all these diverse societies could be viewed as representatives of a single cultural entity, despite their geographic and temporal separation and their varying environmental and social circumstances. At the same time, the focus of his work was clearly and specifically on the topic of religion (ignoring here his distinction of religion from magic).

As stated, the critics of Frazer (and other works of this nature) insisted on the study of particular religious forms, in defined contexts,

seeking the meanings of these forms in those contexts alone. In carrying out field work, their aim was to produce a portrait of the structure
of a given society or community, and to show how religious beliefs and
acts fit into that structure. Two criticisms of that approach developed.
One, already discussed, emphasized the complexity of religious phenomena, which could not be explained only in terms of the threads tying
symbolic expression to social processes. The second criticism was that
this generation of scholars sought to explore the intricacies of individual societies to the point of eschewing cross-cultural comparison.
These workers seemed to lose sight of the original mandate of anthropology, which had stressed the importance of the comparative method.
This may be explained, perhaps, not only in terms of a reaction to the
excesses of the grand theorists, but also in terms of the lack of a theory
of culture or symbolic action which made such comparisons justifiable.
Thus Leach has compared the work of Lévi-Strauss to that of Frazer
(Leach 1970), an image which, in anthropological discourse, cannot but
be ambivalent. While Lévi-Strauss may easily be criticized for the
cavalier fashion in which he has offered his continent-spanning interpretations of myth, it should be appreciated that his return to the comparative method is linked to an attempt to deepen the theoretical
perspective on culture and symbols.

Symbol and Society

The decomposition of the structuralist-functionalist paradigm
moved anthropological work in two seemingly different directions.
One was toward greater interest in the religious and the symbolic,
already discussed, and the other toward more detailed description of
concrete social, political, or economic interaction in specific settings.
This second development, though ostensibly less relevant to the main
issue of the anthropology of religion, must be considered as the
theoretical complement of the first. As will be discussed, the same
anthropologists sometimes figure in pointing to both of these new
directions.

As the detailed study of individual societies progressed, it became
evident that even the notion of "a society" was sometimes too much of
a generalization. A classic study pointing this out is Leach's study of
Highland Burma (1954). It may seem paradoxical that Leach was also

active in developing an awareness of Lévi-Strauss's work on myth among Anglo-American anthropologists.[16] The same paradox may be found in the work of Turner, who, along with others, contributed to the study of local level politics (Swartz et al. 1966). Within a given society there are always different categories of actors, often engaged in competition for wealth, status, and power, who, in the course of these struggles mobilize the various culturally defined resources available, including the manipulation of religious symbols. Thus, the very same studies that often limited the field of study to a unit smaller than the community, focusing on specific scenes and instances of social interaction, also opened up the universe of study from the point of view of symbols, which express and shape the course of action. It became apparent that religious (and, to a certain extent, all cultural) symbols did not have a single meaning in a given situation, but were outstanding in their polysemy or multivocality. Symbols suggest different things to different actors in the same situation, different things to the same actors in different contexts, different things, at varying levels, to the same actors in the same situation, and certainly different things as they crossed cultural boundaries. Symbols, then, when they actually appear in social settings, are most fully understood in reference to the details of those contexts, but also, by their nature, are capable of reaching out beyond those contexts, or, as stressed by Turner, of raising alternatives to the immediate reality. In other words, symbols reach out to bridge both space and time.

An appreciation of the ability of symbols to extend signification beyond the specific context of their appearance in social life is, therefore, a necessary concomitant of the theoretical demand for fine-grained focus on individual social events. Without this recognition, the development of anthropology would involve a kind of reductionism *ad absurdum*.[17] The discipline would involve nothing but a series of ever-more detailed accounts of interaction. That specific instances of interaction make sense in terms of past and future events, and relate to actors and actions not necessarily on the scene at the time of a field worker's observations, only can be explained by the ability of meanings to be transmitted across space and time, which in turn reflects the peculiar properties of homo sapiens as a symbolizing animal. This is made possible, in the first instance, by human linguistic ability, which also lays the groundwork for the ongoing interpretation of words and gestures.

Language and Openness

In comparing humans with related species, two universal features of human life, which are not found among other primates, are often noted: language and religion. Religion is inconceivable without the existence of language,[18] without the refined capacity to establish and to question meaningful images and categories concerning existence in nature, one's place in society, self-worth, sense of purpose, and the like. It is possible to recognize that many religious experiences take individuals beyond language, but it is equally true that the experiences are conditioned by the linguistic/cultural matrix within which they occur, and become historically significant insofar as religious feeling, insights, and commitments are formulated and communicated in language. Religions also communicate through ritual, dance, music, olfactory sensations, and so forth, but each of those forms of communication takes on its specific significance in the context of a religious conceptual (implying the conative and affective, as well) framework which consists, in the final analysis, of a complex linguistic/semantic structure.

It may be argued, therefore, that the openness of religious symbols, that they may be (or perhaps, *must* be) interpreted, stems, in the first instance, from the nature of language itself. Language, on the one hand, contributes to the *regularization*[19] of human thought and action by providing specific and stable categories which guide action among populations of homo sapiens in the absence of genetic fixity. At the same time, language has built into it certain features of indeterminacy which appear at different levels. First is the element of arbitrariness which characterizes most linguistic labels. The phonetic form carrying a given cultural meaning is not the only one that can do so, as is evident when speakers of one language come into contact with speakers of a different language or dialect. Thus, the realization (and anxiety) that one's language (and way of life) is (are) not to be taken for granted is, perhaps, a universal experience in which everyday acts are made ready for the absorption of new significations.

Secondly, there is the dual structure of all human languages (Hockett and Ascher 1964, 139), which permits the production of an infinite variety of sentences (Chomsky 1957), referring in their content to diverse times and places. This may be contrasted with the situationally specific, grammarless vocalizations characteristic of primate communication.[20] The open-endedness, which grows out of these formal features of language, is highlighted when contrasting them with what might be called mimetic features, serving to attach an utterance to a given time and place. Changes in pitch or volume, the (nonphonemic) lengthening of vowels, or the use of pauses, which may appear in a given speech act, function to bring home a message to a defined group of people in a specific context.[21] That these features are inserted into concrete instances of language performance indicates that the formal structure, in itself, is open to various modes of understanding and interpretation.

A similar argument may be made by calling attention to the special ability of human beings to talk about talking (Bateson 1972, 177ff.), indicating that metamessages are often necessary to frame more specific messages in order that the latter be understood correctly. Ricoeur has argued (1970) that certain linguistic forms, such as mythology and poetry, may be defined, in part, by the fact that they require interpretation—in the hermeneutic sense, and it may be suggested that, in a limited way, this is built into ordinary prose speech as well. If this is true of language in general, it would certainly apply to linguistic expressions of concepts like sanctity and divinity (see Rapoport 1980).

If this line of reasoning is correct, then interpretation is not necessarily inferior to other forms of understanding which claim to be close to the facts. Rather, the process of interpretation is built into the interlocking systems of human communication. Physical anthropological and cognate studies of biological characteristics make it amply clear that man may be viewed as an incomplete animal (see, for example, Geertz 1973). It is part of human nature that prenatal development be supplemented by social interactional and culturally mediated experiences after birth. From about the age of two years, language becomes central in this process, and if it is correct that interpretation is an intrinsic component of the ability to use language, then, *a fortiori*, man may be seen as "the interpreting animal" with regard to the manifold modes of human communication.[22]

One may reason that this must be so from an evolutionary perspective. If language and culture were to completely determine man's behavioral responses, then the adaptational advantages gained by the *lack* of genetic fixity in primates, and preeminently in man, would be an evolutionary deadend because of this form of determinism. It is man's ability to interpret, to assign new meanings to conventionally accepted signs and symbols, which, in part, enables him to break out of such determinism. Thus, as Turner (1980) states, myths and some symbols provide the possibility of "going beyond or transcending the languages in which members of societies transact their daily business" and thereby plant "at least the germ of reflexive moral self-critique." It can be asserted that this potentiality may be found, in elementary form, in the existence and structure of language itself, and that interpretation is inextricably part of the process whereby such moments of self-transcendence may be carried over into, and influence, mundane social life.

The Importance of Interpretive Understanding

Interpretive understanding, in which new perspectives are opened up onto old realities (see O'Flaherty 1980), or in which everyday acts become symbols should not therefore, on a priori grounds, be accorded a secondary status as a mode of apprehending the significance of utterances, gestures, or icons, even when the explicit formulation of an interpretation is removed from the original occurrence of the ritual or myth telling. Rather, as an integral part of the communicative process, interpretation is one of the links whereby the "seeds of future possibilities" germinate out of "historical facts."[23] This view of the future potentialities being contained in the symbolic aspects of communication (or perhaps, that all communication has the potential of becoming symbolic, and pointing toward the future) may even be applied to daily interaction. As Sperber maintains (1975, 144): "Today's possibility may become tomorrow's reality. Thus, in interpersonal relations symbolic utterances or behaviors constantly evoke what the relation *may* become and contribute to its transformation" (emphasis added). Human communication, and certainly the communication implied in myth, ritual, drama, and art, always involves interpretation, and hermeneutic disciplines thereby form an indispensable part of the science of culture. Thus, as noted, contemporary anthropology finds itself turning to religious disciplines,[24] or to the study of literature (Boon 1982), for the fullest understanding of its subject matter, and therefore it is not surprising when contemporary indigenous interpretation becomes a source of insights.[25] At the same time, it should be noted, a general consideration of human evolution and a detailed understanding of symbolic capacities carry implications for the way particular societies, cultures, and historical events can be analyzed.

The point of this discussion, it should be emphasized, takes seriously the requirement of detailed and contextual study of individual societies and religions, but attempts, simultaneously, not to lose sight of anthropology's claim to study human development. These two emphases, ideally, should complement and correct one another. For example, the processes of magical thinking (contagious and sympathetic) identified by Frazer, are no longer seen as being present only in a certain type of society, representing an earlier stage of cultural evolution. Rather, they may be shown to be similar to symbolic processes common to all human cultures, and may be elucidated with the aid of the concepts of metonym and metaphor (Sapir and Crocker 1977). This formulation, in turn, allows for a more refined comprehension of particular cultural patterns and their effects on social life.

Comparison between cultures is legitimate, sometimes because of actual historical contact, and sometimes because they may be seen as examples of basic human processes. In the latter case, it is not inevitable that comparisons violate the special quality of a given cultural context. A fine example of such a comparison, which bridges societies and religions of vastly different scale, is Turner's analysis of the meaning of whiteness in Ndembu curing, in Christianity, and in the neopaganism of Moby Dick (1975, 179-203). The three different societies in this analysis are not related in any conventional sense, yet certain similarities in the significance of whiteness may be found in all of them. When different societies and/or periods are related by historical contact and development, the search for parallel meanings and associations is even more justified. A special challenge to anthropological understanding, it would seem, is provided by those cultures and religions which, emerging in one historical period and context, have survived and developed aided by processes of self-interpretation in later periods and diverse social circumstances. The understanding and self-understanding of Judaism certainly is a case in point.

Contemporary scholars of Jewish history, language, texts, law, and so on, usually have been reluctant to relate to Judaism writ large. There is no reason to abandon their insistence on disciplined and responsible research within specialized fields. On the other hand, it is argued, there are discernable threads of continuity, most concretely in text and ritual, linking different historical periods and religious phases of Jewish civilization.[26] That these different ages assign different interpretations to the same texts and practices does not mean that they have to be totally severed from one another. With the appreciation of the nature of symbolic action, and of interpretation and reinterpretation as a basic feature of social life and historical creativity, it may be possible to better understand the threads that link different versions and generations of a given cultural tradition.[27] The final two sections of this essay shall explore this line of inquiry, citing examples from the papers in this volume and other studies of Jewish culture carried out from anthropological perspectives.

Jewish Studies and Anthropological Contributions

Some recent examples

As stated at the outset, there have been many attempts by anthropologists and other social scientists to apply their concepts to Jewish civilization. The Bible, widely available in translation, has been approached from many different perspectives, and theorists continue to utilize it to try out new ideas. Materialists, such as Harris (1974), have sought to explain why the ancient Hebrews avoided pig meat (for one critical reply see Diener and Robkin 1978), and Douglas (1966) has attempted to show the logic of animal categories in Leviticus that explains why some meat is to be considered an abomination.[28] Stimulated by the founder of anthropological structuralism, Leach (1969) published "Lévi-Strauss in the Garden of Eden" in 1961, and since then the number of analyses in this genre has increased rapidly.[29]

Most of these studies are carried out by scholars unfamiliar with the Hebrew text, or with contemporary professional literature written in Hebrew. This does not automatically disqualify their essays, of course, but acquaintanceship with a broader fund of writings would most likely reveal cases where structural analysis has rediscovered insights which were reached by earlier authors and commentators. It should also be mentioned that in a number of instances important contributions have been made by biblical historians who have found social-anthropological ideas congenial to their material, such as Ben Dor's (1982) analysis of the lineage (utilizing Fortes's [1969] work) and Demsky's (1976) study of literacy in ancient Israel (building on Goody [1968]).

It is less common to find an anthropological perspective applied to postbiblical, or rabbinic writings, although this too, is beginning to appear in scholarly work. Fredman (1981) has attempted a generalized (timeless, see Prell 1983) analysis of the Passover *seder* with many examples from contemporary America, while Bokser's more recent historical study based on early rabbinic sources (1984) illuminates the experience of the ancient *seder* with Turner's notion of *communitas* (1969). This section shall mention several attempts on the part of researchers familiar with Judaic texts to enrich the understanding of these texts through the utilization of anthropological points of view.

In recent papers Deshen (1979; 1980) has called on anthropological concepts to help solve the *Kol Nidre* enigma. *Kol Nidre* is a prayer that inaugurates the Day of Atonement, the most solemn day of the Jewish liturgic year, and signifies a ritual moment when the individual reaffirms connections with the Jewish people and heritage, while recognizing one's own frailty at the turn of the year. An examination of the content of this prayer, however, reveals various problems about its meaning and its validity in terms of Jewish law. Deshen follows the development of the prayer from the early medieval period, and shows how the Day of Atonement, as defined from a formal legal perspective, was complemented by an infusion of popular religiosity containing magical elements which often form part of calendrical rituals. In this case, rabbinic authority was forced to accommodate a widespread religious sentiment, although *halakhic* legitimacy for the prayer always remained somewhat doubtful. Deshen's study consists of a complex interweaving of an appreciation of *halakhic* evolution with a sensitivity to folk religion growing out of anthropological study.

Another example, this time by an historian, relates to Douglas's work on the purity laws of Leviticus, and seeks to examine the ideas of purity in ancient Judaism. While purity laws, as outlined in the Bible (mainly in Leviticus and Numbers), relate primarily to the sanctity of the Temple, which was destroyed in 70 C.E., these laws continue to be important in the Mishna (compiled about 200 C.E.), a product of Pharisaic Judaism, and in other contemporaneous groups. Neusner (1973) compares several ways in which the purity rules were interpreted, referring to the New Testament, the Qumran community (as known to us through the Dead Sea scrolls), and rabbinic Judaism. He does not provide a structural analysis of the mishnaic laws themselves, as Douglas (1973, 138, 140) points out in her comments to his monograph,[30] but shows how the same set of text-based rules, which contribute to the definition of group boundaries, acquired different meanings in different periods, and by different groups in the same period, establishing patterns which were important in Judaism and Christianity for centuries thereafter.

The application of anthropological insights to a more recent period

Introduction

is found in Goldberg's discussion of the *mimuna* festival among the
Jews of Morocco (1978). Celebrated on the night which terminates the
Passover holiday, this popular festival clearly resembles other springtime celebrations described for the Mediterranean area from antiquity
through the present. The Jews, of course, do not view the festival in
these terms, but work to interpret it in terms of Jewish tradition, while
anthropological concepts such as "rituals of reversal" and "the power of
the weak," utilized by Turner in his exploration of the ritual process
(1969), underline the logic of this interpretation. At the same time,
structural analysis reveals masked links between the *mimuna* and a
Muslim celebration that takes place at approximately the same period
of time. The *mimuna*, which carries meanings relevant to family life,
communal solidarity, and relations with non-Jews, is delicately balanced between the forces of popular religion, Jewish tradition, and local
Muslim influence.

   These few examples point to several interrelated themes which appear to be central in any anthropological attempt to come to grips with
the special features of Judaic culture. One theme is the centrality of
texts. While other great traditions relate themselves to sacred texts, the
widespread influence of the text in daily life has been a notable feature
of traditional Jewish societies.[31] Secondly, there is the question of *performance*, the realization of rules, tied in mulitplex strands to texts, in
actual practice. This question becomes particularly significant in a
tradition that often has been defined as based on orthopraxy, rather
than orthodoxy. Finally, there is the question of change in the light of
the first two features mentioned. How has Jewish society viewed its
own texts and ongoing performances in changing historical circumstances, while claiming to be faithful to the basic rules of the Pentateuch and its rabbinical interpretations?

*Text in Jewish Religion and Society: Performance, Interpretation, and
Change*

   The study of culture as a text has become a common metaphor in
current anthropological discussion (Boon 1972, 9-15; Geertz 1973, 448-
53). Like any metaphor, it is suggestive of new directions but simultaneously raises problems when placed under scrutiny. The image suggests that anthropologists turn to the interpretive methods developed
by students of literature, drama, and other humanistic disciplines in ad-
vancing the science of culture. While the text of culture is often not

written (literally), the question arises as to whether the anthropologist is to focus on the product of writing, that is, some artifact in which culture has left its imprint (including concrete texts in the restricted sense of the term), or on the process of writing, the actual cultural performances (Turner 1982, 13ff.) in concrete social settings.

In a paper on a performative approach to ritual, Tambiah (1979) has attempted to combine these approaches. He shows why one must take into account the "cosmological constructs and cultural presuppositions" of a civilization in carrying out a formal analysis of the way ritual expresses concepts, images, and values of a tradition, while keyed to a given situation.

When a tradition is expressed not only in oral transmission, but in written texts which are commonly known, the interrelationship between belief system and ritual becomes particularly complex. Anthropologists have always been suspicious of relying on texts to explain actual behavior, claiming that widespread illiteracy, a situation that characterized many peasant civilizations, implies that most members of a society are not influenced *directly* by the written word. One important way that researchers have met that objection is to focus on the importance of *narratives* (Bruner 1984) in cultural life, which may or may not have a written form, but which, in their spoken form, can have a concrete impact on a defined group of actors. When, in addition, the reading of texts and their explanation appear as *part* of ritual, as in the case of Judaism, the linkage between cultural content and ritual form appears to be both intricate and interesting.

The separate focus on themes such as ritual performance, or ritual and narrative, is useful for academic texts and performances, but the study of any particular tradition requires an examination of how these features interrelate in concrete instances. Studying Judaism anthropologically, then, means the necessity of combining several perspectives. Classical texts cannot be ignored, yet it would be foolish to view given performances, linked to these texts, as automatic print-outs of a cultural recipe. As will be illustrated in the papers that follow, intensive symbolic activities have cultural roots far older than any particular social occasion, and may carry with them, as shown clearly by Myerhoff, implications for social settings still to be crystallized in the future. Thus, any given social performance which highlights a particular configuration of cultural form represents a moment which condenses images and meanings from the past (often familiar to the performers and the audience through their exposure to texts), and projects them, with uncertain effect, into situations yet to be born. Relating to the past, as portrayed in texts, through cultural performances, then, may represent a preservation of the past while simultaneously constituting an innovative foray into the future.

The impact of a text, of course, is not necessarily the result of a solitary individual impelled toward behavior on the basis of reading. More often than not, aspects of the text are highlighted through interpretation on the part of prestigious learned figures. It is not surprising that a central project in Zunz's (1832) scholarly efforts was a study of the history of the *derasha*, the lesson/sermon in which ancient texts become relevant to the community of listeners in their existential situation, and thereby perdure in their timeless sanctity. Kugelmass has given us a sensitive analysis of this process in our own days, showing the impact of "Solomon . . . in the South Bronx" (1985). This dialogue between past and present, between the written word and its spoken actualization,[32] may take place during performances associated with study of the text (Heilman 1983), but also occurs in other contexts where the presence of the text is less direct. New readings of a text, through performance, go hand-in-hand with "its" preservation.

Tambiah, in his paper (1979), discussed several ways in which rituals may be seen as performative. One is in the Austinian (1962) sense that ritual action, whether verbal or otherwise, is "doing something." Examples of this process can easily be cited from Jewish life, and it is interesting that in English one often speaks of the performance of a *mitzvah*.[33] It is also noteworthy that it has long become standard in Jewish life to add the accompaniment of verbal blessings, outlined in the standard texts, to *mitzvot* (pl.) which are not intrinsically verbal. Thus the seventh day of the week is the Sabbath by virtue of the cosmic order established at creation, but the Jew also has the opportunity of inaugurating the Sabbath by the twin action of lighting candles and reciting the appropriate blessings. That the study of sacred texts, of Torah, in itself is a *mitzvah*, at the onset of which a blessing may be said, shows the thick intermingling of ritualistic and rational aspects of intellectual *cum* religious endeavor.

Another sense in which ritual is performative, as discussed by Tambiah (1979, 140), consists of the multilayered forms of repetition and redundancy through which ceremonies stress messages on those who participate in them. In seeking links between the cultural content of a tradition and the specific forms that its rituals take, it is striking that the papers contained in this volume, which consider diverse aspects of Jewish cultural and social life, all relate, in one fashion or another, to textual material. Situations are discussed in which people study, memorize, inscribe, cite, interpret, publish, distribute, dream, and even dance with texts. Ritual gains force through the simultaneous use of different sensory modes so that the importance of Torah grows in impact by its association with noncogitational experiences. The hostility of the biblical text and Jewish tradition to plastic representation has not eliminated the tendency to esthetically embellish the performance or paraphernalia of *mitzvot*.[34] Brief mention should be made of music, text, and ritual in Jewish tradition. Textual materials as diverse as Maimonides' articles of faith, Sabbath laws, or messianic imagery have been condensed in popular verse, put to music, and incorporated into ritual in both synagogue and home.

The tendency of ritual to utilize a multi-media strategy in impressing itself on participants/adherents is often linked to the view that the social effect of ritual is to maintain the social status quo. Recent work by Turner (1969; 1980, 20ff.) and others, however, has pointed to the innovative and transformative potential of ritual, developing a line of thought encapsulated in such phrases as "the anthropology of reflexivity." This perspective claims that through ritual/symbolic action a society, or segment of a society, can represent itself to itself, and is thereby able to regard itself. Symbolic forms presented in this manner are available for extension, retraction, or revision: in brief, for interpretation. The papers included in this volume show that this process may form a part of religious rituals, festivals, demonstrations, birthday celebrations, folk-drama, art, study, and humor. Dreaming, too (see the paper by Bilu), may be viewed in this manner. Whether dreaming represents unfulfilled wishes, as in classical analytic theory, or actual past events recollected and reformed, they first of all *represent* a reality, making the representation available for scrutiny.

In sum, texts appear in Jewish life in a multitude of settings, and may be associated both with stability and/or with change. This will be amply illustrated in the papers presented, which are divided into three parts. Part I includes analyses with a diachronic dimension relating to classical Jewish texts and practices. Parts II and III focus on contemporary Jewish communities, in America and Israel, respectively. Some of the research on which these papers are based began with observed behavior and broadened its perspective to consider textual material. In other instances, the analysis of textual material is enriched by embracing social and cultural points of view. Taken as a whole the papers argue for a sensitivity to text combined with insight derived from the more conventional anthropological methods of interview, observation, and participation. The epilogue further explores some of the issues arising from this combined approach with regard to the study of Judaism, and in relation to a comparative framework.

Notes

1. Durkheim and Weber both had knowledge of Hebrew. Biographical accounts of Durkheim often point to his rabbinic family background, but I have not seen any serious study of what this in fact entailed in terms of his early education.

2. It might also be pointed out that the very division into chapters, universally used in printed versions of the Pentateuch, reflects the tradition of Christian translations, rather than a division based on Jewish tradition. The term "Old Testament," in contrast to the "New Testament," obviously is based on the point of view of Christianity. The term *Tanakh* (used, for example by Andriolo 1981), is an acronym based on Torah (the Pentateuch), *Nevi'im* (the Prophets), and *Ketuvim* (the Scriptures) and is the common term used to refer to the Old Testament in modern Hebrew.

3. A distinction must be made between grand theory diffusionism, exemplified by the *kulturkreis* school (Lowie 1937, Ch. 11) and the diffusionism of Boas and his students which was based on first-hand fieldwork and which only attempted generalizations concerning limited cultural regions.

4. See Kaufmann (1960, 208–211) for a brief summary of his views on the compilation of the Torah book, and its relationship to the prophetic books.

5. Cassuto (1973, 1–16).

6. For example, Kaufmann's discussion of religion and magic (1948, 1:286–303) leans heavily on early British and continental anthropological works, but seems not to reflect the influence of Boas and his students, which would have appeared congenial to his point of view.

7. The modern study of Judaism coalesced in a scholarly movement known as the *Wissenschaft des Judentums,* or the "Science of Judaism." Taking shape in Germany in the early part of the nineteenth century, the *Wissenschaft* program was formulated by men steeped in Jewish learning who proclaimed the necessity of applying the standards of contemporary Western scholarship to Jewish studies. Zunz's essay (1818) is generally taken as a comprehensive programmatic statement of this movement (see Glatzer 1964; Dinur 1972; Schorsch 1975, 1983). Wissenschaft scholars had hoped to establish the Science of Judaism within the universities, ensuring its place alongside other academic

disciplines and benefiting from association with them. A positive response, however, from the academic institutions of their day, was not forthcoming.

The challenge to traditional Jewish society and thought, presented by *Wissenschaft* scholarship, did not come from the exercise of rational procedures of inference in the study of texts (see, for example, note 10), so much as from the basic assumptions to which these methods were seen to be wed. Earlier generations of Jewish scholars produced their writings while assuming that the history of Israel was the central arena within which God's purpose on earth was made manifest, but the nineteenth century authors focused on Jewish history while giving primacy to the overall history of the world, which, of course, was seen through European eyes.

8. See the quote by Scholem, pp. 15–16.

9. It is instructive to compare Greenberg's appreciation of premodern culture and speech with the term "restricted codes" utilized by Bernstein (1964), with reference to working-class speech.

10. The word "ten" (*'asarah*) qualifying Joseph's brothers in the verse in Genesis appears in a relatively uncommon grammatical construction. The word *'asarah* in a similar construction is also found in Joshua 17:5, which describes how the land of the Menasheh tribe was divided into ten tracts. The division of Menasheh partially reflects the special decision to allot land to the daughters of Zelophehad (Numbers 27:1–7, 36:2–11). The case of the daughters of Zelophehad reflects a threat to the integrity of the *Makhir* lineage within the tribe of Menasheh, and perhaps the linguistic similarity forms the basis for interpreting Joseph's brothers as being both united and divided. In considering this interpretation, the fact that Menasheh was Joseph's son may also be kept in mind.

I would also like to call attention to the statement of Talmon (1978) who, in discussing the stylistic technique of "resumptive repetition," makes the point that medieval commentators "already remarked on this technique, and defined it in terms which are surprisingly similar to, nay identical with, the ones to which [modern scholars] had recourse" (p. 14). He goes on to say, however, that in applying the stylistic notion to the understanding of text, contemporary scholars distinguish between the work of the authors and the editors, and that "this very distinction betrays a critical attitude to biblical literature which in no way can be taken to represent the view of a premodern exegete." (p. 16).

11. Chouraqui (1952, 264), in describing education among the Jews of North Africa, states: "Pour l'enfant, Abraham s'en allant à Haran ou vers Moriah, c'est le père qu'il voit cheminer quotidiennement sur son ânesse; Hillel ou Gamliel enseignant aux disciples, c'est le rabbin du village: même costume, mêmes moeurs." (To the child, Abraham on his way to Haran or to Moriah resembled his father whom he saw riding along daily on his donkey; Hillel or Gamliel teaching their pupils could have been the village rabbi—with the same dress ar.d same customs.) It should be noted that many of the well-known biblical commentators, such as Abraham ibn Ezra, lived and traveled in Middle Eas-

tern environments. Rashi, the most widely known, lived in France, but it must be appreciated that in this period of time, the majority of Jews still lived in the Middle Eastern world (including Muslim Spain and North Africa). Even in an European environment, it can be argued that intimate familiarity with the text became a force in animating social life, as is evident in this account of *shtetl*-born Shmuel, recalling the beginning of the present century:

> We *cheder* [primary religious school] boys were always together whenever we weren't helping our parents. We were raised on four cultures. We knew Jewish [Yiddish] at home. We knew Polish naturally. After the Czar took over, we had to learn Russian. And there was Hebrew, of course. Hebrew was our spiritual culture. The March of the Kings held us in that tongue. The people were so real for us, the melancholy King Saul, the brilliant singer Solomon, the angry poetic suffering of Jeremiah—he was my favorite. We could always find heroes for us in there. We played our games in Jewish, but from Hebrew came the ideas. Whenever we were free from school, we would play out certain games. We always fell back to the Bible itself and played it out (Myerhoff 1978:58–59).

12. Sahlins (1976, chap. 2) has portrayed the tension in anthropological theorizing between a conception of culture revolving around a "problematic of the symbolic" and views which see culture as the "instrumental realization of biological necessities."

13. See, for example, Firth (1973, 53n). Bloom (1975), basing himself on Scholem, claims to have found the seeds of a modern "theory of influence" in Kabbalistic conceptions. Sharot (1982) has attempted to balance Scholem's approach with systematic sociological comparison.

14. Evans-Pritchard's instructive survey of *Theories of Primitive Religion* (1965) distinguishes between psychological and sociological theories, while recognizing the difference between intellectualist and emotionalist theories in the first category.

15. In anthropological parlance, the structuralism associated with the work of Levi-Strauss is to be distinguished from the earlier structural-functionalism of Radcliffe-Brown (1922), or the functionalism of Malinowski (1922), both of whom laid greater emphasis on the behavioral/institutional side of social life, as compared to their concern with cultural or ideational structures.

16. Leach (1976, 6) takes note of these two different directions in his work.

17. On this point, see Weber (1971, 11).

18. Rapoport (1980) attempts to draw several specific connections between features of language and universal religious notions and sentiments. (See also Bateson 1972, xxv.)

19. The term is used in the sense suggested by Moore (1975).

20. This is not the place to discuss the recent research which has demonstrated elementary linguistic abilities among intelligent primates (Mounin 1976).

21. Silverstein (1976) has emphasized that attention to the indexical mode of signification is important in the contextual understanding of speech. Doleve-Gandelman's paper in part three of this volume, utilizing the notion of "shifter," is an example of that importance.

22. The hermeneutic approach to culture is highlighted in recent works. See, for example, Agar (1980), Babcock (1980), Boon (1982), Frank (1979), Geertz (1973), and Rabinow and Sullivan (1979).

23. The terms are taken from Van Gennep: "Thus folklore produces a feeling that the observed facts contain the seeds of future possibilities whereas the historical fact makes one feel that all its possibilities have already been expressed" (quoted by Belmont 1979, 75). A similar point of view has been expressed by Bauman (1975), in propounding a performance orientation in studying verbal art.

24. Leach (1969, 34) remarks that "the structuralist anthropologist is much closer to the theologian than is the orthodox historian."

25. For example, Levy (1984, 90) states that "Newars were frequently my collaborators, and indeed often my masters in analysis."

26. The study of great traditions over time may have certain methodological advantages with regard to the interpretation of symbolism, even though symbolic analysis has not often dealt with diachronic development (Ohnuki-Tierney 1981). Colby et al. (1981, 433) cite the methodological question that given 3 major symbols with 7 meanings each, there are 343 possible triadic combinations of these meanings, leaving the interpreter a wide open field to find something that fits a hypothesis (see Sperber 1975, 64). In cases where there is documentary evidence of historical development, however, where some symbol combinations and interpretations reoccur in different social and cultural settings, there is more of a basis on which to sort out major (surviving) symbols from minor ones, and to utilize covariation in understanding the relationship of interpretations to particular historical circumstances.

27. Van Gennep, who, as cited in note 23, saw in folk practices "the seeds of future possibilities," was equally willing to entertain the hypothesis that there were enduring and widespread similarities in the work of Jewish artisans from ancient times to the present (1926).

28. See also Soler (1979) and Bahloul (1983). Zenner (1977) provides a general discussion on anthropological explanations of Jewish dietary rules.

29. Andriolo (1981, 277, n. 8) cites about ten studies in this vein, and the list can easily be lengthened. See for example Carroll (1977), Leach (1976, 81–

93), Leach and Aycock (1983), Marshall (1979), Paul (1980), Pitt-Rivers (1977), and Pocock (1975).

   30. Rubin's (1977) study utilizes Douglas's ideas with regard to mourning practices in the mishnaic and talmudic periods.

   31. A recent attempt to construct a new "epistemology of Jewish studies" (Trigano 1984), takes as a starting point that "the Divine, in Jewish conscious-ness, is objectively a social, political and historical relationship to a (Sinaitic) text" (p.35). See, also, Bloom (1983).

   32. Derrida (1974) has claimed that the valorization of speech over writ-ing, as the essential form of language, reflects an ancient cultural bias in Wes-tern thought. Jewish tradition appears to assume a subtle interplay between the two.

   33. The term *mitzvah* in Jewish culture is one that requires "unpacking." See, for example, Heschel 1956, 352–65.

   34. The talmudic concept of *hiddur mitzvah* means to embellish or adorn a *mitzvah*, materially, thereby adding to its honor.

References Cited

Agar,M. (1980). "Hermeneutics in Anthropology: A Review Essay." *Ethos* 8:253–72.

Andriolo, K. R. (1981). "Myth and History: A General Model and Its Application to the Bible." *American Anthropologist* 83:261–84.

Austin, J. (1962). *How to do Things with Words.* Oxford: Clarendon Press.

Babcock, B. A. (1980). "Reflexivity: Definitions and Discrimination." *Semiotica* 30:1–14.

Bahloul, J. (1983). *Le culte de la Table Dressée: Rites et traditions de la table juive algerienne.* Paris: Metailie.

Baron, S. W. (1942). *The Jewish Community: Its History and Structure to the American Revolution.* 3 vols. Philadelphia: Jewish Publication Society.

Bateson, G. (1972). *Steps to an Ecology of Mind.* San Francisco: Chandler.

Bauman, R. (1975). "Verbal Art as Performance." *American Anthropologist* 77:290–311.

Belmont, N. (1979). *Arnold Van Gennep: The Creator of French Ethnography.* Translated by Derek Coltman. Chicago: University of Chicago Press.

Ben Dor, Z. (1982). *The Israelite Bet-ab from the Settlement to the End of the Monarchy.* Ph.D. diss. Hebrew University of Jerusalem. Hebrew, with English summary.

Benedict, R. (1934). *Patterns of Culture.* Boston: Houghton Mifflin.

Bernstein, B. (1964). "Elaborated and Restricted Codes: Their Social Origins and Some Consequences." *American Anthropologist* 66 (2):55–69.

Biale, D. (1979). *Gershom Scholem: Kabbalah and Counter-History.* Cambridge, Ma.: Harvard University Press.

Bloom, H. (1975). *Kabbalah and Criticism.* New York: Seabury Press.

_____. (1983). "Jewish Culture and Jewish Memory." *Dialectical Anthropology* 8:7–19.

Boas, F. (1896). "The Limitations of the Comparative Method." *Science* 4:901–908. Reprinted in F. Boas. *Race, Language and Culture.* New York: Macmillan, 1940.

_____. (1940). *Race, Language and Culture.* Toronto: Macmillian.

Bokser, B. (1984). *The Origins of the Seder: The Passover Rite and Early Rabbinic Judaism.* Berkeley: University of California Press.

Boon, J. A. (1972). *From Symbolism to Structuralism: Lévi-Strauss in a Literary Tradition.* Oxford: Blackwell.

_____. (1982). *Other Tribes, Other Scribes: Symbolic Anthropology in the Comparative Study of Cultures, Histories, Religions, and Texts.* Cambridge: Cambridge University Press.

Bruner, E. M., ed. (1984). *Text, Play and Story: Proceedings, American Ethnological Society.* Washington, D.C.: American Ethnological Society.

Carroll, M. P. (1977). "Leach, Genesis and Structural Analysis: A Critical Evaluation." *American Ethnologist* 4:663–77.

Cassuto, U. (1961 [orig. 1941]). *The Documentary Hypothesis and the Composition of the Pentateuch.* Translated by Israel Abrahams. Jerusalem: Magnes Press.

_____. (1973). *Biblical and Oriental Studies,* vol. 1. Translated by Israel Abrahams. Jerusalem: Magnes Press.

Chomsky, N. (1957). *Syntactic Structures.* The Hague: Mouton.

Chouraqui, A. (1952). *Marche vers l'occident: les Juifs d'Afrique du Nord.* Paris: Presses Universitaires de Paris.

Colby, B. N., J. W. Fernandez, and D. B. Kronenfeld (1981). "Toward a Convergence of Cognitive and Symbolic Anthropology." *American Ethnologist* 8:422–50.

Demsky, A. (1976). *Literacy in Israel and Among Neighboring Peoples in the Biblical Period.* Ph. diss. Hebrew University of Jerusalem. Hebrew, with English summary.

Derrida, J. (1974). *Of Grammatology.* Translated by G. C. Spivak. Baltimore: Johns Hopkins University Press.

Deshen, S. (1979). "The Kol Nidre Enigma: An Anthropological View of the Day of Atonement Liturgy." *Ethnology* 18:121-33.

_____. (1980). "The Enigma of *Kol Nidre:* An Anthropological and Historical Investigation." In E. Etkes and Y. Salmon, eds. *Studies in the History of Jewish Society in the Middle Ages and in the Modern World. Essays in Honor of J. Katz.* Jerusalem: Magnes, 136-53, Hebrew.

Diener, P. and E. E. Robkin (1978). "Ecology, Evolution, and the Search for Cultural Origins: The Question of Islamic Pig Prohibition." *Current Anthropology* 19:493-540.

Dinur, B. (1972). "Wissenschaft des Judentums." *Encyclopedia Judaica.* New York: Macmillan, 16:572-73.

Douglas, M. (1966). *Purity and Danger: An Analysis of Concepts of Pollution and Taboo.* New York: Praeger.

_____. (1973). "Critique and Commentary." In J. Neusner, ed. *The Idea of Purity in Ancient Judaism.* Leiden: Brill, 137-42.

Dubnow, S. M. (1925-1929 [orig. 1901-1905]). *An Outline of Jewish History.* 3 vols. Translated from the Russian. New York: M. N. Maisil.

Durkheim, E. (1912). *Les formes élementaires de la vie religieuse.* Paris: F. Alcan.

_____. (1964 [orig. 1893]). *The Division of Labor in Society.* New York: The Free Press.

Evans-Pritchard, E. E. (1965). *Theories of Primitive Religion.* Oxford: Oxford University Press.

Fahim, H., K. Helmer, E. Colson, T. N. Madan, H. Kelman, and T. Asad. (1980). "Indigenous Anthropology in Non-Western Countries: A Further Elaboration." *Current Anthropology* 21:644-63.

Firth, R. (1973). *Symbols, Public and Private.* London: Allen and Unwin.

Fortes, M. (1969). *Kinship and the Social Order.* Chicago: Aldine.

Frank, G. (1979). "Finding the Common Denominator: A Phenomenological Critique of Life History Method." *Ethos* 7:68-94.

Frazer, J. (1890 [second ed. 1900]). *The Golden Bough: A Study in Magic and Religion.* 2 vols. London: Macmillan.

_____. (1918). *Folklore in the Old Testament.* 3 vols. London: Macmillan.

Fredman, R. G. (1981). *The Passover Seder: Afikoman in Exile.* Philadelphia: University of Pennsylvania Press.

Freud, S. (1913). *Totem und Tabu.* Vienna: Hugo Heller. Translated by James Strachey. London: Routledge and Kegan Paul, 1950.

Fustel De Coulanges, N. D. (1874). *The Ancient City.* Translated by Willard Small. Boston: Lee and Shepard.

Geertz, C. (1973). *The Interpretation of Cultures.* New York: Basic Books.

Glatzer, N. N. (1964). "The Beginnings of Modern Jewish Studies." In A. Altmann, ed. *Studies in 19th Century Jewish Intellectual History* . Cambridge, Ma.: Harvard University Press, 27–45.

Goldberg, H. E. (1978). "The Mimuna and the Minority Status of Moroccan Jews." *Ethnology* 17:75–87.

Goody, J., ed. (1968). *Literacy in Traditional Societies.* Cambridge: Cambridge University Press.

Goshen-Gottstein, M. (1980). "Wissenschaft des Judentums: Bible Research and Jewish Biblical Theology." In U. Simon and M. Goshen-Gottstein, eds. *Studies in Bible and Exegesis.* Ramat Gan: Bar-Ilan University Press, 243–55. Hebrew.

Greenberg, M. (1969). *Understanding Exodus.* New York: Behrman House.

Hahn, H. F. (1966). *The Old Testament in Modern Research.* With a Survey of Recent Literature by Horace D. Hummel. Philadelphia: Fortress Press.

Halivni, D. Weiss. (1986). *Midrash, Mishnah and Gemara: The Jewish Predilection for Justified Law.* Cambridge, Ma.: Harvard University Press.

Harris, M. (1974). *Cows, Pigs, Wars, and Witches: The Riddles of Culture.* New York: Random House, Vintage Books.

Heilman, S. (1983). *People of the Book: Drama, Fellowship and Religion.* Chicago: University of Chicago Press.

Heschel, A. J. (1956). *God in Search of Man: A Philosophy of Judaism.* Philadelphia: The Jewish Publication Society of America.

Hockett, C., and R. Ascher. (1964). "The Human Revolution." *Current Anthropology* 5:135–68.

Hubert, H., and M. Mauss. (1964 [orig. 1904]). *Sacrifice: Its Nature and Function.* London: Cohen and West.

Humphreys, S. C. (1978). *Anthropology and the Greeks.* London: Routledge and Kegan Paul.

Jain, R. K. (1977). *Text and Context: The Social Anthropology of Tradition.* Philadelphia: Institute for the Study of Human Issues.

Katz, J. (1961). *Tradition and Crisis: Jewish Society at the end of the Middle Ages.* New York: The Free Press.

Kaufmann, Y. (1948). *The History of the Israelite Religion: From Early Times Until the End of the Second Temple Period.* 4 vols. Jerusalem and Tel Aviv: Bialik Institute and Dvir. Hebrew.

————. (1960). *The Religion of Israel: From its Beginnings to the Babylonian Exile.* Translated and Abridged by Moshe Greenberg. Chicago: University of Chicago Press.

Kugelmass, J. (1985). "Even Solomon Would Have Trouble: Storytelling in the South Bronx." *Prooftexts* 5:45–65.

Leach, E. (1954). *Political Systems of Highland Burma: A Study of Kachin Social Structure.* Cambridge, Ma.: Harvard University Press.

————. (1969). *Genesis as Myth and Other Essays.* London: J. Cape.

————. (1970). *Claude Lévi-Strauss.* New York: Viking Press.

————. (1976). *Culture and Communication: The Logic by Which Symbols are Connected.* Cambridge: Cambridge University Press.

Leach, E., and D. A. Aycock. (1983). *Structuralist Interpretations of Biblical Myth.* Cambridge: Cambridge University Press.

Levi-Strauss, C. (1955). "The Structural Study of Myth." *Journal of American Folklore* 68:428–44.

————. (1963). *Totemism.* Translated by Rodney Needham. Boston: Beacon Press.

Levy, R. (1984). "Mead, Freeman, and Samoa: The Problem of Seeing Things as They Are." *Ethos* 12:85–92.

Lowie, R. (1937). *The History of Ethnological Theory.* London: Harrap.

Malinowski, B. (1922). *Argonauts of the Western Pacific.* London: Routledge and Kegan Paul.

Marshall, R. C. (1979). "Heroes and Hebrews: The Priest and the Promised Land." *American Ethnologist* 6:772–90.

Moore, S. F. (1975). "Epilogue: Uncertainties in Situations, Indeterminacies in Culture." In S. F. Moore and B. Myerhoff, eds. *Symbols and Politics in Communal Ideology: Cases and Questions.* Ithaca: Cornell University Press, 210–39.

Mounin, G. (1976). "Language, Communication, Chimpanzees." *Current Anthropology* 17:1–22.

Myerhoff, B. (1978). *Number Our Days.* New York: Simon and Schuster.

Neusner, J. (1973). *The Idea of Purity in Ancient Judaism.* With a Critique and Commentary by Mary Douglas. Leiden: Brill.

_____. (1982). *Formative Judaism: Religious, Historical and Literary Studies.* Brown Judaic Studies 37. Chico, Cal.: Scholars Press.

O'Flaherty, W. D. (1980). "Inside and Outside the Mouth of God: The Boundary Between Myth and Reality," *Daedalus* 109:93–126.

Ohnuki-Tierney, E. (1981). "Phases in Human Perception/Conception/Symbolization Processes: Cognitive Anthropology and Symbolic Classification." *American Ethnologist* 8:451–67.

Paul, R. A. (1980). "Symbolic Interpretation in Psychoanalysis and Anthropology." *Ethos* 8:286–94.

Pitt-Rivers, J. (1977). *The Fate of Shechem, or the Politics of Sex: Essays in the Anthropology of the Mediterranean.* Cambridge: Cambridge University Press.

Pocock, D. F. (1975). "North and South in the Book of Genesis." In G. Lienhardt and J. Beattie, eds. *Studies in Social Anthropology,* Oxford: Clarendon Press, 272–84.

Prell, R. E. (1983). Review of *The Passover Seder: Afikoman in Exile* by Ruth Gruber Fredman. *American Ethnologist.* 10:804–805.

Rabinow, P., and Sullivan, W. M., eds. (1979). *Interpretive Social Science: A Reader.* Berkeley: University of California Press.

Radcliffe-Brown, A. R. (1922). *The Andaman Islanders.* Cambridge: Cambridge University Press.

Rapoport, R. A. (1980). "Concluding Comments on Ritual and Reflexivity," *Semiotica* 30:181–93.

Redfield, R. (1956). *Peasant Society and Culture.* Chicago: University of Chicago Press.
_____. R. Linton, and M. J. Herskovits, (1935). "A Memorandum for the Study of Acculturation," *American Anthropologist* 33:149–52.

Ricouer, P. (1970). *Freud and Philosophy: An Essay on Interpretation.* Translated by D. Savage. New Haven: Yale University Press.

Rubin, N. (1977). *A Sociological Analysis of Jewish Mourning Patterns in the Mishnaic and Talmudic Periods.* Ph.D. diss. Bar-Ilan University. Hebrew, with English summary.

Sahlins, M.D. (1976). *Culture and Practical Reason.* Chicago: University of Chicago Press.

Said, E. W. (1978). *Orientalism.* New York: Random House.

Sapir, J. D. and C. Crocker, eds. (1977). *The Social Use of Metaphor: Essays on the Anthropology of Rhetoric.* Philadelphia: University of Pennsylvania Press.

Scholem, G. (1941). *Major Trends in Jewish Mysticism.* New York: Schocken.

Schorsch, I. (1975). "Ideology and History in the Age of Emancipation." In H. Graetz. *The Structure of Jewish History and Other Essays.* Translated and Edited by I. Schorsch. New York: The Jewish Theological Seminary of America, 1-62.

――――. (1983). "The Emergence of Historical Consciousness in Modern Judaism." *The Leo Baeck Institute Year Book* 28:413-37.

Sharot, S. (1982). *Messianism, Mysticism and Magic: A Sociological Analysis of Jewish Religious Movements.* Chapel Hill: University of North Carolina Press.

Silverstein, M. (1976). "Shifters, Linguistic Categories, and Cultural Description." In K. Basso and H. Selby, eds. *Meaning in Anthropology.* Albuquerque: University of New Mexico Press, 11-56.

Smith, W. R. (1914 [orig. 1889]). *Lectures on the Religion of the Semites,* New Edition. London: A and C. Black.

Soler, J. (1979). "The Semiotics of Food in the Bible." In R. Forster and O. Ranum, eds. *Food and Drink in History.* Baltimore: Johns Hopkins University Press, 126-38.

Sperber, D. (1975). *Rethinking Symbolism.* Translated by Alice Morton. Cambridge: Cambridge University Press.

Swartz, M. J., V. W. Turner, and A. Tuden, eds. (1966). *Political Anthropology.* Chicago: Aldine.

Talmon, S. (1978). "The Presentation of Synchroneity and Simultaneity in Biblical Narratives." In J. Heinemann and S. Werses, eds. *Studies in Hebrew Narrative Art Throughout the Ages,* Scripta Hierosolymitana. Jerusalem: Magnes Press, 9-26.

Tambiah, S. J. (1979). "A Performative Approach to Ritual." *Proceedings of the British Academy,* vol. 65. London: Oxford University Press.

Trigano. S. (1984). *La Demeure Oubliée: Genèse Religieuse du Politique* Paris: Lieu Commun.

Turner, V. (1957). *Schism and Continuity in an African Community.* Manchester: Manchester University Press.

――――. (1962). *Chihamba: The White Spirit.* Rhodes-Livingstone Paper No. 33. Manchester: Manchester University Press. Reprinted in V. Turner. *Revelation and Divination in Ndembu Ritual.* Ithaca: Cornell University Press, 1975 , 37-293.

_____. (1969). *The Ritual Process.* Chicago: Aldine.

_____. (1980). "Liminality and Morality." Paper presented at the Annual Meeting of the Israel Anthropological Association, Jerusalem, April, 1980.

_____. (1982). *From Ritual to Theatre: The Human Seriousness of Play.* New York: Performing Arts Journal Publications.

Tylor, E. B. (1871). *Primitive Culture.* 2 vols. London: John Murray.

Van Gennep, A. (1926). "Jewish Arts and Crafts in North Africa." *The Menorah Journal* 12 (1):43–48.

_____. (1960 [orig. 1908]). *The Rites of Passage.* Translated by M. B. Vizedom and G. L. Caffee. Chicago: University of Chicago Press.

Wallace, A. F. C. (1966). *Religion, an Anthropological View.* New York: Random House.

Weber, M. (1952 [orig. 1921]). *Ancient Judaism.* Translated and edited by H. H. Gerth and D. Martindale. Glencoe: Free Press.

_____. (1971). *The Interpretation of Social Reality.* Edited by J. E. T. Eldridge. New York: Scribner.

Wellhausen, J. (1885). *Prolegemena to the History of Israel.* Translated by J. S. Black and A. Menzies. With a Preface by W. Robertson Smith. Edinburgh: Adam and Charles Black.

Zborowski, M. (1955). "The Place of Book-Learning in Traditional Jewish Culture." In M. Mead and M. Wolfenstein, eds. *Childhood in Contemporary Cultures.* Chicago: University of Chicago Press, 118–41.

Zenner, W. P. (1977). "Kashrut and Rationality: The Dietary Laws in Recent Anthropological Writing." *Jewish Folklore and Ethnology Newsletter.* Max Weinrich Center for Advanced Jewish Studies of the YIVO Institute for Jewish Research 1 (2–3):11–18.

Zunz, L. (1818). *Etwas ueber die rabbinische Literatur: nebst Nachrichten ueber ein altes bis jetzt ungedrucktes hebraisches Werk.* Berlin: Maurerschen Buchandlung.

_____. (1832). *Die Gottesdienstlichen Vortrage der Juden, historich entwickelt.* Ein beitrag zur alterthumskunde und biblische kritik, zur literatur-und religion geschichte. Berlin : A. Asher.

PART I

History and Patterning

Introduction to Part I

Few anthropologists have followed the path of Kroeber (1957) in attempting to discuss the development of broad culture patterns, spanning both space and time. This has always been dangerous ground, and even the configurational approach in anthropology, growing out of the work of Benedict (1934), has normally concerned itself with localized cultures in the ethnographic present. Nevertheless, many maintain that questions relating to cultural/historical development constitute a legitimate area of anthropological concern, and that efforts should be made in this direction, the dangers of overgeneralization, subjectivism, and reification notwithstanding. By combining a knowledge of texts with an appreciation of pattern and of interpretive potential it may be possible to trace some of the strands which are part of the make-up of large cultural tapestries over time.

This section consists of three essays of this genre, two of them relating in detail to Jewish law or *halakhah*. Both Cooper and Zohar stress the importance of the link between the biblical text and the oral law culminating in the Mishnah at the beginning of the third century C.E. Before considering the papers in greater detail, however, a sketch of some of the factors prominent in shaping the *halakhah* over the generations must be presented.

The laws of the mishnaic period, originally transmitted orally, were eventually given written form (the period during which this took place is still a matter of debate). Just as the biblical text, viewed as based on divine authority, eventually needed to be supplemented by the oral law, so the Mishnah, and other legal collections such as the Tosefta, required elaboration as social conditions changed, both in ancient Palestine and in other centers where Jewish life developed. The continuing study, discussion, debates, and stories concerning the law on the part of the sages gave rise to the Talmud. One compendium of talmudic study evolved in Palestine, and was redacted in its final form about 400 C.E. A parallel compendium emerged in the other major concentration of Jewish life, Babylonia (Mesopotamia), and took its final form about 500 C.E. The Babylonian Talmud eventually was to spread more widely to other Jewish centers in the Middle East, North Africa, and Europe.

The talmudic laws, and their elaboration by subsequent generations of scholars, formed the basis of internal Jewish life throughout the medieval world, both under Islamic rule and Christian domination. For several centuries after the conclusion of the Babylonian Talmud, Mesopotamia continued to be a major center of Jewish life. The Abbasid empire, with its center at Baghdad, strengthened the office of a Jewish Exilarch (*resh geluta*), supposedly standing at the head of Jewish communities the world over. Side by side with the temporal leadership, rabbinic scholars, given the title of *gaon*, led the religious academies which received funds, students, and requests for guidance in the law from the far-flung communities of the Diaspora (Goitein 1971, 1–40). In a famous epistle of Sherira Gaon (d. 1006), a discussion of the history of the Talmud reached the sages of Kairouan in North Africa who had turned to him with an inquiry. The growth of talmudic scholarship in the Maghreb, in turn, was an important part of the process of its transmission to Spain from where it influenced other European Jewish communities.

The waning of the Abbasid empire and the political division of the Islamic world encouraged the process of decentralization of Jewish authority. Instead of dependence on a single center, rabbis in diverse regions were faced with the challenge of reaching decisions, making ordinances, and promulgating decrees in response to local conditions. The autonomy granted to the Jews, both under Christianity and under Islam, meant that many aspects of daily life could be regulated according to *halakhah*. Personal status, commercial agreements, and taxation, as well as strictly ritual matters, were subject to the scrutiny of rabbinic authority. This, of course, did not preclude influences of the wider environment, which were omnipresent, even when subtle. A classic example is found in Baer's (1938) analysis of the influence of Christian pietism on the Hasidim (pious) of Ashkenaz (the Rhineland) in the twelfth to thirteenth centuries. The instiution of a ban on polygamy in the Ashkenazi world, by Rabbi Gershom of Mayence ("The Light of the Exile," d. circa 1028), and its only partial acceptance among the Jewish communities in the Middle East, is another outstanding example of such influence. The impact of Islamic culture on medieval Jewish poetry and philosophy is also well known.

The wider society had impact, of course, in the everyday realms of food, dress, speech, and popular religion. The dispersion of Jewish communities into different regions gave rise to distinct rabbinic traditions, notably the Spanish (Sephardi) and Ashkenazi (German). This division began to take place at about the beginning of the present millennium. Each tradition, however, recognized the validity of the other in its given geographic orbit.

The development of different rabbinic traditions did not preclude mutual exchange. While there was no central Jewish authority, rabbinic writings spread from one end of the Jewish world to the other, and outstanding contributions became the heritage of communities in diverse lands and regions. The strong internal autonomy which characterized the Jews of Poland/ Lithuania at the time of the Council of the Four Lands (sixteenth century; Ben-Sasson 1976), based itself on communal ordinances of Spanish rabbis of the Middle Ages.

There were several attempts at codifying the complex laws which continued to evolve since talmudic times. The first notable effort was that of Isaac al-Fasi (eleventh century), and Maimonides' (d.1204) compilation, the *Mishneh Torah,* marked a landmark in this direction. Jacob ben Asher of German origin, who grew up in thirteenth century Spain, produced the *Arba'ah Turim,* whose organization is the basis of the last major code, that of Joseph Caro in the sixteenth century (the *Shulhan Arukh*). This latter work is the basis of orthopraxy today, both within Sephardi and Ashkenazi circles.

At the same period of time, the developments in the realm of kabbalah mysticism by Isaac Luria and his school, centered in Safed, furthered this spiritual movement. Caro himself was an active mystic (Werblowsky 1962). Scholem's analysis of the mystical tradition in Judaism has emphasized the interplay of rabbinic authority, expressed in *halakhah*, and the dynamic, vivifying influence of kabbalah (Scholem 1974; Biale 1979). Lurianic kabbalism was the last religious movement to affect the Jewish world in general, and its imprint is evident in many areas of standard Jewish life, such as the traditional prayer book in both Ashkenazi and Sephardi versions.

As Scholem has shown, Lurianic kabbalah made the longing for redemption, which was heightened by the exile from Spain and the apostasy of tens of thousands of Jews there in the fifteenth century, part of the consciousness of the individual Jew. This was accomplished by interpreting the commandments as acts, carried out by the individual, which worked toward bringing about the redemption of Israel and the cosmos. At the same period of time, Marranos, Jews who had ostensibly converted to Christianity but who observed Jewish practices secretly, moved from Spain to various centers in Europe, such as Antwerp and Leghorn. When many of these Marranos returned to Judaism, they naturally introduced the influences of the wider society in which they had learned to function with competence. In the seventeenth century, the Jewish world was rocked by the messianic movement centered on the person of Shabbetai Zvi, who, despite his eventual apostasy to Islam (in 1666), succeeded in raising concrete expectations of relief from the exile, and undermining attitudes toward rabbinic authority on which traditional life was based. Thus, in the eighteenth century, the period when the enlightenment and the political developments in Europe were about to alter, irrevocably, the nature of the Jewish communities in its midst, there already existed some religious and cultural currents within the Jewish world which challenged the rabbinic and *halakhic* bases of medieval Jewish society.

At the beginning of the eighteenth century there were about 2,000,000 Jews in the world, roughly divided equally between those in Europe and the communities of the Middle East and North Africa. From this period of time it is clear that there was the beginning of the break-up of traditional Jewish life, which proceeded at different paces, and in different forms, in the various regions of the Diaspora. In Parts II and III of this volume, some of the developments shaping Judaism in the United States and in Israel, the two most important centers of Jewish life today, will be sketched. Attempts to preserve, adapt, or rebuild Judaism in the contemporary world all refer back to the classic texts which represent Judaism in antiquity and the middle ages. In this first section, three studies with an anthropological orientation will be presented which attempt to delineate cultural patterns having significance in distinct historical circumstances.

The paper by Cooper deals primarily with *halakhah*, rabbinic law. Drawing on structuralist methodology, he demonstrates that there is an underlying logic linking diverse areas of *halakhah* (dietary laws, laws concerning dress, and laws forbidding the planting of grain in the vineyard), which on the surface appear very different from one another. Laws such as these have often caught the attention of anthropological theorists. Frazer (1918, 111ff.) placed the Jewish prohibition on eating meat with milk in the comparative context of taboos which are common in East African pastoral societies. Durkheim (1965, 49) cited the dietetic regulations of the Hebrews, and the prohibition of wearing mixed garments, as examples of "rites which are completely independent of all idea of gods or spiritual beings." Cooper's analysis, which is cautious about conclusions concerning the meaning of the rules, nevertheless points to possible links between these systems of rules and other symbols which are central in Judaism.

His argument implies that the different sets of rules are linked by a logic that has its locus in broad cultural conceptions which are larger than any specific proof-text (an assumption somewhat akin to Katz's [1983, chap. 13] recent allusion to a "ritual instinct" with regard to Sabbath restrictions). These popular cultural conceptions (and not a standard arsenal of anthropological jargon) justify the use of terms such as "sacred" and "profane" for several legal notions which are distinct from one another from the point of view of formal *halakhah*. The logic, he claims, can be teased out of the biblical text, mishnaic rules, and even decisions given in recent times with regard to customary practices. He suggests that the basic notion can best be expressed in the opposition between life and death, a phrasing which can be found in other well-known texts. Cooper's analysis thus suggests a way that the formalistic or legalistic side of *halakhah* may be linked to enduring values and affective responses.

The paper by Zohar is closer to conventional history in that it limits itself to two time periods and tries to understand the links between them. In an attempt to elucidate the significance of the rules governing the Sabbatical year, Zohar delves into the details of the texts of the mishnaic and biblical periods. His analysis of the religious significance of the rules is aided by reference to the anthropological concept of *communitas*, which takes on somewhat different meanings in the two periods discussed.

The interpretive bent of the paper is revealed by its structure. Rather than beginning with the earlier period, and moving on to the later, as standard historiography would dictate, the argument starts by exposing the problematics of the mishnaic (and other contemporary textual) materials. This discussion then leads to a careful consideration of the sources of the laws of the Mishnah in Leviticus. The style of organizing the material is not dissimilar to the manner of traditional talmudic study: the rabbinic law, most directly relevant to the rules of living, is presented first and only afterwards does one scrutinize the biblical text. While at first glance this may seem an intellectually dangerous procedure for an historian, it has its parallels in anthropological argumentation. Evans-Pritchard (1961, 16) once characterized the work of anthropologists, who begin with a contemporary community and try to unravel its past, as "writing history backwards," a formulation apparently approved of by Geertz (1968, x-xii, 59ff.).

Zohar shows the changes that the laws concerning the consumption of food during the Sabbatical year have undergone. Yet, throughout, the rabbis found proof-texts in the Bible to justify their new interpretations. This was neither naiveté nor cynicism on their part but part of a world view, according to Zohar, for reinterpretation "was seen by the sages as being due to an inherent ambiguity and multivocality, intentionally implanted in the text by God as an expression of His divine love and concern for Israel." This same world view gave rise to the notion of the "oral Torah" also originating on Mt. Sinai, whose purpose was to explain, supplement, and even overrule the "written Torah" (see Towner 1982).

Paradoxical as it may seem, this view of the divine text has implications that in some ways parallel the school of thought which challenges the authority of all texts, that of deconstructionism (see Norris 1982). Just as it is possible to argue that each reading of a text is in fact the creation of a new one, so it is possible to claim that the text of absolute authority contains within it, or foresees, all possible interpretations. One famous talmudic story, in which Moses visits Rabbi Akiva's house of study (in the second century C.E.) is an illustration of this view (BT *Menahot* 29b). According to the tale, Moses could not understand what Rabbi Akiva was teaching, but was consoled to hear the lawgiver claim that his interpretation was based on the oral tradition, transmitted to Moses at Sinai.

At the same time, the study of Judaic culture in various periods may present a challenge to an unbalanced deconstructionist position. If threads of continuity and similarity of pattern that bridge different periods and areas can be found, then this would support the position that the text is not infinitely malleable. The text helps shape, and reflects, a value system which is recognizable in its emphases and distinctiveness, despite the various possibilities for interpretation inherent in it and the new meanings which in some instances have been forced on it.

This outlook on text informs Goldberg's essay, which is even freer in its associative license than the two preceding papers, and which relates to a variety of religious forms: dancing with the Torah, customs surrounding weddings, homiletics, and other ritual practices and texts. He attempts to show the frequent symbolic linkage of the text, representing cultural continuity, with expressions of biological continuity, in a range of different settings. The cases cited also span Jewish history, from the biblical narrative to contemporary celebrations of the Simhat Torah festival. The symbolic association highlighted may be seen in comparative perspective, as an example of a nature/culture contrast and linkage, but also as consistently characteristic of a particular tradition. The characteristic association, however, is general enough to take on specific forms and additional meanings in given historic situations.

Goldberg's paper does not focus on *halakhah* per se, although there clearly is a tendency, in traditional Jewish society, for all customary behavior to be subjected to the scrutiny of *halakhic* approval. *Halakhah* thus emerges as an all-pervasive reality in Jewish life, a phenomenon which does not have a precise parallel elsewhere.[1] It is common to speak of contrasts within religious life such as ritual and myth, prophet and priest, mysticism and legalism, but *halakhah* fits none of these neatly. Rather, it may be seen as a potential meeting point of all, particularly when juxtaposed to its natural opposite and complement in Jewish history, interpretive *midrash. Halakhah* can be the realization of a deeply held belief as well as a routine empty gesture. It can be viewed as part of a complex formalistic legal system, but also may be imbued with cosmic meaning, as was the purpose of some of the ritual innovations of Lurianic kabbalah (and, according to Zohar, was also the purpose of some of the innovations of the mishnaic sages). *Halakhah* can also represent a blend of local custom (sometimes based on what is often called "superstition") and principles derived from the great tradition. In short, one might say that *halakhah* has been an ever-present element in Jewish *praxis*, linked by threads of meaning to many other aspects of Jewish social and cultural life.

All three papers make reference to general values and themes, while giving historic examples of their concretization in performance. Parts II and III will show how some of the same themes and rituals are realized in contemporary settings, where the understanding of Jewish practices can be combined with a more detailed consideration of their specific contexts.

Harvey E. Goldberg

Note

1. There clearly is a parallel between Jewish *halakhah* and Muslim *shari'a;* both terms suggest a path along which the adherent must walk. The number of specified obligations and prohibitions in Judaism, however, is far greater than in Islam, and this difference in quantity results in a difference in quality between the two religious systems.

References Cited

Baer, F. (1938). "The Religious-Social Teaching of 'Sepher Hassidim'," *Zion: A Quarterly of Jewish History Research* 3:1–50. Hebrew, with English summary.

Benedict, R. (1934). *Patterns of Culture.* Boston: Houghton-Mifflin.

Ben-Sasson, H. H. (1976). "Autonomy in Institutions." In H. H. Ben-Sasson, ed. *History of the Jewish People.* London: Weidenfeld and Nicolson, 659–90.

Biale, D. (1979). *Gershom Scholem: Kabbalah and Counter-History.* Cambridge, Ma.: Harvard University Press.

Durkheim, E. (1965). *The Elementary Forms of the Religious Life.* New York: Free Press.

Evans-Pritchard, E. E. (1961). *Anthropology and History.* Manchester: Manchester University Press.

Frazer, J. G. (1918). *Folklore in the Old Testament,* vol. 3. London: Macmillan.

Geertz, C. (1968). *Islam Observed: Religious Development in Morocco and Indonesia.* New Haven: Yale University Press.

Goitein, S. D. (1971). *A Mediterranean Society,* vol. 2. Berkeley: University of California Press.

Katz, J. (1983). *The Sabbath Gentile: The Socio-economic and Halakhic Background to the Employment of Gentiles on Jewish Sabbaths and Festivals.* Jerusalem: Shazar Center. Hebrew.

Kroeber, A. (1957). *Style and Civilization.* Ithaca: Cornell University Press.

Norris, C. (1982). *Deconstructionism: Theory and Practice.* London: Methuen.

Scholem, G. (1974). *Kabbalah.* Jerusalem: Keter.

Towner, W. S. (1982). "Hermeneutical Systems of Hillel and the Tannaim: A Fresh Look." *Hebrew Union College Annual* 53:101–103.

Werblowsky, R. J. Z. (1962). *Joseph Karo: Lawyer and Mystic.* London: Oxford University Press.

CHAPTER 1

The Laws of Mixture: An Anthropological Study in *Halakhah*

SAMUEL COOPER

I. Introduction

This paper is an attempt to study Jewish culture in an anthropological manner, using the perception of members of the cultural system as these are reflected in primary sources. By primary sources, is meant, in particular, texts, in their original form, which may be approached using insights gained generally by anthropologists through field research, an understanding which comes to anthropologists as participants in Jewish religion and social life. One notable contribution of this nature is the seminal paper by Deshen (1979) on "The Kol Nidre Enigma,"[1] in which both aspects of anthropological research are featured. Insights gained from personal participation in the Yom Kippur ritual and the ability to understand and evaluate the relevant liturgical and other religious texts were key factors in Deshen's analysis. In addition, his analysis shows a sensitivity to popular religious culture, which sometimes is in tension with official rulings that find more direct expression in texts. The present study will also seek to take these various aspects of anthropological research into account while analyzing the laws of mixture.

This analysis also attempts to demonstrate some of the drawbacks of what might be termed a "closed systems approach." The system to be described here is a tendency or a tension which exists in Judaism. By considering the development of the laws of mixture over time, we observed the tendency of a cultural system to mold elements introduced into it into a particular form or configuration. This is almost always done by expanding the capacity of symbols to absorb new meanings. It is carried out in this case by manipulating certain elements of a legal system to follow the dictates of custom. Both the development of law and the changing customs may be seen as expressions of basic tendencies in Jewish culture. Law attempts to integrate and control custom, but this attempt is never complete and therefore is always open-ended and changing.

The analysis will focus on laws of mixture, an indigenous category, which appears often in the cultural repertoire of the Jews—especially that part of the culture which is recorded in writing in *halakhah* or the body of Jewish law. By showing that halakhah exists, over time, as a system with rules of its own—something that could only happen in a literate culture—this study goes beyond using the laws of the Bible as a metaphor for social/cultural life at a particular point in time (Douglas 1966; Soler 1979). The halakhic system becomes representative of the periodic stresses and tensions in evolving Jewish culture. Halakhah is reflexive; it is written and therefore is always available as a means of comparison between what is (custom) and what ought to be (law). This reflexivity implies that it can always be looked back on and remains in dynamic tension with the actual way people do things.

II. Halakhah

The term "halakhah" refers to the legal side of Judaism and is traditionally viewed as including the written law, the laws which are written in the Bible, and the oral law, that is the law as it is written in the Talmud as well as law generated out of the written and oral laws as they are customarily interpreted. Halakhah is a system whereby basic Jewish legal and cultural premises can be intrepreted and applied to any aspect of Jewish life in order to determine the way in which the observant Jew is to behave.

Elements of halakhah developed and were written down at different times under varying social and cultural constraints. The laws of the Bible are the starting point. Jewish tradition has it that along with the law as it is written in the Bible, there is a second body—the oral law (or oral Torah)—which was given to Moses on Mt. Sinai and was to be transmitted by word-of-mouth. This oral law—what is today called the Mishnah (the term "Talmud" sometimes is used to include the Mishnah as well)—and the Talmud is made up of both substantive law and the system of rules for interpreting and understanding the written law in the Bible.

The oral law was to have remained an unwritten system of interpretation. The concern that much of the oral law would be lost after the destruction of the center of Jewish life in Jerusalem and the dispersion of communities to the Diaspora, probably was the basis for its being written down. The existence of the Talmud in written form gave further impetus to its study and the development of the oral law. Numerous commentaries have been written on the Talmud; among the most important are those of Rabbi Shlomo Yitzhaqi (Rashi) of Troyes, France (1040-1105).

Since halakhah is by and large a system of interpretation, a set of ways and means by which new questions can be broached and answered, there arise differences of opinion in the halakhah—including many arguments which are not resolved. Interpretations of the Talmud have been written in different cultural settings and historical periods and the Talmud continues to be interpreted and explained today by Jewish religious scholars. The study of Talmud is considered to be worthy in its own right, even if there is no immediate application of the legal questions discussed. One aspect of halakhah which does cover the application of the law is the *sh'elot u-teshuvot* or responsa. These are volumes of questions posed to important rabbinic scholars regarding issues in need of clarification. Since these questions are addressed to particular rabbis by particular communities, they present an interesting picture of the kinds of problems Jews of different parts of the world have had to address in different historical periods.

Halakhah is thus a living system which grows and develops with time, geography, and changing conditions of Jewish life. As such, it is of interest from the point of view of the anthropologist. This area is called kind of consistencies which are retained over the vicissitudes of time and place. This paper proposes to examine one small area of halakhic interest from the point-of-view of the anthropologist. This area is called *hilkhot ta'arovot*—laws of mixture.

III. Laws of Mixture

The phrase "laws of mixture" is an established category within halakhah. The Jewish legal system recognizes that certain mixtures are a problem for Jews and need to be addressed formally. In addition to the general category of laws of mixture there are specialized categories of mixtures. These are *kilayim,* mixed species in agriculture; *basar be-ḥalav,* the mixing of meat and milk; and *sha'atnez,* the mixing of wool and linen. The laws of mixture suggest that Jewish law and practice may be based on a system of cultural classification. The fact that this system of classification is overt and clearly stated encourages us to apply anthropological analyses directly.

Investigation of the total range of mixtures prohibited by Jewish law leaves us with a bewildering number of categories. The simple analysis of each type of agricultural mixture recorded in the Mishnah *Kilayim* becomes a most tedious and difficult task. It is appropriate, therefore, to try to discover a means for limiting the field by defining or discovering a subclass of mixtures which would provide a less complicated array of mixtures for an initial investigation. Here, halakhah itself provides an answer by presenting the restriction of *asur be-hana'a.*

Asur be-hana'a means "forbidden from benefit" and is a more stringent restriction than a simple prohibition. Simple prohibition means that a Jew is forbidden to do a certain act. Grafting a fruit of one species onto another is prohibited; but what is to become of the outcome, the fruit that may grow from such grafting? Here the law is that the Jew may eat the fruit. It is the act of mixing which is prohibited, not the act of eating. *Asur be-hana'a* goes beyond the simple prohibition of an act. Not only is the act of making the mixture forbidden, but the use of such a mixture for any purpose whatsoever is strictly prohibited. Thus, the mixing of meat and milk is not only prohibited as an act, but use of the product also is forbidden. One may not benefit in any way from such a mixture. For example, paint made from a meat/milk mixture is forbidden even though it is not eaten but spread on the wall.

An examination of mixtures which are *asur be-hana'a* is much more manageable since there are only three major members of this class of mixtures. All of the three cases are not considered simple mixtures (*ta'arovot*), but have their own special categories and in some way are outstanding.

The three forbidden mixtures which are the subject of this paper are:

basar be-ḥalav—The prohibition against mixtures of meat and milk.

sha'atnez—The prohibition against mixtures of wool and linen.

kil'ei hakerem—The prohibition against mixtures of grape and wheat/barley.

These three prohibitions are grouped together, not because they occur in adjacent biblical verses,[2] but because the law, as it has developed over time, puts them in the category of *asur be-hana'a*. They are treated as what might be called "cultural anomalies." One might approach the subject as follows. In cultural systems where there is a well-defined system of classification, the combination of opposites may be perceived as threatening the stability of the whole system. Where such combinations occur, the formal system of social control (the law) must restrict them. By restricting the threatening anomaly, the system, on the one hand, accepts the possibility of the anomaly occurring, but removes it from the spectrum of options available to members of the society subscribing to the system.

It is important to note that this need not be done in terms of "purity and danger" as Douglas (1966) would have it, but could also be effected, and indeed is effected in the halakhah, in legal-rational terms. Jewish life in the Diaspora implies few applications for the ideas of purity (*tahorah*), except with regard to death ritual and menstrual impurity. This situation has existed since well before the time when the Babylonian Talmud was written. Prohibited mixtures are not necessarily impure (*tame'*), nor are they necessarily seen as dangerous (a term not indigenous to the biblical text), but they do disrupt the system of clear-cut categories and thus the logic of the law must restrict them.

The analysis of anomalies within a system of cultural categories is not simply a matter of recording and interpreting a given system of thought. It is not possible to be sure what stood at the basis of the original prohibitions stated in the text. The practice of the law, however, within a given community, tends to reproduce certain categorical distinctions and augment their importance. An underlying classification is sensed and systematized by the popular practice of rules, but it is not necessarily identical with that which might be arrived at through learned and rational explorations of the original texts. When new situations arise, therefore, it is possible that the development of everyday practice, while preserving the spirit of the original rules, will differ from the correct practice as ascertained by authoritative scholars (see Deshen 1979).

Thus, there may develop a split between the culture as people express it in everyday life—their customary behavior—on the one hand, and the culture as it is written down. The written forms of a legal system have weight and counterbalance and control the tendency of custom. It is possible that were it not for this written aspect of the law and its resulting influence on Jewish customary life, all anomalies would eventually be classified as impure.[3] Given the importance of halakhah in Jewish practice over the centuries, however, respect must be given to the indigenous halakhic categories, rather than imposing on them a theoretical framework which may not be appropriate.

IV. Interpretation of the Laws of Mixture:
The Case of Meat and Milk

The mixing of meat and milk can be understood by looking at the two substances as opposed categories that represent elements which contradict one another and thus must be kept separate as much as possible. It is the nature of the code represented by this contradiction which is the main subject of this paper.

To establish the validity of the code, the following steps are taken. First, the oppositions of meat and milk will be examined in more detail and a suggestion regarding the nature of the opposition will be made. Second, the other two categories mentioned (wool/linen, grape/grain) will be examined in terms of the code, indicating the coherence of the system, Third, the consistency of the system will be further demonstrated by suggesting that in various Jewish communities and during different historical periods, the basic oppositions were maintained as part of custom even when they may have contradicted written halakhah. Although the original written law may not have seen the three mixtures as based on the same code, the force of custom—people interacting with the law over time—has created a convergence. Custom has imposed a meaningful configuration on the law as it developed and continues to exert a dynamic tension on the written legal system.

To begin with the first opposition, meat and milk. The initial prohibition of the mixing of meat and milk in biblical times is limited. The Talmud interprets the fact that since the rule "You shall not boil a kid in its mother's milk," appears three separate times in the Bible (see note 2), and since by the rules of interpretation in halakhic tradition, no repetitions are superfluous, the repetition of the statement is seen to imply an extended restriction, including the prohibition of eating, cooking, or benefitting from milk and meat.

Milk, a life-giving substance, comes from a living animal, but in no way injures the animal when it is taken, nor is the act of taking milk an act of destruction in any way. Tradition has it that milking is beneficial for the cow. Not milking a cow is said to cause the animal pain and is prohibited. Milking a cow is not organized by Jewish law or custom in any special way; it is an everyday act of benefit to both human and animal.

Getting meat on the other hand requires an act of killing, or the spilling of blood. The taking of meat is an act of destruction which at the very least leads to injury. The biblical injunction not to partake of blood is followed by the explanation: "for the blood is the life."[4] This is as if to say that the part of the meat that had a soul or was alive is to be removed. Only the less alive parts of the animal, the flesh, not the blood, are to be eaten. In a sense, these parts are also less dead.

The taking and using of meat are extremely well organized by law and custom. Slaughtering is done in a particular way, by specialists. Various parts, such as the thigh sinew, are considered nonedible (Gen. 32:33), and also must be removed by specialists. After slaughtering, the meat is soaked and salted in a way that is supposed to remove all blood, or else cooked over an open fire to remove the blood by burning.

It will also be remembered that the flesh of kosher (permitted) animals was a major part of the ritual in the Temple in Jerusalem. The Temple was *the* sacred center of Jewish life, and as such, the place in which raw meat and blood were the major elements of the sacrifices. Thus, the aspects of the use of flesh and blood proscribed in everyday life are required in sacred ritual.

Implicit in the foregoing discussion is the notion that the biblical injunction and later developments of Jewish custom and law approach the eating of meat as a problem, and in every case require that the meat be transformed into something which at least appears to be less dead. The eating of meat is somehow associated with death. Milk, on the other hand, has characteristics which are very different from those of meat. Although milk and meat are both nourishing, the taking of milk does not involve the taking of life.

A further distinction may be found between meat and milk in halakhah and custom. No use is made of milk in any sacred ritual; neither is milk included in the things which can become profaned or impure. There is only one case in the Talmud of milk being considered as unusable or impure. The case of *ḥalav akum*—milk produced by a pagan, which becomes suspicious because the pagan might mix drinkable cow's milk with the milk of nonkosher animals.

This presentation of the differences between meat and milk in halakhic terms suggests a model. Halakhah sees meat and milk as opposed to one another and as such not mixable. The difference between meat and milk is seen as parallel to the difference between acts of life-giving and life-taking on the one hand, as well as parallel to the difference between acts where the sacred/profane distinction applies as opposed to everyday acts. It is the claim of this author that the halakhic system imposes this model on all three of the prohibited mixtures under discussion. The written Torah may not have seen the three mixtures as based on the same model, but the force of custom and tradition—people interacting with the law over time—has imposed a coherent configuration on the law as it developed.[5] It will soon be shown how the model derived from the milk/meat case applies to the other two kinds of mixtures.

Meat is always associated with either the very sacred or the very profane[6] and in order to become edible, it must be transformed in some way.[7] This transformation makes it edible, but does not remove it totally from the sacred/profane category; thus it may not be mixed with milk, that is, the act of mixing is prohibited as well as the use of the mixture. This appears to be associated with the opposition between life and death. The other mixtures which are forbidden may also be of the order of the opposition between life and death. In each of the cases, one of the elements of the opposition comes from the living, either animal or vegetable, but its use does not involve the killing of the source. These elements support life without the taking of life, and can be said to represent life. On the other hand, in each case, the second element comes from the living (either animal or vegetable), but the use of this element requires either killing the animal or destroying the plant. This second set of elements will be said to represent death.

Death elements of the prohibited mixtures are used in sacred ritual—either in the ritual of the Temple or in the ritual of death—and when they are used in everyday life (if at all), they are treated ritually in very special ways. Life elements are not used in their natural form in the Temple; indeed, except for grape wine, they are not used in the Temple in any form. The question of grape wine will be discussed after a detailed consideration of the case of *sha'atnez*.

V. Wool and Linen (sha'atnez)

The prohibition of wool and linen is mentioned twice in the Bible (see note 2). In both verses the forbidden mixture is called sha'atnez. Some classical commentators include the biblical laws of sha'atnez among those injunctions which have no rational basis.[8] It is the intention here to show that these laws fit into a pattern of significance consistent with the other cases discussed.

According to the principle of interpreting apparent redundancy, the two biblical verses are meant to prohibit any garment woven of wool and linen together, but to permit the wearing of garments made of wool in one part and linen in another, and sewn together. Later rabbinical injunction, however, prohibits the use of such cloth not only in garments, but for other purposes as well.

If the model discussed is applied to the mixture of wool and linen it is found to follow the parallels. Wool, like milk, comes from the living animal. The taking of wool, too, does not damage the animal in any way. Linen, on the other hand, comes from the flax plant, an annual. Taking the fiber from the plant destroys the plant. Once the fiber is removed it will never grow again since the plant can not renew itself.

In his book on the agrarian history of Roman Palestine, Sperber (1978, 61n) reports that flax is best plucked up by the roots, an act which preserves the full length of the fibers, but which clearly destroys the plant. It appears that this was the common method of harvesting flax by Jewish farmers during the Roman period.

It is possible, then, to associate linen with death as it has been classified here. Similarly, wool is associated with life. It can be found that the traditional use of wool is a matter of everyday life. The tallit (prayer shawl) and the tzitzit (fringes attached to the shawl based on Deut. 22:12) worn in the synagogue were generally made of wool (generalizations are based on Ashkenazic communities), and were worn everyday. Linen has no function in everyday tradition. It is found in only one instance in the life of a plebian (nonpriestly)[9] Jew. Dead bodies are customarily clothed in linen garments. Thus custom may express the life/death opposition in the law, even though tradition has it that the rules of sha'atnez are not explicable in any way.

Moreover, the one case in contradiction to our life–death model, when living persons are commanded to wear clothes of linen, occurs in the Temple. The priests are commanded to wear linen clothing (Ex. 48:42; Lev. 17:4). In the book of Ezekiel (44:17ff.) it is stated: "When they come into the gates of the internal court-yard, they should wear garments of flax; wool should not be worn when they serve within the gate of the inner court-yard." Tucachinsky, whose work on mourning practices will be cited in detail, is aware of the exceptional similarity between the very sacred and extremely profane when he reports that clothes of pure linen are of special significance because the priest wore such clothes while in the Temple (1948, 1:101).

The Talmud reports that the priests were permitted to wear their special clothing only in the Temple. "Priestly garments may not be worn in the town ... in the Temple, during the service or not, such garments may be worn" (BT *Yoma* 69a). Again, as in the case of meat, the ritual use of the element representing death in our model is only in the realm of the very sacred. The elements representing death appear in territories of extreme sacredness and/or extreme defilement and yet these similar elements are kept apart. The priesthood (those who wear linen in the sacred territory) are prohibited by biblical injunction from approaching the dead[10] (those who wear linen in a state of impurity), and are only permitted to attend the funerals of first degree relatives.

The oppositional and problematic associations in the law, indicated by the analysis, are expressed at the level of custom, even when in disagreement with the law. Dead males are wrapped in a tallit according to Ashkenazi custom, although this act is prohibited by law. Tokachinsky (1948, 2:chap. 14) reports that draping the tallit over the corpse and burying the body is definitely prohibited. Indeed, custom has recognized this and in many communities the tallit is made *pasul* (unfit for use) by removing one of the four woolen fringes found on its corners. In an ordinary situation, the tallit thus becomes unwearable for the living since one may not wear a four-cornered garment without the proper fringes. Paradoxically, the dress of the dead thus becomes doubly prohibitive. The tallit of wool is placed over the shroud made of linen and is as such a violation of sha'atnez. Custom here is in violation of the law by creating sha'atnez, by making a tallit become pasul, and by placing the tallit on a dead body for burial. Yet the custom, not the law, is consistent with the system of classification and, like Kol Nidre in Deshen's analysis, the custom may suit the implicit rules of the cultural system more so than the formal law.

The late Rabbi Y. M. Tucachinsky was well known in Israel as an expert on matters of Jewish law regarding death, burial, and mourning.

His two volume work *Gesher ha-Hayim* (*Bridge of Life*, 1948) is a standard reference work on matters concerning death. The second volume is comprised of a long series of responsa regarding questions raised during his lifetime. The fourteenth chapter deals with questions forwarded to Tuckachinsky by two leading rabbis, both asking whether the dead may be buried in a tallit. The second of these questions is presented in some detail.

The questions are asked because the ancient custom in the Land of Israel was not to bury in a tallit, but to remove the tallit before the body was placed in the ground. For some people this was disappointing. The custom of burying in a tallit pasul (an unfit tallit), from which one of the four fringes has been removed, thus making it unwearable as a four-cornered garment without four fringes, was common in the Ashkenazi diaspora. The following is part of the text of a letter from one Shlomo Ish Emunim of Tel Aviv, forwarded to Rabbi Tucachinsky by Ashkenazi Chief Rabbi Herzog.

> From my youth . . . I cannot remember a night that went by without *tzitzit*. I was born in Pinsk and my forebearers were members of the burial society. Upon their passing on, I became head of the burial society . . . and we always kept the custom of burial in a *tallit*. Even those who did not wear the *tallit* (during prayers) in their lifetime were buried in a *tallit*. I took care that, in the case of one who did not cover his head with a *tallit* (a custom of piety) during his lifetime, we did not cover his head with the *tallit* in death. . . . From the day that I reached seventy, every time I reached the prayer *Shema Yisrael* I cover my head with the *tallit* to remind me of my last day of life. I cannot rest knowing the custom in Israel. As a result, I have come into contact with religious authorities in search of written permission to request from the burial society that I be buried with a properly fringed *tallit*.
>
> Shlomo Ish Emunim

Tucachinsky's response covers about six pages. He acknowledges the fact that there are variations in custom, but at the same time makes an extremely strong legal/rational case for the custom of not burying in the tallit. Here are some of his points:

> The view that one should render the *tallit* unfit by removing one of the fringes makes a mockery of the dead since we dress him in a *tallit* which is four-cornered and, therefore, should have all four *tzitzit* . . . and does not, and is, therefore, not to be worn.

Tucachinsky goes on, mentioning two cases:

We know the two cases of great Jewish scholars, both of whom desired that they be buried in a fit *tallit*, and in both cases a "sign" occurred that their will was not [to be] carried out. In the case of the first, the *tzitzit* were entangled with the ropes used to lower the body into the grave and were torn. In the second case, the student who was entrusted with the order to bury the scholar in a suitable *tallit* became ill; by the time he arrived at the graveside, the grave was already covered.

Considerable detail is used here because the debate is significant. First, the request of Shlomo Ish Emunim demonstrates the considerable importance given to this particular custom by the burial societies in Europe, which required disregarding the various issues raised in Tucachinsky's response. Second, the mode chosen by European Jews for solving the problem of the tallit is of interest. By removing some significant part of the tallit (the tzitzit), the tallit was transformed into something which could be buried. Certainly, it was no longer a tallit which could be associated with the living since it was a four-cornered tallit with only three fringes and thus was not to be worn. Yet, this is the very nature of the transformation made when we wish to transform meat into the category of everyday life. Some element of the material to be transformed is *removed* or *destroyed* and the category of the material is thus changed. A special characteristic is assigned to one aspect of the thing to be transformed and it is removed, thereby allowing for the change of category. It shall be shown how this logic is used once again in approaching the third case of forbidden mixtures.

VI. Grain and Grapes

The third opposition comes from the general category of mixtures called *kilayim* (see note 2). Generally, these are mixtures of various types of agricultural products which are the result of grafting, sowing together, or using together in other ways. The principle is clearly that of not mixing breeds, but the specification of what types of plants and trees may be mixed with one another, and which are prohibited from mixture, is a complicated task of talmudic research and will not be attempted here. Interest here will focus on one type of *kilayim* called *kil'ei ha-kerem* (mixed breeds in the vineyard). There is some talmudic argument regarding what constitutes *kil'ei ha-kerem*, but most sources agree that if one were to cast a grape seed along with wheat and barley into the vineyard, this would be a clear violation of the law, and that whatever might grow in the vineyard would be unsuitable for any purpose. This is then a third area in which a restriction is found of *asur behana'a*. The Talmud clearly makes a comparison between *kil'ei ha-kerem* and meat/milk mixtures (BT Ḥullin 116b).[11]

An examination of three components of the prohibited mixture demonstrate that this prohibition, too, conforms to the proposed model. Grape, coming from the vine, is a fruit which, having been picked, has no effect on the life of the vine itself. Man reaps benefit from the fruit without harming the vine in any manner. In this way, the harvesting of grapes is similar to milking the cow and shearing the lamb. The harvesting of wheat and barley is different. Here, as in the case of linen and slaughtering, the source must be destroyed. Once the product has been taken, living things in this category cannot renew themselves. Sperber (1978) notes that there is evidence that wheat, like linen, was harvested by plucking from the roots. Not only is the destruction of the plant a result of harvesting, but the very act of harvesting by plucking (or slaughtering) is an act of eradication.

The elements of this third instance also conform to the sacred/ profane aspect of the previous two oppositions. The element representing death in each of the earlier cases had a place in sacred ritual; grain was an integral part of Temple services. The *lehem ha-panim* or shew bread[12] had a special place in the Temple and was renewed every week. Several of the Temple offerings had grain as an important component, and grain exists in the profane state as well, in the form of new grain from which the first fruits have not yet been given to the Temple.[13] Most important, however, is the newly prepared loaf, before it has been baked. In the time of the Temple, the priesthood was granted a gift of a fistful of dough before baking; this was called a gift of *ḥallah* (Num. 15:20). Today, since there is no Temple, and no practicing priesthood, ḥallah is removed from a loaf of kosher bread before baking, and is burned. As in the previous cases, the transformation of something from the class of sacred or profane into the class of everyday life requires some kind of removal. The taking of ḥallah on this level is similar to the removal of blood from meat to make it edible, or the removal of one of the fringes from the tallit to make it interrable.

The similarities of the three cases are shown in the diagram, which also indicates certain differences. The opposed elements are classified as belonging to either life or death categories. In each case the death category has two expressions, one sacred and one profane, and in each case there is a mechanism of transformation from one category to its opposite. In each case the mechanism involves removal of some part of the transformed product and the destruction of part of what is removed.

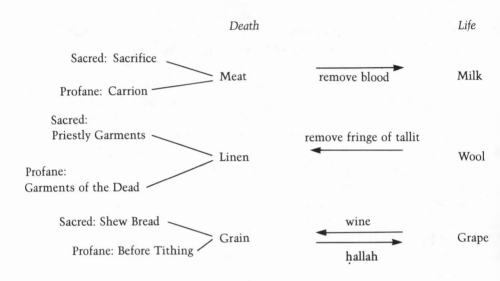

Thus, meat in its death category is either sacred as sacrificial meat, or profane as carrion meat. In order to be transformed to the category of edible, it must have the blood soaked out or burned out and then it becomes edible: less meat(death)-like and not absolutely opposed to milk. It remains opposed to milk, however, in that mixture of the two is forbidden; the opposition is relaxed only in the sense that meat may be eaten at all. It thereby may exist in the category of everyday things.

Linen follows this model. It is either sacred as in priestly garments or profane as in the garments of the dead, and although it may be used in the everyday world for clothing, the rabbinic injunction makes such use very difficult since it cannot be worn in association with woolen garments. Wool, on the other hand, is used in the tallit, an everyday garment,[14] and when the tallit is placed in the category of death, by burying it with the dead, it must be profaned by the removal of one of its fringes. Here the life element is transformed to the class of death elements.

The last part of the diagram shows the grape/grain contrast. Grain, which is placed in association with death, has both its sacred (shew bread) and profane (new grain) forms. It is introduced into everyday life by removing ḥallah or by tithing or both. The case of grapes does not fit the model precisely since it exists in both sacred (Temple sacrifices)[15] and everyday forms.

It is not the purpose here, however, to show that there is a closed system in operation. Rather, this study indicates a trend which seems to lead to a convergence of cases which are not altogether identical. Thus the problem of the place of grapes in the scheme may be resolved by distinguishing between the grape and grape wine and recognizing that it is grape wine that can be seen as part of the sacred/profane category, after undergoing a transformation logically similar to the first two cases. This logic, formalized in the model, is made explicit in one traditional commentary which suggests interpretations of various laws and customs.

A text found in *Pirkei de Rabbi Eliezer* (Friedlander 1965), discusses the significance of the term *'arel* or (*'orlah*), which, when referring to circumcision, means foreskin. In general, *'orlah* can be translated as a heaviness or an extra area attached to any living thing. The text states: "There are five *'oralot* (S. *'orlah*) in the world, four in man and one in the trees." The text goes on to cite the four sources for *'orlah* in the human body by quoting biblical texts. For example: "I will remove the heart of stone from your flesh and give you a heart of flesh" (Ez. 31:21) or "cut away, therefore, the thickening (*'orlah*)about your hearts" (Deut. 10:16). "There is one (*'orlah*) in a tree since it is written ... when you come to the land and plant any tree for food, you shall regard its fruit as forbidden" (Lev. 19:23). "Rabbi Zeriqa says the tree being referred to is the grape vine. If one does not remove its *'orlah*, all of its fruit will come out shriveled and not good looking and its vine may not be used in the sanctuary. If one cuts the *'orlah*, all the fruit will be pretty and the vine will be chosen to be sacrificed on the altar" (see Friedlander 1965, 206–207).

Rabbi Zeriqa's image is similar to the suggested model. The ability to take wine and use it for sacred needs in the Temple is seen as contingent on removing the *'orlah* from the grape. In fact, what this *'orlah* refers to is the four years of first growth in which none of the fruit may be used. The midrash phrases the prohibition and its outcome in terms of removal and transformation. Such a midrash makes explicit the process whereby different laws are, at symbolic and interpretive levels, compared with one another and placed within a single framework. The model attempts to point to and illuminate this dynamic process in rela-

tion to halakhah. Whether it will prove useful for the other laws of mixture, or indeed, may be extended to other areas of Jewish law, such as
circumcision (as suggested by the midrash), is a matter for more
detailed study.

VII. Discussion

In presenting the case for an anthropology of halakhah the following steps were taken. A definition of halakhah was put forth and
various types of halakhic texts were presented which reflect different
periods of Jewish history and different types of Jewish communities.
The chronological order of the texts discussed was not considered
significant for the purposes of this paper since an historical study was
not intended. This paper does not point to the historical conditions at
each point in time, in each community, to explain specific reasons for
the development of the rules of opposition. Rather, it hopes to show
that the various sources form a consistent whole which reflect the pre-
disposition of the cultural system to deal with particular types of oppositions, defined here in terms of life and death. Life and death are applied as metaphor, a convenient tool to describe the structure of the
oppositional system and to demonstrate its consistency. It may very
well be that some other oppositional metaphor will be more suitable
when all the rules of mixture are examined as a whole and in more
extensive detail.

In the halakhic system there are two kinds of responses to change.
The first appears to be similar to the way in which most traditional
cultures cope with changes in the world around them; by changing or
adapting custom to new conditions, and making the system more simplified and understandable to the people who live in it. The other aspect
of the halakhic system, the textual side, also responds to change.
Halakhah is basically a conservative force which, through its permanence, can always be turned to check and balance the force of custom. The text itself is immutable, but changes in textual interpretation
reflect different sets of cultural rules, such as those hinted at in the case
of the explanation of 'orlah and grape wine.

It becomes necessary therefore for the anthropologist who wishes
to study a literate system to become familiar with the texts of the culture as they have been preserved and to describe the place of legal texts

as both reflections and mechanisms for control of cultural change. The use of models to describe the workings of the system must be generated from within. Here halakhah presented a key concept—that of mixture—which allowed the development of the present model. Other oppositions—aside from life and death—come to mind as mechanisms for dealing with the three mixtures discussed. Nature/culture is a well-known example. Detailed examination of the texts, however, leads to the conclusion that this opposition simply does not work in the present case. The nature/culture opposition would separate between those elements which may be used in their natural state, such as milk, and those elements which are generally used in a modified state and are in some way processed by man, like meat which must be cooked. This opposition would not hold for wool/linen, since both must be processed as fibers before their use or for grape/grain, since both may be used in their natural states and may be used in their processed states (wine/bread). Similarly milk, coming from domesticated animals, is not easily classified as nature or culture as opposed to meat. The researcher is forced to recognize the existence of the text as a cultural force and thereby is limited in the kinds of interpretations he may apply.

Close examination of textual sources also makes the system appear much less consistent than might be recognized. A living cultural system with an adaptive capacity could not be otherwise. If the system were to be completely closed and totally coherent internally, it would soon reach the limits of its capacity to adapt to new conditions and become fragile, leading to disintegration. Total consistency of the customary and legal/rational systems is not proposed here. Rather, there exists a basic tension which is a matter of reflection on the text and manipulation on both customary and legal/rational levels.

It is impossible at this stage to discuss the meaning of the oppositions as they are represented in halakhic texts. The research presented is only intended to demonstrate the level of consistency in the material. The question of meaning or essence must be left for much more detailed examination, since it would have to be pursued from both an historical and structural point of view. Here the existence of the text further complicates matters since a vast amount of material must be taken into consideration. It is suggested that whereas structure may tend toward internal consistency and stability, meaning may vary with situation and it is more likely that the halakhic system carries with it a repertoire of alternative meanings for dealing with similar problems.

Notes

1. See the Introduction, p. 27.

2. The relevant verses are as follows:

  a. Meat and milk: Ex. 23:19, 34:26; Deut. 14:21.

  b. Wool and linen: Lev. 19:19; Deut. 22:11.

  c. Grape and grain: Lev. 19:19; Deut. 22:9.

3. One example may be the custom of a menstrual hut which was found among the Jews of Kurdistan at the middle of the last century (Brauer 1947, 133), but which goes beyond anything required by biblical or rabbinic law. Similarly, there developed among the Jews of the mountainous Jebel Nefusah region (and other regions) in Tripolitania, an extreme avoidance of mourners, which was criticized by rabbis who became aware of the practice (Hakohen 1980, 17, 129).

4. See Lev. 3:17, 7:26ff., and 17:10. In Deut. 22:23 the motivation for the prohibition is given. The equation of blood with life or "soul" (nefesh) also is presented in Gen. 9:4, and the rabbis of the Talmud differed as to whether or not the prohibition of eating blood should be considered a universal (panhuman) prohibition, like murder.

5. This coherence is never watertight and always has a dynamic aspect to it. For example, the prohibition of eating meat from hoofed animals together with milk was extended to fowls, but, according to talmudic evidence, this stricture was not observed for a while in the Galilee (BT Ḥullin 116a).

6. I consider sacred/profane to be an opposition, and view the profane to be diametrically opposed to the sacred. I therefore assume the existence of a cultural-religious category of everyday things, which are neither sacred nor profane. This may be a departure from the original formulation of sacred/profane found in Durkheim (1965, 52), but I find this departure necessary for dealing with the present material.

7. Meat becomes profane when it is carrion, that is, when it is not properly slaughtered, as a result of the animal having died a more natural death. It also becomes profane when the slaughtered animal is found to have a defect, especially in the lungs, as well as when the blood has not been extracted from the meat by soaking and salting, or when it has not been washed periodically after slaughtering. The rules regarding the treatment of meat are complex and it is not my purpose to write a long explication here, only to indicate the plausibility of a general pattern.

8. Rashi comments that the laws of Lev. 19:19 are like "enactments of the king, for which no reason is given."

9. The descendants of Aaron, Moses' brother, are the priests (kohanim). They continue to have certain ritual privileges, despite the fact that their main

ritual tasks and rights, associated with the Temple worship, are no longer in force today. A partial (and historically late) exception to the generalization about the wearing of linen is referred to in the paper in this volume by Goldberg, which cites the custom whereby a young male is placed on a linen cloth on the day of his circumcision, eight days after birth. This might also be seen as a confirmation of the general point, for the child at this time is clearly in a liminal state, having moved from prelife, and is in the process of becoming a participant in the Jewish community. It was customary in some Western Ashkenazi communities to make a (sacred) Torah-binder from this linen.

10. Lev. 21:1ff.

11. It is interesting that the text prohibiting *kilayim* uses the term *tiqdash*, meaning that the resultant mixture may not be used, but which is based on the stem *q-d-sh* meaning "set aside" or "holy."

12. Ex. 35:13 and 39:36.

13. See Lev. chap. 2, with regard to the Temple offerings, and Lev. 23:9–14 and Deut. 26:1–12 with regard to the contribution of the first fruits.

14. The original meaning of *tallit* is a sheet, or cloak, that is, an everyday garment. The biblical precept requires that fringes be put on standard clothing. The fashioning of a special prayer shawl to meet this requirement is a later development.

15. Num. chap. 28.

References Cited

Brauer, E. (1947), *The Jews of Kurdistan: An Ethnological Study.* Compiled and edited by R. Patai. Jerusalem; The Palestine Institute of Folklore and Ethnology.

Deshen, S. (1979). "The Kol Nidre Enigma," *Ethnology* 18:121–34.

Douglas, M. (1966). *Purity and Danger.* Harmondsworth: Penguin Books.

Durkheim, E. (1965 [orig. 1912]). *The Elementary Forms of Religious Life.* New York: Macmillan, Free Press.

Friedlander, G., trans. and ed. (1965). *The Chapters of Rabbi Eliezer the Great.* New York: Herman Press.

Hakohen, Mordechai. (1980). *The Book of Mordechai: A Study of the Jews of Libya.* Translated and edited by H. Goldberg. Philadelphia: Institute for the Study of Human Issues.

Soler, J. (1979). "The Semiotics of Food in the Bible." In *Food and Drink in History*, R. Forster and O. Ranum, eds. Baltimore: Johns Hopkins University Press, 126–38.

Sperber, D. (1978). *Roman Palestine 200–400: The Land.* Ramat Gan: Bar Ilan University Press.

Tucachinsky, Y. M. (1948). *Gesher ha-Hayim.* Jerusalem, Hebrew.

CHAPTER 2

The Consumption of Sabbatical Year Produce in Biblical and Rabbinic Literature

ZVI ZOHAR

I. Introduction

In some recent anthropological writing the image of culture as text has been presented as a means for gaining an understanding of a society subject to study. An examination of institutional and cultural trends in Jewish society ought to be of particular interest, from this perspective, for Jewish tradition views the text as the mold in which the people's life should be formed. The way in which the people lived was conceived as an attempt to realize what was set down in the text, and the culture's bearers evaluated the people's deeds, according to the extent in which they succeeded in doing so.

Obviously, no society or culture remains frozen, absolutely unchanged by the passage of time. Thus, a unique kind of tension between text and historical reality resulted for the Jewish people. On the one hand, the people's attempt to fulfil the ancient text (which was preserved against any kind of change or alteration of its language or content by the observance of a strict set of scribal norms), was viewed as its raison d'etre. On the other hand, circumstances often made it impossible (or even undesirable and impractical), to observe literally the rules of the text without any deviation from the original practices and precepts. The Jewish sages who lived during the first centuries of the Common Era were well aware of this tension. This is reflected in complex and sophisticated ways, both in their conceptual metaphors and in their reformulation of the details of ancient practices. They attempted simultaneously to retain the instructions of the eternal Mosaic law and to relate to the social and religious needs of the Jews of their time.[1]

To complement the written Torah, the divine Torah of Moses, changeless and eternal in its language and precepts, the sages posed the religious concept and symbol of the oral Torah. This, though also divine in origin, was revealed only through an interpretive process, through the sages' discussion of how the implications of the eternal divine utterances recorded in the written Torah could be applied in contemporary circumstances.[2] The desire to realize the unchanging written Torah in dynamic everyday life thus became central to the consciousness and identity of the Jewish people. Its religious and social institutions were able simultaneously to maintain, throughout, both an impressive internal continuity and a significant degree of freedom. This enabled them to respond productively to changing circumstances and to needs that arose as a result of new sociohistorical situations.

Two texts are outstanding in their importance to Hebrew/Jewish culture in general, and to this study's topic in particular. The first is the Pentateuch, the Torah of Moses, composed of five books which existed in their present form in the sixth century B.C.E., and whose cultural and literary roots go back some hundreds of years earlier. This text was defined as the written Torah. The other is the Mishnah, or *Mishnat Rabbi Yehuda ha-Nasi*, which was edited under the supervision of Rabbi Yehuda the Prince toward the end of the second century C.E. and contains material whose formulation was begun in the preceding centuries. The Mishnah was viewed as the primary concretization of the oral Torah.

These books, like any other major culture text, were not of folk origin; they were authored by the Jewish people's cultural and religious elite and therefore reflect, first and foremost, the values and ideas of that elite. However, it may be stated with a fair degree of certainty that for the greater part of the 1500 year period in which a Hebrew/Jewish agricultural society flourished in Palestine, this class of literati maintained profound ties with the less educated people.

The possession of these two major literary texts, separated by an interval of over 700 years, gives the researcher a relatively rare opportunity to analyze patterns of continuity and change in the religious institutions and values of an ancient culture.

This paper will analyze these patterns of continuity and change as reflected in aspects of a central institution of the agricultural life of ancient Israel: the *shevi'it* (sabbatical year). This case study provides an example of the general processes and dynamics of the religious life of the people of Israel, perennially seeking to relate actual practice to the divine text.

The *shevi'it* was an important socioeconomic institution to the people of Israel in ancient times. Despite the fact that Israelite society was overwhelmingly agricultural, its members were required to abstain from cultivating their land in the seventh year. Produce which grew of itself was not considered the property of the owner of the field or orchard that had produced it, and everyone alike was entitled to help himself to it. It was a year when debts could not be collected,[3] and when Hebrew slaves, both male and female, were set free.[4]

To the Jewish world view, the *shevi'it* is bound up with the people's ancestral land. However, a decline in the size of Palestine's Jewish population began in Judea after the defeat of the Bar Kokhba rebellion and spread, with added impetus, to the rest of the country. This decline, caused by the severe economic recession in the Roman Empire in the third century C.E., had the effect of making the *shevi'it* less significant to Jewish life and consciousness. Though it was never formally discontinued, its influence on communal life dwindled considerably. With the renewal of Jewish settlement in Palestine in the nineteenth century, attempts were made to revive it.[5] However, even momentarily disregarding the processes of secularization that have alienated broad segments of present-day Jewry from observation of ancient Jewish traditions, the fact that the sabbatical year relates mainly to agriculture makes it of only marginal significance to a modern society in which so few people farm.[6]

What is known of the sabbatical year derives from the study of literary sources produced in those periods when this institution was vital and influential in the people's life. The Torah provides a reasonable faithful portrayal of the *shevi'it* as it existed during the latter generations of the first Temple period (up to 586 B.C.E.), and throughout the subsequent century. The Mishnah does the same for the latter generations of the Second Temple period (up to 70 C.E.), and those of the subsequent 150 years.

The present study has several parts. First, it shall begin with the later texts and locate in the Mishnah and other *tannaitic*[7] literature several basic norms governing the ways in which the produce that grew during the *shevi'it* was to be prepared and consumed. This paper shall demonstrate the resemblance between these rules and the tannaitic norms concerning two other realms: (a) the consumption of *ma'aser sheni*—the second tithe, which was designated for consumption in Jerusalem—and (b) the eating of *terumah*, produce set aside for the priests.

Second, it shall study the norms expressed in the earlier text (the Torah) regarding these various kinds of produce, to discover that despite a clear continuity linking the Torah to the Mishnah, the unique and distinctive character that each of the three institutions (*shevi'it*, *ma'aser*, and *terumah*) have in the Torah is replaced, in the Mishnah, by a significant degree of normative resemblance.

In order to facilitate an understanding of the basic elements of the biblical *shevi'it*, this study shall make use of the concept of *communitas* and its essential characteristics, drawing on the insights of Victor Turner.

Third, an attempt will be made to explain why these three institutions, which display a relatively large degree of normative differentiation in the Torah, should later have acquired the significant normative resemblance evident in the Mishnah. In this context, this study shall undertake an analytic critique of the relationship between *communitas* and *societas* (as defined by Turner), and shall attempt to explain the differences between the Bible and the Mishnah, taking into account the differences between the community's social and religious consciousness in the two periods in question, and the differences between the people's social and religious needs as understood by their religious leadership in each period.

The analysis of the biblical *shevi'it* will be based on Turner's ideas. This paper shall, however, make use of the results of a comparison between biblical and tannaitic *shevi'it* practices to formulate a critique of some of the finer points of Turner's understanding of *communitas*, thus modifying his original concept. It is hoped thereby to contribute to the productive dialogue that has begun to develop between specialists in cultural and religious anthropology, on the one hand, and scholars of Jewish studies (especially those involved in studying the history of Jewish law), on the other.

II. Resemblances between Tannaitic Norms Governing the Consumption of the Fruits of *Shevi'it,* of *Ma'aser Sheni,* and *Terumah*

The norms regulating the consumption of *shevi'it* fruits resemble those governing the consumption of *terumah* and *ma'aser sheni* in many ways.[8] While the differences between them are by no means negligible,[9] this study will focus on their similarities and try to suggest possible reasons for them. Also taken into account will be the biblical roots of these practices, which appear to be much farther apart from one another than the norms of *shevi'it, terumah,* and *ma'aser sheni* were in rabbinic times.

Those aspects of *shevi'it* with which this study is concerned include norms of the following types:

1. The normative definition of "consumption";

2. Utilization norms governing permissive modes of consumption;

3. Processing norms governing the *degree of sophistication* permitted in processing the produce for consumption;

4. Group boundary norms concerning:
   a. *who was permitted* to partake of the food and
   b. *who was forbidden* to partake of the food;

5. Geographical-spatial norms governing *where* the produce could be consumed;

6. Temporal boundary norms governing the *period of time* during which the consumption of the fruits was permitted.

These norms governing the use of *shevi'it* agricultural produce are largely analogous and sometimes even identical to those governing the consumption of *terumah* and *ma'aser sheni,* in these six realms. A comparison between them will illustrate their similarities.

1. The normative definition of consumption

It is permissible to eat sabbatical produce. This license was extended to include not only eating in the literal sense, but also drinking and use for purposes of anointment (that is, for rubbing into the skin).

There is a tannaitic source for this in the Mishnah, tractate *Shevi'it* (chap. 8, 2):

> Sabbatical year produce is intended to be used as food and drink and unguent. . . . The same is the case with the priest's share of the produce and the second tithe.

On what grounds did the sages determine that the biblical precept regarding the consumption of *shevi'it* produce includes drinking and anointing as well? Several solutions have been suggested in their discussions. It will not be elaborated on here,[10] but rather take note of the following facts:

a. The Mishnah accepts this extension of the biblical precept without question, as an established fact.

b. The Mishnah itself points out that the laws for *shevi'it, terumah,* and *ma'aser sheni* are identical in this respect.

2. Utilization norms

The same passage of the Mishnah says:

> Sabbatical year produce is intended to be used as food and drink and unguent—to be eaten: whatever is usually eaten . . . and to be used as unguent: whatever is customarily used as unguent. One may not use wine and vinegar as unguent, but one may anoint with oil. The same is the case with the priest's share of the produce and the second tithe.

The statement that "one may not use wine and vinegar as unguent" seems to be an illustration of the preceding rule. Since vinegar and wine are not ordinarily used for anointing, one may not make such use of sabbatical vinegar and wine; but since oil is ordinarily used for anointing, it is both permissible and proper to do so with sabbatical oil. The Mishnah thus seems to be referring to accepted social convention; the right way of consuming a particular *shevi'it* fruit is the way in which it is most commonly used for sustenance.

The Mishnah portion cited points out the similarity between the norms of *shevi'it* and those of *ma'aser sheni* and *terumah* in this respect. This is confirmed by the following passage from tractate *Ma'aser Sheni* (chap. 2, 1):

> Second tithe was intended for eating, drinking and anointing: to eat that which it is usual to eat . . . and to use for anointing that with which it is usual to anoint. One may not use for anointing wine and vinegar, but he may anoint with oil.

There is no parallel passage to this one in the Mishnah of tractate *Terumot*, but something similar is found in the Tosefta[11] (*Tosefta Terumot* chap. 9, 10):

> *Terumah* is intended to be used as food and drink and unguent—to be eaten whatever is usually eaten, and to be drunk whatever is ordinarily drunk, and to be used as unguent whatever is customarily used as unguent.

The continuation of this passage gives several illustrations to clarify these rules, and it would appear from them that the thrust of the above statements is not quite the same as what has been concluded from our analysis of the parallel passage in tractate *Shevi'it.*

> What is meant by "to eat that which it is usual to eat"? One is not required to eat cuttings that have been trimmed off a vegetable. Or a food whose appearance has been spoiled. What is meant by "to be drunk whatever is ordinarily drunk"? One is not required to swallow *el-aigaron*[12] or *oxygarum*[13] or drink the lees along with the wine.

The Tosefta's examples, rather than stressing that one's consumption of edible agricultural produce should be restricted to modes that were socially conventional, emphasize exemptions from that duty.

If we examine the Tosefta of Shevi'it on the same subject, it shall be seen that there, too, the laws are phrases as an *exemption from a duty*, rather than as a *restriction on what is permissible* (*Tosefta Shevi'it*, chap. 6, 1–3).

> Sabbatical year produce is intended to be used as food and drink and unguent to be eaten whatever is usually eaten, and to be drunk whatever is ordinarily drunk, and to be used as unguent whatever is ordinarily used as unguent. What is meant by "to be eaten whatever is usually eaten"? One is not required to eat cuttings that have been trimmed off a vege-

table or a bread that has become moldly or a food whose appearance has been spoiled. What is meant by "to be drunk whatever is ordinarily drunk"? One is not required to swallow *elaigaron* or *oxygarum* or to drink the lees along with the wine.

The requirement to consume this produce in the ordinary way thus has two complementary aspects:

a. exemption from the duty to eat produce that is not fit for human consumption;

b. restriction of the consumption of the produce to the most commonly accepted way(s) of doing so.

What the two have in common is that both define eating in terms of social convention. Vegetable trimmings are not, after all, devoid of nutritional value; moldy bread would be eaten with gusto by starving men. This, however, is not considered food, but repulsive, unappetizing nutritive matter. Similarly, of course, using wine as an unguent has the formal characteristics of anointment, but the society (in which the sages lived) was accustomed to using oil, not wine, for this purpose.

3. Processing Norms

In tractate *Terumot*, normative restrictions are found on the mode of preparation of the produce (chap. 11, 3):

> They must not make grapes into honey, or apples into cider, or winter-grapes into vinegar, nor may any other fruits be changed from their natural state (*mi-briatan*) if they were priest's due (*terumah*) or second tithe (*ma'aser sheni*) with the exception of olives and grapes.

This restriction appears to supplement the one described. Ordinarily, people did make dates into honey, apples into cider, and winter grapes into vinegar, and all of these products were undoubtedly considered delicacies. The passage quoted from the Mishnah thus distinguishes between different ways of using the produce as food, some of which, however, leave it *ki-vriatan* and others which do not. The word *ki-vriatan*, it seems, ought to be translated here as meaning "in the original primary way"; *shelo ki-vriatan* would thus refer to processing the food or making secondary use of it. The term (derived from *briah*, a form of the verb meaning "create"), would thus seem to be used here in a naturalistic sense. This interpretation ought not to be taken simplistically, however, if only because of the exception granted in the case of olives and dates. Two alternative explanations for ki-vriatan seem possible: either it is the most simple and direct way in which this fruit is customarily used, or it refers to the specific use for which this fruit was originally created.

The first of these explanations takes us back to the realm of social convention. The second one does too, but by an implication, having a theological overtone. All produce used by man, according to this explanation, was created for this purpose by God. When the Holy One was creating each specific fruit, He preordained a particular *original* use for it, and this is therefore the natural way of using it. However, it is the sages, as teachers of the oral Torah, who must identify just what the original way of using each of these fruits is, and they do this by observing what is customary in a good, well-ordered society—like the Jewish society in which they lived. In other words, this explanation, too, rests both theoretically and practically on what is customary and accepted within society, but it endows these ordinary modes of consumption with theological/ontological authority.

It would appear, then that the word ki-vriatan has some of the same meanings as is attributed today to the word "natural": primariness, originality, lack of artificiality, closeness to the state of things before man's intervention.

There is a close relationship between the concept of ki-vriatan and the restrictions on permitted modes of consumption which were shown in the preceding section. Thus, while the Mishnah explicates the demand that fruits be used ki-vriatan only in relation to terumah and ma'aser sheni, Maimonides notes that it extends to shevi'it fruit as well, and integrates the utilization and the processing norms discussed (Mishneh Torah, Hilkhot Shemittah ve-Yovel, chap. 5, 1–3):

> Sabbatical year's produce may be used for food, drink or anointing...
> How for food and drink?
> To eat that which is customarily eaten, and to drink that which is usually drunk,
> *as is the rule for heave-offering (terumah) and second tithe (ma'aser sheni).*
> One may not divert shevi'it product from its natural use, just as one may not divert heave offerings or second tithe.

4. Group Boundary Norms

A. EXCLUSION OF OUTSIDERS

There are instructions prohibiting certain groups or kinds of people from partaking of the kinds of produce with which this paper is concerned, namely *terumah*, *ma'aser sheni*, and *shevi'it*.

The most prominent example of this is *terumah*, which may be eaten only by priests and members of their immediate households, and then only if they are in a state of purity. There are also certain categories of people who are forbidden to partake of *ma'aser sheni*, including: (1) anyone in an impure state; (2) anyone who is uncircumcised (both Jews and Gentiles); and (3) any mourner whose departed relative has not yet been buried. Because of the biblical prohibition against partaking of *ma'aser sheni* while in an impure state, the sages imposed an injunction against giving *ma'aser sheni* produce to members of the uneducated common people, the *'am ha-aretz*.[14] Restrictions on the consumption of *shevi'it* fruit were less exclusive: only Gentiles were prohibited from participating in the eating of the produce of the seventh year.[15]

For each of these special kinds of produce (*terumah*, *ma'aser sheni*, and *shevi'it* fruit), then, there is a phenomenon of the outsiders. In this they differed not only from ordinary, unconsecrated produce, but also from other ritual gifts, such as *ma'aser rishon* (first tithe) and *ma'aser 'ani* (tithe for the poor), which might be eaten by all.

B. DEFINITION OF INSIDERS

The Bible contains clear instructions in this respect with regard to *ma'aser sheni* (Deut. 12:17–18):

> Thou mayest not eat within thy gates the tithe of thy corn, or of thy wine, or of thine oil ... but thou shalt eat them before the Lord thy God ... *thou, and thy son, and thy daughter, and thy manservant, and thy maidservant, and the Levite that is within thy gates* (Emphasis added).

With regard to sabbatical fruits, too, there is an injunction to extend dining privileges beyond the immediate circle of the man and his family, and the extension here seems even broader than that specified for *ma'aser sheni* (Lev. 25:7):

And the sabbath-produce of the land shall be for food for you: for thee, and for thy servant and for thy maid, and for thy hired servant *and for the settler* by the side that doth sojourn with thee; *and for thy cattle, and for the beasts that are in thy land,* shall all the increase thereof be for food (Emphasis added).

There is no such positive injunction with regard to *terumah.* One explanation for this is that those who were designated to eat of it were a clearly defined, small and privileged group (the priests).

5. Geographical-spatial norms

Ma'aser sheni could be eaten only inside Jerusalem. *Terumah* and *shevi'it* fruit could be eaten outside Jerusalem, however they could not be removed from the land of Israel and eaten abroad (Mishnah *Shevi'it,* chap. 6, 5):

Contaminated oil of *terumah,*[16] and *shevi'it* fruit, may not be taken outside of the land of Israel to another country.

This clear restriction of sabbatical fruit to the borders of the land of Israel led the tannaim to the following dispute over what a person should do if he came into possession of sabbatical fruit which nevertheless had somehow been removed from the land of Israel (*Tosefta Shevi'it* chap. 5, 1):

Sabbatical fruits which have been removed from the land of Israel— according to Rabbi (Yehuda ha-Nasi), one must burn them in the place where they are. Rabbi Shimon ben Elazar says: One must bring them to the land of Israel and burn them there, as it is stated in Scripture: *"in thy land shall all the increase thereof be for food."* (Emphasis added.)

6. Temporal Boundary Norms

There was a time restriction on the consumption of both *terumah* and *ma'aser sheni,* and of *shevi'it* fruit. This restriction is defined by the concept of *bi'ur,* the precise interpretation of which is in dispute.[17] According to one opinion, once the time of *bi'ur* has arrived, one may not keep the produce in one's home, but must put it outside for the taking and use of anyone who wishes. Another opinion holds that this produce must be destroyed. In either case, the time of *bi'ur*—and such a time exists for all three kinds of produce under discussion—transforms the possibilities for making use of this produce.

Our survey of the tannaitic rules shows that the use of *shevi'it* fruit was characterized, from the point of view of halakhah, by a series of norms defining modes of processing and utilization, spatial and temporal boundaries, and out group/in group boundaries. One of the central functions of these norms is to emphasize the special and exalted character of the partaking of this produce. No wonder, then, that these categories of produce are defined in the texts as "sacred." Interestingly enough, *terumah* and *ma'aser sheni* produce is termed sacred by the Torah; sabbatical fruit, however, is explicitly characterized as such only in rabbinic sources.

III. Differences between the Written and the Oral Torah: From Distinctiveness to Resemblance

The use of the term "sacred" is not the only realm in which the biblical passages on this subject differ from those in rabbinic literature. A comparative analysis will show that the norm similarity found in rabbinic literature is significantly at variance with what may be inferred from the biblical text. The following table summarizes these differences:

Textual Sources of Norms Relating to *Terumah, Ma'aser Sheni,* and *Shevi'it*

| | Textual Source of Norm | | |
Norms governing:	Terumah	Ma'aser Sheni	Shevi'it
Method of processing	Mishnah	Mishnah	Torah
Method of utilization	Mishnah	Mishnah	Torah
Spatial boundaries	Mishnah	Torah	Mishnah
Temporal boundaries	Mishnah	Torah	Mishnah
Consumer group exclusion boundaries	Torah	Torah	Mishnah
Communal inclusion boundaries	none	Torah	Torah
Ritual purity of consumers	Torah	Torah	none

If the mishnaic norms are disregarded, then, the resemblance that is seen between *terumah*, *ma'aser sheni*, and *shevi'it* fruit was not originally as great as would appear from rabbinic literature. The sages of the oral Torah obviously filled in normative gaps thereby achieving an almost complete overlap between the norms governing consumption of produce in these three ritual categories. By doing so they also significantly modified the original distinctiveness and characterization of each. To better understand the thrust of rabbinic activity in this sphere, this paper will now briefly analyze each of the three ritual institutions in the relevant Torah texts.

IV. The Biblical Norms in Context

1. Terumah

The main passage formulating the nature of *terumah* and how it was to be eaten is to be found in Numbers, chapter 18, beginning with verse 8. *Terumah* is one of several gifts the people of Israel are directed to give to the priests. These gifts are portrayed as belonging by right to the Lord. He, however, has allocated them to the priests, the children of Aaron (Num. 18:8):

> And I, behold, I have given thee charge of my heave-offerings, even of all the hallowed things of the children of Israel unto thee have I given them for a consecrated portion, and to thy sons, as a due for ever.

He who was entitled to partake of the priestly gifts including *terumah*, thus had a right to eat from the table of the Lord, that is, to eat food that belongs to God, which He has graciously bestowed on those who are close to Him. This right was a sign of the high status ascribed to Aaron and his sons on account of their having been anointed with the oil of consecration. Not without insight, then, do the sages interpret the words "for a consecrated portion" as meaning "for a sign of greatness."[18]

What distinguishes *terumah*, then, is not when and how it is to be eaten, but the fact that those who may eat it have a special, high status. This right to eat sacred produce was linked explicitly to the fact that the priests performed the sacred service in the sanctuary. According to a statment in rabbinic literature, eating *terumah*, even outside of Jerusalem, was of the same ritual status as service in the temple.[19]

To sum up, according to the biblical source text the most important characteristics of the consumption of *terumah* are its links to the sacred, to the ritual service of God, and to a special, highly esteemed in-group.

2. Ma'aser Sheni

A primary quality of the consumption of *ma'aser sheni* is that of joy (Deut. 7:7):

> and there ye shall eat before the Lord your God, and ye shall rejoice in all that ye put your hand unto . . . wherein the Lord thy God hath blessed thee.

It is the blessing of God, manifested and embodied in the fruits of their labors, in which the people rejoice. This rejoicing occurs in the context of the thrice-yearly pilgrimage, and the celebrant is enjoined to draw many fellow pilgrims into his company (Deut. 12:12):

> And ye shall rejoice before the Lord your God, ye, and your sons, and your daughters, and your manservants, and your maidservants, and the Levite that is within your gates.

The consumption of *ma'aser sheni* thus brings together all levels and classes of society, from wealthy landowners to impecunious Levites, manservants, and maidservants, to eat in joy before the Lord. It is an expression of satisfaction and largess. Pilgrims coming from afar were allowed to sell their *ma'aser sheni* produce at home and bring the money thus obtained to the sanctuary center, where they were to put it to festive use. The verse dealing with how the money may be used, seems to indicate that the celebrant might spend it on anything that would help to increase his joy (Deut. 14:26):

> And thou shalt bestow the money for whatsoever thy soul desireth, for oxen, or for sheep, or for wine, or for strong drink or for whatsoever thy soul asketh of thee; and thou shalt eat there before the Lord thy God, and thou shalt rejoice, thou and thy household.

The reiteration of "whatsoever thy soul desireth . . . whatsoever thy soul asketh of thee;" seems to express not a limitation on what the celebrant may eat, but, on the contrary, an encouragement to him to fulfill this joyous and exalted experience of eating before the Lord in an entirely personal way.

3. Shevi'it

The biblical directive regarding the consumption of produce from the year of *shevi'it* seems incongruous with the firm restrictions on agriculture explicated in the Torah. Let us analyze this issue in the context of the central biblical text about *shevi'it,* Leviticus, chapter 25, which includes (Lev. 25:4-5):

> thou shalt neither sow thy field, nor prune thy vineyard. That which groweth of itself of thy harvest thou shalt not reap, and the grapes of thy undressed vine thou shalt not gather.

These verses would appear to contain two complementary prohibitions:

1. It was forbidden to sow or cultivate agricultural produce.

2. That which grew spontaneously could not be gathered in from the field.

A look at the conceptual context of these prohibitions confirms the prima facie impression that doing anything involving the land and its fruits during the seventh year was utterly forbidden (Lev. 25:4-5):

> but in the seventh year shall be a sabbath of *solemn rest* for the land, a Sabbath unto the Lord;
> thou shalt neither sow thy field . . . it shall be a year of *solemn rest* for the land (Emphasis added).

The phrase "a sabbath of *solemn rest,*" which appears in this verse, is laden with significance. It appears elsewhere only in connection with the weekly sabbath and the Day of Atonement.[20] Those who knowingly transgressed the strict prohibitions associated with those days, according to the Torah, are to be judged very severely. The prohibition against growing or utilizing crops during the sabbatical year was placed, terminologically, in the context of these two other sabbaths of solemn rest so that the reader was directed toward viewing it as having the utmost authority and severity. Immediately following this strict injunction, however, comes a verse which describes eating the fruit that grows during this sabbath of solemn rest (Lev. 26:6–7):

> And the sabbath-produce of the land shall be for food for you:
> for thee, and for thy servant and for thy maid,
> and for thy hired servant and for the settler by thy side that sojourn
>   with thee;
> and for thy cattle, and for the beasts that are in thy land, shall all the increase thereof be for food.

Considering the severity of the previously mentioned prohibitions, these permissive lines might seem to convey that it would, indeed, have been more appropriate not to allow the consumption of any sabbatical produce. However, due to the scarcity and dire need that might prevail during this period of agricultural inactivity, the legislator, acting to stave off famine, permits the people to eat of sabbatical fruit. This contrasts with the consumption of *terumah* and *ma'aser sheni*, which are similar in that both stem from a positive, deliberate directive from God regarding the sacramental consumption of the fruits of the land. Thus the permission to eat sabbatical fruit would seem to be an after-the-fact concession to the needs of the people, who, being earthly, flesh and blood creatures, are unable to fulfill the land's sabbath of solemn rest in its full, true sense.

If the same chapter in Leviticus is read further, however, one finds that the Bible had anticipated certain difficulties as potentially hindering the Jews' fulfillment of the seventh-year sabbath of solemn rest (Lev. 25:20–22):

> And if ye shall say: "What shall we eat in the seventh year?
> Behold, we may not sow, nor gather in our increase";
> then I will command My blessing upon you in the sixth year,
> and it shall bring forth produce for the three years.
> And ye shall sow the eighth year, and eat of the produce,
> the old store; until the ninth year,
> until her produce come in, ye shall eat the old store.

God is portrayed as aware of the problems that were likely to arise for want of a whole year's crop, and as promising to prevent them by providing an extra-large harvest in the sixth year. Thus the people would have enough to sustain themselves comfortably thoughout the *shevi'it* period until they had gathered in the new crops in the ninth year.

This solution is curiously analogous to the treatment of the non-provision of food on the sabbath day in the time when the people of Israel were living on manna alone. Then the people were commanded to gather manna for six days and told that there would be more on the Sabbath (Ex., 16:26). And if the people protested, "but what shall we eat on the seventh day?" God had a ready solution that "He giveth you on the sixth day the bread of two days" (Ex. 16:29). As God knows that the weekly sabbath can be kept only if extra food is provided on the sixth day, so He knows, too, that the sabbath of solemn rest in the seventh year can be kept only if extra food is provided in advance. In both cases, He promises to provide the children of Israel with sufficient stores to enable them to keep the sabbath. According to the chapter in Leviticus, it is not by permitting the people to eat what grows of itself in their fields that solved the problem of scarcity anticipated in the seventh year, but rather the provision of surplus crops in the sixth. In context it now appears incorrect to interpret verse 6 ("and the sabbath-produce of the land shall be for food for you") as a grudging exception granted only in order to solve pressing problems of want; the instruction to eat the fruits of the seventh year must have an entirely different explanation.

4. Why Sabbatical Fruit is Meant to be Eaten

According to the Bible a man is strictly enjoined against doing anything in the seventh year to induce the land to bring forth its crops, and against relating to what does grow in this year as his possession. This now appears not as a post facto concession contrary to the spirit of shevi'it, but rather as an a priori divine invitation to partake of fruit that really belongs to God Himself. And who is it that God invites to dine at His table?

"And the sabbath-produce of the land shall be for food for you" says the text, which immediately details those included:

for thee, and for thy servant and for thy maid,
and for thy hired servant and for the settler by thy side that sojourn
    with thee;
and for thy cattle, and for the beasts that are in thy land,
shall all the increase thereof be for food.

It is not only the owner of the field who is entitled to eat the shevi'it fruit, but also members of the lower classes, including members of his own household (servants and maids), for whom he is obliged to provide, and even hired servants and settlers, who have no claim to the land or right to enjoy its crops. In this year, the right to eat the land's produce is entirely severed from the right to own and work the soil; everyone may benefit equally from these fruits which sprout of themselves by the grace of God. The end of the verse gives this intention added emphasis: the permission to eat sabbatical fruit applies equally not only to men, but even to animals, and not only those which are beneficial to man ("thy cattle"), but all "the beasts of the land," including those which are of no use to man.

These scriptural guidelines thus create a fellowship of all those who are permitted to eat the fruits of the table of the Lord in the sabbatical year; rich and poor, human beings and all other creatures of the earth, share in it equally. What better demonstration of the verse, "Thou openest Thy hand, and satisfieth every living thing with favor" (Ps. 145:16)? The phrasing of the permission to eat *shevi'it* fruit intentionally emphasizes that which all creatures share in common. This important element of commonality would seem to be reflected in the parallel passage regarding the jubilee year (Lev. 25:11–12):

> Ye shall not sow, neither reap that which groweth of itself in it,
> nor gather the grapes in it of the undressed vines....
> it shall be holy unto you; ye shall eat the increase thereof from the
>   field.

Man is required, in these holy years, to refrain from controlling the land and its produce, but the benefit of spontaneous growth is not denied to him. When he partakes of it, however, he must not do so in an artificial way; he must approach the fruits in the natural way in which all creatures eat of the hand of God: "ye shall eat the increase thereof out of the field." This primary mode of eating is consistent with man's return to the brotherhood of all God's creatures. The appearance of "the beasts that are in thy land" is thus no trifling matter: they characterize the mode of consumption of the fruits which grow during the sabbath of solemn rest.

To summarize, then, the distinctive aspect of the consumption of *shevi'it* fruit according to Leviticus 25, seems to be this consciousness of the fellowship of all creatures, who in togetherness and in a primary and natural way partake of the fruits which God graciously causes to grow in the fields of the land.

V. The Biblical Sabbatical and the Experience of *Communitas*

What has been seen of the biblical seventh year suggests the characteristics of *communitas*, the term Turner uses to describe that state—to be found amongst numerous cultures and religions—in which the members of a society share in an experience of brotherhood and equality, brought about by the temporary abolishment of barriers and divisions which have their source in the everyday social order. A more detailed comparison between certain aspects of the sabbatical year and the typical manifestations of *communitas* confirms that the biblical sabbatical does indeed represent a very characteristically Jewish expression of the general human desire for *communitas*.

1. Striving to Maintain the Divine Order amongst the Jewish People

The tone of the whole twenty-fifth chapter of Leviticus reflects the basic assumption that all the children of Israel are brothers, as expressed in the sociolegal institutions outlined in the chapter. In principle, this brotherhood binds all of the people's members to one another. It is not self-evident; rather it is explained as stemming from the equality of all Israelites in their basic relationship with God, who took them out of Eygpt in order to give them their inheritance, where they will live together in His presence and do His will.

Consider, for example, the reason given for keeping the institution of the jubilee year, which provided that each man, in the fiftieth year, regain possession of the land handed down to him by his forefathers, irrespective of his economic situation on the eve of the jubilee (Lev. 25:23):

And the land shall not be sold in perpetuity;
for the land is Mine;
for ye are strangers and settlers with Me.

No one may truly own the land, and the people must express this principle in action by dealing fairly and honestly for the purchase or sale of land, and by relating to their fellow-men as brothers (Lev. 25:14–15):

And if thou sell aught unto thy neighbor, or buy of thy neighbor's hand,
ye shall not wrong one another [lit: each his brother].

> According to the number of years after the jubilee thou shalt buy of thy
>   neighbor [lit: brother]
> and according to the number of years of the crops he shall sell unto
>   thee.

The proper attitude prescribed for treating a person who has become impoverished also derives from the concept of brotherhood and from the idea that all are equal in relation to God (Lev. 25:35–38):

> And if thy brother be waxen poor, and his means fail with thee;
> then thou shalt uphold him; as a stranger and a settler shall he live
>   with thee.
> Take thou no interest of him or increase;
> but fear the Lord thy God;
> that thy brother may live with thee.
> Thou shalt not give him thy money upon interest,
> nor give him any victuals for increase.
> I am the Lord your God, who brought you forth out of the land of Egypt,
> to give you the land of Canaan,
> to be your God.

Even the Hebrew slave, who no longer participated in the equality and brotherhood of the free, had however a very different status from the Gentile bondsman. His basic equality with the other members of the Jewish people could never be eradicated, even though his function in society might be that of a slave (Lev. 25:39–46). The laws of a Hebrew slave are motivated in the following terms:

> For they are My servants, whom I brought forth out of the land of Egypt;
> they shall not be sold as bondmen. Thou shalt not rule over him with
> rigor; but shalt fear thy God . . . over your brethren the children of Israel
> ye shall not rule, one over another, with rigor.

The fact that Israel's God is the God of history gives a special tone to the kind of order that is meant to be expressed by the society described in scripture. It is not so much a cosmic order as a divine one, revealed through the history of the people.[21] Nevertheless, it seems that the examples examined from the twenty-fifth chapter of Leviticus, and especially those concerning the ritual-symbolic periods of the sabbatical and jubilee years, are typical of the primary element in the ritual experience of *communitas*:

persons deeply divided from one another in the secular or nonreligious world nevertheless in certain ritual situations cooperate closely to ensure what is believed to be the maintenance of a cosmic order which transcends the contradictions and conflicts inherent in the mundane social system. Here we have an unstated model of communitas, an operational model (Turner 1974, 238).

2. The Absence of Ownership: Togetherness based on Symbolic Poverty

One of the most central, if not the most central, aspects of the sabbatical year is the people's absolute renunciation of property ownership. All members of the society thus become equal, for all alike are landless. Of course, the structure of the society was not abolished in favor of an egalitarian anarchy. What happened, rather, was that the outward manifestations of this structure were ritually suspended to make way for the ritual adoption of symbols of equality, which were borrowed from the world of poverty and scarcity. All became equal; and this did not express itself in their "all alike behaving like rich men and princes," but rather in their "all alike behaving like poor people who had nothing at all."

In this sense, too, the qualities reflected by the biblical institution of shevi'it resemble the characteristic nature of other communitas rituals, which give expression to "the bond that exists between communitas, liminality, and lowermost status" (Turner 1974, 243).

3. Emphasis on "Naturalness" and the Natural Dimension

The Torah states that shevi'it fruit is not to be harvested in the same manner as the fruit of other years, but rather "ye shall eat the increase thereof out of the field"; that is, it is to be eaten in a direct and immediate way, without the intervention of those stages of processing characteristic of more sophisticated methods of human consumption. This mode of eating also follows from the definition of the circle of those who may partake of sabbatical fruit; rich and poor, free and indentured—all are invited to dine on it, together with the domestic animals and the beasts of the field. Moreover, the produce which makes up their meal has grown of itself in the course of the year, entirely naturally and spontaneously, without any human intervention or initiative.

This relationship between eating sabbatical fruit, and simple, immediate methods of preparation, also demonstrates the resemblance between the *shevi'it* year and institutions designed to evoke the experience of *communitas* in other human cultures and societies. What Turner (1974, 252–53) has to say about the cultural nature of the symbols of naturalism is relevant in this context:

> In a sense, when man ceases to be the master and becomes the equal or fellow of man, he also ceases to be the master and becomes the equal or fellow of nonhuman beings. It is culture that fabricates structural distinctions; it is culture too that eradicates these distinctions in liminality, but in so doing culture is forced to use the idiom of nature, to replace its fictions by natural facts—even if these facts themselves only possess what reality they have in a framework of cultural concepts.[22]

4. The Confirmation of Ordinary Social Structure

Finally, if a proper understanding of the institution of *shevi'it* is to be gained it is important to recall that despite its emphasis on the equality and brotherhood of the people of Israel and their essentially equal status in relation to possession of the land, it does not express a desire to revolutionize the existing order of society, or a challenge to the very institutions of property and land ownership. There is no essential conflict between the six years of productive work, in which land is owned and society is structured around class differences, and the sabbatical year, in which ownership is suspended and the unity and togetherness of society are emphasized. The seventh year is the converse of the preceding six, the opposite side of the same coin, the dimension of *communitas* which, together with the social structure of society, completes the social existence of the people on its land. As Turner says: "'Societas,' or 'society' as we all experience it, is a process involving *both* social structure *and* communitas, separately united in varying proportions" (1974, 238).

VI. Biblical and Mishnaic Norms Regulating the Consumption of Sabbatical Produce

If we look once more at the normative characteristics of the consumption of *shevi'it* fruit, it will be seen that the regulations to be found in the Bible are those governing (1) methods of processing (in the natural state); (2) methods of consumption (in the ordinary way); and (3) eating in company. It was the sages, however, who framed the temporal, spatial, and group boundaries which appear in the oral Torah as limiting the consumption of sabbatical produce. Manifestly, the qualities of the sabbatical year listed in the Bible are those characteristic of *communitas* modes of behavior, while the norms added by the oral Torah have their source in other considerations.

This study has concluded that in order to gain a good understanding of what the sages had in mind in formulating similar norms of consumption for *terumah*, *ma'aser sheni*, and *shevi'it* fruit, the relevant passages in the scriptures should be examined. It has been seen that originally each of these three realms had its own independent, and distinctive, and original characteristics. Nevertheless, it appears that the sages saw these three institutions as expressing a powerful common element, which could create a normative convergence toward a common halakhic focus. What, then, is this common factor?

1. Before Communitas: What Ground for Brotherhood?

To answer this question, it is necessary to first discuss what appears to be a nonsequitor in the argument regarding the experience of *communitas*. As Turner describes it, once the barriers and divisions characteristic of an ordered social structure have been removed, people will naturally enter into a state of *communitas*. In other words, all one has to do in order to evoke in people a deep sense of brotherhood is to remove the ordinary social structure. However, it is not at all a matter of course that this will come about. Without a social structure, what is to bring people together? On what basis will they experience a sense of brotherhood and equality? Is it not just as likely that they will experience isolation, loneliness, and alienation?

The concept of *communitas* thus seems to be in need of completion, and this study proposes to do so. Every society has its ideals of unity and commonality, ideals which function to keep this human association a living reality. These ideals vary from society to society, so that the uniqueness of each appears in its own group-formative ideals as well as in its structure and institutions. The vitality of these ideals in the consciousness and feeling of the members of a given society will be a precondition for the experience of *communitas*, or at least will be reflected in the particular expression of *communitas* emerging in that society.[23] To the extent that these group-formative ideals characterize a society's members, the removal of ordinary social barriers will enable them to unite on the basis of the sense of commonality and so achieve an experience of *communitas*. If these ideals are weak, however, it is doubtful whether the removal of social barriers in itself will lead to that experience. The reverse would be more likely: the removal of barriers would lead to a disintegrative experience of alienation and anomie.[24] There is thus an interdependence between the experience of *communitas* and group-formative ideals. Experience of *communitas* can come about only if group formulating ideals have some significant pre-existence among the members of a society. However, the experience of *communitas* itself contributes to a strengthening of the emotional and spiritual devotion of the group members to these fundamental ideals. This relationship may be represented as:

$$\text{group formative ideals} \rightleftharpoons \text{communitas}$$

With this approach to the concept of *communitas* in mind it is possible to return to the discussion of the consumption of sabbatical produce.

If the twenty-fifth chapter of Leviticus is examined once more, it will be seen that the group-formulating ideals of Israelites society are clearly expressed: the equality and essential brotherhood of all Israelites stem from the fact that all are equal in their relationship to God and in their status before Him. All are servants of God, and therefore all are free in relation to one another. All of them live in the land with the status of strangers and settlers on God's earth—and so all have an equal right to possess a share in the land forever.

The social structure of the people of Israel, with its divisions between rich and poor, master and slave, landowner and landless must thus be viewed, according to these passages, as purely functional in nature, so that it does not express the true relationships obtaining among the members of the society and between them and their land. The structural division of society according to class, status, and role is really only a surface phenomenon, for all alike are servants of God, and are alike, too, in their essential relationship to the land. The nature of this relationship stems from the bond between God and His people. He brought them out of Egypt in order for them to serve Him after they settled in the land of Canaan.

Leviticus 25 gives the impression that this link between God and His people was entirely obvious and clear to the author. His intention was to show what implications this religious-experiential state of affairs ought to have in the social and human realm. The passages dealing with the consumption of *ma'aser sheni* in Jerusalem, or with the consumption of *terumah* by the priests, reveal an analogous phenomenon. Their religious, ideological, and experiential element is a matter of course, a given; the people need only to be informed of the behavioral norms by which this religious and experiential dimension will find expression. The religious experience and ideas in all three areas are similar: all are concerned with gifts God gives to man in grace, and with the fact that it is He who gives and has always given daily bread. However, there is a high degree of differentiation as to how this expression is formulated, as it is adapted to different social and human functions. In the *shevi'it* year, it is manifested in the suspension and symbolic annulment of economic dichotomies, strengthening the people's sense of brotherhood and *communitas*; with *ma'aser sheni*, in buttressing the status of the central place of worship and the brotherhood of the tribes of Israel, and in the joy of the harvest; and with *terumah*, in the enhancement of the priests' unique and exalted status and in emphasis on their closeness to God.

In the scriptural stratum of Jewish tradition, in other words, it can be seen that: (1) the original group-formative experience/consciousness is very clear; and (2) this clarity serves as the ground for the formulation of social institutions, each with its particular purpose. The situation becomes more complex, however, in texts from the rabbinic period.

2. The Rabbinic Stratum: Communitas and the Attempt to Reconstitute Group-Formative Consciousness

In the laws formulated by the sages in the oral Torah one finds, as has been seen, an integration of various elements drawn from biblical norms relating to *terumah*, *ma'aser sheni*, and *shevi'it*.

The idea of spatial and temporal boundaries of consumption has been extended from *ma'aser sheni* to *terumah* and *shevi'it*. The idea of limitations on the way food may be processed and utilized has been extended from the sabbatical to *terumah* and *ma'aser sheni*.

The ideas of the sanctity of the fruits and of boundary norms limiting access to the fruits have been extended from *terumah* and *ma'aser sheni* to *shevi'it*.

These extensions of the characteristics of each of the three halakhic institutions increased the normative overlap among them; they became less distinct. The biblical *shevi'it*, with its outstanding qualities of unity, equality, and *communitas*, thrust in the direction of release from the extant social structure, from interpersonal barriers, and from the limitations of the ordinary. In the oral Torah, it acquired some limiting properties as well: restriction to an in-group which included Jews alone and a temporal restriction (until the *bi'ur*). These limitations entailed a positive correlate as well: sabbatical produce now was characterized as holy, a description which, while the Bible may have hinted at it,[25] became explicit only in the oral Torah. The consumption of *terumah* as described in the Bible, on the other hand, was the exalted activity of a special, high status group. Not for nothing were the words "for a consecrated portion" interpreted as meaning "for greatness," and therefore was it said of the priests that they ate like kings. What *terumah* received from *shevi'it*, then, were its qualities of simplicity and primariness: the requirement that the produce be eaten in its natural state and in the ordinary way. However, the group-extending norms characteristic of *shevi'it* and *ma'aser sheni* were not applied to *terumah*; eating *terumah* remained the province of a small, high status in-group. While *terumah* retained its royal quality, however, the kings drew closer, at least symbolically, to nature and their ways partially resemble modes of eating common to all. *Ma'aser sheni*, too, acquired some of the properties of *shevi'it*. Limits were placed on the absolute subjectivity previously allowed the celebrant in Jerusalem, so that even as he set about experiencing the great joy of the festival, he was asked to refrain (again, symbolically) from moving too far away from nature and from the conventional eating habits of his fellows.

In sum, *terumah* and *ma'aser sheni* acquired the sabbatical year's quality of naturalness and its attribution of religious significance to social eating conventions, while the sabbatical acquired qualities of boundary maintenance and sanctity that had previously been applicable only to *terumah* and *ma'aser sheni*.

This paper asked how this normative convergence might be explained. It is possible to now offer a solution, which rests on an understanding of the basic problems which the sages faced and the ways in which they generally coped with them. The sages did not create Judaism. Its traditions were already ancient, well developed, and institutionalized when they came on the scene. These traditions, however, had lost much of their vitality. The original group-formative consciousness of God's current involvement in the people's life and of the dependence of all creatures on His immediate mercy, which had been so strong in biblical times, had dimmed. Conjointly, the institutions and regulations of the Jewish religion, and particularly the norms connected with the sanctuary and the priesthood, had become elaborate and formalized. They emphasized the sanctity and exaltedness of the sanctuary and the priests, but the ordinary lives of the masses of the people now seemed pale in comparison, for they were marked neither by the ritual grandeur of the sanctuary nor by that immediacy and primariness which had been the Israelite religion's source of vitality in its earlier stages.

It may be said that one of the major (if not the major) goals of the sages' endeavor was to restore a sense of value and religious vitality to the life of the community at large, especially outside of the priesthood. One of their primary ways of accomplishing this was to stamp the principal areas of daily life with an element of ritual, which was intended to create the same kind of impression, in everyday life, as had been created by the elaborate rituals of the sanctuary; that is, it was to strengthen the people's sense of God's presence and of man's vital relationship with Him.[26]

While in biblical times the issue had been one of how to make the transition from the people's fairly clear group-formative religious consciousness to the creation of distinct social institutions, in the rabbinic period the situation had, to a large extent, been reversed. The problem now was how to revive religious consciousness by means of the existing religious and social institutions. What the religious leadership had to do during this period was not to build different institutions on the basis of a single, unified religious consciousness, but rather to exploit the multitude of existing institutions and rituals to restore a homogeneous, commonly held group-formative consciousness. The fact that the rabbis were working in this direction is highly visible in the realm of food and dining. They surrounded the mealtimes of every Jew with a wealth of rituals and norms, concerning what he could and could not eat; how he was to prepare foods in accordance with the appropriate ritual forms; and how he was to behave before, during, and after a meal. Numerous blessings were formulated, and their recitation, subject to detailed and elaborate norms, was made obligatory before and after partaking of various foods. The sages advocated that priestly norms of purity concerning the eating of sacral food (such as *terumah*) be applied, in toto, to the daily eating and drinking habits of every Jew. Those Jews who took on themselves these priestly norms with regard to eating were called *Pharisees*.

VII. Conclusion

To summarize this analysis of rabbinic halakhah, it was found that the requisite modes of eating the produce of *shevi'it, ma'aser sheni,* and *terumah* became more similar to one another, while each of these institutions lost something of its distinctive character. It was the sages' desire to conscript existing institutions to strengthening the people's consciousness of God's presence and their closeness to Him, that made them shape the norms connected with these institutions to resemble one another more closely. Thus, for example, while *shevi'it* norms had previously stressed the commonality of all living creatures, this was now played down, as the experience of *communitas* was directed toward reaffirmation of the brotherhood of the people of Israel alone, and the sanctity and status of eating *shevi'it* produce gained greater emphasis. Conversely, *terumah* acquired the sabbatical year's qualities of simplicity and primariness, so the unique status of the priestly class lost some of its emphasis, and the resemblance between the sacramental priestly consumption and the eating before the Lord, which could be done by any Jew anywhere, became more pronounced. In both cases, then, there was an attempt to combine aspects of simplicity and primariness with those of a sanctity and uniqueness that applied to the whole community of Israel.

When the rituals connected with the sabbatical year were formulated, they were shaped in such a way as to effect a transition from the prevailing state of the people's society and consciousness to a different one which was deemed desirable. In the scriptural stratum of tradition, rituals were designed to create, in the people's awareness of their common Israelite-religious foundation, that experience of equality and brotherhood characteristic of *communitas.* In the mishnaic period, on the other hand, these rituals underwent modification, so that they could serve toward restoring and revitalizing the people's fundamental sense of the presence of God in the land and the closeness of all the people of Israel to Him. The same socio-religious institution was thus channeled to serve different purposes, by means of its adaptation to the current social and religious needs of the Israelite (Jewish) community, as these were understood (whether consciously or intuitively) by those responsible for molding the institutional and ritual dimension of the people's life.

Notes

1. The openness of the Torah text to significant and even radical reinterpretation was seen by the sages as being due to an inherent ambiguity and multivocality, intentionally implanted in the text by God as an expression of His divine love and concern for Israel. "R. Jannai said: The Torah which the Holy One, blessed be He, gave to Moses was delivered to him in forty-nine aspects of uncleanness and forty-nine aspects of cleanness, as it is stated, *And his banner* [*vediglo*, Can. 2:4], the numerical value of its letters being 49." *Masekhet Soferim*, chap. 16, rules 5–6, English version taken from Cohen (1965, 290–91)

2. See, for example, *Seder Eliyahu (Tanna de-Bei Eliyahu) Zuta* (chap. 2) in which the divine source attributed to the Mishnah, and the relationship of the Mishnah to the Torah, is explained thus: "both Bible and Mishnah are the words of God. What, then, is the difference between the Bible and Mishnah? This can be learned from the parable of the king who had two servants. He loved them very much, and he gave to each a measure of wheat and a bundle of flax. So what did the clever one do? He took the flax and wove it into a cover, and he took the wheat and made it into flour; he sieved and milled it, kneaded it and baked it. Then he arranged it on the table, spread the cover over it and put it aside to await the king's arrival. As for the foolish one, he did nothing at all. Eventually the king came into his house and said to them, 'My sons, bring me what I gave you.' The one brought out [the bread that he had made from] the flour upon the table, with the cover spread over it; and the other brought out the wheat in a basket, with the bundle of flax on top of it. Oh, the shame of it! Oh, the disgrace! Now, you must admit which of them would be the more favored—he who brought out the table with [the bread that he had made from] the flour upon it. . . . For when the Holy One, Blessed be He, gave the Torah to Israel, what he was giving them was wheat to be made into flour, and flax to be made into cloth."

3. In the literature of the oral Torah, the cancellation of debts in the seventh year is viewed as absolute. Once the sabbatical year has begun, in other words, the creditor can no longer collect his debt from the borrower. The internal logic of the scriptural text, however, would seem to indicate that the effect of the sabbatical cancellation of debts ought to parallel what happens in the relation to the land—a temporary suspension of a person's right to realize his ownership. This makes sense, for how could a farmer, in an agricultural society, put together the sum he needed to repay his debt at a time when he had no income from the sale of his produce? It thus appears that originally, in scripture, the cancellation of debts in the sabbatical year meant that the creditor would have no right to collect his debt, nor would the debtor be under any obligation to repay it during this time. Once the sabbatical year was over, however, the economic world would recommence functioning as before; the farmer would resume ownership of the produce of his field, and the creditor would once more have the right to demand payment of the debt (see Deut. 15:1–11).

Incidentally, the view that the Torah demanded the absolute cancellation of debts, made it impossible, de facto, to keep this commandment. As a direct consequence of it, the sages of the Second Temple period were impelled to institute a number of rules which limited the application of the principle of cancellation of debts.

4. I have intentionally avoided taking a stance on an issue that has been the subject of an enormous amount of scholarly controversy, namely, whether the seventh year mentioned in connection with the liberation of slaves was identical with the agricultural sabbatical—in which case all slaves would have gone free in that same year, regardless of how long they have served until then; or whether, despite the linguistic similarity and proximity of this passage to the commandment concerning the sabbatical cancellation of debts, each slave was to go free in the seventh year after his purchase, regardless of the seven-year agricultural cycle affecting society as a whole.

5. A highly significant ideological controversy sprang up around the attempts to revive the sabbatical year in modern Israel. Was the good of the new agricultural settlement to establish exemplary communities, which would dedicate themselves to the service of God regardless of socioeconomic considerations, or was it, rather, to bring about the national revival of the people through the establishment of farming communities, for which sake the renewed fulfillment of ancient religious practices might be sacrificed? (see Friedman 1974:455–80).

6. As things stand in Israel at present, the sabbatical year is formally considered binding, but the prohibition against working the land is in fact circumvented by a halakhic/legal fiction recognized by the chief rabbinate and acceptable to all except a few ultraorthodox groups which demand that the requirement to abstain from working the land be carried out in practice.

7. The *tannaim* (sing. *tanna*) were the rabbinic authorities of the mishnaic period, and some of their traditions are preserved also in extramishnaic sources such as the Tosefta (see note 11).

8. *Terumah* is the portion of a farmer's agricultural produce which is given to the priests. *Ma'aser sheni* is the tenth of the farmer's agricultural produce (or its monetary equivalent) which must be brought to the place where God's sanctuary is located, and consumed there (Deut. 12:17–18).

9. These laws are highly complex. The clearest and most systematic classical summary of this area of halakhah, in its rabbinic configuration, was composed by Maimonides in his magnum opus, the *Mishneh Torah*. See in that work, *Mishneh Torah, Sefer Zera'im, Hilkhot Terumot, Hilkhot Ma'aser Sheni*, and *Hilkhot Shemittah ve-Yovel*.

10. See Jerusalem Talmud, *Ma'aser sheni*, 2:1.

11. Tosefta is a collection of oral law arranged similarly to the Mishnah, often including material which expands and illustrates matters given only a brief, summary treatment by the latter. The Tosefta was edited around the same

time as was the Mishnah (toward the end of the second and the beginning of the third centuries of the Common Era).

12. A sauce of oil and vinegar.

13. A sauce of vinegar and garum.

14. For the sources and proof-texts of these laws, see the relevant chapters of the *Mishneh Torah* of Maimonides (see note 9).

15. The biblical verse states that "the sabbath-produce of the land shall be for food for you" (Lev. 25:66), and the rabbinic legal exegesis to the Bible interprets this as meaning "for you—and not for others." Moreover, according to Tosefta Shevi'it 5:21: "A Gentile may not be given ... sabbatical produce to eat."
Whether a Gentile who was also a member of a Jewish household could eat sabbatical produce was a matter of dispute among the rabbis. This problem may also be approached from the perspective of the fundamental issue of *communitas*: are those who customarily eat together considered to belong to the same group; or must one belong to the larger community in order to justify his partaking of sabbatical produce along with the rest?

16. Oil which is to be burnt is oil that had been given to the priests as *terumah* but became impure. It was agreed by all that pure *terumah* oil may not be removed from the land of Israel.

17. The dispute over this issue is lengthy and complex. See *Encyclopedia Talmudit* (1976, 4:55ff.), in the entry on "Bi'ur Shevi'it."

18. In the *Sifre* to Numbers (18:8) this verse is commented on as follows: "for a consecrated portion"—"consecration" means greatness (see Horowitz, 1917, 135, line 7). See also BT *Sotah* 15a, *Hullin* 132b.

19. *Midrash ha-Gadol*, Numbers, (Rabinovitch, 291).

20. See, for example, Ex. 31:15; Lev. 16:31.

21. Yehezkel Kaufmann identifies the "consciousness revolution" of biblical monotheism with the realization that there is no "cosmic order" governing the whole universe, to which all—including the gods—are subject; rather, God precedes and transcends the cosmic order, and He governs it with an absolutely free will (Kaufmann 1948; 1:244ff.; and Kaufmann 1960).

22. From this we can also gain a clearer idea of the inner logic underlying the specifying of certain methods of preparing and eating food as simple or natural according to the conventional modes of preparation used in ancient Jewish society.

23. Da Matta (1977) also implies that *communitas* in a given society should be seen in relation to its particular social structure and values.

24. Turner (1969), in discussing *communitas*, also notes that it is an alternative to the dissolution of society into the Hobbesian war of every man against

every man. I have here attempted to suggest a factor whose influence is central in determining which alternative—the Hobbesian one or that of *communitas*—a society will fall into, after dissolution of structure.

25. In connection with jubilee fruits, see Lev. 25:11–12, 19.

26. An outstanding example of this is the formulation of the institutionalized prayers according to a structure expressly intended to parallel that of the Temple service.

References

Cohen, A. ed. (1965). *The Minor Tractates of the Talmud.* London: Soncino.

Da Matta, R. (1977). "Constraint and License: a Preliminary Study of Two Brazilian National Rituals." In *Secular Ritual,* S. F. Moore and B. Myerhoff, eds. Assen: Van Gorcum, 244–64.

Encyclopedia Talmudit (1976). Jerusalem: Talmudic Encyclopedia Institute.

Freidman, M. (1974). "On the Social Significance of the Polemic on *Shemita.*" *Shalem* (Studies in the History of the Jews in Eretz Israel) 2:455–80. Hebrew, with English summary.

Horowitz, H. S. ed. (1917). *Sifre D'Be Rab.* Leipzig: G. Fock. Hebrew.

Kaufmann, Y. (1948). *The History of Israelite Religion: From Early Times until the End of the Second Temple Period.* 4 vols. Jerusalem and Tel Aviv: Bialik Institute and Dvir. Hebrew.

_____. (1960). *The Religion of Israel: From Its Beginnings to the Babylonian Exile.* Translated and Abridged by M. Greenberg. Chicago: University of Chicago Press.

Rabinovitch, Z. M. ed. (1967). *Midrash ha-Gadol, Numbers.* Jerusalem: Mosad Ha-Rav Kook. Hebrew.

Turner, V. (1969). *The Ritual Process.* Chicago: Aldine.

_____. (1974). *Dreams, Fields and Metaphors.* Ithaca: Cornell University Press.

CHAPTER 3

Torah and Children:
Some Symbolic Aspects of the
Reproduction of Jews and Judaism[1]

HARVEY E. GOLDBERG

He who teaches Torah to his companion's son is considered by scripture
as if he had sired him
—Babylonian Talmud, *Sanhedrin* 19b

I. Introduction

A major challenge to anthropological scholarship is the integration
of the findings of contemporary field research with the study of classic
world civilizations. The problems and possibilities of this challenge
were explored by Redfield (1955) in his discussion of anthropology's
growing involvement with peasant societies. Since then, notions of
"great tradition" and "little tradition" have become standard in anthropological vocabulary. Despite the program formulated by Redfield, and
the work on Hinduism and Islam cited by him, the challenge of understanding the cultural interchange between cosmopolitan and paro-
chial expressions of a tradition evoked limited immediate response.
Most anthropologists (with some notable exceptions as in the case of
India) carrying out work in the areas of major civilizations focused on
questions of peasant society and economy, seeking to understand the
integration of village communities with urban, regional, or national
networks, rather than on elucidating the symbols and meanings which
animated these societies at their various levels.

Since the early 1970s, however, there have been important attempts to understand the links between the concepts and values embodied in the classic texts and the details of contemporary behavior observed at the local level. Dumont (1970) has attempted to show the

correspondence between the details of caste structure and classic Hindu religious ideas. His position has been criticized by Marriot, and Inden (1977, 229), who nevertheless suggest an alternative interpretation based on a "combination of authoritative texts with field observation." Gombrich has studied "precept and practice" in Sinhalese Buddhism and found "what people [monks] say now has turned out ... to be remarkably similar to what was being said about 1,500 years ago" (1971, 318). With regard to the Middle East, Antoun (1976) has argued persuasively that anthropologists should have a greater familiarity with the classical languages and texts (see Meeker 1976, 421) and Geertz's study of bazaar life in a Moroccan town views some of the central notions evident in bazaar activities in terms of classical Islamic conceptions (Geertz, Geertz, and Rosen 1979).

If, in fact, isomorphism can be demonstrated (and one should not ignore instances of lack of it) between ancient text and contemporary daily life, a central question is: how does this correspondence come about? The answer that people behave in a certain way because they read and believe (see Needham 1972) certain books is obviously inadequate, and anthropology has always recommended separating the study of customary behavior from native explanation of that behavior. On the other hand, the proverbial divorce of the study of text from the study of context, which was said to have characterized anthropology's relationship to the classics (Redfield 1955), is likewise unsatisfactory because there clearly are interesting influences between the two.

A related question, and one that makes the problem even more complex, concerns the wide diffusion of these great traditions to people speaking diverse languages and characterized by different social structures. Obviously, literacy is one important factor here. In the case of Judaism, the resemblance in the mode of traditional basic schooling among Jews in Eastern Europe (Zborowski 1954, 125), Kurdistan (Brauer 1947, 200–202), Yemen (Goiten 1953, 141–42), and North Africa (Zafrani 1972, 129ff), even when being taught to translate the biblical text into different languages, is striking. At the same time, this traditional education involved heavy emphasis on rote learning, so that an understanding of the text, in the contemporary sense of the word, cannot explain, in itself, the widespread diffusion and historic continuity. The problem is even clearer in the case of Islam, where millions of devotees speak languages entirely different from Arabic, but develop a deep attachment to the Quranic text and what it stands for. In the case of Catholicism, direct popular access to the written text was not normally encouraged, even though the religion is ideologically based on the text. In Hinduism, while the religion relates to ancient texts, a knowledge of these is not at all central in the ongoing practice of tradition (see Gombrich 1971, 18); ritual seems to be much more important. Ward (1977) has argued, with regard to traditional China, that despite the importance of literacy in elite formation and maintenance, drama, in addition to the written word, has to be viewed as a critical mechanism in the transmission of Chinese civilization to large segments of the population.

An important area of research appears to be, therefore, the interrelationship of schooling, or textual teaching, to other forms of communication in establishing and diffusing commitment to major religions. Judaism provides a case in point. Side by side with the stress on study in Jewish tradition is the explicit educational purpose of certain rituals. For example, the motivation of the Passover sacrifice appearing in Exodus (12:26) is as follows: "And when your children ask you— 'What do you mean by this rite?,' you shall say—'It is the Passover sacrifice to the Lord, because he passed over the houses of the Israelites in Egypt when he smote the Egyptians, but saved our houses.' " A similar reason is given for eating *matzot* or unleavened bread (Ex. 12:8), and both these rituals have been incorporated in the *seder* ceremony of Passover, in which many activities are saliently oriented toward children (see Fredman 1981, 17, 18). A direct association is found, therefore, between ritual and education, which in Judaism has meant, preeminently, textual education.

In other civilizations textual study may be less important, and other symbolic processes more crucial, in establishing commitment to religious traditions among individuals and groups (Ward 1977). Recent advances in the anthropological study of the symbolic dimension of social life bring it within the purview of concepts taken from drama, literary criticism, semiotics, and other areas. This makes it possible to link the field observation and analysis of ritual to textual scholarship in ways which were not possible before. It is now feasible, therefore, to heed Redfield's call for the "social organization of tradition" with a deepened sensitivity to cultural form. It thus seems promising to explore the role of ritual and other activities heavily invested with meaning, in their relationship to texts, as socializing agents capable of bringing about widespread devotion to world views, and corresponding patterns of behavior, in several of the classic literary civilizations.

With these general thoughts in mind, it is possible to turn to a consideration of the centrality of scripture in Judaism. Stimulated by modern work on symbolism, the question may be approached in the following way. Turner (1964; 1968) has stressed how dominant symbols are characterized by two poles—an ideological one, focused on the central values of a society, and an orectic (sensory, psychobiological) pole, which anchors symbols in the affective processes of individuals. Book learning and writing are cognitive processes par excellence, and Judaism's conception of the revealed and written word as vehicle of the sacred, in opposition to plastic representations of the divine (Ex. 20:4; Deut. 4:25, 5:8) is well known. It may be asked, therefore, is there any way in which the stress on book learning, on *Torah*, is attached to other symbols which relate to the more biological or emotional concerns of the individual (and society).

In answering this question, this paper will first present some ethnographic (and historical) examples dealing with the treatment of the *sefer Torah*, the scroll of parchment on which the Five Books of Moses are written for the purpose of public ceremonial reading. Next will be suggested interpretations of these customs and rituals, and an evaluation of these interpretations in light of other related data, including the interpretations of traditional practitioners of these rites. Following this, it will be argued that some of the symbolic associations revealed in the later ethnographic material are similar to those implied by the biblical narrative.

The presentation of ethnographic and textual materials moves back and forth between different historical periods. This reflects, to a large extent, the manner in which the hypothesized symbolic connections were first conceived, and how the conception was refined, but not fundamentally modified, in the light of new data. The retention of this organizational form parallels Sperber's (1974, 63ff) discussion of how structuralist explanations of symbolic forms are empirically tested. Similarly, following Sperber's general argument, the textual materials cited are not treated as the interpretation or meaning of the symbolic acts discussed, but both ritual and text are viewed as part of a single field of significant (but not signifying, in the referential sense) elements. This paper will find that, despite the obvious differences in the data bases examined, and the vast separation of these cultural manifestations in space and time, similar associations are evident in many different instances, reflecting common Jewish conceptions of the dynamic relationship of Torah, or Jewish culture deriving from God's inscribed commandments, to the natural world, in particular to the realm of reproduction and biological continuity.

II. The Torah Scroll and Children: Some Ethnographic Examples

A. Simḥat Torah

The holiday of Simḥat Torah is celebrated each fall by traditional Jewish communities throughout the world. In Israel, the holiday coincides with the Shmini Atzeret festival, prescribed by the Bible to follow immediately the Feast of Booths (Sukkot), while in the diaspora, Simḥat Torah is an extension of Shimini Atzeret, falling two days after the Feast of Booths (*EJ, 14; 1571*). The term *Simḥat Torah* means joy of the Torah. On this day, the annual cycle of reading the entire Five Books of Moses is terminated, and at once begun again with the reading of the first section of Genesis. As on all such occasions, the reading is done from a handwritten parchment scroll, and not from a printed Pentateuch.

A central feature of the holiday is the dancing and singing with the Torah scrolls, after they are taken from the adorned cabinet in which they are stored, and the parading around the synagogue prior to the ceremonial reading. Many of the men take part in this dancing. In the center of the festivity are those individuals who hold the Torah scrolls as they dance (men take turns dancing with the scrolls). They may be surrounded by others who dance empty handed. In addition to dancing with the Torah scrolls, it is common for men with young children to dance with their children, particularly males, in their arms or on their shoulders. The author has observed, and participated in, this dancing on numerous occasions within Ashkenazi (European-derived) communities, but has been told that dancing with children was found among some Middle Eastern communities as well[2] prior to migration to Israel, where there is an easy diffusion of many customs. There is no rule that one must dance with children, and, to the participants, this act is a natural expression of festive feeling. From the point of view of the outside observer, the question may be raised—is there any association between the two items carried by the dancers—Torah scrolls and children?

B. Torah Scrolls

The Torah scroll is written on parchment and wound round two wooden poles. The common Sephardi tradition is that the scroll is built into a round wooden case which holds it in place. In Ashkenazi practice, the scroll is kept from rolling apart by binding it with a cloth tie. In some western Ashkenazi (Central European) areas, it was the custom to take the liner cloth that was placed under a male child on the day of his circumcision (when a baby boy is eight days old), and make it into a form that may be used as a Torah binder (Pollack 1971, 25; Abbink van der Zwan 1979; Kirshenblatt-Gimblett 1982). A metonymic relationship between male children and the Torah scroll is, therefore, strongly suggested.

The Torah scroll is the central cult object of Judaism. It takes on importance in the context of the communal life of the Jews. According to the biblical account, God's revelation at Sinai was witnessed by the entire people. The public reading of the Torah in the synagogue on Mondays, Thursdays, Sabbaths, and festivals, while routinized in religious law, is also suggestive of a reenactment, in quotidian life, of the revelation at Sinai.[3] As in other realms of Jewish practice, the communal and the individual or family are easily merged (Savishinsky and Wimberly 1974, 282), so that along with the communal importance of the Torah and the Torah scroll, interesting ties are also found between the Torah and the individual or, perhaps better, the family.

A Torah scroll is normally housed in a cabinet within a synagogue, called the Holy Ark (a common Ashkenazi term) or a similar epithet. The scroll itself, however, may be the property of an individual, or a family, who paid a scribe to prepare it according to established rules. Among the Jews of Tripolitania and elsewhere, men who had no children were among the most common purchasers of Torah scrolls. Providing such a Torah scroll, which bore the name of the owner, for the use of the community thus, partially, took the place of the sons that were kept from him. Perpetuity of seed, and perpetuity of the Torah are closely associated.

III. Discussion and Interpretation

Thus far three ethnographic examples from Jewish practice have been given suggesting that, symbolically, the *sefer Torah*, or Torah scroll becomes, inter alia, identified with the perpetuity of seed, or particularly, the siring of male children. This is not viewed as a dogmatic association, nor is it being insisted that the association exists consciously or unconsciously in the minds of all traditional Jews. Rather, given certain central values and conceptions within traditional Jewish thought, there is a potentiality of this association being made, and remade, an association which, therefore, might be understood better as a recurring process rather than as an established category. This potentiality may or may not be realized in a given socioritual context. At the same time, because the link between the two conceptual domains is suggestive rather than definitive, alternate, but often parallel, associations are found. While these associations differ from the sefer Torah = male children equation, they do not thereby invalidate it. Rather they reinforce the general thrust of the argument, but also show that the realm of symbolic linkages is open-ended and dynamic. Several of these alternative but parallel associations will now be discussed.

To begin with, it does not require a stretch of the imagination to suggest that the sefer Torah may be viewed as analogous to a human being. One of the basic laws with regard to the treatment of a sefer Torah directly suggests the parallel. A sefer Torah which is no longer fit for use (public reading) may not be casually discarded or burned. Rather, it is put away in a manner parallel to the burial of humans.[4] Thus, it is not surprising to discover in other contexts the symbolic association between the sefer Torah and human beings in general, or specific kinds of human beings in particular.[5]

One kind of human being that the sefer Torah may represent is a king.[6] In the Ashkenazi tradition, the scroll (in addition to being bound) is dressed with a velvet covering. In both the Sephardi and Ashkenazi traditions, the sefer Torah is often adorned with silver ornaments, which are sometimes shaped like a crown. When the sefer Torah is removed from the Holy Ark and paraded around the synagogue at the time of a public reading, it is treated with acts of respect such as standing in its presence, kissing, and mild bowing, as might be accorded a royal personage. It is therefore reasonable to suggest another equation: sefer Torah = king.

The association of the sefer Torah with royalty does not necessarily inhibit its association with the ordinary Jew.[7] After hearing an earlier version of this paper, a colleague suggested to me[8] that the traditional festive garb of many traditional Eastern European Jews—a round hat, satin coat, and sash around the middle—may be likened to the dress of a sefer Torah—a round head covering, a velvet outer garment, and a tie around the midsection. At the same time, it is possible to metaphorically link a sefer Torah and a female.[9] A Libyan woman, in describing her early years, during which she did not go out of the house to school or to work until she left her father's home at marriage, likened herself to a sefer Torah, guarded in a closed cabinet.[10] Thus, if it is argued that the sefer Torah is symbolically associated with male progeny, then it must be claimed that it is not the only way in which the Torah is likened to people,[11] but certainly as a plausible one among others. Part four of this paper shall argue that this particular association has great historical depth and may also be found in the biblical text.

Similarly, if the link between Torah and the siring of male children is interpreted as one example of the grounding of ideology in orectic processes, it does not mean that this is the only such link. Another sensory region often (and naturally?—Torah literally means that which is taught) linked to Torah is the oral-alimentary zone. In seventeenth-century Germany, a Jewish male child, on his first day in school, would lick honey smeared across the verses of a book of the Pentateuch, from which he would be taught to recite (Pollack 1971, 54). At the parallel occasion in Kurdistan, the teacher would write letters of the Hebrew alphabet on a piece of paper, smear honey on them, and give them to the child to lick.[12] The image of the ingestion of the Torah, too, has a long history. In the biblical text, Isaiah is consecrated to prophecy by touching his lips (Is. 6:6–7),[13] and Ezekiel is commanded, in a vision, to eat a scroll containing the words of the divine message (Ez. 3:1–3).[14] In the latter instance, Ezekiel finds the words "sweet as honey," so that the biblical text easily serves as a model, or at least as a source of legitimation, of the cited customs.

The metaphor of the transmission of the Torah by ingestion and the image of Torah as biological reproduction, may not be totally unrelated. When this researcher began considering the custom of Ashkenazi Jews to make Torah binders out of circumcision cloths, he began to ask acquaintances within the Libyan community about customs concerning a sefer Torah in infancy. It was not surprising to find that such customs exist. One custom[15] concerns the silver pointer, which often decorates a sefer Torah, hanging from a chain around one of the wooden poles. This pointer typically is made in the shape of a hand, with an outstreched index finger. Since one should not directly touch the parchment of the Torah scroll with one's hands (so as not to smear the letters?), the reader (or a helper standing alongside), often uses the pointer to follow the closely written lines to help keep the place. Among the Jews of Libya it was sometimes the practice to give this pointer to a teething infant, as it was hard (but not sharp), and clean, being made of silver. The pointer, which comes into direct contact with the sefer Torah and its letters, directly enters a child's mouth. The metonymic incorporation of the Torah is easy to see.

At the same time, the pointer is easily viewed as phallic in likeness. Recently, some attention has been paid to demonstrated cases of ritual fellatio (cited by Schneider 1976), in which a young boy is seen as receiving spiritual *cum* material sustenence from an older male relative. In the custom of giving the Torah pointer to a baby, this may also be a case of symbolic phallic (male reproductive) oral transmission. Whether this interpretation in fact corresponds to the unconscious associations of any specific (set of) individual(s), it illustrates that with the process of elaboration of a tradition, one line of symbolic elaboration can easily coexist, and intermingle, with another.

It is unlikely that this interpretation (teething on the torah pointer = ritual fellatio) would be spontaneously offered by a native informant, or accepted if offered by someone else (a nonnative or uninformed native). Nevertheless, the parallel between oral transmission and phallic/reproductive transmission may not be wholly foreign to rabbinic tradition, and appears to have some prominence, perhaps reflecting systematization, in later kabbalistic thought. Fellatio, per se, is not explicitly prohibited in the biblical text, as are, for example, homosexual intercourse and relations with animals (Lev. 18:22–23). According to the later rabbinic views, however, phallic/oral intercourse would be forbidden because it involves the "vain emission of seed" (see Feldman 1968, chap. 6). This expression (in Hebrew, *hotza'at zera le-vatalah*) has the same form as the prohibition of the vain mention of the divine name, such as in an inappropriate blessing (*berakhah le-vatalah*). A correctly executed blessing must be audible to one's ear and to the ears of others, so that they may respond amen. A structural parallel between the case of an uttered blessing and the case of male intercourse may be that *emission* is ideally linked to *transmission.* It can also be seen that rabbinic tradition views the emission of seed as an act which potentially can be sanctified and not simply as a biological function, and thus subjects this act to detailed laws regarding its execution.

Ancient Jewish (and Greek) physiological conceptions linked the emission of semen to the brain (Scholem 1966, 147). The kabbalistic tradition has viewed the prohibition of the vain emission of seed with

particular severity, and, according to one interpretation, the appropriate
penitence to correct this transgression is to immerse oneself in the
study of Torah (Feldman 1968, 116). One practice that has been institutionalized on the basis of this theory is that of ta'anit dibbur, a fast
of speaking. In such a fast, one does not refrain from eating, but spends
the whole day reciting psalms and studying,[16] and refraining from any
secular speech. In Hasidic literature from Eastern Europe, the fast is explicitly recommended as being useful penitence for the sin of vain emission of seed.

While one would not expect an average native informant to make
explicit the precise formulations put forth by the anthropologist, it is
not surprising to find interpretations given by individuals with a classic
textual education that seem to fit into the general argument that the
transmission of the Torah may be likened to procreation. The following
excerpt from field notes (slightly edited) shows an example of such an
interpretation. Moshe Ji'an, born in Libya, and presently a resident of
Netanya, Israel, began (without being asked) to tell of the celebration of
the purchase of a sefer Torah, and its contribution to a synagogue, by
two women in town. Moshe was asked to give the derasha (sermon/
lesson) at the celebration,[17] which he recounted as follows:

> The two women lived together in Tripoli, and continue to live together
> in Netanya. Neither of them ever married. One's brother had been
> married to the second's sister. The married couple was killed during an
> air raid in World War II, and then the two women took in the orphaned
> children and began to live together. Sometimes people joked about them
> saying that they lived together as husband and wife. The other day there
> was a celebration in the Dakkar synagogue over the sefer Torah they
> had purchased. The celebration began with a gathering, eating, and
> singing from 4:00–6:00 P.M. in their house and then continued with a
> procession carrying the sefer Torah to the synagogue.
>
> Moshe told of the derasha he had given at the synagogue. He con-
> nected the event to the weekly Torah reading—dealing with Noah. The
> portion begins: "This is the line of Noah. Noah was a righteous man; he
> was blameless in his age" (Genesis 6:9). Rashi (an eleventh century
> scholar whose commentary on the Bible is a standard appendage to
> traditional editions of the biblical text) says that the main "offspring"
> (that is "line"—Hebrew toladot) of righteous people are their good deeds.
> The way Moshe explained Rashi is as follows.
>
> Rashi asked: Why does the phrase "Noah was a righteous man,"
> come immediately after the phrase "This is the line of Noah"? It should

immediately mention Noah's descendants" Shem, Ham . . . (as in other instances when the term *toladot* is used in Genesis). The answer that Rashi gives is that good deeds of righteous people are their descendants. This, Moshe said in his derasha, applied to the case of the two women. They performed the *mitzvah* (fufillment of a commandment) of acquiring a sefer Torah which is the equivalent (k'neged) of all the rest of the Torah. It is said that at Sinai, when the Torah was given, it was like a marriage—in which the children of Israel were the bride and they became wed to the Torah. These women are not married, but this occasion (their acquiring of the sefer Torah) is *like their wedding* (italics added). At this point, Moshe claimed, there was tremendous approval from the crowd, and shrill ululation (*zgharit*) on the part of the women gathered.

This account was given to this author approximately half a year after presenting the initial version of this paper. On hearing it, it occurred to him that Lévi-Strauss's (1969, 13) notion about myths speaking through people may not be total mystification.

Marriage, in the traditional understanding, is the first step toward (or better, the first step of) procreation. This is evident in the elaborate biblical account of Abraham's search for a wife for his son Isaac (Gen. 24). It is a custom among Sephardi Jews that on the Sabbath after his marriage, a man (the bridegroom) is honored by being called to recite the blessing while one of the sections of the weekly portion is being read from a sefer Torah.[18] It is also common that, when a bridegroom is called, a part of Genesis 24 (Isaac's marriage) is read as well. Currently, this special section from Genesis is usually read from a printed text. Formerly, it was a widespread practice to take out a special Torah scroll for this reading and to read the account of Isaac's marriage directly from the sefer Torah (Zimmels 1958, 181). This practice is no longer common, but it is still found in some of the Libyan Jewish synagogues in Israel. This was witnessed during the summer of 1980, on a Sabbath when there were two bridegrooms in the synagogue. On that occasion, two separate additional scrolls were taken out and read, one for each bridegroom (even though the special reading was identical in each case).[19] After the services were ended, there was some disagreement among the congregants as to whether this was proper, whether it was necessary to take out a sefer Torah (something that is not done frivolously) for each person, or whether one scroll would have been enough. It is possible that those who argued that each bridegroom should have his own scroll perceived some sort of link between the concrete person and the concrete scroll, indicating, once again, close association of marriage (and the siring of children) and the sefer Torah.

This discussion will end where it began, by considering the holiday of Simḥat Torah, which now clearly can be shown to express the perpetuation of the Torah in the metaphors of marriage and intergenerational continuity. First of all, allusions are directly made by the terms used to designate the men called to the most honorific readings of the holiday—the readings from the end of the Book of Deuteronomy and the opening section of Genesis. These men are referred to as the *hatanim,* or the bridegrooms, of the respective portions of the Torah, (*hatan torah, hatan bereshit*). Another expression is found in the custom of calling young boys, below the age of bar mitzvah (13 years) to the reading of the Torah.[20] Normally, these youngsters, who are in the status of religious minority, are not permitted to recite the blessing of the Torah. It is one of the relaxations of rules, characterizing the festive mood, that the young boys are called up together, and recite the blessing in unison (accompanied by an adult male who recites the blessing with them, to make sure it is not an instance of *berekhah le-vatalah*). When all the children are gathered at the reader's lecturn, on which the Torah scroll is placed, a large prayer shawl is spread over their heads by men who surround them. This is the precise way that a bridal canopy (*hupah*) is formed in many traditional weddings. Although this researcher has never heard anyone spontaneously liken the event to a wedding (having been involved in the ceremony many times), the association is apparent. After the youngsters conclude the blessing of the Torah, they themselves are blessed by the reader (as is customary for anyone after having been given the honor of going up to the Torah). This blessing has a special version for the festive occasion, and concludes with the words of Jacob, on blessing Joseph and his sons (Gen. 48:16):

> The Angel who has redeemed me from all harm
> Bless the lads.
> In them may my name be recalled,
> And the names of my fathers Abraham and Isaac,
> And may they be teeming multitudes upon the earth.

IV. Torah and Procreation: Culture and Nature

The previous two sections presented three ethnographic examples illustrating metaphoric and metonymic associations between Torah and procreation, and then attempted to explore and further demonstrate this association by reference to other examples. Two general points emerged in this discussion. One is that variant symbolic forms, and attendant interpretations, do not necessarily invalidate one another, and may, in fact, reinforce one another. The second point is that people often have recourse to the biblical text in formulation and interpretation of ritual forms. The first of these points is ostensibly methodological, and the second, substantive or ethnographic. These points may be interrelated, at a theoretical level, by Sperber's view (1974) that the interpretation of a symbol is best seen, not as an explanation of that symbol, but as an extension of the symbolic process. They may also be interrelated by the specific manner in which Judaism *cum* Jewry sees itself and acts as the perpetuation and the embodiment of the text.

It is possible to argue that there are certain conceptions and values which have been central in Jewish tradition, as is evident by both their antiquity and ubiquity. The antiquity is attested to by the presence of these conceptions in the biblical text (see below), and their ubiquity by the ethnographic (and historic) material presented. This does not mean that these central notions are unaffected by historical changes or shifting configurations of social life. What it does claim is that there exists a level of structural continuity in Jewish tradition which does not immediately reflect the vagaries of historical and social changes. At the same time, however, within shifting social circumstances, there may be a variety of situational expressions (or repressions) of these enduring notions. The link between the enduring and concretely expressed levels is often provided by the known structuralist mechanisms of metaphor, metonomy, inversion, and so forth. These operate, it appears, in the realm of ritual and ceremony, no less than in the realm of myth.

The enduring structure is shaped by (but is not identical with) the biblical and other classic texts and becomes established both by the study of text (which is always selective and interpretive), and the set of widespread rites and customs interwoven with the text (of which examples have been given).[21] Given the basic notions which characterize this structure, an elaboration (and transformation) is found in various surface expressions, reflecting both the processes of individual creativity and the sociocultural matrix within which that creativity operates. These processes of elaboration can produce variant, confused, or even contradictory forms, but this does not disprove the fact of their rootedness in enduring cultural conceptions. In the previous section of this paper, examples were given of this elaboration while arguing that the variety of expression found does not necessarily challenge the existence of a consistent structural link between Torah and procreation.

Admittedly, recourse to a concept like enduring structure is notoriously undefined. It may be likened to the notion of the deep structure of a grammar of a specific language, which has also been summoned to designate panhuman cognitive characteristics, whether in respect to language, mythmaking, or other cultural realms. In this argument, it has been used to refer to an ancient and enduring relationship in Jewish tradition. This relationship might be considered, on the one hand, deep, but on the other, it has been stressed how it is constantly reinvented, and is manifest in eminently public settings, such as texts and socioritual situations. Structuralist theory, which aims to find the basis of symbolizing in the human mind, also raises the question as to whether the values of Jewish tradition that have been analyzed here can be related to comparative or cross-cultural issues. In attempting to do so, it seems helpful to view this discussion in light of the general categories of nature and culture.

There are different opinions as to what Levi-Strauss means by the nature/culture opposition. From our point of view, the opposition may be interpreted as follows: that all human beings (cultures) sense, on the one hand, the continuity between themselves and animal (natural) life, and the chaos that this continuity suggests, but on the other hand, recognize (desperately need to recognize) a special dimension of human existence. Each culture phrases (and thus structures) this contrast/dilemma in its own fashion, thereby partially shaping the way the dilemma is dealt with in cultural form. That opposition in Judaism, briefly stated, may usefully be compared with those oppositions in other cultures conveniently labeled nature/culture (see Fredman 1981).

The account in Genesis pictures the natural world, and the world of human beings as deriving from the same divine project of creation. Continuity between men and animals appears (man giving names to the animals; the snake duping the woman), yet, at the same time, man is clearly put in a special category—with dominion over nature and duties toward God who granted that dominion. Culture, defined as that which distinguishes man from the rest of the natural world, is of divine origin, and therefore, inevitably involves obligations toward the divine, that is, the obeying of God's commandments.[22] In obeying God's commandments, human beings have the ability to sanctify nature (Buber 1952), including the natural functions (eating, defecating, sexual relations) of their own bodies. Thus, man, as part of the overall creation, has the special ability, and obligation, to sanctify nature and, thereby, to make the natural world a partner in their joint testimony to a common divine origin.

This formulation of the relationship of humans (who bear culture) to nature, within Judaism, is not particularly new (although the academic context within which the formulation is placed is relatively novel). Parallel formulations have been offered by philosophers, theologians, preachers, and others attempting to explicate central concepts of Jewish tradition. In this academic form, the formulation is not likely to be communicated to more than a handful of readers sharing the same intellectual background as the author. In contrast, this same message (if the analysis is correct) may be found in the biblical text, which has had much greater success publishing itself. The power of the text, in making itself public, may be attributed to the quality of the text itself, but also, as has been shown, to the situational contexts in Judaism, within which the importance of the text and its continued study are reinforced. Thus the text, and the bearers of the text, have succeeded in creating extra-textual mechanisms to perpetuate involvement in the text, even as these mechanisms (as discussed in parts two and four) partake of the same concepts and values embodied in the texts themselves. If this argument is correct, at least one set of mechanisms has been delineated whereby a text becomes a living force within the life of a social group, allowing a view of the culture of that group which embraces both text and context.

To conclude the argument, it will be briefly demonstrated that the associations discussed earlier, in which biological continuity and spiritual continuity (embodied in the Torah) are closely intertwined, may be found in the biblical narrative. It is thereby seen that this particular statement of the relationship of nature to culture is of great antiquity in Jewish tradition and has reproduced itself over the generations.

According to the biblical account, the central figure in the initial formation of the people of Israel is Abraham. Abraham predates the giving of the Torah at Mt. Sinai, which took place in Moses' time, but is still considered the spiritual father of the Jewish people, as well as its progenitor. The biblical narrative highlights Abraham's moral and religious qualities, even though these were not associated with a written code. Both in the text itself, and in the midrashic (rabbinic homiletics) elaborations of the narrative, stress is placed on the personal and religious qualities which made Abraham worthy of being the father of the people of Israel.

While it is thus common practice to scrutinize Abraham's career as a cultural model, a plain reading of the text shows an equal emphasis on the biological drama of reproduction. From the outset of Abraham's career, when he is still called Abram, it is stated that his wife, Sarai, is childless. Nevertheless, the divine promise unhesitatingly states that Abram will sire a multitude of nations. The promise of progeny, and the parallel promise of possession of the land, are repeated and developed throughout the chapters of Genesis before Abraham has children, highlighting the discrepancy between God's word and the natural reality. This promise with regard to nature, that is, reproduction, in itself implies culture, in the form of faith—a test of Abraham's acceptance of the divine revelation. The tension between the promise and the reality continues through the stories of the birth of Ishmael, the birth of Isaac, and Isaac's emergence from the trial of Moriah unscathed. At this point it finally becomes clear that God's promise of progeny (and the perpetuation of Abraham's moral and religious tradition) will be fulfilled. This is marked by a brief section following the Mt. Moriah climax, which lists the descendants of Abraham's brother Nahor, naming Rebecca who eventually becomes Isaac's wife (Gen. 22:20–24). At every point in the plot, the seemingly biological (natural) process of reproduction is dependent on divine (cultural) intervention and purpose, both with regard to its actual occurrence and its significance.

It is now necessary to consider the generation of Moses, the point in biblical history when God's message and purpose become embodied in a written form, and eventually in a book. The original revelation of the Ten Commandments involved God's writing of the commandments on stone tablets. The term *book* (sefer), too, appears in the narrative, close to the Sinai revelation, in two contexts that are suggestive with regard to this thesis. One instance concerns the crisis of the golden calf. In God's wrath over the rebelliousness of the children of Israel, He threatens to destroy the whole people, save only Moses and his progeny, and to make Moses into a great nation (Ex. 32:10). Were this to occur,

Moses would have the status both of the natural progenitor of the people and the chief propagator of the written word of God. Moses opposes this threat, and in his appeal, states that if God destroys the whole people, then Moses, too, wishes to be erased from God's book[23] (Ex. 23:32). The crisis of physical continuity and the question of preservation in a written book go hand in hand.

Just before their arrival at Sinai, the children of Israel experience their first confrontation with an armed enemy. The Amalekites attack Israel at Refidim. At this point Israel is faced with the possibility of total destruction. After the defeat of the Amalekites, Moses is commanded to write in a book, and orally instruct Joshua,[24] that he should "utterly blot out the name of Amalek from under heaven" (Ex. 17:14). Here, too, the permanence of writing and the question of biological continuity are juxtaposed, this time with regard to Israel's enemy. This association is preserved today in the classic curse of an enemy of the Jewish people: "May his name be blotted out." Paradoxically, the written commandment to blot out Amalek's name ensures the eternity of his memory.

V. Conclusion

The examples cited have attempted to show that there is a long-standing association, in texts, customs, and rituals, between the biological perpetuation of the Jewish people, wherein procreation becomes a central concern, and the perpetuation of the religious tradition, embodied in scripture.[25] The incident of Amalek, as well as many of the stories in Genesis (the patriarchs' encounters with Pharaoh, the warring kings, Abimelech), demonstrate that the history of Israel, within which God becomes a dominant actor, is to be understood as taking place on the broader stage of history. The Torah's message is relevant to all humankind, but is aimed directly at a portion of it, and is handed down from generation to generation in a manner closely associated with, but not identical to, biological reproduction. In the story of Abraham, as has been seen, it is clear that even biological continuity is contingent on religious continuity—Abraham's steadfastness in his loyalty to God. Abraham is the beginning, in the biblical view, of a special new tradition, and it is also of Abraham that it is said (Gen. 12:3): "All the families of the earth shall bless themselves by you."

The special tradition beginning with Abraham, then, is to be viewed in counterpoint to the traditions and moral histories of other nations. This means that a cross-cultural perspective is built into the biblical narrative, as well as into the world view of those religions which claim to derive from it. The association, in Judaism, of a universal religious message encoded in a public document, with a particular group of people to whom recruitment is mainly (but by no means only) biological, has been a puzzle and a challenge to the other monotheistic religions. Christianity sought to sever commitment to God from Jewish descent, with Paul claiming that "it is men of faith who are the sons of Abraham" (Galatians 3). Islam remained closer to traditional Jewish assumptions, even while combating the claim of the continued validity of Judaism. Thus, Ibn Khaldun's claim that the Israelites of his day delude themselves about the nobility of their descent (1967, 102–103), may parallel the standard Islamic charge that the Jews forged part of the Torah (see Rosen 1984, 157). In any event, these interlinked religions hold variant but related views on the separation and ties between nature and culture.

The comparative perspective may be expanded beyond those traditions which have direct contact with one another. Ward has pointed to the culturalization (author's term) of Chinese ethnicity, in which being Chinese is perceived in cultural terms (1977, 187). Here, too, being something by descent is conceptually merged with carrying a certain tradition. At the same time, Ward argues persuasively that it is not literacy alone that is responsible for the widespread diffusion of Chinese civilization. There appears to be, therefore, ample room for comparison among various great traditions as to the specific role of literacy in spreading a given view of the world.[26] At the same time, these traditions appear to differ as well in their conceptualizations of literacy in relation to their own central values and in relation to the bearers of their particular message.

Notes

1. In addition to its initial presentation, versions of this paper were presented at a symposium on "The Future of Structuralism" held under the auspices of the International Union of Anthropological and Ethnological Sciences, Amsterdam, April 1981, and at a Seminar of the Department of Social Anthropology, Cambridge University, May 1981, and has benefited from discussions on both occasions. I am also grateful for the comments of Moshe Idel.

2. The custom of parading with the scrolls around the raised platform from which the Torah is read, seems to have originated in Austria (Zimmels

1958, 360) and presumably spread to Sephardi communities later. A detailed investigation of the distribution of the customs to be cited, through the Ashkenazi and Sephardi communities, is beyond the scope of this paper. With the required caution understood, I present a fair amount of material on the Jews of Libya, with whom I have the greatest field work familiarity. Using them as representative of North African and Sephardi Jewry generally, I simply hope to show, for the purpose of this paper, that the symbolic processes discussed were widespread. Whether the precise customs mentioned are (were) to be found in any given community, however, is a matter of careful ethnologic investigation.

3. See Y. M. Epstein, *Arukh Ha-Shulhan, Orah Haim*, cap. 141, subcap. 1 (Vilna: Garber, 1907–1924), where the motivations offered for several laws and customs relate the readings in the synagogue to the situation during the revelation at Sinai.

4. See Joseph Caro's *Shulhan Arukh, Yoreh De'ah*, cap. 282, subcap 10. Various forms that this custom takes are surveyed by Cohen and Stillman (1985).

5. Two other examples from field work may be cited. There is a pilgrimage festival among Libyan Jews associated with a saintly sefer Torah called *zghair derna* (the "little one" of the town of Derna; see Noy 1967) to which are attributed powers commonly associated with sainted rabbis. A man from Tripoli, while speaking to me once, said, "There are a lot of [saintly] rabbis, Rabbi Shim'on [Bar Yohai], Rabbi Meir [Ba'al ha-Ness], *Zghair Derna*, and others." This was a clear anthropomorphization of the sefer Torah. Idel (1981) has shown the anthropomorphic conception of the Torah in the kabbalistic tradition.

6. This was suggested to me by Jeffrey Tigay. Kirshenblatt-Gimblett (1982) suggests the image of a queen.

7. The law of Deuteronomy (17:18ff) requires that the king have a copy of the teaching (Torah) written for him by the levitical priests and that "it remain with him and let him read it all his life." The motivation of this law is that the king "not act haughtily toward his fellows." The mishnaic law is that a king write a sefer Torah for himself (*Sanhedrin*, chap. II). This requirement is democratized in the Babylonian Talmud (*Sanhedrin* 21b) which, basing itself on another verse (Deuteronomy 31:19), requires that every man write a sefer Torah.

8. The suggestion was made by Samuel Cooper.

9. See the paper by Prell in this volume. In Agnon's (1960) story, "Legend of the Scribe," the writing of a sefer Torah replaces both children and a deceased wife. The conclusion of the story poignantly merges a sefer Torah with the scribe's deceased bride.

10. Typically, the cabinet in which the Torah scroll is kept is locked. In a community which has many scrolls, that is, more than are needed for the required ceremonial readings, it is sometimes the custom to rotate the use of the

different scrolls, so that each sefer Torah is given a chance (another anthropomorphization).

11. A traditional song, commonly sung on the Simḥat Torah festival, is based on the refrain: "Israel [meaning the people] and the Torah are one."

12. These examples can be multiplied. The sweetness of the Torah conveyed by this custom does not exclude the opposite: namely the rigor of its demands. In the Kurdish case cited, the father, on the same occasion, tells the teacher in a proverb not to refrain from striking the child if it is necessary for his education (Brauer 1947, 200).

13. The biblical text does not explicitly indicate that this is the meaning of the touch on the lips, but the ancient Aramaic *targum* (translation) interprets the verse in this sense. Demsky (1976) discusses the dual images of oral and written transmission which characterize classical prophecy.

14. The Torah, and Jewish book learning in general, are taught both through the study of the written word and through oral repetition and transmission (Demsky 1976). We cannot go into an extended discussion of the notions of the written Torah and the oral Torah. (See Neusner 1979, chap. 3 and Zohar's paper in this volume, p. 103, notes 1 and 2).

15. Another example is the draping of kerchiefs over Elijah's chair during a circumcision in the same manner that a sefer Torah is draped on festive occasions.

16. This is based on my observations of such a fast in a village of Tripolitanian Jews in Israel in 1964 (Goldberg 1972).

17. Deshen (1970) has provided descriptions and analysis of such events, as they become intermeshed with election campaigns. The present celebration was of such a purer traditional form, though this is not to say that there are no sociofunctional aspects of the ritual, as the presentation of a sefer Torah always brings prestige to the donors.

18. The corresponding Ashkenazi custom is that a bridegroom is called to a reading on the Sabbath before his wedding.

19. If a reading from different sections of the Torah is required, it is preferable not to roll the scroll from one section to another in front of the public, but to prepare different scrolls in advance, so that they are open to the correct sections. If a given section is to be repeated, there is no reason to take out an additional Torah scroll from the Holy Ark.

20. This is a common Ashkenazi practice. It was not found among the Jews of Libya, and I do not think that it was common in other Sephardi communities.

21. Smith (1980) has forcefully argued that historians and students of religion have ignored the ways in which scripture can become a living force in social action.

22. The religious/moral dimension of the universe, and its demands on nature, are so powerful in the biblical account of creation that even animals are sometimes seen to have moral accountability, as in the story of Noah and in the Book of Jonah.

23. This reflects a belief concerning a divine book in which the destiny of each individual is written (see Mal. 3:16 and Ps. 139:16). While its primary referent is, therefore, not the book of the Torah, the appearance of the term *sefer* in this context is still suggestive.

24. See the reference in note 14 on parallel written and oral transmission.

25. Another ethnographic example, in which Torah, children, and survival appear in the same context may be found in the *kittab* ceremony among the Jews of Ghardaia in Algeria. This ceremony concerns the initiation of young boys to the study of the Torah, and is described as a "unique Saharan custom" (Briggs and Guède 1964, 28ff), even though it contains elements and expresses values common to other Jewish communities. As part of this ceremony, "each father took his son in his arms and carried him up onto the platform running along the far wall, beneath the Tablets of the Law (most likely a decoration above the cabinet in which the Torah scrolls are kept). Here they all strutted back and forth showing off their progeny to call attention to them" (30). In interpreting this custom, a former inhabitant of Ghardaia, currently a resident in Strasbourg, said that it has to be understood in the light of the high rate of infant mortality in the Algerian town. The celebration marked, in part, the boys' survival of early childhood diseases, and their having reached the stage where they could begin to study Torah.

26. As an example of a comparison, Ward (1977, 190) states that in traditional China, "in the eyes of the uneducated (and many of the educated too) . . . reading as such was not an important activity." For practical purposes writing was more important than reading." This may be contrasted with Goitein's analysis of Medieval Jewish society, based on his study of the Cairo *genizah* documents, wherein being a "business clerk" (writing) was different from, but carried less prestige than, a knowledge of the sacred texts (Goitein 1971:179). This may not be unrelated to another remark by Ward (1977, 200 n.28) about how "any piece of paper with written characters on it was meticulously collected and burnt up in order to prevent its being used for unclean and therefore polluting and mystically dangerous, purposes." The normative Jewish response in such an instance would be to preserve the Hebrew characters by placing them in a *genizah*. An anecdote in my notes, from life in Tripolitania, tells of a Jewish man who saved a piece of paper with mysterious letters on it, and used the paper for profit by writing protective amulets (many of his customers were Moslems) based on the written characters.

Another interesting comparison to the sefer torah = people symbolism may be found among the Maori (Best 1924,65ff). In traditional Maori society, the lore was passed on in seasonal schools to adepts who were skilled at

memorization. In the last generation of the transmission of Maori esoteric culture, the priests-teachers found that the scholars were writing down the
knowledge they acquired in notebooks, rather than committing it to memory.
The priests, who formerly performed rituals over the scholars' persons to stabil-
ize the information in their memories, opposed the innovation, but accom-
modated themselves to the new reality by performing a ceremony with regard
to the notebooks that parallel the former rituals with regard to people.

References Cited

Abbink van der Zwan, P. J. (1979). "Ornamentation on Eighteenth Century
Torah Binders." *The Israel Museum News* 14:64–73.

Agnon, S. Y. (1960). "Legend of the Scribe." In *Elu va-Elu*. The Complete Works
of Shmuel Yosef Agnon. Jerusalem: Schocken, II:131–145. Hebrew.

Antoun, R. (1976). "The State of the Art in Middle Eastern Anthropology." In
*The Study of the Middle East: Research and Scholarship in the Humanities
and Social Sciences*. L. Binder, ed. New York: Wiley and Sons, 137–
228.

Best, E. (1924). *The Maori*, vol. 1, "Memoirs of the Polynesian Society."
Wellington, New Zealand: H. H. Tombs.

Brauer, E. (1947). *The Jews of Kurdistan: An Ethnological Study*. Compiled and
edited by R. Patai. Jerusalem: The Palestine Institute of Folklore and
Ethnology.

Briggs, L. C., and N. Guède (1964). *No More For Ever: A Saharan Jewish Town*.
Papers of the Peabody Museum of Archaeology and Ethnology, Harvard
University, 55(1). Cambridge, Ma.: Peabody Museum.

Buber, M. (1952). *Israel and Palestine: The History of an Idea*. London: East and
West Library.

Cohen, M., and Y. Stillman (1985). "The Cairo Genizah and Genizah Customs
among Middle Eastern Jews." *Pe'amim* 24:3–35. Hebrew.

Demsky, A. (1976). *Literacy in Israel and Among Neighboring Peoples in the
Biblical Period*. Ph.D. diss. Hebrew University of Jerusalem. Hebrew, with
English summary.

Deshen, S. (1970). *Immigrant Voters in Israel: Parties and Congregation in a Local
Election Campaign*. Manchester: Manchester University Press.

Dumont, L. (1970). *Homo Hierarchicus*. Chicago: University of Chicago
Press.

Feldman, D. (1968). *Marital Relations, Birth Control and Abortion in Jewish Law*. New York: New York University Press.

Fredman, R. G. (1981). *The Passover Seder: Afikoman in Exile*. Philadelphia: University of Pennsylvania Press.

Geertz, C., H. Geertz, and L. Rosen. (1979). *Meaning and Order in Moroccan Society: Three Essays in Cultural Analysis*. Cambridge: Cambridge University Press.

Goitein, S. D. (1953). "Jewish Education in Yemen as an Archetype of Traditional Jewish Education." In *Between Past and Future*. C. Frankenstein, ed. Jerusalem: Szold Institute, 109–44.

――――. (1971). *A Mediterranean Society: The Jewish Communities of the Arab World as Portrayed in the Documents of the Cairo Genizah*, vol. 2, "The Community." Berkeley: University of California Press.

Goldberg, H. (1972). *Cave Dwellers and Citrus Growers: A Jewish Community in Libya and Israel*. Cambridge: Cambridge University Press.

Gombrich, R. (1971). *Precept and Practice: Traditional Buddhism in the Rural Highlands of Ceylon*. Oxford: Clarendon Press.

Ibn Khaldun. (1967). *The Muqaddima: An Introduction to History*. Translated by F. Rosenthal, abridged and edited by N. J. Dawood. Princeton: Bollingen Series, Princeton University Press.

Idel, M. (1981). "The Concept of Torah in Heikhalot Literature and Kabbalah." *Jerusalem Studies in Jewish Thought* 1:23–84. Hebrew.

Kirshenblatt-Gimblett, B. (1982). "The Cut that Binds: The Western Ashkenazic Torah Binder as Nexus Between Circumcision and Torah." In *Celebration: Studies in Festivity and Ritual*. V. Turner, ed. Washington, D.C.: Smithsonian Institution Press, 136–46.

Lévi-Strauss, C. (1969). *The Raw and the Cooked*. Translated by J. and D. Weightman. London: Jonathan Cape.

Marriott, M. and R. B. Inden. (1977). "Toward an Ethnosociology of South Asian Caste Systems." In *The New Wind: Changing Identities in South Asia*. K. David, ed. The Hague: Mouton, 227–38.

Meeker, M. (1976). "Meaning and Society in the Near East: Examples from the Black Sea Turks and the Levantine Arabs (II)." *International Journal of Middle East Studies* 7:383–422.

Needham, R. (1972). *Belief, Language and Experience*. Chicago: University of Chicago Press.

Neusner, J. (1979). *Method and Meaning in Ancient Judaism*. Brown University Judaica Series X. Missoula, Montana: Scholars Press.

Noy, D. (1967). *Seventy-One Folktales of Libyan Jews.* Jerusalem: Folklore Archives. Hebrew.

Pollack, H. (1971). *Jewish Folkways in Germanic Lands (1648–1806): Studies in Aspects of Daily Life.* Cambridge, Ma.: The M.I.T. Press.

Redfield, R. (1955). "The Social Organization of Tradition." *Far Eastern Quarterly* 15:13–22.

Rosen, L. (1984). *Bargaining for Reality: The Construction of Social Relations in a Muslim Community.* Chicago: University of Chicago Press.

Savishinsky, J., and H. Wimberley. (1974). "The Living and the Dead: A Cross-Cultural Perspective on Jewish Memorial Observance." *Jewish Social Studies* 36:281–306.

Schneider, D. (1976). "The Meaning of Incest." *Journal of Polynesian Society* 85:149–69.

Scholem, G. (1966). *Les Origines de la Kabbale.* Traduit par J. Loewenson. Paris: Aubier-Montaigne.

Smith, W. C. (1980). "The True Meaning of Scripture: An Empirical Historian's Non-reductionist Interpretation of the Qur'an." *International Journal of Middle East Studies* 11:487–505.

Sperber, D. (1974). *Rethinking Symbolism.* Cambridge: Cambridge University Press.

Turner, V. (1964). "Symbols in Ndembu Ritual." In *Closed Systems and Open Minds: The Limits of Naivety in Social Anthropology.* M. Gluckman, ed. Chicago: Aldine, 20–51.

——. (1968). "Myth and Symbol." *International Encyclopedia of the Social Sciences.* New York: Macmillan, X:576–81.

Ward, B. (1977). "Readers and Audiences: An Exploration of the Spread of Traditional Chinese Culture." In *Text and Context: The Social Anthropology of Tradition.* R. K. Jain, ed. Philadelphia: Institute for the Study of Human Issues, 181–203.

Zafrani, H. (1972). "L'enseignement traditionel juif au Maroc." In *Mélanges Abraham Elmaleh.* H. Z. Hirschberg, ed. Jerusalem: Comité de la communauté marocaine, 123–39. Hebrew, with French summary.

Zborowski, M. (1955). "The Place of Book-Learning in Traditional Jewish Culture." In *Childhood in Contemporary Cultures.* M. Mead and M. Wolfenstein, eds. Chicago: University of Chicago Press, 118–41.

Zimmels, H. J. (1958). *Ashkenazim and Sephardim: Their Relations, Differences and Problems as Reflected in Rabbinical Responsa.* London: Oxford University Press.

Judaism in America

Introduction to Part II

While at the beginning of the eighteenth century most of the Jewish world continued to function in the framework of what Katz has called a "traditional society" (1961; 1982), by the end of the century, the forces causing the breakup of that world had unmistakably left their mark. These changes were both internal and external. The developments in science and philosophy in western Europe had their echoes in the Jewish intellectual movement known as the *Haskalah* (enlightenment; see Mahler 1971, chap. 13), with Moses Mendelssohn, the most prominent figure signaling the beginning of this movement (Altmann 1973). Mendelssohn advocated that Jews begin to participate in the general culture of their times.

Political developments were equally, if not more, important. The development of the national state brought into question the accepted status of the Jews as a corporate community, living according to a basic set of norms that legitimately separated them from the surrounding society. A major development marking the new era was the emancipation of the Jews of France a few years after the issuance of the Declaration of the Rights of Man (Hertzberg 1968). In 1806 Napoleon convened a council of rabbis, called the "Great Sanhedrin" (after the body of seventy-one elders holding supreme religious authority in mishnaic times), posing critical questions to them concerning the Jews' view of themselves in relation to the civil law. It was clear from these questions that the Jews were expected to be loyal, first and foremost, to their native country, and abandon time-honored notions of the messianic yearning to return to their ancient homeland. Judaism was to become a religion severed from the traditional Jewish body politic scattered in the diaspora. From its inception in France, at the beginning of the nineteenth century, political emancipation spread consistently eastward, not without reversals, as the principle that persons of the Mosaic persuasion could be full citizens in a modern national state came to be accepted.

While the emancipation provided the Jews the opportunity of moving out of the ghetto (Katz 1973), the involvement in the wider life of the society also presented an enormous challenge to Judaism. One reaction was that of assimilation. In the early nineteenth century, assimilation often meant, not a natural process of erosion because of lack of involvement in Jewish life, but an explicit ideology to abandon the religious and social burdens of Judaism and to join the universalist majority. The end point of this process often was conversion to Christianity. There are various estimates concerning the number of Jews converting in the first half of the nineteenth century, but all agree it was considerable.

Another response to the challenge of western culture was the *Wissenschaft*[1] movement, which established the modern study of Jewish history and civilization within Jewish life. While this was an intellectual movement, its proponents did not enjoy university positions, but often worked within the framework of Jewish communal life. While all shared a commitment to the modern science of Judaism, the *Wissenschaft* savants were divided as to what implications their new understanding of Judaism had for their time. For example, some scholars concerned themselves with synagogue life, which, in Central Europe, was undergoing a process of reform. Various changes were made to rationalize the traditional form of worship and to add a dimension of decorum to the synagogue service to bring it in tune with accepted Gentile conceptions of worship. Reform philosophy also criticized halakhah, opposing its ritualistic aspects, which tended to overshadow the basic moral and social concerns which characterized Judaism. The universal aspects of Jewish religion were thus stressed at the expense of the traditions which gave Judaism its distinctiveness and identity.

The more extreme expressions of reform, often associated with the names of Samuel Holdheim and Abraham Geiger, later led to a reaction on the part of other *Wissenschaft* figures, who felt that time-honored Jewish practice was being abandoned in too wholesale a manner. A leading figure here was Zechariah Frankel, who led the rabbinical seminary in Breslau (established in 1854). His approach, labeled "historic Judaism," aimed to combine enlightenment with adherence to tradition. This point of view claimed that halakhah does indeed evolve, and adjust itself to the times, but that this has to take place in a responsible and controlled manner. The point of view formulated by Frankel and his school became the basis of what was later called, in the United States, Conservative Judaism (as opposed to Reform Judaism).

Another important development in modern Jewish culture was the rise of large-scale organizations aimed at the social, civic, and cultural betterment of the Jewish people. The first of these to have important international significance, was the *Alliance Is-raélite Universelle*, established in Paris in 1860. About half a century after Napoleon had insisted that the Jews give up their loyalty to the Jewish nation, the Jews of France found a way of combining their patriotism with a reformulated sense of peoplehood and ties to Jews everywhere. Local committees of the alliance were set up in many countries, particularly in Eastern Europe and in the Islamic world, to defend the political rights of Jews and to seek their social, educational, and moral advancement. Similar organizations emerged among the Jews of England, Germany, and, later, the United States.

The Jews active in these organizations often had achieved prominence in general social and cultural life, and acted, in a sense, as emissaries of their newly adopted countries. The alliance's efforts on the part of the Jews in North Africa, for example, went hand-in-hand with the French *mission civilisatrice*, and the schools it established were crucial in creating a European-oriented elite. The colonial background of the alliance activities reinforced the assumption that the Jews of Middle Eastern lands had to be guided into the modernity that had been shaped in Europe. Little thought was given to the possibility that the Jews in non-European communities might themselves evolve creative responses to the challenges of emancipation. The indigenous religious responses to modernity only recently have become a subject of sustained scholarly attention.

Another important response to emancipation and modernization was that of orthodoxy. While orthodox movements within Judaism view themselves, and present themselves to outsiders, as the preservers of Jewish tradition as it has been kept over the generations, any serious historical consideration of orthodoxy shows it to be one response to modernity and, thereby, part of modernity. Samet (1971a; 1971b) indicates a number of areas in which orthodoxy differs from traditional Judaism, from which it must be distinguished: (a) as a retreat from the commitment to the unity of the Jewish community, which had included both the observant and lax Jew, in favor of a policy of separatism, which allowed the orthodox adherents to establish institutions fitting their own particular ideological orientation; (b) with a stress on strictness in the observance of halakhah, including an emphasis on nonessential details of the law (the careful ritual observance which had characterized pious individuals in traditional society became a marker separating the orthodox from the non-orthodox); (c) with a negative and suspicious attitude toward modern culture leading to the establishment of autonomous orthodox schools in which contemporary secular education was presented selectively and sharply curtailed. (An exception to this was the neoorthodoxy of Samson Raphael Hirsch [1808–1888] who combined strict observance of halakhah while encouraging Jews to familiarize themselves with wider European culture.) Within Jewish studies, emphasis was placed on the study of the Talmud, as the basis of rabbinic law, to the detriment of subjects such as Bible, Jewish philosophy, and Hebrew language and literature, which presented Judaism as a civilization in which religion was one part; and (d) with the establishment of *yeshivot* (academies of talmudic study), drawing on students from many different communities, to engage in the theoretical study of Talmud with little practical orientation.

Orthodoxy, like the other religious movements already mentioned (Reform and Conservative), had its origins in central Europe in the first half of the nineteenth century. It cannot be considered apart from its reaction to reform within Judaism, as well as its stand on modernization per se. Later, its influence spread to Eastern Europe, America, and Israel. It must be distinguished, historically, from movements arising from within the dynamics and problematics of traditional Jewish life, such as the Hasidic movement (Scholem 1941; Ettinger 1976), which arose in Poland and the Ukraine in the eighteenth century. Today however, the Hasidic movement, as well as its historical opponents (the *mitnagdim*), are clearly part of the orthodox camp. It is nevertheless true that orthodoxy is internally diverse, and even divided. In section three, further consideration will be given to the concept of the *ḥaredim*, or ultraorthodox.

Along with the development of new ideas and institutions, the history of modern Jewry is also a history of population movements. The growth of national states in Europe, and later in the Middle East, often created an atmosphere in which the presence of a Jewish population was problematic and uncomfortable. The consolidation of national identity, and its political ramifications, therefore, often were factors in the process of large numbers of Jews leaving one country for another. Perhaps the earliest example may be found in Spain, where, in 1492, both the Jews and Muslims remaining in the country were required to leave (or submit to conversion to Catholicism). This was a major event in expanding the Sephardic diaspora,[2] and also set the stage for the first movement of Jews to the New World.

The first Jews to establish a community in North America were twenty-three Sephardic Jews, refugees from Brazil, who arrived in New Amsterdam in 1654 (at the time of Peter Stuyvesant). At first, Sephardic Jews were the dominant element in the small Jewish communities existing in America, but they were later surpassed in number by the Ashkenazim. The middle of the nineteenth century saw the flow of Jews to the United States begin to increase, and German-Jewish immigrants became an important element on the American Jewish scene. These Jews provided a natural ground for the growth of the Reform movement within the United States. A union of Reform congregations was organized in 1873, and a school for the training of rabbis, the Hebrew Union College (in Cincinnati), was established in 1875 (Glazer 1957, chap. 3).

During the nineteenth century, Eastern European Jewry had undergone a population explosion, perhaps quadrupling in the course of the century. Toward the end of the nineteenth century, nationalism combined with revolutionary ideas and movements in an atmosphere of social and political ferment in Eastern Europe. From the beginning of the century Jews of Russia, Lithuania, and parts of Poland under Czarist rule had been confined to the Pale of Settlement, resulting in growing impoverishment and misery. Pogroms erupted in several parts of Russia in 1881 and after, apparently with official encouragement. The physical insecurity caused by the pogroms, added to the difficult economic situation, increased the flow of East European migrants, which had numbered in the thousands in the 1870s, to a mass migration of hundreds of thousands. These migrants reached Western Europe and the New World, with the most important destination being the United States.

While modern Jewish movements, particularly the Haskalah, has begun to spread in Eastern Europe, the bulk of the Jewish immigrants to the United States came from a traditional background, although among some of them the bonds of tradition had already begun to weaken. They tended to group themselves, religiously, in small congregations where they could continue familiar forms of worship. Similarly, burial associations were formed, along with the setting up of *landsmanschaft* organizations. The existing reform synagogues were quite foreign to these immigrants, and Sabato Morais, a prominent Sephardi rabbi, aligned with some of the leaders of the newcomers to seek an approach that combined tradition and modernity. In 1886 they established the Jewish Theological Seminary, which was to become the rabbinical seminary of Conservative Judaism (see Sklare 1972). A decade later, a central Orthodox yeshiva, the Rabbi Isaac Elhanan Theological Seminary (today, Yeshiva University) was set up as well, building on the continuing influx of Eastern European Jews. Both these institutions gained prominence and influence only in the second decade of the twentieth century.

As in Europe, the religious response was only one of the modes of relating to the new challenges. America proved to be fruitful soil for a variety of ethnic organizations (B'nai B'rith, founded in 1843; Young Men's Hebrew Associations, first founded in the 1850s; the American Jewish Committee, 1906; the American Jewish Congress, 1917; and so forth), which concerned themselves with a range of social political, and cultural matters (Elazar 1976). Socialist thinking, which had also been attractive, in various forms, to the newly emerging Jewish proletariat in Eastern Europe, had a certain success among the masses of the lower East side in the early twentieth century. The role of Jews in organizing garment workers is well known. According to some estimates, nearly two-thirds of the Jewish immigrants entering the United States between 1880 and 1914 began their careers by working in the needle trades.

The mass immigration of Jews was attenuated after World War I, and limited by the Johnson Act of 1924. In the interwar period, the institutions and patterns which took form in the earlier decades crystallized and developed as America turned into a major center of world Jewry. The importance of American Jewry was tragically enhanced by the Nazi policy to liquidate the Jews during World War II. Among the survivors of the Holocaust in Europe were some groups of Hasidic Jews, who immigrated to the United States in the postwar period. This introduced the relatively new element of ultraorthodoxy into the panorama of American Jewish life.

The three selections presented in this section give some sense of the variety of religious and cultural expression found among Jewish groups in America today. The elderly described by Myerhoff were mostly born in *shtetls* (small towns) of Eastern Europe, and immigrated to the United States at a relatively early age. They quickly became involved in the struggle for social mobility, dignity, and Americanization, and their cultural background seemed to become less and less important. More than half a century later, however, with the blessings and dilemmas of longevity, their childhood culture, preserved in memory, became crucial in maintaining their identity and even their physical survival. They now combine their intimately shared shtetl experiences with a sophisticated American contemporaneity in ways that could hardly have been envisioned even a decade before. Religion is not a highly explicit aspect of the performances and texts described by Myerhoff, but a taken-for-granted element of the overall cultural background which makes these performances possible. Facing few problems of authenticity, these shtetl *cum* Californian octogenarians weld together elements of the past and of the present in novel ways which seem legitimate to their audiences as well as to themselves.

The minyan participants, described by Prell, could easily be the grandchildren of the old people of Venice, California. They reflect some of the dilemmas of the partially successful implantation of Judaism in America. College educated, some have also received systematic modern Jewish schooling (in Reform or Con-

servative educational frameworks), while others have little formal training with regard to Jewish religion, culture, and history.
As a group, they constitute a *havurah*, forming part of a movement which has attempted to challenge establishment Judaism
(in its religious and organizational aspects) in the 1970s (Elazar
and Monson 1979).

Clearly a reflection of the counterculture of that period, the
havurot (pl.) stress an ethos of equality among the worshipers,
which, in the case of the minyan, implies an ideology of full participation on the part of women in all formal religious roles. At
the same time, havurot also include a central feature of the
talmudic institution from which they take their name—the
study of the Torah. Members of the minyan described by Prell are
committed to the effort of blending the values of their upbring-
ing in America with Jewish ritual and study in the assumption
that these can be mutually relevant and even enriching. The effort
does not achieve instant success however. An honest look at
authentic Jewish practice does not mesh completely with cherished ideals of equality of the sexes. In their synagogue humor,
their perplexity is highlighted. The Simḥat Torah festival, which
traditionally features the relaxation of norms, and even contains
elements of reversal, becomes problematic because of their commitment to Torah-based texts, which they have not been able to
fully reconcile with their other values.

The uncertain path on which the minyan has embarked
reflects a general situation within the worship patterns developed by havurot, where "doubt and ambivalence [are] as ax-
iomatic a part of worship as faith once was" (Weissler 1986). The
question of the place of women in religious ritual is much more
general. A decade ago the Reform movement in America under-
took to ordain women as rabbis, and a parallel decision has recently been taken by the Conservative movement's Jewish
Theological Seminary. Within Conservative Judaism as a whole,
however, the issue of women as rabbis still is debated, and it appears, as in the case of Prell's havurah, to be intimately linked to
the question of the authority of halakhah and the mechanisms
by which it changes. The women in religion debate has also had
some impact on left wing American Orthodoxy.

The Bobover Hasidim, discussed by Epstein, exemplify a
very different American experience. The strict separation of

religion and state has not been utilized as an opportunity for social mobility and cultural integration, but as the basis of building
their own religious-communal life in order to minimize outside
influences. Their ability to do so is reinforced by their location in
Boro Park, Brooklyn, which has become a center of Orthodoxy,
partially reflecting the successful claims, based on ethnic interest and self-consciousness, put forth in America of the 1960s
(Mayer 1979).

While the Bobover reject the goal of integration into American culture, they do adopt new technological devices while per-
petuating their own way of life. This may be seen in their production of the *purim-shpil* (Purim play), which dramatically sets
them off, not only from other Americans and secular Jews, but
even from other Hasidic ultraorthodox groups. Thus, various
levels of interpretation, from the general Jewish to the specific
Bobover, are given to the Purim story based on the Book of
Esther.

An ancient tradition claims that even when all the other
holidays are no longer celebrated, in Messianic days, the holiday
of Purim will continue to be feted. Perhaps this reflects a sense of
the eternity of its theme, the senseless hatred of the Jews as a
minority group. The Kabbalah has created a link between Purim,
with all its gaiety, and the most solemn day of the year, *yom ha-
kippurim.* The phonetic similarity betweeen the names of the
holidays supports this closeness-by-opposition. This inversion of
a holiday, itself based on inversions, is given further special
meaning in the Bobover Purim play, as Purim is a day in which
they solemnly remember the Nazi Holocaust. The Purim holiday,
based on a book which celebrates the survival of the Jewish people, is shared with Jews everywhere, while it takes on meanings
reflecting the history and circumstances of a particular group.
The power of purim-shpil undoubtedly lies in the fact that these
distinct layers of interpretation, as analyzed by academics, are ex-
perientially merged by the Bobover actors and audience.

Harvey E. Goldberg

Notes

1. See the introduction, note 7.

2. Large numbers of Jews began leaving Spain for Algeria and elsewhere

after massacres in the area of Seville in 1391. The same events led to many conversions and the growth in the number of New Christians or Marranos.

References Cited

Altmann, A. (1973). *Moses Mendelssohn, A Biographical Study.* London: Routledge and Kegan Paul.

Elazar, D. (1976). *Community and Polity: The Organizational Dynamics of American Jewry.* Philadelphia: Jewish Publication Society.

Elazar, D., and R. G. Monson (1979) "The Synagogue Havurah—An Experiment in Restoring Adult Fellowship to the Jewish Community."*Jewish Journal of Sociology* 21:67–80.

Ettinger, S. (1976). "The Internal Struggle in East European Jewry." In H. H. Ben-Sasson et al., eds. *History of the Jewish People.* London: Weidenfeld and Nicolson, 764–76.

Glazer, N. (1957). *American Judaism.* Chicago: University of Chicago Press.

Hertzberg, A. (1968). *The French Enlightenment and the Jews.* New York: Columbia University Press.

Katz, J. (1961). *Tradition and Crisis: Jewish Society at the End of the Middle Ages.* New York: The Free Press.

———. (1973). *Out of the Ghetto: The Social Background of Jewish Emancipation, 1770–1870.* Cambridge, Ma.: Harvard University Press.

———. (1982). "Traditional Society and Modern Society." In S. Deshen and W. Zenner, eds. *Jewish Societies in the Middle East.* Washington, D.C.: University Press of America, 35–47.

Mahler, R. (1971). *A History of Modern Jewry, 1780–1815.* London: Valentine, Mitchell.

Mayer, E. (1979). *From Suburb to Shtetl: The Jews of Boro Park,* Philadelphia: Temple University Press.

Samet, M. (1971a). "Neo-orthodoxy." *Encyclopedia Judaica.* Jerusalem: Keter, 12:956–58.

———. (1971b). "Sofer, Moses." *Encyclopedia Judaica.* Jerusalem: Keter, 15:77–79.

Scholem, G. (1941). *Major Trends in Jewish Mysticism.* New York: Schocken.

Sklare, M. (1972). *Conservative Judaism: An American Religious Movement.* New York: Schocken.

Weissler, C. (1986). "Making Davening Meaningful: Worship in the Havurah Movement." In: D. Lipstadt, J. Woocher, and D. D. Moore, eds. *Sacred People, Secular World.* New York: Rossel Books.

CHAPTER 4

"Life Not Death in Venice": Its Second Life

BARBARA MYERHOFF

The whole earth is the sepulchre of famous men and ordinary men, and their story is not graven on a stone, but lives on woven into the stuff of other men's lives. . . .

Pericles's funeral speech

The power of breadth of our own life, and the energy of reflection upon it is the foundation of the historical vision. It alone enables us to give second life to the bloodless shades of the past.

Dilthey, *Pattern and Meaning in History*

In a recent article on "the refiguration of social thought," Geertz (1980, 167-178) points out the growing vitality of interest among social scientists in "the anatomization of thought" as indicative of "a move toward conceiving of social life as organized in terms of symbols . . . whose meaning we must grasp." How people make sense out of themselves, for themselves, and how we as anthropologists develop our interpretive skills in unpacking their symbolic systems becomes a central concern in our discipline.

One of the most persistent but elusive ways that people make sense of themselves is to show themselves to themselves, through multiple forms: by telling themselves stories; by dramatizing claims in rituals and other collective enactments; by rendering visible actual and desired truths about themselves and the significance of their existence in imaginative and performative productions. Self-recognition is accomplished by these showings and is, as George Steiner says, a "formidable, difficult, and perpetual task." More than merely self-recognition, self-definition is made possible by means of such showings, for their content may state not only what people think they are but what they should have been or may yet be. Evidently, interpretive statements are mirrors for collectivities to hold up to themselves; like mirrors, such statements may lie, reverse, and distort the images they carry, and they need not be isomorphic with "nature."

In this paper, I will present two instances of cultural mirroring, one event which I call a "definitional ceremony," the other an inscribed text, a self-portrait of a collectivity. Both of these are found in a highly self-conscious community which continually interprets, depicts, and performs its self-determined reality; both forms are strikingly symbolic and can be unpacked to elucidate the community's understanding of itself; and both are reflecting surfaces and reflexive, demonstrating the creators' consciousness of their own interpretive work.

The cases I cite, ceremony and inscribed text, were exceptionally successful in the persuasions about the reality they asserted. Their success may be judged by the fact that they reached beyond convincing and moving their own members about the claims they made. They succeeded in interesting and captivating outsider-witnesses as to the validity of their interpretations. These outsider-witnesses—anthropologist and the media—served as further reflecting surfaces, broadcasting, re-presenting what they had been shown, and thus enlarging the people's original interpretations and giving them a greater public and factual character than they had in their primary form. By pressing into service others who believed, to restate their versions of themselves, they amplified their claims. The people involved eventually succeeded in bringing about actual changes, in reversing to some degree their political impotence and invisibility, by the canny deployment of their symbols, consciously manipulated; by their skillful operation on public sentiments; and by their sheer conviction that although they understood their manipulations fully, they were innocently, utterly correct. Ultimately, they displayed "facts" of their life and their meaning, knowing full well that the facts they portrayed were about life not as it was but as it should have been.

"Life Not Death In Venice": Background

In 1971 I began an anthropological study of ethnicity and aging, concentrating on a community of very old immigrant Jews from Eastern Europe, whose social life was focused on the Israel Levin Senior

Adult Center in Venice, California.[1] My work there brought to my attention a singular and dominant theme: the people's severe invisibility
and the consequent disturbing psychological and social consequences
of being unnoticed. It is a truism that severely marginal people are
stigmatized and neglected by the mainstream society, subject to dis-
missal that is usually not even the result of hatred or conscious disdain.
Often, it is merely that such people are not *seen;* they are treated as
invisible.

Among very old people—those with fading sensory acuity, deprived of natural intergenerational continuity, and hence unable to
transmit their natal culture or personal histories to their absent, acculturated progeny—people who are facing death and utter disappearance, the problem of social inattention is especially serious. They
may come to doubt not only their worth and potency, not only their
value, but the very fact of their existence. It became clear to me that
these particular elders were intent on presenting themselves to the
world and being noticed; on interpreting the meaning of their history
and culture to a wider outside world that would remember them after
they had died; on possibly transmitting something of their lives to
younger people. Many of their struggles were intractable: extreme
poverty, poor health, inadequate housing and transportation, insuffi-
cient medical care, dangerous surroundings, loss of social roles, and
outliving spouses, family, and friends. But their invisibility proved not
be be irreversible. Through their own ingenuity, imagination, and bold-
ness, aided by outsiders who publicized their activities, they learned to
manipulate their own images, flying in the face of external reality,
denying their existential circumstances.[2] They displayed and performed their interpretations of themselves and in some critical respects
became what they claimed to be. By denying their invisibility, isolation,
and impotence, they made themselves be seen, and in being seen they
came into being in their own terms, as authors of themselves.

The elders had created an entire culture of their own making, one
of great complexity and richness that was shot through with contradictions, paradoxes, and fantasies. It had been built up over the course of
some three decades spent together on the beach in Venice. They had
come to this neighborhood in their mid-sixties, after retirement, leaving the industrial centers of the North and Northeast, where most of
them had lived and worked since emigrating to America from Eastern
Europe around the turn of the century. Here, in an age-homogeneous
ethnic enclave, surrounded by the carnival-like life along the board-

walk, they revived some features from their childhood history in the cities and shtetls of the Old World. Particularly important was their return to their natal language and culture, Yiddishkeit, and to some extent to the religious practices they had discarded on arriving in America, when rapid assimilation for themselves and education for their children were the most singular concerns.

The culture they had invented to meet their present circumstances in old age was bricolage in the best sense—an assortment of symbols, customs, memories, and rituals, blending in a highly ecumenical spirit; they used something from all the layers of their history: Old World, Yiddish, Jewish, modern, American, Californian, secular, and sacred. They knew that improvisation and invention were essential, but like all people they also needed to convince themselves that these solutions were proper, authentic, believable, and occasionally traditional. Their need for such persuasions, and for being visible, coincided with their naturally performative bent, resulting in a highly dramatic self-presentational culture that was extroverted and often touched with the frenzy of desperation. (And, of course, things had to be loud, clear, and exciting since most of these people were in their mid-eighties to mid-nineties; it was often difficult for them to see and hear some of the quieter displays.) The way of life devised by these elderly Jews was a major accomplishment, one that proved successful in dealing with their everyday circumstances and with numerous internally and externally generated crises.

Exegesis and self-examination were ancient religious and secular customs for the elders; textual analysis was taught them as part of the scripture. A long history as pariah people, at least since the biblical dispersion from Israel, in the Old World, and repeated now in their old age, further heightened their self-consciousness. Performance and self-commentary were natural to them. Life in a constructed world (one that they knew to be constructed) was characteristic of their past as well as their present. The power of the imagination, when publicly stated and collectively experienced, was understood by many to be a necessity, a gift, and a potential danger.

Following a precariously contrived ceremony that wedded an Old World religious event with a secular modern one (with which it had little in common), a great argument ensued among some of the Center's elders as to whether or not the ritual had been "proper," "successful," indeed, whether it had been "real" (Myerhoff 1980, 106). "This is nonsense, completely made up. Nothing like this could ever happen," protested Shmuel. Moshe's comment was finally accepted as authoritative, however.

> This is a story I am getting from Martin Buber, the great Hasidic philosopher.[3] I am showing it to the ones who say [the ceremony] was not proper. It tells about two men who are worried about the holiness of the Sabbath. "What is it that makes something holy?" they ask. They decide to make a test to see what happens when they have a Sabbath on a weekday. So they make the Sabbath in the middle of the week. Everything they do is right, and it feels the same way as on a Saturday. This is alarming, so they take the problem to the rabbi to explain. Here is what the rabbi tells them: "If you put on Sabbath clothes and Sabbath caps it is quite right that you had a feeling of Sabbath holiness. Because Sabbath clothes and caps have the power of drawing the light of the Sabbath holiness down to the earth. So you need have no fears." (1980, 68).

On another occasion, the dangers of a life lived imaginatively were discussed vividly by Shmuel, who described his childhood in a little town in Poland:

> Now it is strange to say that we belonged there.... The beautiful river, forests, none of these are ours. What did we have but fear and hunger and more hunger? Hidden in a foreign land that we loved and hated. A life made entirely from the imagination. We say our prayers for rains to come, not for us here in Poland but for the Holy Land. We pass our lives to study the services in the Temple. What Temple? Long ago finished. Where do our priests make offerings? Only in our minds. We feel the seasons of Jerusalem more than the cold of Poland. Outside we are ragged, poor, nothing to look at, no possibilities for change. But every little child there is rubbing elbows with the glorious kings and priests of the Holy Land.... In this we find our home.... Would you say this is insanity? It could be. If we lived more in Poland and not so much in the Holy Land, would all our people now be buried in pits along the river? (1980, 69).

Here, then, are two illustrations of the group's capacity to describe their own lives imaginatively and consciously, questioning their own inventions while proceeding to believe in and enact them. Alongside their verbal reflections, however, was their often startling capacity to shape their physiological lives no less than their thoughts and acts. It was remarkable that they continued to survive, as individuals and as a collectivity, far beyond the norm, beyond predictions of sociology, history, and physiology. And not a few proved able to tailor their deaths as well as their lives, according to their own designs, dying naturally but precisely in the moments and manners of their choice. These people inscribed their self-interpretations on the spaces and surfaces they touched—walls, neighborhoods, media—sometimes even pressing their own bodies into service as statements of meaning, the most final and most dramatic of all.

Definitional Ceremonies

Definitional ceremonies are likely to develop when within a group there is a crisis of invisibility and disdain by a more powerful outside society. Let me state briefly why visibility was such a critical issue among these people. As immigrants, they had no natural witnesses to their past lives and culture. They lived in a world of strangers who "had to be told everything." Moreover, since the Holocaust had eliminated their natal culture, these elders felt an especially great obligation to transmit their firsthand experiences in Eastern Europe to others. They were the last ones who could explain "what it really had been like." And because their children were assimilated into another culture, there was no one to receive and preserve their memories and tales. Also, because they were marginal, disdained people, outsiders knew nearly nothing about them. The absent witness/missing progeny feature, then, was a serious, multidimensional problem.

While marginality, extreme age and the proximity of death, the shock of immigration and the loss of a natal culture (suggesting personal and collective obliteration) all contribute to a sharp self-consciousness, pain and discontinuity are essential contributors as well. Only through the assimilation of experience into a form that endows meaning can such a history be rendered bearable. "Because both our fortunes and our own natures cause us pain, so they force us to come to terms with them through understanding. The past mysteriously invites us to know the closely woven meaning of its moments." (Dilthey 1961 [1910], 100). But the sense of continuity, of being a member in a chain of being with an inherited history that can be transmitted, may contribute as much to reflexive consciousness as rupture, pain, and loss.

This point emerged very clearly in a discussion[4] with some of the elderly artists who participated in the cultural festival (see note 2). Sherrie Wagner, a graduate student in history, queried the artists about their sharp awareness of being "in history," saying:

One of the things that I often asked my grandmother was what she thought about historical events, like Pearl Harbor, the Second World War, and things like that. She never really had a sense of having been a part of history or a part of the important events of her time. I could never get her to talk about where she was or what she felt. It was as though they had no impact on her. But the people sitting here today seem to have a much clearer sense of history and I wonder if it is because they are painting and sculpting and that makes them more aware? Or is it being in this show? Do you now have a greater sense of being a part of history?

Ida Bernstein replied: "Well, to tell you the truth, I had it before, I always had this very strongly. This may sound very pompous, but I have certain traditions, values that I can transmit."

Not being noticed by children or the outside "serious world" was exacerbated among these elderly by the loss of some of their sensory acuity. Clarity of consciousness tended to fade, memories fused with the present, dreams with desire, sleep with wakefulness. There were few kinesthetic cues as to their continuing vitality since there were no kin, spouses or children to hold, and it was not their custom to embrace each other. Sensory deprivation was often severe. When both the outside and inner world deprive us of reflections—evidence that, indeed, we are still present and alive, seen and responded to—the threat to self-awareness can be great. Definitional ceremonies deal with the problems of invisibility and marginality; they are strategies that provide opportunities for being seen and in one's own terms, garnering witnesses to one's worth, vitality, and being. Thus, it was the custom for Center members to display and dramatize themselves in many forms, informal and formal, planned and spontaneously: by storytelling, creating difficulties, making scenes; by positioning themselves to be noticed, recorded, listened to, and photographed.

Definitional ceremonies were the elders' most regular and formal patterns of display. These were quite predictable, marked by considerable momentum leading up to a crisis, after which, when things had settled down, it appeared that nothing had been accomplished. No internal conflicts were settled, no social realignments made. At first these events seemed to resemble what Turner (1974) described as social dramas—they had a natural sequence, a beginning, a middle, and an end, and there was the same progression from breach of a norm to crisis and resolution, with displays of common, powerful, and binding symbols. Certainly the style was agonistic; much adrenalin had flowed and a good fight indeed offered clear-cut evidence of continuing vitality. Heroes emerged, pro- and con-, and there were antagonists, accessories, and always a sizeable chorus. Parts were discovered and developed so that everyone was heard from, seen, authenticated. And as with Turner's social dramas, the ends of these affairs were always marked by the enunciation of the participants' collective symbols, reiterating their common membership and deepest shared commitments. That the ceremonies changed nothing was signal, and is what distinguished them from social dramas. It seemed, in fact, that their purpose was to allow things to stay the same, to permit people to discover and rediscover sameness in the midst of furor, antagonism, and threats of splitting apart.

Here, the performative dimension of definitional ceremonies was the critical ingredient. Within them claims were made that were frequently unrelated to any palpable "reality," which was often evident to all of those involved. To merely assert such claims would be ludicrous and utterly unconvincing; but to enact them was another thing. Mounted as dramas they became small, full worlds, concrete, with proper masks, costumes, gestures, vocabularies, special languages, and all the panoply that made them convincing rituals. Our senses are naturally persuasive, convincing us of what the mind will not indulge. Presentational symbols have more rhetorical power than discursive ones (the latter require exceptional skill and some veracity); in ritual, doing is believing, and we become what we display. Detail may substitute for artfulness. Kenneth Burke might refer to definitional ceremonies as another example of "dancing an attitude." Like string quartets and Balinese cockfights, as Geertz (1973) points out, such symbolic dramas are not "mere reflections of a pre-existing sensibility, analogically represented"; they are "positive agents" in the creation and maintenance of the subjectivity they organize into a proper, coherent tale. Considering the freqency with which this particular population engineered such opportunities for appearing and enacting their dreams, we are tempted to describe definitional ceremonies as more like stages than mirrors. They did not merely show the people to themselves; rather, they provided scenes into which the people could step and play their parts. If others were watching, so much the better. Their attention, belief, and possibly recording would become evidence in the future of the "truth" of the performance, solid corroboration of what began as desire and through enactment came into the world as fact. If no one else noticed, the Center members watched each other and themselves, bearing witness to their own story.

The Parade

The boardwalk which the Center faces had been used for some time by bicyclists, though a local (unenforced) ordinance prohibits wheeled traffic. More recently, roller skating enthusiasts have joined the stream of bicyclists, making the boardwalk as heavily trafficked and dangerous as a major street. Several collisions have occurred; old people have been struck down and injured. All of them were growing frightened and angry, but no one had succeeded in seeing to it that the law against wheeled traffic was enforced. Old and young competed fiercely for space, dramatically enacting their opposing concerns in regular shouting matches:

"This isn't an old people's home, you know!"

"I worked hard all my life. I'm a citizen. I got to have a place to put my foot down also."

Thus the stage was set for the precipitating event that led to a crisis. A bicyclist struck Anna Gerber, aged 86, as she left the Center one Sunday morning. The youth who hit her was reported to have said in defense of himself, "I didn't see her." His statement outraged the old people, for Anna evidently had been directly in front of him. Clearly, it seemed a case of "death by invisibility." When Anna died as a result of her injuries, the Center members organized a protest march. The event was carefully staged and described in advance to the media, which appeared to cover it. An empty, unmarked "coffin'" made from a paper carton painted black was in the middle of the procession. Members carried placards reading "S.O.S. = Save Our Seniors," "Let Our People Stay," and "Life Not Death in Venice." Two blind men led the procession, and people with walkers and canes placed themselves prominently alongside the coffin. The members dressed in particularly bright, nice clothing, "so as not to look poor or pathetic," said one member.

Roller skaters, bicycle riders, and the concessionaires who rented skates and bikes all heckled the elders, who spoke up sharply to be sure that the television cameras and microphones caught the moral outrage they articulated: "See this sign, 'Let Our People Stay'? That goes back to the Bible, you know. We were driven out from Europe already. We don't want to be driven out from here." The group proceeded several hundred yards down the boardwalk, to the small orthodox synagogue that recently had been acquired by a group of young people. The elders did not regularly visit the synagogue because most were not observant and many objected to the orthodox practice of separating women and men during prayer, regarding it as "too old-fashioned, the kind of thing we got away from when we left the Old Country." Now everyone crowded into the little *shul*. Men and women were seated together, Jew and non-Jew, young and old, members and media people, as many of those who had joined the parade as could fit inside. It was a splendid moment of communitas, a profound and moving celebration of unity, as the prayers were said to "bind up the name of Anna with the ancestors."

The ceremonies did not end there, however. The members returned to the Center for an afternoon of dancing to celebrate the birthday of Frances Stein, aged 100, a woman of singular strength, a symbol of successful longevity, always in good spirits, clear-headed, unencumbered by cane, hearing aid, or illness. The continuity of life was acknowledged as vividly as the presence of death had been earlier in the day. "It's a good way to finish such a day," people agreed, clearly aware of the symbolic propriety of juxtaposing a funeral and a birthday to assert their continuing vitality and power despite injury and loss. The ceremony had been an enactment of their historical vision and their rejection of the assigned position of helpless victim. It was a profoundly reflexive occasion, the kind that, as the opening epigraph by Dilthey notes, gives human experience its "second life."

What were some of the specific symbols deployed in the definitional ceremony? Most were clearly identifiable with the people's layered, long history, ranging from ancient times to the most recent developments. "Let my people stay," the reference to the Jews' exodus from Egypt, came from the oldest layer of history, signifying their capacity to achieve freedom and leave slavery behind in a return to their homeland. Certainly the motto referred as well to the repeated form, a procession, or in recent terms, a protest march, a demonstration. That freedom in ancient times meant "going out" and in contemporary times meant "staying put" was a satisfying bit of opposition that gave that motto a pungent, ironic flavor. The placard that became "the name" for the parade, "Life Not Death in Venice" similarly reasserted the life-over-death message and was in response to a newpaper clipping announcing the coming protest march under the heading "Death in Venice." Some members become irate by this suggestion of defeat and, recognizing its danger, used a counterslogan; they employed placards, printed words speaking to other printed words (the newspaper headline), as a means of erasing or out-shouting the statements made by outsiders about them. It was another instance of literally "making a scene" to make sure that their message was seen and heard.

The use of the prayer for Anna, "binding her up with the ancestors," came from a historical layer that was equally old. The Jewish prayer for the dead, Kaddish, makes no reference to death.[5] It is a statement only about continuity and perpetuity; it elevates the individual who has died to the quasi-sacred position of the Patriarchs and Matriarchs, mythic figures with whom he or she becomes bound, suggesting the removal from history and time, sounding again the theme of renewal and transcendence, of deathlessness. Note as well that no official reference was made to the most recent and powerful historical episode of all: the Holocaust. While it was briefly, obliquely cited verbally, it was not used on a poster or displayed in any way. It is my impression that, as a rule, these people avoid using that experience or exploiting it, except in rare circumstances, and then usually to each other but not outsiders. The experience seems too strong and sacred to put to immediate practical purposes.

The note of renewal and denial of death were repeated in the association of a coffin and a birthday party. The incorporation of the synagogue into the procession was a fortunate choice, for it symbolized the inclusion of all Judaism in this local event and touched the particular circumstances with sacrality. That outsiders and nonmembers were included within the synagogue was a fine symbolic note that their cause went beyond them, beyond other Jews or old people. It was essential that outsiders be brought into the protest for the definitional ceremony to succeed. If it were limited to only those like themselves, there would have been no audience to register the elders' message. While they might have succeeded in convincing themselves, there would have been no hope of making the impact they aimed for on the outside world.

Finally, within the procession the elders displayed themselves as symbols, dramatizing precisely how they wished to be and how they wished to be seen. They exploited signs of their fragility—canes, walkers, blindness—but deliberately dressed well. They wished to be viewed as strong presences, angry but not defeated; yet they were too

cagey to omit the message about their vulnerability and the implicit ac-
cusation it stated. At once they dramatized strength and weakness in a
brilliant, accurate paradox. Moral superiority and structural inferiority
so commonly deployed by liminal people, as Turner has pointed out,
was particularly well stated here.

The comment made by the youth on the bicycle after he struck
Anna was often repeated and called to the attention of outsiders as
highly symbolic. All the old people knew why he hadn't seen her; their
determination to make themselves visible was the specific impetus for
the parade. That they succeeded in altering more than their own vision
of themselves was beyond question when a few weeks later barricades
appeared on the boardwalk, on either side of the Center, providing a
four-block section where the old people could walk without fear of traffic. A limited but decisive victory! The elders had transformed their
assigned role as helpless, unseen people into their chosen one as people
to be reckoned with. The definitional ceremony had defined them as
such and was sufficiently convincing to outsiders as well. All entered
into collusion to agree that the elders did indeed exist and should
have been seen.

It was, of course, real or anticipated popular pressure that finally
caused local politicians to erect the barricades. This pressure was
generated by media coverage that amplified the elders' visibility, making it larger, clearer, and more public than it would otherwise have
been. Hence, the media must be included in this analysis of reflecting
surfaces. Publicity afforded by the parade was a significant mirror that
showed the old people's culture to themselves and to outsiders. Nevertheless, the elders originated the image that was broadcast, and it was to
their image that they successfully drew their witnesses. They not only
created an imaginary existence for themselves but for those who
watched them. Geertz has described ritual as that form which allows
the "dreamed-of" and "lived-in" orders to fuse. Indeed, they fused in
this event. The authors of the ritual stepped into the single reality made
of the two orders and took part of their audience there with them.

The Center Mural: An Inscribed Text

Paul Ricoeur tells us that "inscriptions fix meaning." A social event
read as a text is slippery, as though the words flew off the page before
we could finish reading them. An "inscribed" social text is easier to

read, however. Like an object, it sits still while we look at it; it allows us to re-present it to others, as I do here in discussing the meaning of the second symbolic form used by the group of elderly Jews in California.

The Center members all came from a tradition that forbade portraiture and the depiction of images. Nevertheless, many were attracted to visual art and themselves enjoyed painting. Their self-expression in this form was encouraged by their art teacher, Mrs. Betty Nutkiewicz, herself an Eastern European Jew and a refugee from the Holocaust, somewhat younger than most of the members but still what Americans would call a senior citizen. She organized some of the most enthusiastic students in her regular art classes in the Center to paint a mural the length of one hall there (see Figure 1). Many people participated in the project, but three of the members were the major designers and artists. Those who did not paint instead witnessed, criticized, kibitzed; and finally the painting took shape. It is not possible to determine precisely how many or who contributed particular themes and ideas, though Mrs. Nutkiewicz remembers some especially striking contributions. The mural is unquestionably a collective self-protrait, showing the elders' social history freely interspersed with their myths.

The mural begins at the west end of the hall with a drawing of the Mayflower. An American flag flies on top, jutting out of the confining frame. Mrs. Nutkiewicz notes: "This was Bessie Mintz's idea though I do not think that most people in this group came over on the Mayflower. She made the boat very big because it had to carry so many Jews here."[6] The next scene depicts the Statue of Liberty: like the American flag a beloved symbol to these immigrants, marking the beginning of a new life of freedom. Mrs. Nutkiewicz comments: "You notice they made Miss Liberty a little heftier than usual. You might think that is because she is strong. That's true, but also because the artist who made it thought that women who were a little bit fat looked healthier, more attractive."

A market scene in a village square, fusing New York and Eastern Europe, follows, prompting Mrs. Nutkiewicz to tell us: "What is interesting here is that these little houses you wouldn't find in New York. They brought them from their past probably. They carried these ideas and memories from their little shtetls and put them right up here on the wall." The secular associations of Yiddish and the sacred associations of Hebrew are alluded to by two written signs in the scene: "Fresh herring can be bought here" in Yiddish over one of the stalls in the marketplace scene; "Synagogue" in Hebrew over the House of Prayer. She continues: "This scene you would find in the Lower East side, all right, it's mixed up with Europe. [The Center elders] identified themselves with these people. Some had sisters, mothers like this, sitting all day in front of a little pile of fruit, vegetables. And of course, there are peddlars. You see one very talented artist made that horse, a beautiful skinny horse, had to be skinny because it shows that everyone was poor."

Next is a segment on the elders' middle years in America, in the sweatshops where so many passed most of their working lives and which represents a significant portion of their collective social history; whether or not experienced individually, the experience is "borrowed" as a historical moment and regularly incorporated into accounts of personal histories. (The same is true for having lived as a member of a shtetl rather than in a town or city. When pressed, many members indicate that they were not actually born or raised in shtetls, those largely Jewish hamlets and villages of Eastern Europe. Rather, they use the term to signify their childhood experiences as members of a religious community of their own people, in contrast to their later lives in secular, pluralistic America.) Mrs. Nutkiewicz remarks: "And this is, you know, the Liberation movement. It started to grow up at this time. Here are the suffragist women with their signs, 'Strike,' 'Fight,' 'Eight Hours of Work,' 'Arbeiten,' all in Yiddish. You see, they are in long dresses, heels, the old-fashioned dress but they are modern people, fighting for the improvement of their working conditions. Because after the sweatshops come the unions. That was their doing. They fought for themselves, for freedom and social justice, but everyone benefited." The merging of strikers and suffragettes is an interesting note, suggesting the peoples' identification with common causes for which they must struggle in their pursuit of freedom and social justice. Trade unions and the fight for women's rights merge here. That primarily women are depicted in the protest march is not unusual when we consider that all of the painters of the mural were women. Clearly, it is the privilege of artists everywhere to personalize and localize their great themes, embuing the Great Tradition with the specific forms and personnel that give the Little Tradition its vivacity.

The portion of the mural that follows this displays the citizens as middle-aged in the sweatshops. "This has a great history in the life of the Jewish people," says Mrs. Nutkiewicz. "Because you see here the worker sewing, in very poor conditions, on the sewing machine. And

Figure 1. Mural at the Israel Levin Senior Adult Center in Venice, California. The woman in the photograph is a member of the Center who refused to move for the photographer, so she has been included, which is in keeping with the spirit of this essay. Note that the ship is the Mayflower, which dates from 1620, but that it is carrying an American rather than a British flag; also note that the flag breaks the frame at the top of the mural. This and the sequence of photographs on the following pages are courtesy of Andrew Bush.

you see standing over them, the foreman who is supposed to be very strict, selfish. You can see how hard everyone works. But at least we are together."

Then come the elders in Venice, already retired, dressed in modern American garb and seated outside the Israel Levin Center on the boardwalk benches.

> Here you see the people sitting on the benches. Look, one is feeding a hungry dog. You see the woman is almost falling down but she didn't want to sit because she had to feed the dog. They painted this picture but they were unhappy with it because they identified themselves with this picture. You see they are a little apart from each other and they look kind of desolate.So what can we do to make the picture happy and the conditions happy? So somebody said, "Let's make the Israel Levin Center." And here we began to build a center.

> Now here is something interesting, I would say almost surrealistic. People walk through the Center and the Center became almost transparent. You see one figure is inside, one figure is half outside. But they show that they are going through the Center. Even the figure is still in the Center but we can see it. And naturally, they dance, the "eternal Hora" dance, and they're all happy. And it was Friday. We finish with the Oneg Shabbat [the welcoming of the Sabbath] with the blessing of the candles.

The hallah [braided Sabbath loaf] is there, and the beautiful table cloth with fringes.

The half-inside-half-outside figures are two individuals who are holding hands, drawn in outline, not colored, shaded, or given any detail. They look unfinished. Indeed I assumed that someone had simply failed to complete them, until I heard them referred to as the "ghosts" or "spirits" in the mural. Explained one of the members: "We have here ghosts because, you see, even though we are old, we are not yet finished. We still come into new things and could change yet a lot before we die." Intrigued, I asked several other people about the possibility of ghosts, and there were various interpretations: "These are not ghosts. No, it's because you see, people don't come fully into their life without holding their comrades' hands. This we learn from our history. United we stand. You can see how lonely they look over there [on the benches] before they took hold of each other."

A woman standing nearby overheard our conversation and countered: "You always got to put politics into things. It was much simpler. I know the woman who did this part of the painting. Esther Wolfe was her name. You would be standing outside and so naturally you couldn't

see the people inside the Center already. So you have to show them coming out into the world, which they couldn't do with their bodies. So they don't get their bodies until they come out into the sunshine." Mrs. Nutkiewicz didn't like the suggestion that these outlined figures were in any way "not real":

> Oh, no! They are not ghosts or spirits. They're very real. They are the people going through the Israel Levin Center. And our artists are primitive, I would say. They didn't know how to solve the problem to show that the person is inside and you can see the person, half in and half out, if you are standing outside looking in. But they are real. Real living members of the Center, not ghosts, everything is real. If someone wants to say they see ghosts, all right, but that would be gloomy. They are very much alive.

> Here's another thing. You can be naive but it doesn't mean you are always realistic. Chagall would have a cow flying in the sky. That doesn't make it senseless. So maybe if the people weren't inside or weren't dancing the Hora, they are pale, a little anemic you could say. They became alive when they join hands and danced in a group. This could be, too. Esther said that in the Center when they participate in the activities, they look much brighter. I thought this was very interesting. You see, one person inside is really pale, like a shadow, and the other one joined hands and became already colorful. It is like a little fantasy.

This carries over into the Oneg Shabbat. You see how everyone here is inside now. Everyone is together and peaceful and very happy.

This is a significant set of comments. The overall discussion at several points makes explicit the elders' free interpretation of history, shaping and idealizing it, bringing it to the level of near-myth. Many of their most strongly held ideals are portrayed, particularly working for others through social change and philanthropy, which is somewhat pathetically expressed by the woman feeding a hungry dog even though she herself was too frail and poor to stand alone. Another important theme is the returning to the peace of the Sabbath, the sacred, expressed primarily in the realm of women and the home, usually at a heavily laden table. The importance of community is another theme that is implicit throughout the mural. And Mrs. Nutkiewicz's statements are interesting for their near explicit claim that the mural does not merely reflect, it actually creates the peoples' reality: "They painted this picture but they were unhappy with it because they identified themselves with this picture," and later, by "making the picture happy the conditions depicted are also made happy."

The argument about ghosts is, however, the outstanding element here, establishing with certainty a truly reflexive attitude on the part of

the creators of and witnesses to the mural. Their analysis and argument, sorting among the possible symbolic implications of the empty figures, is a metatext, a commentary on the original commentary. In more abstract terms, it is a second-order signification. The mural becomes fully contextualized in this argument, for we hear the creators' exegeses of it. Texts require multiple contextualization to be well read (see Geertz 1980, 176–77). In this segment we have such contextualization: the relation of the parts to each other within the text; to the creators of the texts; to the realities lying outside the text; and to those associated with it. What, then, is the meaning of the ghosts? All the suggestions made are valid and germane: the people are unfinished; they continue to grow and change and therefore have a future, for which they need each other, coming fully into their humanity only when they are seen in public, though they never stray too far from the place of their beginning, to which they always return—the Center and all that is associated with it, Yiddishkeit, home, hiddenness, and community.

The Parade Comments on the Mural, and Vice Versa

Since both the parade and the mural are regarded here as symbolic statements, as texts to be read, it is suitable now to read each in relation

to the other, intertextually. Do they merely repeat the same message? Do they distort, contradict, reinforce, expand, refine, or shift each other's messages? Do we find in them any information about differences between performed and inscribed texts? Since one is behaved and the other is a picture of ideas, can we draw any conclusions about the relations between action and ideas? Can we go beyond considering both as mirrors and attribute causality or influence of one statement to the other? Finally, can anything be said about the relations of these texts to the existential circumstances in which they occur? These are some of the more interesting questions raised by the data, and they are worth noting, though not all of them can be fully answered or explored in depth with the materials on hand.

Both statements, Parade and Mural, were made for the same purpose—self-knowledge, self-creation through display—and roughly by the same people. Presented diagrammatically (see Table), it is clear that both the mural and the parade have a parallel form. In each case the members depart from the safety and familiarity of home, here associated with childhood, family, and exclusively Jewish communities and made sacred through local custom and deep embedding in culture. These are the profoundly familiar and intimate settings in which daily life takes place. With all its limits, poverty, and conflict, unques-

Diagram of the Parade and Mural

	Departure from "home" Primary ties Exclusively Jewish Sacred; familial	Protest for social justice Public activity Secular; amid strangers	Liminal zone Venice community Neighbors, lantzmen Strangers, intimates	Return "home" Primary ties Exclusively Jewish Sacred; familial
PARADE	Center	March with coffin, placards	Synagogue	Center: celebrating life (birthday party)
MURAL	New York/shtetl	March with placards	Boardwalk benches	Center: celebrating life (Sabbath)

Note: I have begun this reading with the New York/shtetl instead of the Mayflower/ Statue of Liberty because of the fusion of New York and shtetl, New World and Old. The story which the mural tells is about America, but it suggests the peoples' reluctance to omit or leave behind their past in Europe. Read as a pilgrimage, the mural suggests a set of nesting circuits: from the Old World to the New, from the East Coast to Venice; and in miniature, the same form is enacted whenever they depart from the Center for an outside public event in which they enact their self-definition, and then return to the Center. The format and message are reiterated.

tionably it is *home* in the fullest sense. The people depart for a zone of strangers, a secular world to which they do not truly belong but which they try to improve nevertheless through protest for social justice. They are active, resolute, and performing. Then they pass into a liminal zone, betwixt and between, partaking of public and private, strangers and intimates, in their made-up community in Venice where they live with neighbors and *lantzmen* (fellow immigrants). They are midway between inside and outside, somewhat lost. The benches are not truly theirs, nor is the synagogue (for reasons too complicated to discuss here; see Myerhoff 1980). They are described and depicted as "desolate," sitting apart from each other in the mural, not yet having established the Center. In the synagogue they are similarly uncomfortable, partly because they are not habitual visitors, partly because it is being used for secular as well as sacred purposes and includes a great many non-Jews. In both cases the elders are passive, witnessing the activities of others rather than performing themselves.

The circuit is completed in both cases by a celebration back "home" in the Center. At the end of the march a birthday is marked, that of an exceptionally vital, exceptionally old person, a clear rejoicing in ongoing life. Similarly, the end of the mural shows a celebration, the Oneg Shabbat,[7] a holiday customarily celebrated at home which includes women and children and is associated with all that is intimate, safe, and loved. The Sabbath begins when the woman of the house lights the candles, bringing in the Sabbath and with it a foretaste of Paradise, for a Jew enters Paradise for this twenty-four-hour period.[8]

Together, the mural and the parade sketch the same shape: birth, struggle, and death; movement from home, into the world, and returning home; a rite of passage showing separation, liminality, and re-aggregation. These are variations on the same theme, marking the movement through the primary stages of life, individually and collectively, macro- and microcosmically.

Clearly, we are justified in noting that the mural and the parade replicate each other; the mirrors show the same image. As texts, they are redundant. The performed text, the parade, was preceded in time by the inscribed one, the mural, which may have had some influence in shaping behavior. Certainly, no one consciously constructed the parade to conform to the mural. But remember that these people spend all day, every day, within walls that broadcast messages about who they are, what they do, how they do it, where they have come from, and where they are going. This must make a silent, steady impact on them. One might say that the idea of the mural shaped the behavior of the parade; but it is more fruitful, I think, to see them both as symbolic statements, performance and icons ricocheting off each other, dual reflecting surfaces that do more than merely mirror. The parade and the mural are mutual shapers of thought and action.[9]

In these texts we see a group of people creating themselves. The inner world, the more real world, they know they have made up. It is invisible to the outside world, sometimes even invisible to them, as many of its most important features are shadowy memories from the remote past. The membrane that separates the real invisible world from the unreal daily world of the present is permeable, like the curtain that separates the Balinese Topeng dancer from his audience, or the Indonesian *wayand kulit* screen on which shadows appear and dance, reflections of the "real" invisible world of heroes, gods, and demons. Just before he leaps into view, the Topeng dancer daringly shakes the curtain that separates the daily world from the world of illusion. When he bursts forth, we are reminded of the fragility of such boundaries. The imagination incarnated in action does not give us time to pause and consent. It is palpable and must be addressed. No matter how secular the setting, stepping from one world into another is a numinous moment, a hierophany, when the sacred shows through.

These old Jews know exactly what they are doing. Their highly developed reflexive consciousness does not impede their capacity to believe in their creations. Long ago they learned to make hidden, safe, self-determined worlds from within. To quote Shmuel again on his little town in Poland: "In that little town, there were no walls. But we were curled up together inside it, like small cubs, keeping each other warm, growing from within, never showing the outside what is happening, until our backs made up a stout wall." This was an important lesson, one that serves them well in American in their old age. Here, they do not remain inside, however. By enacting their dreams publicly, they have altered the world in which they live. As a result of their ceremonial parade, something has changed externally; through self-display, their commentary has persuaded outsiders to their own truth. Skillfully using strong symbols drawn from relevant, abutting social fields, the old Jews have managed to convey their statement to outsiders, to witnesses who then amplified and accredited their claims. Quite literally, they were taken in. A self-fulfilling prophecy and then some: the reality created by the elders' imaginative statements is not limited to their own minds and beliefs but has become true for nonbelievers, for nonmembers. As a result, the real world has been brought into conformity with imagination, by means of imaginative statements.

Lansing (n.d.) describes the Balinese as remarkable for their ability to "make up an invisible world, watching themselves make it up and still believe in it so strongly that they can enter it." These old Jews do likewise, separating the curtains between real and unreal, imagined and actual, to step across the threshold and draw with them, pulling behind them, witnesses who find, often to their surprise, that they are somehow participating in someone else's drama. They may not "believe" in the claims being made, nevertheless they are incorporated. Having stepped over the threshold, they become the "fifth-business," witnesses who push a plot forward almost unwittingly; their story is not wholly their own but lives on, woven into the stuff of other people's lives.

Notes

This project was part of a larger study entitled "Social Contexts of Aging," funded by the National Science Foundation and administered through the An-

drus Gerontology Center of the University of Southern California. A full description of the group appears in Myerhoff (1980). A film about the group, entitled "Number Our Days," was produced and directed by Lynne Littman for
public television station KCET, Los Angeles, based on my fieldwork. The
cultural festival referred to in note 2 was entitled "Life Not Death in Venice,"
after the parade. I would like to acknowledge the people who made it possible
and to thank them for their generosity in helping to produce the festival and for
assisting me in gathering the written and visual materials I needed to do this
preliminary analysis. At the University of Southern California, Center for
Visual Anthropology: Alexander Moore and Denise Lawrence; College of Continuing Education: Barbara Perrow; Department of Anthropology: Sherrie
Wagner and Vikram Jayanti. Partial funding for portions of the festival was provided by the Ford Foundation and the California Council for the Humanities.

After much deliberation I decided to use real names in this paper, for the
Center, the community, and the pertinent individuals. This is not consonant
with general anthropological practice, which seeks to preserve the anonymity
of the populations it studies. In this case, however, the group's urgent desire to
be recorded suggests that it is appropriate to name names; it is also consistent
with the approach that they have pressed me to take and that I have agreed is
suitable. In view of the wide distribution of the film about them, anonymity is
not genuinely possible, in any case. Since I live in close proximity to these people and continue to be in contact with them, I regularly submit my writings and
photographs to them for comment. There is usually some disagreement about
my interpretations; sometimes I amend the original statements, sometimes I
merely note that our views do not concur.

1. When I first began my work here, there were approximately ninety official members, though a great many more used the Center. At present there are
close to four hundred members, due in part to increased publicity and activity
and in part to the Center's relatively recent provision of daily, hot, inexpensive
meals. At its farther reaches, the community of elderly Eastern European Jews
within walking distance of the Center is estimated at between three and four
thousand; thirty years ago there were approximately eight to ten thousand. Inadequate housing has helped to diminish the population and prevents others
like them from moving into the area. The recent surge in membership of the
Center does not represent recruitment either of people outside the neighborhood or of younger people. New members seem to be formerly peripheral individuals, nonjoiners, and the like who have decided to become affiliated for a
variety of reasons.

2. Aware that these people sought attention above all, my own efforts were
naturally directed toward promoting their visibility within the community and
in relation to the outside society. By establishing life history classes and the like
at the Center, I was able to offer additional arenas for them to present themselves to each other. By sending my students to work with them, further channels for publicizing themselves were opened. The publication of my book about
them helped, as did the "Life Not Death in Venice" art and cultural festival held
at the University of Southern California in 1980, where the elderly and their art
works, and scholars and artists who had worked in the same Eastern European

cultural traditions, were brought together. The older people served as docents to their art works, and their life histories, collected by students, were presented along with the art. The subtext of this festival was to provide circumstances not only for the elderly to be seen and appreciated, but for them to be there when this occurred, seeing the public, artists, and scholars *seeing them*, thus assuring them of some of the cultural transmission which they so ardently sought. Perhaps the most important aspect of this part of my work came through the KCET film, shown on national television several times, which portrayed this community of elderly Jews to the largest audience available. The film sensitized outsiders to their presence, their difficulties, and their accomplishments, but it did not give the members the direct experience of becoming visible in the eyes of people immediately around them; hence the arrangement for this offered in the festival.

3. An interesting depiction of Buber who is more accurately described as a philosopher of Hasidism (ed.).

4. The discussion was organized and videotaped in connection with a grant from the California Council for the Humanities, to assess the impact of the artists and scholars involved in the festival on one another and to evaluate the effects on the artists of both themselves and their works being displayed in public.

5. The Kaddish is not formally a prayer for the dead, but a doxology which "Magnifies and sanctifies the Name of the Almighty" and terminates with a petition for peace in the universe. In slightly variant versions it marks junctures in the daily public prayer services, and when reached toward the end of each service it is recited by people who are marking a year of mourning or who are commemorating an anniversary of the death of a relative. It thus is metonymically associated with memorialization of the dead to the extent that in some areas of Eastern Europe the eldest male child in a family was sometimes referred to as his parents' Kaddish. The idiom of "binding up the soul in . . . life," which is the basis of the previous phrase quoted, comes from a prayer which can properly be called a prayer for the dead. (ed.).

6. This commentary was recorded on videotape and transcribed for inclusion of excerpts in this essay.

7. Oneg Shabbat usually refers to a celebration during the course of the Sabbath while the term *kabbalat Shabbat* is the normal way of referring to ceremonies which inaugurate the Sabbath. Because it was unsafe for the elderly of Venice to be outdoors after nightfall, their Oneg Shabbat was celebrated on Friday afternoons, before the actual onset of the Sabbath (ed.).

8. The association of fire, the lighting of candles, with entering Paradise is very widespread. Here Paradise is clearly associated with a symbolic set: renewal, the transcendence of time and change, *illud tempus*, the return to eternal beginnings and origins, completion, fulfillment, and finally death, at least in mortal, temporal terms.

9. In a Nov. 1, 1982 letter to Ed Bruner, in reponse to his editorial suggestions, I wrote: "Certainly feel free to say that the parade and mural are not
isomorphic—that is quite accurate. There is a metaphoric relation between
them, with possible modeling of behavior—the parade—based on an image or
story—the mural. Influence and metaphor, but not cause or isomorphism. And
by all means do stress the openness and tension between these two forms of expression. That is indeed what makes it complex and interesting."

References

Dilthey, Wilhelm. (1961 [orig. 1910]). *Pattern and Meaning in History*. Edited by
H. P. Rickman. New York: Harper Torchbooks.

Geertz, Clifford. (1973). *The Interpretation of Cultures*. New York: Basic
Books.

_____. (1980). "Blurred Genres: the Refiguration of Social Thought," *American
Scholar*. Spring, 165–79.

Lansing, Stephen. (n.d.). "Reflexivity in Balinese Aesthetics." MS. Author's
files.

Myerhoff, Barbara. (1980). *Number Our Days*. New York: Simon and
Schuster.

Turner, Victor. (1974). *Dramas, Fields, and Metaphors: Symbolic Action in Human
Society*. Ithaca, N.Y.: Cornell University Press.

CHAPTER 5

Sacred Categories and Social Relations: The Visibility and Invisibility of Gender in an American Jewish Community*

RIV-ELLEN PRELL

American Jews, like some of their European counterparts have, for more than one hundred years, devoted themselves to altering their rituals while attempting to preserve their essence. The definition of that ritual essence varied with ideology and historical period, but innovators consistently sought balanced religious experience that preserved continuity while modifying what they viewed as inappropriate.

This paper will consider the case of ritual innovation, focused on the question of gender, in an American Jewish community. In Jewish tradition, where careful distinctions between cultural categories are of paramount importance, clear gender divisions are found in every arena of experience. Therefore, a Jewish group committed to altering gender relations raised crucial issues inherent in the paradox of maintaining continuity while initiating change. What constraints do tradition and innovation place on one another?

A community is described which sought simultaneously to be traditional, and generally observant of the Jewish legal code, but also to change the practices which make religious gender equality impossible. In this group, gender is the most significant area in which the reformulations of religious rules have attempted to equalize social relations. This paper will analyze how complex these reformulations are. It will present an example of a breakdown of the group's ideology and vision of traditional yet altered Judaism, showing that ritual innovation constrains participants' enactment of tradition, and tradition constrains members' realization of gender equality.

Their attempts to achieve both continuity and change alternately demanded the restructuring of certain traditions, and the maintenance of others. Tradition served the ends of change; change underscored the importance of tradition. The community's attempt to alter gender relations within the framework of Jewish law and ritual is particularly paradoxical. For members sought equality; women were to become more observant than the law permitted. The more they changed the tradition, the more they seemed to value it. Yet, this traditioning process was to create a series of conflicts as well. On occasion, covert and insidious expressions of hostility to any form of change were expressed by male members of the community, who were closely associated with the traditional observance of Judaism. It will be suggested, in light of the paradox addressed, that alterations of tradition which seek continuity are more likely an ideal than an achievable possibility. Those disadvantaged by the tradition (in this case women), remain vulnerable even with change.

The community to be discussed calls itself a *minyan* (Hebrew for prayer quorum). It meets for prayer on the Sabbath and the religious festivals of the Jewish year. They began meeting in 1972 and continue to meet.[1] As innovators, they made some significant changes in Jewish worship services, such as including women as full and equal participants,[2] deleting or shortening certain prayers, and introducing secular materials into the service. Another aspect of their innovation was, in their own perception, traditioning, making their worship more traditional.[3] They rejected the contemporary American synagogue as an appropriate place for worship and tried to change forms of worship. They did not use a formal service leader on a regular basis, despite the four rabbis and five rabbinical students who belonged to the minyan at the time of this study. They owned no building and met either at one another's homes or in a campus religious center in the West Coast city where they are located. Finally, as cultural innovators allied with their generational peers (of the late 1960s and 1970s), they emphasized informality, equality, and spontaneity. The minyan is one of several such groups in cities with large Jewish populations. They are usually called *havurot* (fellowships), and those writing about American Judaism in the

1970s recognized these groups to be a significant effort to revitalize Judaism by older adolescents and young adults.[4]

Havurah (sing.) members are innovators in three senses. They change traditional Judaism by liberalizing it and they change American Judaism by rejecting synagogues and corporation-like forms of religion. They change their parents' Judaism by attaching to their practice what they consider a more authentic traditionalism which appears to them to resemble the Judaism of prewar Europe. Their innovations are thus both religious and organizational. Paradoxically, they accomplish these changes by making use of countercultural norms of spontaneity and equality (cultural innovation). The tradition becomes part of innovation, and the innovations have as their purpose, as in Reform or Conservative Judaism, a conserving quality, to conserve what they believe to be the essence of traditional Judaism.

Minyan members held a general view of tradition and found it difficult to articulate their particularized sense of innovation. The changes they made in prayers, service order, and participation were not dictated by a clear and systematic ideology. When it was necessary to make changes in the tradition, the correct ones seemed apparent. Only when members disagreed about what should or should not be changed were they called on to articulate some abstract principles of change. Precisely because the principles of change were difficult to articulate, the minyan always perceived itself as primarily committed to tradition, even though some fundamental changes were made.

Because minyan members in particular, and havurah members in general, think of themselves as traditional Jews, *halakhah* (Jewish law) is always a major concern to them. Consequently, none of the changes minyan members made had implications as radical as their implementation of gender equality in ritual. Contrary to traditional law, women were given all the same ritual rights and obligations as men. Not only were they allowed to read and bless the Torah (to have an *'aliyah*), and lead prayer services, they also were invited to wear male ritual garb. The minyan, in essence, produced a generic Jew, male or female, whose religious participation no longer depended on gender. Gender is a central category in Jewish law. It determines which laws are obligatory and which are not, underlining the differences in access to the fullest expression of a Jewish life. The minyan members' decision to include women was made without recourse to any principle of Jewish law. The group's founders emphasized that the decision to include women was not rationalized. Those who could not accept the violation of the law did not join the group. It was a given to these students, rabbis, and young professionals, male and female, that, in the America of 1972, women should and would have equality. Although their actual participation was not as extensive as that of a few of the most active male members, there was not a single responsibility women did not assume or an event in which they did not participate.

Their explicit commitment to gender equality was nevertheless countered systematically during the year the community was observed, 1973 to 1974. On each Sabbath, men and women shared responsibilities for leading the service and for bringing food for lunch. However, on several festivals and in other informal occasions, men not only dominated formal roles, but engaged publicly in humor that by any account was sexist. Above all, these occasions were ones in which gender became a prominent category as the source of humor and of divisions and conflicts. Whereas the Sabbath celebration in the minyan all but erased gender, festivals brought it to the forefront of social and ritual action. The symbolic and social association of men and women with separate domains, which the minyan was formed to overcome, reappeared at these times.

What unfolds in the ethnographic cases presented is the sheer difficulty in reshaping traditional texts and performances. The forms of innovation already mentioned were still tied to ideas and emotional experiences that were not easily left behind. The weight of Jewish tradition repeatedly dominated on those occasions when conscious ideology weakened its control. The result was the exclusion of women.

The problem presented itself, at first, in a somewhat trivial instance. On this occasion the group, in a joking manner, made manifest its own apparently frivolous classification system. During the festival of Simḥat Torah (Rejoicing in the Law), minyan members joined with other members of the university community where they resided to complete the annual cycle of the weekly reading of the Torah. On this festival the final verses of the Book of Deuteronomy and the first verses of the Book of Genesis are read to mark the end and beginning of the Torah cycle. The festival is also the climax of the three weeks in autumn that include the New Year and Sukkot harvest festivals. The entire period is an intensely holy time. Simḥat Torah stands in contrast to these events, because its sacredness, celebrated joyously, entails a relaxation of solemnity. The synagogue, normally a place of restraint, which carefully prescribes distance from the Torah scroll and detailed etiquette for all who come near to it, is transformed. Dancing occurs, in which people merrily carry all of a synagogue's Torah scrolls around the sanctuary, while children wave flags and eat candy and fruit during the procession. In some settings, adults drink alcohol, although drunkenness is not encouraged. In the evening, along with parading, the Torah is read, the only nighttime reading in the yearly cycle. In the morning, the gaiety continues and the Torah cycle is begun anew as Genesis is read following another series of circular processions (*haqafot*) around the synagogue.

As part of the minyan's evening celebration, one of the men leading the service humorously assigned verses of a hymn, sung at the introduction to the Torah service, to various groups of minyan members. His wit cleverly played on oppositions which, after being called out by the leader, were elaborated by other participants. In this way, he distributed verses among different categories of persons and called out:

Graduate students and undergraduates

People living together (married or not) and single people

Women and men

Rabbinical students

People living in a Jewish commune/people living in a Jewish suburb/people living in a Jewish inner city area

People named David (there were many)

Kohanim (the inherited priestly class of men)/*Levi'im* (the inherited assistants to the Kohanim)/those wearing levis.

Everyone laughed at these oppositions and categories, particularly as they grew more absurd, as in the Hebrew/English word play on Levite and Levi jeans. But this classification contained a series of categories and oppositions that every aspect of minyan life was devoted to excising. In their three forms of innovation—religious, organizational, and cultural—they purportedly had obliterated the exclusiveness of the priestly classes inherited patrilineally, the hierarchic relations of rabbis and nonrabbis, and the distinctiveness of males and females (an opposition also embodied in the categories of married and single). The classification, so utterly ordinary by any American Jewish standards, is almost reactionary in light of normal minyan interactions.

Virtually all changes of Jewish law on the part of the minyan members resulted from the group's commitment to change social relations in the direction of equality. Their innovations as Jews rested less on the transformation of texts or rituals per se than on the reformulation of who participates in the rituals and in what way. They viewed their success as providing wider access to the tradition to those who previously were excluded, particularly women and individuals with a minimal formal Jewish education. They believed that they had made more people come close to normative Judaism and had made normative Judaism sensible to a greater number of contemporary Jews. Minyan members saw themselves as encompassing and equalizing categories of people that the law excludes. Their vision of innovation was to equalize and harmonize a religion built on differentiation.

During minyan activities which sanctioned humor, however, members enacted and articulated differentiation of all kinds. On these occasions, the humor was both formally structured, and improvised in bantering, joking, and teasing. The butt of the humor was women. Actual women were not overtly the targets. Rather, female attributes, stereotyped female qualities, and women as predators were woven into the humor. Whether the male participants joked about their fear of women or the suitability of women for participation in ritual, they made visible the connection between gender and differentiation, the denial of which was so critical to their ideology of innovation.

Minyan members were committed to equality, thereby undercutting traditional Jewish categories of differentiation. Their humor articulated the very categories of the traditional formulations that they rejected. If the carefully and delicately wound strands of secular ideologies and Jewish tradition that characterize their community are examined, it will be seen that women in particular, and gender in general, came to express the conflicts inherent in religious innovation. The struggle for (and perhaps impossibility of) a well-engineered balance between tradition and innovation was acted out around women, who represented one set of meanings in the tradition and another in the minyan.

Two examples will illustrate this point. They concern the celebrations of the festival of Simḥat Torah in 1973 and 1974, which contrasted with one another in two important ways. Members believed that the first was considerably more constrained than the second because it coincided with the Yom Kippur War in Israel. The events of the war dominated every conversation and circumscribed the holiday cycle from Yom Kippur to Simḥat Torah. Minyan members were very tied to Israel, both personally and ideologically. Every member had friends and family in that nation and most had lived or visited there. Although it was not apparent at the time, the 1973 holiday was subdued.

The second contrast between the two celebrations involved major shifts, both in the identity of the participants and in the way humor was expressed. The 1973 celebration had precipitated a series of discussions and protests. A number of women had flatly called the event sexist and informally suggested to other minyan members that things should change.[5] The result was an altered celebration in 1974. The contradictions in the group's own constructions of ideology and tradition were revealed in these events.

Celebration and Distinction

Simḥat Torah in the minyan is celebrated with the larger university Jewish community in the evening, and in the more intimate minyan setting during the morning portion of the festival.[6] Because work is prohibited on the festival, there is no competing activity for minyan members and the service is a long, leisurely one. The celebrations, focused on the Torah, are basically identical in both evening and morning services. There are haqafot, dancing, expressions of happiness, singing, and drinking. The morning differs in that the beginning section of Genesis is also read and special honors are extended to the people who recite the blessings over the final portion of Deuteronomy and the first portion of Genesis. The honored ones are called *hatan* or "groom" of the Torah and of Genesis.

On the fall morning of 1973, members gathered at Jacob and Rachel's home. A distinct sense of celebration was in the air, more lighthearted and happy than at a regular Sabbath service. The members prayed the morning service of the festival together, until the Torah service. At that point a drama unfolded in which women, sacred knowledge, and the Torah itself were targets of jokes and abuse.

What initially struck me about the merriment was that although all members participated in praying and then received *'aliyot* (pl.) to bless the Torah, only a few actually participated in any of the joking. Rather, there was an event within an event, and while one was inclusive the other was exclusionary. The chief actors of the inside event were the *gabbai* (officiant charged with assigning ritual honors), the Torah reader, and the two men designated as *hatan Torah* (groom of the Torah) and as *hatan bereshit* (groom of Genesis). The two Torah service leaders who orchestrated the event were not rabbis; the two honorees were.

From the moment that the Torah was unwrapped from the prayer shawls that cover it during a service and separate it from even the holy activity of prayer,[7] it was the target of uncharacteristic physical attention. The usual stately march of the Torah around the room by the reader, Harvey, was replaced by his race-walking the scroll around the room, dodging furniture and people until it was put on the table with some jostling. At that point Michael, the gabbai, intoned a complex series of rules.

> Each person who takes an 'aliyah will then have a drink (he pointed to the bottles of hard liquor on a table standing nearby). The gabbai will then have a drink and the reader will follow him in a drink. After an 'aliyah a person is free to take as many drinks as he or she likes.

Michael emphasized that he and Harvey would have as many drinks as there were people in the room, which would have totaled about fifteen drinks each before 11 A.M. They did not consume half that amount of liquor, but by establishing the rules they linked their subsequent behavior to the effects of alcohol. Michael also took the center stage by introducing his rules as a contest between him and Harvey to see who would consume the most alcohol. In this way their roles were transformed from ritual functionaries to key actors.

Each minyan member was serially called to receive an 'aliyah. Because there were more people than verses to read, Harvey read the verses again and again, stopping short of the last verses of Deuteronomy. He chanted until his voice was so hoarse that he could barely be heard. In addition to chanting with a *trop*, the traditional melody with which the biblical Hebrew verses are read, he occasionally used nursery melodies that verged on the taunting songs of preschoolers. Each minyan member took his or her 'aliyah, had small sips of liquor, listened to the lengthy Torah reading, and occasionally chatted with a friend quietly amidst the jovial and relaxed atmosphere.

At times, Sima or Donna, two founding members of the group, played a prank of the sort children might have done in a *shtiebel* (a small, traditional, storefront synagogue). While the reader read the scroll, or the gabbai called up members, one of them would tie the ritual fringes of his *tallit* (prayer shawl) to the *bimah* (the reading table). When he tried to move he found himself tied to the table and had to unknot the fringes to get free. Everyone laughed at the awkward predicament in which the men found themselves and the prank was repeated several times until the participants tired of it.

After all the other members were called to their 'aliyot, Jay, one of the group's rabbi members, was called up as the bridegroom of the Torah to bless the reading of the final section of Deuteronomy. A large man, Jay strode authoritatively to the bimah after his Hebrew name was called, his long prayer shawl gently swaying about his body as he walked. When he reached the table he told the gabbai, "Call me *rav* (rabbi); you have not shown sufficient respect." And then, when Michael complied, he laughed and said "Don't call me rabbi; I still owe the Seminary a paper." Harvey responded, "You're not married, Jay, how can you be the Torah's bridegroom?"

Jay then approached the scroll, covered with the Torah cover. He slowly and suggestively picked up a tiny corner of the velvet cover and peeked beneath it. His face registered a look of shock and then a leer. He cleverly affected the behavior and expression of a man peeking beneath the dress of a woman. His pantomime was so effective that the woman seated next to me whispered, "Is he going to fuck it next?" Her tone expressed her anger.

"She is a poor bride," Harvey commented in response to Jay's gesture, acknowledging the worn and faded condition of the cover. Jay chanted his 'aliyah and as Harvey read the final verse, the bridegroom crawled around under the table on his hands and knees, slightly shaking the reading table, and distracting attention from the much-repeated readings of the verses.

Jay remained at the bimah while Jacob, another rabbi, was called to be the Bridegroom of Genesis. The words of praise and honor the gabbai is prescribed to read after bestowing the honor were read with ridicule and mockery, so that Jacob's 'aliyah in fact became a debased honor. As he approached the bimah, Michael and Harvey teased, "You are so old to be a bridegroom. Can you make your way up here? Can you manage?" Jacob, in his early thirties and one of the older members, feigned the behavior of an old man. He walked stooped over, pantomimed carrying a cane, and struggled to the Torah. Jacob read the blessing seriously and remained at the bimah.

Harvey then read the first verses of Genesis. He announced another set of rules. "Each time we read one day of God's creation we will pause and sing this melody." He then introduced a nursery melody.

And the group followed suit. After properly chanting, for example, "And God called the light day, and the darkness He called night. And there was evening and morning, one day"; the people paused and sang a tune using "la, la, la," disrupting the continuity of reading. After Harvey read about the creation of man and woman, he said in an aside to Michael, "It is clear that men are superior. It says so right here." Beth retorted, "It's odd we didn't have a female bridegroom in the minyan." Harvey answered, "A female bridegroom is impossible and women in the minyan should be pleased that they are even allowed near the Torah. You should know your place." Harvey exaggerated his statements with pomposity and everyone laughed, some louder than others, at this continuing parody of sexism. In fact, throughout the day, Harvey had feigned the role of the stern Torah reader who, in the face of noise and whispers in a synagogue, pounds his fist on the bimah shouting, "Quiet, quiet, you must be quiet or I will not read." And on occasion he added, "The women in the gallery must stop the gossiping," referring to the separation of the sexes during traditional worship and his own memories of immigrant-dominated synagogues where women, curtained away from the proceedings of prayer, were labeled as disruptive talkers.

Following the Torah reading, the section from the prophets (haftarah reading) was read in English. The service then ended routinely. Everyone stayed for a brief lunch, during which the atmosphere changed. Harvey's hoarse voice prevented him from much conversation. The Yom Kippur war in Israel was still under way and there was little else anyone discussed at lunch. The group broke up immediately following the service and over the year several people reflected on the service as a somber one because of the war.

What I witnessed resembled a classic rite of reversal (Babcock 1978). I had not anticipated such an event because none of my reading about American Judaism had indicated that such events would occur. In fact, such behavior on this occasion generally is associated with the orthodox, and little has been written about it. The content of this humor is usually scholarly, based on puns and parodies of classical texts. But from what I knew about rites of reversal, religious innovators would not be likely to participate in them.

These men and women had chosen by their own behavior and beliefs to break with many of the norms of traditional Judaism. Some Jewish laws were ignored by everyone in the group, and the observance of other ritual requirements and prohibitions varied considerably among the members. Minyan members, therefore, did not require ritual license to challenge the social norms or sacred demands of normative Judaism. Their own parents, if not their grandparents, had begun the process of change long ago with immigration to the United States. Change was not difficult for them to imagine. Yet, ritual license, in its most outrageous forms, normally is associated with societies where stability and timelessness are viewed as holding sway. These rituals diminish in importance, and often disappear, in pluralistic societies where norms are not uniform, nor attacks on them straight-forward.[8]

In addition, it was subsequently learned that the minyan humor was in many ways idiosyncratic. Although the occasion for merrymaking was shared with other Jews, the actual content of minyan humor and intimacy with the Torah was not. The Torah was handled in an un-thinkable manner for either more observant Jews, or more acculturated Jews, who would find such antics undecorous. The explicit attribution of sexuality to the Torah was particularly unprecedented. And the content of the humor, rather than resting on esoteric wit aimed at the clever parodies of texts, was unique to the people involved.

While status jokes aimed at rabbis, teachers, and cantors are common on Simhat Torah, the most idiosyncratic and common butt of the day's jokes in the minyan was the feminine in general, and female qualities of the Torah in particular. The feminine associations with the Torah, largely derived from the noun gender of the Hebrew word, were made highly sexual and transformed the sacred object of reverence into a sexual object. Actual women were marginalized in the event as well, by their exclusion from active participation and joking. Despite the fact that they received 'aliyot, as was generally accepted in the minyan, their minimal participation was highlighted by the fact that they only performed what were recognized as immature pranks. The only other humor of the day was also derived from the introduction of a categorical distinction—rabbi/laity. This hierarchical distinction was parallel to gender in the minyan in that it too had lost its salience in minyan practice. Those who made the jokes relied on categories normally absent in minyan worship and social interaction.

The joking about gender, however, had rather different consequences than the banter about status differences. Those who used gender in humor excluded real members of the community. The use of "rabbi" in humor did not exclude rabbis. Particular rabbis were ridiculed, and honorific titles and prayers were debased. But the actual rabbi members participated, joked, and ridiculed as well. They even participated in self-parody, joining the nonrabbis in a ridicule of tradition. The effect of gender-based humor was radically different. Women did not participate, did not parody themselves or others. They were silent.

Of course, not all men participated equally in the jokes, and some made no gender-derived comments. The humor was dominated by a particular group of men. They were minyan founders, those learned in Jewish texts, and also formed a friendship network. But women who shared these qualities did not participate. The humor may have exposed a category, "founders and learned," which was hidden from formal minyan ideology but apparent in minyan interaction, and also exposed categories denied in minyan interactions but potent in Jewish tradition. Those who constantly emphasized gender in their humor focused on categories which were both crucial in Jewish tradition and in social relations within the group. They made visible a category normally kept invisible, while simultaneously making invisible women members who regularly participated in Sabbath worship.

The effect on women members was real enough. Some of them spoke to the principal participants. As I was told later, they talked to these men privately about the sexism of their remarks. One particularly sympathetic man, Mark, a rabbi and minyan founder, who held that the 1973 Simhat Torah celebration was "unsavory," vowed to make sure that these events would not be repeated in 1974. In addition, the women who found the event objectionable organized a Sabbath service in the spring called the "Women's Service," to address in liturgy and ritual the whole issue of inequality (Prell 1978a).

Even with the enactment of the dramatic women's service little explicit attention was ever paid again to Simhat Torah. But true to his word, Mark worked behind the scenes to make sure 1974 would be different. Since there is no regular procedure in the minyan for assigning ritual roles for festivals, as there is for the Sabbath, he could easily control what would happen simply by asserting a plan. He assigned both men and women to the roles of gabbai, reader, hatan Torah, and hatan bereshit. Indeed, the celebration and joking on Simhat Torah 1974 were different. While the service offended no one in 1974, it was an interesting variation of the 1973 performance.

The morning portion of Simhat Torah was again held at Jacob and Rachel's large apartment. The English and Hebrew hazzanim (prayer leaders) were far more prominent in the humor than were the previous year's service leaders. The Torah service no longer dominated the festival as the source of celebration. The less subdued atmosphere was most noticeable in how much of the liturgy was sung rather than chanted. The humor was more inclusive than in the previous year. This humor mainly consisted of puns and word plays between two languages, Hebrew and English. All Hebrew words that sounded like English words were repeated again with English references. When, for example, the hazzan (sing.) led the passage that begins with the syllables o *say shalom*, members repeated back, "Say what?" The humor moved from person to person in the room. The only other consistent use of a joke form was engineered by the hazzan. He led the entire service using Ashkenazi Hebrew.[9] The sound was rather different from the Sephardi pronunciation to which they were accustomed and provided a base of constant dissonance, which members found very funny.

The Torah service provided the most dramatic contrast to the previous year. Mark had asked Sima to be gabbai, thereby taking it from the hands of a man who would be in a position to make gender directed jokes. Now the reader was a man and the gabbai was to be a woman. But Beth also wanted to be gabbai so the position was shared by two women. Harvey again read the Torah. Sima and Beth attempted to begin the Torah service very much as had their counterparts in 1973. Beth announced,

> After your 'aliyah take a drink from one of those bottles. But wait for us to drink along with you.

Sima added, "We ought to be in good form after a few 'aliyot." The jokes fell flat. No one laughed and the joking failed to extend to other members. There were few allusions to liquor as there had been last year.

Sima and Beth tried again to dominate the joking. Together they held up a sheet of paper and Beth said,

> This confession has been signed by Harvey. Here are listed all of his sins. With this evidence can we consider him an acceptable reader of the holy Torah?

Harvey made no response to them. He ignored the effort to engage him in banter, looking bored and distracted. Again their joke fell flat for lack of engagement and the service continued.

As during the previous year, each man and woman were given an 'aliyah, so once again Harvey repeated the Torah verses until his throat

grew hoarse and he was barely audible. But there were more people attending in 1974 and the forty 'aliyot seemed interminable. As one after
the other came to the Torah others wandered off to talk. Except for
those standing at the reading table, the ritual frame of the event was
broken. Harvey asserted his role in that setting; he elaborated the role
he had taken as the day's chief humorist. He once again imitated tradition as he did when he led the service using an Ashkenazi pronunciation. At the completion of each person's 'aliyah Harvey embraced him
or her saying "y'shar kohakha, may you grow in strength and knowledge
as a righteous person." He said this with much flourish, exaggeration,
and in a sing-song tone. After five of these elaborate parodies his speech
changed. He embraced the honoree, said "y'shar kohakha" and then
added, "mumble, mumble, mumble." He was uncharacteristically affectionate and very physical in his embrace of male members.

The final 'aliyah of Deuteronomy and the first of Genesis were not
given to rabbis, as had occurred during the previous year. Mark also engineered their selection, extending the honors to a man and a woman,
and honoring the woman as the bride of Genesis rather than the
bridegroom. Mark told me later that he chose these people because "the
Minyan means so much to them" but publicly Harvey said these people
were honored because they were "representative of the community."
They were called with seriousness and their honorific call to the Torah
was not ridiculed. Only Harvey continued his embrace and formulaic
"y'shar kohakha." The service then continued in much the same way as
in 1973. Many people had left during the long series of 'aliyot. Harvey
again used a silly trop when reading about the days of creation. The additional portions of the service were quickly completed and the
service ended.

Obviously, the significant contrast between 1973 and 1974 rested
on the carefullly engineered assignment of roles and the privately
agreed on decision to avoid humor connected with gender. Participants
did not overtly express categories of gender or hierarchy. As such, the
1974 event successfully maintained the minyan's ideology of equality.
The social relations that dominated a Sabbath service, which carefully
balanced male and female, and both learned and nonlearned, in positions of authority were maintained. No specific category of participants
was marginalized. No specific category of participants dominated. The
humor that worked had as its butt the American synagogue and the
Judaism that the members grew up in, which was associated with their
parents. It mocked formality, rabbinical lofty tones, and the Hebrew of

childhood. The celebration, rather than primarily expressed through jokes, was dominated by singing, embracing, and some dancing with and around the Torah.

In 1974 there were no individuals who became the butt of jokes. The jokes changed and the efforts of Sima and Beth to imitate the antics of the previous year failed. No one would take up their offer for a "joking license."[10] Just as the social relations of the holiday paralleled more closely those of the Sabbath services, the humor and celebration of Simḥat Torah were transformed.

While seemingly different, these two events are similar in significant ways. On neither occasion were the texts nor the holiday itself subject to innovation. To the contrary. They provided the scenario and the license for the humor,[11] but the subjects and objects of the humor were supplied by the ideology of the innovators. Normative Jewish tradition provided the occasion and outline for the humor, but virtually all of its content grew out of the minyan ideology. In the 1973 performance, the ideology was inverted and potentially subverted. In the 1974 performance, the ideology was reasserted. Yet in both performances tradition constrained the commitment to innovate in the realm of social relations, that is, to substitute the equality of men and women for their asymmetry. As the group fought to maintain innovation within a traditional formulation, so the men continued, in their efforts to keep the minyan a recognizable Jewish prayer group, to assert control.

In this conflict one sees the teeter-totter of tradition and innovation, the pull and push between acknowledged continuity and acknowledged change. Tradition established the scenario for humor and provided the script for distinguishing between male and female categories, while separating actual men and women. In their ridicule, the men enacted their antagonisms and continued to control the humor. Innovation was criticized in jest with each parody of the stereotypic male-female interaction. Even with the revised 1974 Simḥat Torah, which adhered to a traditional script, women never succeeded as the primary jokers.

The 1973 event, which seemed to resemble a shared sense of what Jewish tradition is, expanded and distorted the holiday's license and celebration. In the riotous celebration of the Torah cycle, they veered toward the sacrilegious in some of the participants' attacks on the Torah and its sexual attributes. Yet in pursuing, imitating, and even parodying tradition, the very social relations the minyan members sought to alter were enacted due to the fact that women were excluded and that the status differentials of rabbi and laity were emphasized and controlled by men.

In the 1974 performance, which seemed to resemble a shared sense of what the minyan holds dear, the innovation of social relations muted humor during the Torah reading and thereby left out many traditional associations. The egalitarian gesture to include an 'aliyah for every member allowed only the reader and gabbai to remain engaged in the service. There was no inversion of status hierarchies and little humor; and gender as a category within the service was obliterated. The female Torah was associated with a bride of Genesis. If the minyan's innovations were meant to more effectively maintain continuity or tradtion, the result was not apparent. Rather, male-female equality seemed to strain against ritual celebration, asserting conscious ideology, and undermining the role of tradition.

Cultural Classification and Innovation

The most significant implication of these events for the innovative program of the group is that during these two celebrations every category and classification of minyan life and Jewish life were hardened and rigidified. Simḥat Torah, an occasion when the permeability of categories, such as male/female, humor/sacrality, high status/low status, and even tradition/innovation become most apparent, through playful celebration, was utterly transformed. Instead, the two minyan celebrations undermined the possibility of permeability by exaggerating the categories and distinctions, tightening and hardening them. Either the stereotypically female exhibited vulgar sexuality or she became nonexistent. Women were either made invisible or carefully equalized with men. Hierarchic differences were treated in a similar manner. Educated men eclipsed all others or they did not engage in interaction. The dilemma thus comes to the fore in that tradition is either debased or it controls the scenario through those actors who best claim ownership of it. For only those who are most traditional can parody Hebrew language, text, Torah, and ritual. They attack the tradition not through the humor of innovation, but through the tradition itself. As those associated with hierarchy parody themselves, they do it not with a shared and equalized humor, but through their version of a traditional humor. Hence they harden tradition to encompass both the oppressive

Judaism of childhood, which they view as requiring innovation, and those aspects of Judaism that only the learned can control.

The result of such hardening is that the generic Jew of the Sabbath celebrations of the minyan was transformed by male members into the hypermale traditionalist of the 1973 Simḥat Torah. The palliative adopted for the 1974 Simḥat Torah was only partially successful. While all differences, parodies and categories were reined in to some extent, returning them to a genderless Judaism, social relations were not transformed. Not all people could engender humor; who the potent actors were remained clear.

Insofar as the basic innovation concerned social relations, the alteration of those relations did not spawn their own forms of humor, engaging gender categories in new and nonhierarchic forms that allowed a relationship to the Torah, informed by altered gender categories, to emerge. In short, expressive forms of religious life, particularly those that elaborate, reverse, or invert fundamental categories and distinctions, are often hardened by innovators adapting and remolding religious ideology and practice. Innovation, based on ideology and conscious manipulation of beliefs and practices, undercuts possibilities for the freedom occasioned by such festivals, during which social and pyschological constraints are relaxed.[12]

Gender is a particularly poignant example of just this process. The literature on saturnalia abounds with examples of cross-dressing and exaggerating gender differences by the attribution of stereotypic qualities.[13] Mary Douglas has interpreted the ubiquity of such behavior to the symbolization of relations between "parts of society" rather than "expressing something about the actual relation of the sexes" (1966, 14). Yet, in the minyan, the transformation of the social relations of the sexes is intricately caught up in the symbols of the occasions that have been discussed. Male/female relations and innovation/tradition are linked to one another in powerful ways. The minyan asserts a perfect equilibrium between both pairs. But as innovation must exist within a traditional ritual and textual framework, women are contained by a traditional, explicitly male, religious status. Occasions other than the very well-structured Sabbath celebration seem to allow the balance to be disrupted. When participants are not carefully assigned roles, when the minyan scenario and the traditional Jewish scenario are not carefully meshed, the perceived traditional scenario, controlled by particular men, dominates in fact. Women cannot participate in this scenario. Even when (as in 1974) conscious ideology is asserted by members who carefully enforce innovation, the results are constricting with regard to women. Women participate, but are not engaged by the men in behavior (the Simḥat Torah humor) that resembles their representations of tradition. The content of gender relations is thus exposed; the hierarchic nature of relations is made explicit. In this case, contrary to Douglas, examining the gender categories reveals a great deal about actual gender relations. Every time gender relations are reintroduced in the minyan, when the generic is partitioned into male and female, hierarchy and exclusion result.

Whether these are the personal views of forty men and women is to some extent beside the point. The categories, male and female, and their link to hierarchy, have, over the generations, been continually central in Jewish life. Innovators committed to the maintenance of the tradition seem to have limited options in changing the most salient categories of the tradition. Men and women who seek to innovate feel they must constantly choose between having a gender or being Jewish in the way they believe is appropriate. Hence, for women, no humor emerges, no counterceremony, no self-parody. They do not invert group norms. They simply cling to them as a way to see themselves as both traditional and full participants. When the compromise is put off balance, women lose their visibility. In short, the women's deepest stake is in innovation. But men appear to be torn between the tradition that assures continuity, place, and status, and the innovations to which they maintain a commitment.

In the performances discussed, the assertion of distinct and overt gender categories expresses associations to the tradition as it is represented and understood by innovators. The associations evoke childhood, orthodoxy, and an authentic past. Hence it stands for what innovation was aimed to change. Invoking gender division alters the social relations sought by the group, and hence tends to subvert the innovation. To assert distinction is to undermine the principal innovation of the minyan that attempts to include some men and women as equals.

Throughout, this analysis has focused on three pairs of contrasting oppositions as they appear in social interaction, in ideology, and in many humorous formulations. First, an examination was made of how minyan members deal with tradition versus innovation, and secondly, how they relate to male and female as categories of normative Judaism. Finally, it has been noted that Jewish text is treated as unchanging while the alteration of social relations is critical to the minyan's innovations. Overall, text/altered social relations and tradition/innovation appear as homologous pairs. Male and female are treated as oppositions in the tradition, but as alike by these innovators.

While the minyan lives out its religious life as a community, one side of each constrasting pair consistently constrains the other. Tradition and text mark out a structure, which constrain and temper all actions aimed at innovation. Similarly, the male Jew is the pole of the contrast which defines piety; his ritual garb, prayer language, and obligations constitute the model that is called the "generic Jew," a model which women must imitate.[14]

In the humor described, there is evidence of the failure of the innovative strategy which explicitly claims that balance is possible, that social relations may be altered with a minimal transformation of tradition. To say that the humor or ritual failed on both occasions is to say quite simply, someone was not laughing. In the first instance, public enjoyment of the ceremony excluded all women participants. In the second event, women could not engender laughter and male participation was constrained. To look at it another way, simply changing the occupants of particular roles did not produce a balance of innovation and tradition.

In the minyan humor, tradition, text, and males are associated; they constrain action in a particular direction. Ideology, innovation, and women are also associated, again constraining action in another direction. The result is a clash made apparent during non-Sabbath events when spontaneity is more common.[15]

Ritual occasions which employ humor are inevitably events wherein the critical categories of experience are displayed and upended. In the minyan it is those categories, tradition, innovation, gender, and text, which men fix and tighten. Even as they parody themselves, so they parody the traditions, undermining themselves as innovators and as traditionalists. But they nevertheless hold tight to their centrality and attack the most significant of all minyan asprirations, to restructure the social relations of their own community.

During the Simḥat Torah rituals, and while reflecting on them, I found myself returning repeatedly to an image derived from Max Gluckman's work on rites of reversals (1965, 253–58). I visualized his description of Zulu women dressed in their husbands', and brothers', clothing, brandishing warriors' weapons, threatening males, expressing every form of aggression and lewd behavior, and then returning to a rather circumscribed role in everyday life. He warned against a psychological interpretation, offering instead a social one focused on the control of conflict built into the structure of society. What an odd tradeoff for minyan women. They were caught between the hammer and the anvil. Their innovations gave them a significant measure of control over their religious lives, putting them in the position of asserting rights that, Gluckman argued, Zulu women never would. However, their occasions for inversion and reversal, even ones they sought to control, seemed consistently to marginalize them. Given the tradition/innovation balance, they sought an indigenous form of humor that never emerged. As actors on the public stage of religious life they sought neutrality. It was their only choice.[16]

Notes

*An earlier version of this paper was presented at the first International Interdisciplinary Congress on Women in Haifa, Israel, 1981. Grants from the University of Minnesota and the American Council of Learned Societies allowed me to attend.

1. A fuller description of this group may be found in Prell-Foldes (1978b).

2. Traditional Jewish law differentiates male and female obligations. Women are freed from the positive *mitzvot* (commandments) which obligate adults to time-bound duties, such as reciting prayers three times a day, or wearing a fringed garment, which is obligatory during daylight. Women must observe all negative mitzvot with minor exceptions. Positive mitzvot which are not time bound are also required of women, again with some exceptions. Because women are not obligated to participate in prayer activities, they are not counted in the minyan (see Berman, 1976).

3. See Heilman (1983, 62–63).

4. *Havurot* (fellowships) are a North American Jewish phenomenon that gained prominence in the early 1970s. Sleeper and Mintz (1971) and Neusner (1972) describe the initial movement. Bubis and Wasserman (1983) and Reisman (1979) describe the later development of havurot within synagogues. Weissler (1982), in addition to the author, has conducted an ethnographic study of such a group. Like the minyan, most havurot were made up of graduate students and faculty members. The Minyan had a number of nonacademic professionals, many of whom were alumni of the university near which they met.

5. Such a charge was unprecedented in the minyan. In the group not all

women were feminists, and none were radical. Their sense of outrage was considerable; the charge was not casual.

6. In Jewish time reckoning, the day begins at nightfall, terminating in the next night.

7. In a permanent synagogue the Torah is housed in a Holy Ark. In a room, temporarily used for prayer, it should be covered in the manner described.

8. A useful discussion of the differences between plural and traditional societies and the rituals of each may be found in Turner (1977).

9. The Ashkenazi pronunciation is characteristic of Eastern European Jews. The Hebrew spoken in comtemporary Israel has adopted some salient features of Sephardi speech, and has thus come to be known as "Sephardic." Since the establishment of the State of Israel, there has been a trend among Jewish communities in the United States to switch from an Ashkenazi pronunciation to modern Israeli Hebrew. In the synagogues of the parents of minyan members, however, the prevalent pronunciation was most likely still Ashkenazi.

10. Handelman and Kapferer (1972, 484), in their analysis of the generation of the "emergent form of joking itself," explain why some actors control, or fail to control, joking in groups.

11. Handelman and Kapferer (1972) also discuss "category routinized humor," occasions on which humorous scenarios are predetermined.

12. Some examples of the freedom of such events may be found in Davis (1978) and Da Matta (1977), and with regard to a less ritualized context, in Basso (1979).

13. Some classic examples are Bateson (1958), Bricker, (1973), and Gluckman (1966). In Jewish tradition, the Purim feast is an occasion during which it is permissible for men to dress as women, and vice-versa (see paper by Epstein in this volume).

14. Naomi Goldenberg (1979) addresses this point in her book on women and religion.

15. During a minyan Sabbath retreat outside of the city I heard many jokes similar to those made after a Friday night celebration. I asked a woman founder of the group, seated next to me, about these jokes. She said, "They joke like this on all the holidays." Her expression and tone were of mild dismay. I analyze other such events in "Laughter that Hurts: Ritual Humor and Ritual Change in an American Jewish Community" (Prell, ms.).

16. Some of the ethnographic events in this paper are described in my manuscript (see note 15). What I explore in this paper, the relationship between tradition and gender, is of only minor importance there. I would also like to acknowledge the insightful comments of Amy Kaminsky and Steven Foldes on earlier drafts of this paper.

192   *II. Judaism in America*

References

Babcock, B., ed. (1978). *The Reversible World: Symbolic Inversion in Art and Society*. Ithaca: Cornell University Press.

Basso, K. (1979). *Portraits of "The Whiteman": Linguistic Play and Cultural Symbols Among the Western Apache*. Cambridge: Cambridge University Press.

Bateson, G. (1958). *Naven*. Palo Alto: Stanford University Press.

Berman, S. (1976). "The Status of Women in Halakhic Judaism." In E. Koltun, ed. *The Jewish Woman: New Perspectives*. New York: Schocken Books, 114–28.

Bricker, V. (1973). *Ritual Humor in Highland Chiapas*. Austin: University of Texas Press.

Bubis, G. and H. Wasserman. (1983). *Synagogue Havurot: A Comparative Study*. Washington D.C.: The University Press of America.

Da Matta, R. (1977). "Constraint and License: A Preliminary Study of Two Brazilian National Rituals." In S. F. Moore and B. G. Myerhoff, eds. *Secular Ritual*. Assen: Van Gorcum, 244–64.

Davis, N. Z. (1978). "Women on Top: Symbolic Sexual Inversions and Political Disorder in Early Modern Europe." In B. Babcock, ed. *The Reversible World: Symbolic Inversion in Art and Society*. Ithaca: Cornell University Press, 147–90.

Douglas, M. (1966). *Purity and Danger: An Analysis of the Concepts of Pollution and Taboo*. London: Routledge and Kegan Paul.

Gluckman, M. (1965). *Politics, Law and Ritual in Tribal Society*. Chicago: Aldine.

Goldenberg, N. (1979). *The Changing of the Gods*. Boston: Beacon Press.

Handelman, D., and B. Kapferer. (1972). "Forms of Joking Activity: A Comparative Approach." *American Anthropologist* 74:484–517.

Heilman, S. (1983). *The People of the Book: Drama, Fellowship, and Religion*. Chicago: University of Chicago Press.

Neusner, J., ed. (1972). *Contemporary Jewish Fellowship in Theory and Practice*. New York: Ktav.

Prell-Foldes, R. E. (1978a). "Coming of Age in Kelton: The Constraints of Gender Symbolism in Jewish Ritual." In J. Hoch-Smith and A. Spring, eds. *Women in Ritual and Symbolic Roles*. New York: Plenum Press, 75–100.

_____. (1978b). *Strategies in Conflict Situations: Ritual and Redress in an Urban Jewish Prayer Community*. Ph.D. diss. University of Chicago, Department of Anthropology.

Reisman, B. (1977). *The Chavurah: A Contemporary Jewish Experience*. New York: Union of American Hebrew Congregations.

Sleeper, J., and A. L. Mintz, eds. (1971). *The New Jews*. New York: Vintage Press.

Turner, V. W. (1977). "Variations on a Theme of Liminality." In S. F. Moore and B. G. Myerhoff, eds. *Secular Ritual: Forms and Meanings*. Assen: Van Gorcum, 36–52.

Weissler, L. (1982). *Making Judaism Meaningful: Ambivalence and Tradition in a Havurah Community*. Ph.D. diss. University of Pennsylvania, Department of Folklore and Folklife.

CHAPTER 6

Drama on a Table: The Bobover Hasidim *Piremshpiyl**

SHIFRA EPSTEIN

Our players here are all amateurs at acting, as they were amateurs at
surviving.
—Arthur A. Cohen: *In the Days of Simon Stern*

Purim is a Jewish holiday celebrated annually on the fourteenth
and fifteenth of the month of Adar (February/March). The second
day of Purim is referred to as Shushan Purim (Purim of Susa). Chron-
icled in the Book of Esther, it commemorates the deliverance of the
Jews of Persia during the fifth century B.C.E. from a plot to annihilate
them. From early accounts of its celebration, Purim emerges as the most
enigmatic of all Jewish holidays. It has become an occasion for masquerading, for drinking to the point of intoxication, for genial satire,
and for performing and attending plays: all forms of behavior which are
in contradiction to normative Jewish conduct.

The license given to the inverting of everyday norms is inherent in
the original Purim text: The Book of Esther. A central ideal underlying
the Book of Esther is *venahofokh hu* (in Hebrew: "and it was reversed"
[Esther 9:11]) referring to the inversion quality of the story of Purim.
Accordingly, Haman, the king's vizier, who wanted to hang Mordecai,
himself is hanged, and Mordecai becomes a minister. The Jews take
revenge on their enemies rather than being harmed by them, as
originally planned.

Throughout the ages in Jewish tradition, Purim has become
associated with the celebration of inversion. At the same time, it has
taken different forms in accordance with historic circumstances and
cultural movements within Judaism. This allowed the kabbalists of
Safed in the sixteenth century and their successors, the Hasidim (in the

eighteenth century), to draw on this concept for strengthening their ideology and traditions. Playing on the Hebrew word *Kippurim* (Day of Atonement) to mean also "like Purim" (Ki-Purim), they elevated Purim to be as important as the Day of Atonement, the most solemn of all Jewish holidays.[1] For them, a central theme prevails in both: repentance is requested and granted, and on these days, God is more attentive to supplication.

Purim has also become a paradigm of other events in the Jewish experience. Since the twelfth century more than one hundred communities and families who survived minor or major catastrophes have established a local or family Purim in commemoration of their survival. This study examines the Purim celebration as a cultural performance in a contemporary Jewish community, that of the Bobover Hasidim in Brooklyn, New York.

The Bobover dynasty originated in southwestern Poland in the mid-nineteenth century in the town of Bobowa (known in Bobover Yiddish as Bobof). The contemporary Bobover leader, Shloyme Halbershtam, is a direct descendant of the founder of the group, Hayyim Halbershtam (1793–1816). Shloyme Halbershtam, who survived the Holocaust, established a Hasidic court in Boro Park, Brooklyn. Today, the community numbers approximately one thousand families in Brooklyn with several hundred families in Europe, South America, and Israel.

In Judaism there is a continuum from the great traditions, those observed and celebrated by the whole Jewish people, to the more specific, little traditions, such as those confined to the Bobover Hasidim. Bound by the great traditions of Judaism, the Bobover, like other Jews, read the Megillah (the Hebrew Scroll of Esther) twice in their *besmedresh*[2] (house of study, a synagogue), exchange presents, and eat a festive meal on Purim. This study focuses, however, on a distinct and self-conscious Bobover tradition for Purim, the performance of a *piremshpiyl* (Purim play) on Shushan Purim (second day Purim). The performance of the piremshpiyl will be analyzed in detail in order to show the inversion quality inherent to Purim and its relevance to the Bobover situation.

Purim plays, known in standard Yiddish as *purimshpiyl*, were the most common form of folk drama among Eastern and Western European Jews until the Second World War.[3] Written accounts from the early sixteenth century, and probably even earlier, recount performances of purimshpiyl based on biblical and nonbiblical themes by artisans and *yeshiva* (talmudic academy) students. The plays took place at the homes of rich people, in the synagogues, or even in special halls.

Purimshpiln (pl.) were still popular in Eastern Europe and Palestine during the late nineteenth and early twentieth centuries. Folklorists, ethnographers, philologists, literary historians, and artists have recorded, annotated, revived, and interpreted purimshpiln from oral tradition. In some *yeshivot* (pl.) and small towns of Eastern Europe and Palestine the purimshpiln continued to be performed until World War II. Scholars were especially interested in these folk dramas because they saw in them the origins of modern Yiddish theater.

The Bobover Piremshpiyl

The Bobover Hasidic community is perhaps the only community today that both continues the tradition of performing a folk drama on Purim and makes it an important community event. Although the Purim play was always an important part of Bobover folkways in Poland before World War II, it has acquired even greater significance in the United States. Those who survived the Holocaust and settled in New York City continue the Purim play tradition to this day. From the early 1950s until 1966, the Bobover Hasidim lived in Crown Heights, Brooklyn, New York, where they did not have their own yeshiva. During this period they performed Purim plays together with other Hasidim and non-Hasidim on Ocean Parkway, Brooklyn. Since 1966/1967, when they settled in Boro Park, the performers of their Purim plays have been recruited from their own community. They perform a *piremshpiyl* (Bobover Yiddish) annually in their besmedresh on the night of Purim also known as Shushan Purim.

This study is based on the plays that were performed in the Bobover Hasidic community in 1976 and 1977. However, information gathered in the course of fieldwork on earlier and later plays is also included.

The two plays to be discussed here, like most, but not all plays in the Bobover repertoire, deal with biblical themes. Genesis 22 provided the theme of the play performed in 1976, entitled *Akaides Yitskhek,* "The Binding of Issac." The primary plot deals with Abraham's ultimate devotion to God when ordered to sacrifice Isaac, his beloved son. Only after Abraham had bound Isaac and was ready to slaughter him, did God command Abraham not to touch the boy. Several episodes from midrashic literature embellish the biblical account, including Abraham's lie to Sarah that he was taking Isaac to a Babylonian yeshiva, Eliezer's and Ishmael's quarrel over Abraham's inheritance, Satan's attempt to prevent Abraham from fulfilling God's command to sacrifice Isaac, and Sarah's death after Satan tells her that Isaac was dead and her subsequent revival on Isaac's return. These episodes also appear in the piremshpiyl.

The Book of Daniel serves as the basis for the play performed in 1977, whose title consists of the names of the protagonists—*Hananiah, Mishael, ve-Azariah—Daniel—Nevukhadnetser Melekh Buvel.* This play focuses on the Babylonian exile and the attempts of Nebuchadnezzar, the black king of Babylonia, to convert to idolatry three Jewish children—Hananiah, Azariah, and Mishael. When they refuse to be converted, Nebuchadnezzar throws them into a fiery furnace. In the last scene of the play, they are saved by God, and Nebuchadnezzar acknowledges that their God is the most powerful. Additions to the biblical account include scenes in which the children reveal their wisdon through clever answers to the king's riddles, and Daniel's lamentation to God about the destiny of the Jews. The two plays, performed in 1976 and 1977, were recorded on audio tapes by the author. The 1977 play has been more extensively documented, with videotapes, audio tapes, and photographs. This fieldwork provides the first and only detailed information available regarding the production and the performance of the Purim plays—the writing of the script, the personnel, the rehearsals, the costumes, the physical setting, the musical arrangement, and the interaction between the actors and the audience. These data serve as the basis for an analysis of the social and cultural significance of folk drama in a contemporary Jewish community.

The Production

More than any other high-intensity event in the Bobover calendar of special days, the piremshpiyl engages the community in ludicrous playful behavior, antithetical to everyday norms. In effect, it is the only occasion during the year which is almost completely dedicated to disorder. Their world is temporarily inverted: married men become actors and wear costumes; the members of the besmedresh, now the audience, view a play on this one and only occasion of the year; the division between male and female is relaxed and women chide men and draw aside the *mikhitse* (the curtain separating the women's and men's sections of the prayerhall).

Underlying the production of the play is the idea of *venahafokh hu*, the paradigm of Purim inversion. The Bobover believe that the performance of the play can have an influence on the course of events, a phenomenon known to anthropologists as "sympathetic magic." This idea can best be illustrated by the following anecdote provided by an elderly Hasid. According to him when the Jews of Nemirov could not pay a salt tax, they received an edict expelling them from the city. Since it was the time of Purim, the Hasidic *rebe* of the city suggested that his followers perform a piremshpiyl based on this particular problem, and that they conclude with a plea to the aristocracy for leniency. The play had a happy ending and so did the real-life situation of the Jews of Nemirov.

Another central inversion occurs within the production of the play. The production of the piremshpiyl provides a rare opportunity for the junior male members of the community to participate in the ritual inversion and to express their gratitude for the rebe's services during the year. "Gladden the rebe" (*misemaiekh zan dem-rebm*) provides the chance to present an extravaganza in the rebe's honor. In the production of the play, the major ritual inversion involves the rebe, because the laity—that is the administrators of the Bobover school system, the faculty, and the students—take over all aspects of the production.

Normally it is the rebe who presides at major religious rituals; his participation, presence, and performance are more desirable than that of any other member of the community. For the Bobover, whether it be the Sabbath collective religious work, his conducting of *tishn* ("tables," see below), his lighting the Hanukkah candles, his sounding the *shofar* (Hebrew: ram's horn) on Rosh HaShanah (Hebrew New Year) and Yom Kippur, his reading of the Megillah on Purim, or his leading the procession with the Torah on Simhat Torah (Hebrew: Joy of Torah festival), his activity transcends and enhances the spiritual quality of the rituals for the community. However, in the preparation and production of the piremshpiyl, the rebe's role is much more limited than in other activities during the year.

An ad hoc committee of craftsmen, scene painters, musicians, writers, and actors—often veterans of other Bobover piremshpiyln—is organized. Each member of this committee is talented in special aspects of the production and is accustomed to teamwork. The committee selects a theme for the produciton, submits it to the rebe for his approval, and proceeds with the production when they receive his blessing.

Considerable discussion, however, takes place within the committee during a number of informal sessions. Several think-tank members suggest themes and discuss whether or not to use an old text or to write a new one. When they submit the ideas to the rebe, he may remind them of previous texts or inform them of aspects of the play with which they should be concerned.

Preparation for the production is limited to a short time before Purim—never more than seven to ten days before the event. Sometimes even less time is provided because of the frivolous nature of the event; some individuals regard it as a waste of time (bitl-toire)—certainly less important than studying.

However, several committee members and yeshiva students actually study and research the piremshpiyl text within the great and little traditions of Judaism—studying the Bible and rabbinic and Hasidic literature and teachings. After preparing trial sketches of the roles and after selecting musical segments, they are ready to schedule the first rehearsal. (If the play is completely new and requires more work than would an older play with an available text, it is possible to arrange for a little more time.) Usually, only four rehearsals take place.

At the rehearsals, the actors continue to adapt to alterations in the script, such as the addition of pages with assigned melodies and the changing of parts of the text (often in the format of jokes and other humorous routines). About a week before the production, the script is typed, mimeographed, and distributed. However, it is still not a final text. Changes appear up to the actual performance of the play.

The play is always written in Yiddish with several Hebrew sections. Although in recent years English has made noticeable inroads into Bobover everyday life—men and women read English newspapers and English is increasingly used at home—the piremshpiyl remains loyal to Yiddish, the language in which the Hasidic movement was born.

Although the entire committee takes part in the various aspects of the production, the principal of the Bobover elementary school for boys performs the most important tasks related to the play. As an exceptionally learned man, a talented cantorial singer, and a prolific rhymster, he plays the role of the hero in the play. He is the major contributor in developing the texts and selecting the music. Sometimes he even writes the entire text by himself.

The director or supervisor of the production is a middle-aged Hasid who has had theatrical experience and who is respected for his ability to move an audience to tears with his production. While he can direct actors to play authentic and convincing parts, the director himself is subject to supervision from the principal script writer so that the production will not deteriorate into excessive emotionalism.

The coordinator is in charge of all technical aspects of the production. He also coaches the actors during the rehearsals and serves as prompter during the performance. He moves up and down on the stage, and even assists in quieting the audience when necessary. Several yeshiva students help him select costumes (perhaps rented from a professional costume company such as the one in Forest Hills, New York). They also help the coordinator rent a professional sound system. They may also assist in the installation of the electrical units in the besmedresh.

The design of the backdrops is the special assignment of a talented yeshiva student who consults his teachers and friends. They not only advise him, they also bring him or give him photographs of actors as models for inspiration.

What makes the piremshpiyl a unique community event is that, with the exception of the fiddler, the entire production is done by the Bobover members. As the Bobover do not have an old time fiddler (they do have a young, though unexperienced one), they welcome the participation in the event of a talented non-Bobover fiddler. As this fiddler has participated in many Bobover Purim plays and loves their music and production, he fits into the performance quite naturally.

Time and Space

By incorporating the piremshpiyl into the rebe's tish on Shushan Purim, the event is elevated into a major event in the Bobover religious life. The rebe's tish is a unique Hasidic ritual which takes place on Sabbaths and on most Jewish and Hasidic holidays. On this occasion the rebe and his Hasidim are gathered around a table (from which the event derives its name) for a communal meal, singing and dancing, and hearing the rebe's sermon. Since the piremshpiyl is part of the rebe's tish on Shushan Purim and more men and women, including many guests, come to be entertained than on any other tish, the piremshpiyl is always a very well attended and crowded event. The besmedresh, the largest space for religious work, is therefore the most appropriate place for the event—the peoples' tish.

The *play frame*, a Purim prerogative, is of particular significance because it transforms the besmedrash setting from a place of prayer to a place of entertainment. Normally a house of worship, study, and assembly, the besmedresh, through the license associated with Purim in general, becomes a theater. The yeshiva students, under the supervision of one administrator, are responsible for the theatrical paraphernalia and the construction of the stage. However, their activities are confined to the afternoon of Purim *only* so that their tasks will not interfere with the normal functions of the besmedresh.

The stage itself is a small platform of desks assembled to cover an area approximately twelve feet in width, six feet in length, and two feet in height. It stands on the south end of the ark (housing the Torah scrolls), partially blocking the audience's direct view of the ark. A movable curtain hangs from a semicircular aluminum rod and several papers rolled up in towels rest in loops suspended from the ceiling. The stage is lit simply with red, white, and blue ceiling lights which contribute to the mood of the play.

During the performance the backdrops are rolled up and down to change the scene. At this time, the Holy Ark is entirely out of the audience's view. When the actors perform on the stage, they face the audience but stand with their back to the ark. (Turning one's back to the ark or blocking its view would, on any other occasion, be regarded as unseemly or disrespectful behavior.)

The rebe occupies the best seat in the house. He, his relatives, and community elders sit in a good viewing area. As the stage is an extension of the U-shaped arrangement of tables of the rebe's tish, the event may be called the "drama on the table." The rebe sits, as he does on other tishn, at the horizontal line of the U, while his relatives and the elders sit along the position of the vertical lines.

On Shushan Purim, as on every tish, young married men and yeshiva students pile up three of four tiers of benches on which they stand. The number of children in the audience increases at this time. In keeping with the inversive quality of the occasion, several young men and children masquerade in costume.

The Audience

The piremshpiyl, like most cultural events, is indeterminate, in the sense that it does not prescribe one type of behavior but rather encompasses a variety of experiences involving different degrees of role involvement in the event. It is of value here to identify these behaviors in terms of Kenneth Pike's distinction between "spectacle" and "game" (1955, 48).

Pike observes that in a football game the "spectacle" includes all activities and involvements which, while related to and dependent on the existence of the official "game," are not, strictly speaking, part of the "game" itself. The football game itself remains the "predominant focus unit" (1955, 48) in spite of the pre- or post-game activities and the events at half-time.

So, during the several segments of the play, certain activities can be seen as part of the spectacle, as opposed to the game or actual performance on stage. For example, a spectacle develops as men and women go to great lengths to secure a good viewing position.

During the play, which never starts before midnight and may last more than three hours, the traffic often seems endless as people drag benches into the viewing area at official and nonofficial intermissions. Benches are brought from the yeshiva dining room, from the classrooms of the yeshiva itself, and even, as a last resort, chairs and benches are taken from the nearby Bobover elementary school for boys.

Viewing arrangements can be precarious. Often the benches, perched on top of each other in three or four tiers, are a particular hazard. If the first tier collapses, people tumble down with such commotion and disorder that they cause the performance to stop. Some people stand on ladders used for procuring books from high shelves; others balance on window sills or hang from the ceiling after removing the acoustical tiles. Still others, in the men's section, stand on inverted garbage cans and on water fountains. A single gesture may topple any one of a number of unreliable arrangements. When a person tries to keep or tries to enlarge a viewing area, a chain reaction can occur destroying decorum within the audience.

On occasions of such commotion, the *gabuim* (the rebe's assistants) will attempt to restore order by pointing a cane from the stage at the trouble area. Usually a degree of order will return. But in other instances, the *shtraml* (fur hat) of the troublemaker is taken away from him and tossed far away so that he must leave his place to retrieve it. During the interim, decorum is reestablished until the next accident or disturbance.

Clifford Geertz observes that "every people ... loves its own form of violence" (1973, 449), and even severe instances of violence which frequently erupt during the play do not prevent people from coming again. An example of Bobover legitimized violence is when one of the rebe's assistants loses his temper and strikes someone with a large cane. If a beating becomes too severe, blood may flow.

Order, however, is not always restored in violent ways. The actors, and especially the one who plays a humorous part, the antihero, may on occasion, reestablish order and silence by incorporating the disruption into the play. He might say: "I have time (I can wait) ... I am being paid by the hour ... if I stay longer I will be paid more." Or on other occasions during the play, he may include the audience in the game when, as Nebuchadnezzar, he says, "I have met many animals in my life, but this kind [referring to the audience] I never met." In both cases, order is restored in good humor.

Women do not participate in the game because physical contact in public between adult men and women, even relatives, is against the norms of the community. Men, forbidden to hear women sing in the piremshpiyl, must play female roles and wear women's clothing and make-up.

Women are restricted to the spectacle aspect of the event. They arrive early at the besmedresh, preceding the men, in order to reserve an adequate viewing position in the women's section. Women arriving very early may stand on the first row of tables near the mekhitse. However, those who arrive only an hour or two before the play begins must take positions further back in the third or fourth row from the mikhitse. Unlike the men, who sit on tiers of benches during the performance, the women must stack benches on tables so that they can see the play.

The curtain, separating men and women's sections during normal communal events, is now pushed aside and raised—an indication of the license generally associated with the piremshpiyl.

As the tiers in the men's section occupied by seated children and yeshiva students block much of the women's viewing spectrum, it is particularly annoying to the women when some individuals move into a standing position and further cut off the view close to the pole and the fence separating the women's section.

At this time, some women will reverse their normal social behavior toward the men by commenting aggressively: "Sit down immediately!" "Take off your shtraml!" or "Don't block the view." Occasionally, a woman may reach through the fence touching a man or pushing him with an indication to sit down. Her behavior, less tolerable in normal circumstances, at this time becomes merely a woman's reaction peculiar to the situation. Others, both men and women, eventually attempt to restrain the individuals involved by echoing a long *"sha!"* (an exclamatory word which is the plural command form of *shat* meaning hush or be quiet). While the occasion provides women with a unique opportunity to chide the men and to dispense with the mikhitse, the exchange itself contributes to a communal feeling of *haimishkait* (hominess) of the event and increases comaraderie within the group.

The Bobover Piremshpiyl: A World of Oppositions

The inversion quality of Purim is apparent in the fixed oppositions expressed in the structure of the plays. A dialectic emerges in the plays which is indicative of the Bobover world view and which provides a strategy for survival. The salient oppositions in this world view are:

Jew	:	non-Jew
culture	:	nature
civilized	:	savage
sacred	:	profane
monotheism	:	idolatry
good	:	bad
white	:	black
mind	:	body
clever	:	stupid
poor	:	rich
physically weak	:	physically strong
faithful	:	fickle
persecuted	:	persecutor

The plays are thus constructed around the conflict of opposites. In "The Binding of Isaac," three Jews, Abraham, Isaac, and Eliezer, are in conflict with a non-Jew, Ishmael, who appears as an Arab villain. In the "Play of Daniel," four Jews, Azariah, Hananiah, Mishael, and Daniel, are in conflict with the black king Nebuchadnezzar and his court, who attempt to convert the Jews. In "Joseph and His Brothers," performed ten years ago, the conflict between Joseph and Pharoah is in the foreground. In the "Children of Teheran," performed as recently and 1973, Jews in the Warsaw ghetto struggle against the Germans. In "The Three Revenges," also recently performed in 1975, a Czarist overlord in Russia falsely accuses a Hasidic Jew of a crime.

Within the context of the plays, the polarities between Jew and non-Jew become more apparent. For example, in "The Binding of Isaac," Ishmael, the non-Jew, wears a stereotypical Arab costume so padded that the villain appears grossly fat. As Ishmael enters the scene, the sound of belly-dancing music is heard and his exaggerated body movements and obviously suggestive gestures evoke laughter in the audience. Because Ishmael goes about barefooted, Abraham's servant Eliezer calls the man by the biblical term *pere-udem* (savage). The contrast to Ishmael is Isaac, the prototypical Jew, who dresses like a Bobover child and who studies the Talmud. Isaac resists Ishmael's temptation to learn archery and to become a hunter. Isaac prefers to study the sacred text, while Ishmael wants to conquer the world, even to exploit it through his oil fields.

In the "Play of Daniel" the polarities are expressed in extreme characterization. Nebuchadnezzar, a black king, and his soldiers are stupid and rough people. They are preoccupied with food, with wondering about strange dreams, with converting the Jews, and with conquering the world. On the other hand, Daniel and his friends are God's obedient servants who, although lacking in physical strength, are strong spiritually and pursue a religious way of life. In both these cases of conflict with outside forces, the Jews have to face the challenge of self-sacrifice and martyrdom.

It is difficult to assess how much the actors and audience are conscious of the blackness of Nebuchadnezzar's physical appearance. When the director of the play was asked why Nebuchadnezzar was black, he explained that the actor wore black make-up in order to disguise his identity. Since he is a well-known performer, the cast wanted to puzzle the audience by making it difficult to identify him.

The great and little traditions of Judaism do not describe Nebuchadnezzar as black. It may be suggested that in the case of the Bobover piremshpiyl, the black make-up of the antihero is a sign for a conglomeration of elements, including both the darker powers of evil and the constant threat to Hasidim from Blacks in their neighborhood and in New York.

The contrast between "us" (Bobover) and "them" (non-Bobover) is further worked out in the comic domain. Jokes become inter/intracultural boundary markers. They help to maintain the polarities between Jews and non-Jews and Bobover and other Jews.

During the rehearsals the actors may improvise jokes for particular scenes or may suggest jokes, which the director will accept or reject. The only actor who has permission to improvise jokes during the actual performance is the one who plays the antihero in such parts as Nebuchadnezzer, Pharoah, or Ishmael.

A typical joke that Nebuchadnezzar might tell involves a pun on a Yiddish word *grob* (deep, crude):

> When I was about to build my new palace, I wanted to have a choir for the inauguration. I put an ad in the newspaper asking singers with bass (*grob*) voices to audition. I asked one of the candidates to sing as low as possible. He tried several times and each time I asked for a deeper and deeper note. Finally, he angrily declared: "Go to *hell!* Is that obscene (*grob*) enough for you?"

In the piremshpiyl, a favorite target of jokes, either directly or indirectly, are other Hasidim. The Jew/Jew contrasts may be analyzed as follows:

Bobover	Other Hasidim	Other Jews
Scrupulous observance	Ignorant observance	Non-observance

The Bobover comment on the observance of the Satmar Hasidim in the "Play of Daniel," when Nebuchadnezzar tests the wit of the three children in his capture by asking riddles: "What is the significance of seeing a cow in one's dream?" A child answers that is is proof of success in making a living (*parnuse*). "How?" the king asks. The child answers: "You feed the cow 500 liters of nonkosher milk (*khulev akum*) and you milk 500 liters of kosher milk (Yiddish: *khulev yisruel*)."

The term *khulev yisruel*, which refers to milk produced under careful Jewish supervision, appears on the Golden Flow milk containers which are prepared in a factory owned and supervised by the Satmar

Hasidim. The criticisms implied in the joke is that the Satmar Hasidim are remiss in their supervision of the milk.

The Lubavitcher are the target in "The Three Revenges," where a sick Jew visits a Turkish physician who wraps a blood pressure meter around the Jew's arm. The Jew pushes the doctor away, explaining that the blood pressure meter is a reminder of an experience the Jew had several years ago when he was a member of a tank corps in Russia: "A Hasid asked the man if he were a Jew. When the man replied affirmatively, the Hasid told the Jew to put on *tfilin* (phylacteries)." The implication of the joke for an audience in New York in 1975 was the extreme form of the Lubavitcher Hasidim missionary efforts in both New York and Israel. In their zeal to bring Jews back to their faith, the Lubavitcher Hasidim would try to persuade the Jews to enter their *mitsve* tanks and there to perform mitsves (precepts)—especially the putting on of tfilin.

The jokes in the piremshpiyl are not limited to other Hasidim— esoteric and private jokes about Bobover individuals and institutions are also popular. In these jokes little-known aspects of a person's character emerge: for example, a Bobover's stinginess or extravagance and perhaps other indiosyncrasies. References to a Bobover institution, company, or organization can provide an inside joke to the members of the audience. Such a joke occurs in "The Binding of Isaac."

> Ishmael complains that his father blames him for buying hard *matsos* [sing. *matse*: unleavened bread] every year from the baker of the *koilel* [a fraternity group]. The father says that the *matsos* are so hard they could break one's teeth.

At this point the audience laughs and yeshiva students hiss. The *koilel* is the study fraternity of young married Bobover men. The students hiss at the mention of the matse bakery that provides most of the income for the group.

But the repertoire of comic element in piremshpiyl is not limited to jokes; funny body movement and to a lesser extent transvestitism are also popular elements in the play. For example, when the actor playing Ishmael, and antihero, appears in "The Binding of Isaac," he dances a gross belly dance to Arabic music. He introduces himself with a joke about his adventures as a hunter:

> Several months ago in the forest I saw a huge lion but I did not run away from him. I drew closer and closer to him until I could see his eyes.

> When a smart-aleck asked me why I did not knock the lion's head off, I
> answered him that the lion's head was already cut off!

The humor of transvestia can also provide a number of incongruous
situations in the piremshpiyl. For example, when a man playing a
female part tries to imitate a woman's voice but slips into his regular
voice, the audience immediately notices the discrepancy and responds
with laughter. In the production of "The Binding of Isaac," the actor
playing the part of Sarah had a long red beard. He covered it with a
woman's kerchief. However, the kerchief made it difficult for him to
talk. Every time the actor started to speak his lines over the kerchief, the
audience burst into laughter.

The repertoire of comic elements in the piremshpiyl is another example of the license of reversal characteristic of the Bobover pirem.
Consistent with Bobover world view, the plot of the piremshpiyl must
be serious, sad, and didactic, an aspect which is by itself an inversion of
the Purim mood, which is subversive, burlesque, and antinormative.
However, the humorous elements, both spontaneous and less spontaneous, are capable of placing a Batesonian (1972) frame around the
serious saying, "all which is inside is not serious, but a play." Hence, the
humor of the play reversed the already inverted aspect of Purim to the
original Purim frame, that of burlesque and fun.

The Piremshpiyl as a Literature of Martyrdom

The notion of Purim-Kipurim, that the festival of Purim is like the
most solemn day of the year, will become apparent when unpacking the
meanings of the piremshpiyl texts. A central idea in Jewish experience
throughout the ages is that of martyrdom. The readiness to sanctify the
divine name by committing oneself unreservedly to death rather than
giving up one's faith is called *Kiddush Ha-Shem* (Hebrew: the sanctifica-
tion of God's name). The theme appears in the sacred service of Yom
Kippur (Day of Atonement). Many of the plays in the Bobover repertoire dwell on this theme to some degree. The stories of Isaac and
Daniel, the two plays discussed here, are among the earliest accounts of
martyrdom in Jewish tradition.

The ideology of martyrdom continued from an early formulation
in the second century B.C.E. through the Middle Ages and into the
modern period. New martyrs sanctified The Name in the course of such

catastrophes as the slaughter of Jews in the Rhine Valley during the First Crusade, the blood accusations and subsequent pogroms in the Ukraine and Poland at the time of Chmielnicki (1648–1649), when countless thousands were massacred. Hence, martyrdom becomes a major thematic element in a variety of literary genres in every period: elegies, dirges, poetic narratives, *selihot* (Hebrew: penitential prayers), historical chronicles, and folk dances. In this way heroic acts can be commemorated, recommended, reenacted, praised, and lamented. Like other genres in the literature of martyrdom, the Bobover piremshpiyl serves as a model for the ideal martyr. When the heroes in the play of Daniel, for example, prefer to die rather than to commit idolatry, one of the boys, Azariah, recites the martyrdom blessing: *al pi din mizn mir makhn a brukhe, aniy mekadesh shmo berabim* (according to the law we must recite: I sanctify the Name of God in public). Connoisseurs of Jewish tradition will immediately recognize the words as a sacred incantation which is very rarely heard. During the scene, a fiddler plays the hymn *aniy maamin* (I believe in the coming of the Messiah), which in modern times was the credo chanted by Jews before their death in the ghettos and concentration camps. The evocative power of the martyr's blessing is intensified by the musical accompaniment.

Within the great tradition of Judaism, the binding of Isaac is an example of a person's self-sacrifice and obedience to God's will. Isaac is a prototype of one kind of Kiddush Ha-Shem, or readiness for martyrdom. In Akaidas Yitskhek, Abraham also pronounces a blessing, declaring: "I am ready to perform the sacrificial duty." Like Azariah, Abraham is also saved from the actual performance of the sacrifice when God responds: "Touch not the boy."

In modern times, Jewish martyrs, victims of the Nazi ghetto and concentration camps, including many Bobover, continued to sanctify The Name in the same spirit as those martyrs who preceded them. For the Bobover the theme of martyrdom is normally a part of the liturgy recited on Yom Kippur and on days of national mourning. But, just as the Bobover paradoxically associate Yom Kippur, the most solemn holiday, with Purim, the most joyous holiday, so they include martyrdom as a thematic element on both occasions. For example, on Yom Kippur the prayers refer to the sacrifice of Isaac and other martyrs, a commemoration that is peculiar also to the piremshpiyl. Just as selihot and elegies become part of the prayers chanted on the fasts of Yom Kippur, the Tenth of Teveth, and the Ninth of Av, so too is the theme of martyrdom a part of the Bobover celebration of Purim.

Music

For the Bobover, like other Hasidim, music has a special meaning in their world view. It is through music that Hasidim believe that they can reach ecstasy and thus also God. Consistent with this idea, Bobover tradition is filled with stories about the musical talent and beautiful composition of the Bobover rebe. These compositions, called *nigunim* (melodies), are known and loved by the members, who are always looking forward to a festival tish in which the rebe will introduce his latest compositions. Singing and chanting are part of the tish, daily worship, and weddings. During weddings and festivals instrumental music is played by a Bobover ensemble consisting of a drummer, an accordionist, and a fiddler.

The music sung both during the rebe's tish and the piremshpiyl is conducive to the realization of the Purim paradigm with its inversion quality. (It is helpful to view these two as different musical events even though they are considered by the Bobover as one event. According to the program, the tish may start several hours before the play, the latter never earlier than midnight).

As on other tishn, the repertoire of *zmires* (liturgical songs) is associated with the occasion that they mark; in this case they include zmires from Purim and Yom Kippurim. The members around the rebe's tish sing together *pirem luni* (Purim is to us) and *Shoshanas Yankev* (The Rose of Jacob) with specific Bobover melodies, and they also sing melodies for Yom Kippur. These are wordless solemn melodies composed by the famous Hungarian folk rebe, Yitskhak of Karlow (d. 1828). The melodies are sad and pastoral and were learned by the Karlower rebbe from shepherds in the villages of Hungary. They have become not only favorite Bobover melodies for Yom Kippur, but also for Purim.

The session of singing around the rebe's tish before the performance of the piremshpiyl has the potential of bringing several individuals, especially among young yeshiva students, to experince ecstasy. However, reaching this point takes some warm-up. The yeshiva students in their tiers are usually more active in the singing, while the participation of the rest of the audience varies from relative silence to some level of participation. The rebe's *gabe* coordinates the singing while standing or sitting on a bench close to the rebe's table, by cuing with his hands, "start," "continue," or "stop."

Each *zmiyre* (sing.) lasts from two to three minutes. They are sung repeatedly, sometimes for seven or eight minutes. After a period of warm-up, which may last up to ten minutes, the entire body of Hasidim around the U-shaped table starts moving. The yeshiva students on the tiers sway from side to side and slightly forward and back in almost perfect synchronization while singing and clapping hands. One way to describe this is to compare the crowd to a huge wrapped *tfiln*,[4] a continuous undulating black-and-white spectrum; this impression is conveyed by the Hasidic clothing, black *bekeshes* (silken gowns), *shtramlakh* (fur hats), and white tucked socks.

Those who achieve a degree of ecstasy are few, and can be identified almost as being somewhere else during the event: they do not talk to their neighbors, they do not stop singing, but continue to sing with steady force, all the while looking toward the rebe.

As in an opera, so too in the piremshpiyl "music comes to be employed consistently as part of the drama rather than an occasional embellishment" (Pauly 1970, 51). It has been shown elsewhere (Epstein 1979) that the musical frame of the piremshpiyl is not a random collection of sound. It has its own logic with elements drawn from liturgical and paraliturgical songs, Eastern European Jewish and non-Jewish songs, and recorded and sound effect music. For the purpose of this paper, several examples will be given of how the music of the piremshpiyl provides the Bobover with another opportunity to draw on the license of reversal characteristic of Purim. In the "Play of Daniel," in the scene where Daniel elicits God's attention after the expulsion from Jerusalem, he synchronizes his lips to a tape of Yossele Rosenblatt, a noted cantor, singing *habait mishamayem irey* (Lord, look down from Heaven) (Psalms 33:13), to organ accompaniment.

For Hasidim, who believe in individual prayer, the appearance of a professional cantor in the besmedresh violates their religious norms. It is, however, consistent with the general license associated with Purim, that organ music—which, as the epitome of the *goyishe* (Gentile) domain is rejected in everyday practice—should no longer present a problem for the audience of the play.

The use of sound effects manifests a license similar to that shown in the case of cantorial music. It also shows the Bobover fascination with army and uniform; for example, fife and drums playing an Irish tune, which announce the arrival of Nebuchadnezzar on the stage, are typical of music which the Bobover consider licentious, a Purim reversal.

The theme of fascination with the military is followed through in the costumes of the play, such as that of Nebuchadnezzar who is dressed as an early nineteeth-century general. During the year, most Bobover do not hear goyishe and secular Jewish music on the radio, television, or in the theater. The yeshiva students who select this music are not familiar with its nature or origin. They select their sound effects from records that they have borrowed from the Boro Park Public Library or recorded off the radio. On every other day of the year, it is improper to listen to this music because it is forbidden to imitate non-Jewish ways. Nevertheless, consistent with the license associated with Purim, it is acceptable to listen to such music on the occasion of the Purim festival.

The piremshpiyl music is also effective in transmitting the themes of martyrdom and religious devotion associated with Yom Kippur and Purim. As in Europe, so today, these themes have strong emotional associations for the members of the audience who recall the tragic events of past and recent Jewish history. Today, for example, the Bobover audience, the middle-aged and elderly members, survivors of the Holocaust, are moved by the fiddler who plays *aniy maamin* during the scene where the children are thrown into the fiery furnace. Many of them actually heard this credo chanted by their brethren when they were led to their death in the ghettos and the concentration camps. The audience is extremely attentive during these scenes, some humming the melody along with the violin. Men and women experience an intense feeling of sadness—they can be seen wiping tears with their handkerchiefs. In interviews, Bobover identified the hardships of the heroes in the play with their own experiences. One informant also observed: "The later misfortunes [Holocaust] cause the former ones to be forgotten."

The Bobover piremshpiyl, as a people event, is conducive to the acting out of what psychologists call a "psychodrama." Through the dramatization of themes laden with anxiety: survival, martyrdom, and redemption, the audience can experience catharsis—which standard psychological and functional theories recognize as the "bursting out of emotion," or in Aristotle's terms: "the purging of pity and fear."

Conforming with the formal Jewish code while preserving a unique Bobover world is characteristic of the Bobover Purim. Creating and precipitating such a world is particularly difficult on Purim because on this holiday other Jews also wear costumes, drink, play, and make fun. Only by drawing on all their spiritual and artistic resources can the Bobover make within Purim a world of their own. Making the piremshpiyl, once an Eastern European Jewish folk tradition (not necessarily Hasidic), into a unique Bobover ritual is only one way of creating such a world.

The Bobover Purim illustrates that there is a constant negotiation between the great traditions of Judaism and the little traditions, including that of the Bobover. Creativity and individualism are permitted as long as they are within the framework of tradition.

For the Bobover the celebration of Purim is also a continuity ritual, a local Purim commemorating their survival of minor and major holocausts. The piremshpiyl, the focus of this study, as one event in the celebration of the Bobover Purim, is a continuation of Eastern European Jewish traditon and as such dramatizes the remembrance of things past; it is a celebration of community survival; it is a reaffirmation of the oath to accept martyrdom in the face of future trials.

Epilogue

For the Bobover Hasidim the annual performance of the Purim play is not a form of entertainment, it is rather part of their sacred work for the festival. Because the status of Purim, for Hasidim, is as important as that of Yom Kippurim (purim-kippurim), the performance of the piremshpiyl acquires a special meaning in the Bobover cosmological year. They believe, like their forefathers, in the power of the piremshpiyl to change the course of regular events. The piremshpiyln discussed in this paper represent this notion in that they underscore forces in Bobover and Jewish history on which their future depends. Each play creates an appropriate atmosphere to enact a human drama, whether the story of the binding of Isaac, of Joseph and his brothers, or of the Nazi Holocaust, dealing with the central theme of survival. All are reenactments of their intimate partnership with history. The daily threat that the outside world, whether in Babylonia, Egypt, or pre-World War II Poland, poses for the observant Jew, is boldly dramatized in the plays. Because the piremshpiyl organizes time and space in a special way there is no conflict between the synchronic and diachronic points of view. The piremshpiyl neutralizes the opposition between synchronic and diachronic occurrences and mediates time and place. The play is a presentation of a moment in and out of time, an enactment of the eternal now which is an integral part of the piremshpiyl as a ritual of incorporation and camaraderie.

It is helpful to view this activity through Lévi-Strauss' (1970, 16–

22) formulation of *bricolage*. The Bobover, like the *bricoleur* (do-it-yourself man), may use whatever costumes, music, sacred, and non-sacred texts are available, without regard for inconsistencies in historical perspective or conventional dress code. Thus in the piremshpiyl an actor may appear wearing the dress of a Bobover child, while presenting Isaac, the son of Abraham. And as Isaac did in the midrash, the actor portraying him might also study from the Talmud or be sent to a talmudic academy although the story takes place almost two thousand years before the Talmud was completed and the talmudic academies were established in Babylonia and Jerusalem. It may also happen that the actor, playing the part of Nebuchadnezzar in his court, would wear the uniform of an early nineteenth century general for an event that took place more than two thousand years before.

By altering, interpreting, contradicting and abrogating the great and little traditions of Judaism, within the context of the piremshpiyl, the Bobover preserve a value system in their own way. They use the piremshpiyl to define and maintain relatively clear boundaries between themselves and others. Indeed, the piremshpiyl can be seen as folk midrash, and as such, it dramatizes the essence of the midrashic transmission of law which "in order to be preserved, must be interviewed, opened up, violated" (Mehalman 1972, 34).

Notes

This paper is a version of a chapter from my dissertation (Epstein 1979). An abridged version of the paper was presented at the World Congress of Jewish Studies in Jerusalem (1976). Fieldwork was conducted between 1976 and 1979, while I was a Fellow at the Max Weinreich Center for Advanced Jewish Studies, New York. Special thanks are due to Professor Barbara Kirshenblatt-Gimblett of the Hebrew Institute for Advanced Jewish Studies and the Performance Studies Department at New York University, and to Professor Richard Bauman, University of Texas at Austin, who encouraged me through my years of research. In 1977 I received a grant from the International Endowment for the Arts and the YIVO Institute for Jewish Research to videotape the entire Play of Daniel. An edited version of the play, with English subtitles, is available to the public through the YIVO Institute.

1. For Hasidic literature concerning the concept of Purim/Ki-purim see J. Issac of Przysucha, (1908, 35–36) and A. I. Sperling (1957), 378, article 892. For kabbalistic literature see Tiqqunei Zohar, tiqqun 21, p. 86.
2. Italicized words without an indication of the language represent spoken Bobover Yiddish, a subvariant of Central Yiddish. Eastern European Yiddish

may be divided into three main regional variants: northeastern, southeastern, and central Yiddish, popularly known as "Lithuanian" Yiddish, "Ukraine" Yiddish, and "Polish" Yiddish,respectively. In a few instances the pronunciation of standard Lithuanian Yiddish is presented. Hebrew, especially as used in the names of holidays, is represented in the standard pronunciation of contemporary Israel.

3. For a comprehensive study of the history of biblical plays in Yiddish, including many extant versions of Purim plays, see Shmeruk (1979). Many works on the history of the Yiddish theater also include material on Purim plays. See B. Gorin (1923, 19–63); I. Shipper (1923–1925, 104); and Zimberg (1975:311–44).

4. These phylacteries consist, in part, of long black leather straps wrapped around the left arm, in such a manner that a man's "white" skin alternately is exposed between the straps.

References

Bateson, G. (1972). *Steps to an Ecology of Mind.* San Francisco: Chandler.

Epstein, S. (1979). *The Celebration of a Contemporary Purim in the Bobover Hasidic Community.* Ph.D. Diss. University of Texas.

Geertz, C. (1973). *The Interpretation of Cultures.* New York: Basic Books.

Gorin, B. (1923). *Di Jeshikhte Fun Yidishn Teatr* (The History of Yiddish Theater). New York: Mar N. Mayzel. Yiddish.

Jacob, Isaac of Przysucha (1908). *Ha-Yehudi Ha-Kadosh.* (The Holy Jew) Petrokew: Zederboyn.

Lévi-Strauss, C. (1970), *The Savage Mind.* Chicago: University of Chicago Press.

Mehalman, J. (1972). "The 'Floating Signifier': From Lévi-Strauss to Lacan." *Yale French Studies* 48:10–37.

Pauly, R. G. (1970). *Music and the Theater: An Introduction to Opera.* Englewood-Cliffs N. J.: Prentice-Hall.

Pike, K. L. (1955). *Language in Relation to a Unified Theory of the Structure of Human Behavior.* Glendale, Cal.: Summer Institute of Linguistics.

Shipper, I. (1923-1925). *Geshikhte Fun Yiddisher Theater-Kunst und Drauna fun di Eltste Tsaitn biz 1750* (The History of the Yiddish Theater and Drama from Early Times until 1750), 2 vols. Warsaw: Kulture Lige. Yiddish

Shmeruk, Ch. (1979). *Mahazot miqraiyim beyidish: 1697–1750* (Yiddish Biblical Plays: 1697–1750). Jerusalem: The Israel Academy of Sciences and Humanities. Hebrew.

Sperling, A. I. (1957). Taáme Ha-minhagim (Explanations of the Customs). Jerusalem: Eshkol. Hebrew.

Zimberg, I. (1975). *A History of Jewish Literature*, vol. 7. Edited and translated by Bernard Martin. New York: Ktav.

Judaism in Israel

Introduction to Part III

The reformulation of traditional Judaism into the directions of Reform, Orthodox, and Conservative Judaism, all took place, at first, in Central Europe and as has been mentioned, underwent further developments in the United States. Of the three religious currents, it was only Orthodoxy that had a serious impact on Eastern European Jewry, and ultimately on Judaism in Israel (Deshen 1978). As indicated (p. 132), the Haskalah movement also moved from Germany eastward, and in doing so underwent a process of nationalization. While the earlier Haskalah literature was in German, and generally exhorted the Jews to become literate in the language of the land in which they lived, the Eastern European Haskalah turned to Hebrew, as a language that potentially could be understood by Jews in all lands, and in so doing contributed significantly to the revival of the ancient tongue. This section shall point to some of the main threads linking contemporary Jewish religious forms to nationhood, as a background to the papers in part three which look at Judaism in Israel.

Traditionally, Judaism has always had a nationalistic component. The principle of separation of church and state, which became basic in the West, was not part of the Jewish experience where religion and community, including widespread intercommunal and even interregional ties, had always remained a densely intertwined set of notions. The expression of hope for a return to Zion was built into the daily prayers, the blessings at meal times, the festivals, and wedding ceremonies, to mention a few examples. Emancipation, as has been seen, demanded that the Jews accept the western formula, that their religious commitment be severed from any political or nationalistic loyalty. This demand resulted in a range of reactions during the course of the nineteenth century.

The initial Reform position accepted this demand as legitimate and eliminated, or at least downplayed, the aspects of Judaism which stressed messianic aspirations or a return to Eretz Yisrael. Orthodoxy, or course, could not do away with such an integral part of established Jewish life, but their commitment to the age-old ideal of a messianic return did not directly imply an activist stand in terms of contemporary national movements. To Jews moving on the path of assimilation, either purposively, or through lack of interest in Judaism, the national dimension of Judaism understandably had no import.

During the second half of the nineteenth century, however, it became clear that assimilation on the part of Jews did not bring automatic acceptance by the wider society. This lay the groundwork for the emergence of ethnic consciousness and organization, which, when combined with the natural nationalistic response of Eastern European Jews, who had had limited experience with emancipation, provided the social and spiritual bases of modern Jewish nationalism.

Legal emancipation did not affect the Jews of Russia until 1917; but in Eastern Europe, the religious basis of the traditional order had already begun to be challenged from within. Haskalah writers, at the same time that they tried to bring knowledge of the wider cultural world to the Jewish masses, attacked the narrowness and legalisms of the rabbis. As stated, this literature was created in Hebrew, and also in Yiddish, so that the very media used, had the affect of bolstering ethnic or national awareness, even if some extremist Haskalah writers saw the use of these languages as only a transitionary tactic on the path to participation in the wider society. Most of the Jews in Eastern Europe, however, were not yet enticed by the wider society to change the nature of their self-definition. The phrase "Russians of the Mosaic persuasion" would have been meaningless to them. Even when socialist ideas came to be adopted, fervently by a certain portion of the population, this new ideology was combined with a nationalistic identification linked to Hebrew or Yiddish.

The emphasis on Yiddish dovetailed with the emergence of a modern Yiddish literature, with the works of Mendele Mokher

Sforim, Sholem Aleichem, and Y. L. Peretz being the most outstanding examples (Shmeruk 1971). Yiddish culture was stressed by the Bund, a workers' organization claiming that socialism could be combined with nationalism, which continued to struggle for this view in the context of the Bolshevik revolution and in interwar Poland. The notion of Jewish nationalism in the diaspora was given an ideological basis in the writings (in Russian) of Simon Dubnow (1967–73), who stressed the importance of communal and social institutions throughout Jewish history as compared to the importance of ideas given prominence in the works of the earlier Science of Judaism authors. The emphasis on Yiddish, of course, had little chance of appealing to Jews outside of Eastern Europe, in particular the Jewish populations in the Middle East, but few were aware, at that time, of the potential future significance of these communities.

By the latter part of the nineteenth century, the impulse of the Haskalah, with its main emphasis on universal values, had spent itself in Eastern Europe, but the legacy of modern Hebrew writing was available for attachment to Jewish nationalism. Mendele Mokher Sforim wrote in Hebrew as well as Yiddish, providing new standards for naturalistic Hebrew prose, and Chaim Nachman Bialik, still known as the national poet, evoked a great sensitivity to the traditional world, while pointing clearly to the need for spiritual and political renewal. The poetry of Shaul Tchernichovsky, which reflected a closeness to nature, evoked sentiments of national revival based on secular and naturalistic conceptions which turned their back on sacred history (see the paper by Doleve-Gandelman in this volume).

These cultural expressions were paralleled by the development of political theories and programs. While there had been forerunners of Zionist ideology earlier in the nineteenth century, such as the religious writings of Y. Alkalai and Z. H. Kalischer, and the analysis of the German Jewish socialist Hess (1862), the more proximate figures in the actual emergence of modern Zionism were the Hovevei Zion movement in Russia and the Zionist organization established by Herzl.

Like the mass migrations to the West, the organization of activities aimed at bringing Jews to Eretz Yisrael, was directly stimulated by the pogroms in Russia in 1881. Groups were organized throughout the country, calling themselves Hovevei

Zion (Lovers of Zion), forming the Hibbat Zion movement. Within this movement, there quickly emerged a conflict between those with a more secular orientation and those more committed to religion. The former found ideological leadership in the writings of Ahad Ha'am (literally, "One of The People," a pen name of Asher Ginsburg), who advocated the return to Zion as the spiritual center of the Jewish people, conceived in national-cultural terms. The year 1882 saw the organization of the first modern 'aliyah (ascent immigration) to Palestine, which was consciously aimed at creating a new Jewish society in Eretz Yisrael. This was the beginning of the First Aliyah which, though small in number, and treated suspiciously by Turkish authorities, succeeded in establishing farming settlements in various parts of the country.

The term *Zionism* was coined in the 1890s and received prominence, when, under the leadership of Theodor Herzl, the First Zionist Congress was convened in Basel in 1897. Herzl himself was paradigmatic of the Central European Jew who had integrated himself into the general environment, even gaining some cultural prominence, but who reached the conclusion that Jews would never be fully accepted by European society. His experience of the Dreyfus trial in Paris undoubtedly had an effect on him, encouraging the conclusion that a political solution must be found to the Jewish question. The Zionist Congress called for participation from all walks of Jewish life, and attracted groups with diverse and competing images of a new Jewish polity.

The Zionist idea that the Jews must have their own state, side by side with other nations, was so self-evident to Herzl that he was convinced that world leaders would readily recognize its merits as a solution to a European problem. His plan of action on an international level, seeking formal recognition of a Jewish state before any immigration began, was at odds with the emphasis of many Eastern European Zionists, who saw the practical settling of Palestine, in any way possible, as the only sure way to bring about the return of the Jews to the Land. In 1901 the Zionist Organization established the Jewish National Fund to begin a program of purchasing land in Palestine to permit eventual settlement. Jewish immigration to the country took a new turn when young, secular, and socialist-oriented immigrants began to arrive in 1904 and continued to do so until the beginning of World War I, constituting what is now known as the Second Aliyah. It was during this period that the first collective settlement (popularly known as the kibbutz) was founded (1909).

Views on religion were another matter that divided members of the Zionist movement. The secular-oriented education program suggested at the 1901 meeting of the congress stimulated the formation of the Mizrahi party in 1902, whose aim was to combine religion and Zionism. Zionism was at first rejected by the Reform religious movement, but many Orthodox also found it an anathema. The notion that the prayed-for return to Zion would be brought about by political leaders, many of whom had turned their back on religion, could not be accepted. At the same time, Central European Orthodoxy (as opposed to traditional Judaism) was spreading its influence eastward. In 1912, the Agudat Yisrael party was formed, linking the Orthodox leadership of Frankfurt-am-Main with prominent Eastern European rabbis. The Agudat Yisrael party was distinctly non-Zionist, and between the two wars competed vigorously for influence among the Jewish communities of Poland.

The issuance of the Balfour Declaration in 1917 encouraged both Zionist activities in the diaspora and actual immigration to Palestine. The main 'aliyah to Eretz Yisrael after World War I represented a continuation of the ideals of the Second Aliyah, stressing socialism, secularism, and a return to the soil. This turned out to be the dominant ideology within the Jewish community (the Yishuv) during the prestate period, being expressed in collective settlements, political parties, the organization of the General Federation of Labor (Histadrut), and other economic and social organizations. At the same time, the other 'aliyot (pl.) of the interwar period introduced a middle-class component to the Yishuv, based on immigrants coming from Poland and Germany. They formed the basis of parties with more centrist and economically liberal views. The growing conflict with the Palestinian Arabs over the ultimate claim to the territory stimulated the growth of the revisionist movement, which insisted on a more activist stance concerning Jewish sovereignty. The local clashes and Arab pressure brought the British to stop Jewish immigration into the country in 1939, the same year that the Jews throughout Europe came directly under the Nazi threat. Through the various migrations, including the illegal immigration taking place during and after World War II, the Jewish population in Palestine grew to about 650,000 by 1948.

The ideological variation within the Yishuv gave shape to different educational trends. The Jews organized their own educational system while Arab education was administered by the Mandatory government. Jewish children studied either in the Labor Zionist trend, the General Zionist trend (centrist, liberal), or the religious (Mizrahi) trend. While the Labor Zionists, and many of the General Zionists, stressed secular education, this was a Jewish secularism, which sought, consciously, to reinterpret many of the texts and symbols of the tradition in a manner appropriate to a national community settled naturally on its land. This ideology might be viewed as the basis of the civil religion of Israel (see Liebman and Don-Yehiya 1983), and is amply illustrated in the paper by Doleve-Gandelman. The religious Zionists shared many of these notions, but attempted to combine nationalism with the maintenance of religious observance and ideology.

The majority of Zionist immigrants came from Europe, but there was also a significant Jewish population not affiliated with the Zionist mainstream. The old (pre-1882) Yishuv had contained both Ashkenazi and Sephardi communities, many of whom became absorbed in the nation-building activities of the newcomers. Other Ashkenazim moved in the direction of ultraorthodoxy, which viewed living in Eretz Yisrael an an important religious commandment, but did not identify themselves with the new political orientation (Friedman 1978). Some of the Sephardim continued to live a traditional life, and remained relatively self-enclosed, socially, neither resisting Zionism nor actively joining it.

One year prior to the first Zionist 'aliyah (1881), a group of Jews from Yemen arrived in Eretz Yisrael, and until World War II there was some immigration from Middle Eastern lands, such as Syria-Lebanon, Iraq (including the Kurdistan region), as well as further migrations from Yemen and Aden. Zionist organizations also existed in the countries of North Africa and the Middle East, but their activities were limited and often forced to focus on education and the teaching of modern Hebrew. Zionism in Middle Eastern countries was, of course, a sensitive issue, and normally was not encouraged by the colonial regimes. In North Africa, for example, the French tried to limit attachment to British-ruled Palestine

The cataclysmic events of World War II, in which six million Jews were purposely destroyed, brought about the resolve within the Yishuv in Palestine, and in the Zionist movement, to press for a fully independent Jewish state. The mounting tension in Palestine, plus growing international sympathy for the Jewish plight, led the British to return the mandate to the United Nations, and, in November 1947, the General Assembly recommended that the territory of Palestine be divided into a Jewish and an Arab state. This recommendation was accepted by the Yishuv and by the leadership of the World Zionist Organization, but was rejected by the Arabs in Palestine and the neighboring Arab states. Hostilities broke out before the official end of the mandate, and escalated when Arab armies invaded Israel after its independence had been officially declared in May 1948. An armistice agreement (the second of two) was reached in June 1949. During the fighting, about 700,000 Arabs fled the area which came under Israeli rule. The establishment of Israel opened the way for large-scale Jewish immigration into the country, which began soon after the declaration of independence, resulting in a significant change in the composition of the Jewish population.

Between May 1948 and the end of 1951, over 600,000 immigrants entered Israel, doubling the Jewish population in the course of three and one-half years. The first immigrants were mostly survivors of the European Holocaust, but soon they were joined by arrivals from Middle Eastern countries. In some instances, such as in the cases of Iraq, Yemen, and Libya, there was close to a complete exodus of Jews from these lands; in other cases emigration was more gradual and selective. For the decade thereafter, most of the newcomers were of Middle Eastern provenance, notably North African. Subseqently, immigration has tended to reflect political conditions in the country of origin, such as the emigration of Jews from the Soviet Union, beginning in the late 1960s.

The influx of newcomers from Middle Eastern cultural backgrounds became one of the major issues facing the new society, whose institutions had been developed, for the most part, by Jews of East European origin. While there had always been a certain romanticism associated with these populations, stemming from the notion that they represented some early authentic Jewish or Hebrew culture, the dominant view of the country's leadership was that their original way of life was to be sloughed off, so that they could be absorbed into a newly emergent modern Israeli society. In addition to the pressing problems of defence and economics, including housing and employment for the newcomers, the question of education, which had always been linked to competing ideological conceptions of the Zionist enterprise, became central.

Under the leadership of Ben-Gurion, a philosophy called *mamlakhtiut* was formulated, which stressed the preeminent place of the state, as against the various ideologically based groups within the society. One expression of this philosophy was the attempt to abolish the various trends in education which had characterized the essentially voluntaristic educational system of the mandate period. There was success in abolishing the difference between the Labor and General Zionist trends, so that in 1953 the parliament legislated a unified system of education, which stressed Zionist values acceptable to a range of segments within the society. The values stressed in Doleve-Gandelman's analysis of preschool celebrations were an important component in the emerging educational establishment of Israel, even though the socialist and pioneering elements began to be attenuated.

Mamlakhtiut was only partially successful, however, because the same law established a parallel system of state religious schools, which, while based on Zionism, also taught the students about a religious way of life. In the early 1970s close to 30 percent of the nation's children attended these schools, while today (mid 1980s) the percentage is in the vicinity of 20 percent. The law also allowed the existence of private schools, outside of the national system of education, which permitted the development of ultraorthodox, non-Zionist elementary education. Many of the children attracted to the state religious schools were from families of Middle Eastern origin, among whom it was taken for granted that schooling should include a religious dimension. Neither trend of Zionist schools, however, paid much attention to the fact that the cultural backgrounds of the new immigrants were quite different from that in which European Zionism had developed. The children, like their parents, came into full-scale contact with major institutions which, for the most part, ignored their cultural and religious heritage, or tended to take for granted that their spiritual patrimony was irrelevant to life in the new society.

The division of the national education system into two trends, one religious, and the other secular (nonreligious), stems from a basic conceptualization of Israeli society being divided into two sectors: *dati* (religious) and *lo-dati* (not religious), respectively. The most salient and public indication of religious affiliation in everyday life has become the wearing of a head covering (*kippah*), and different sizes, styles, and colors of these head coverings often signal different modes of religious identification. In actual practice, however, many non-dati Israelis will selectively observe various aspects of religious tradition. Some sort of celebration of reaching religious majority at the age of thirteen (*bar mitvzah* for boys, and *bat mitzvah* at age twelve for girls) is very widespread, as is the observance of the Passover night celebration (*seder*) in one form or another.

The bipolar conception of religious commitment in the society in a sense represents an acceptance of the orthodox view by the lo-dati that their own involvement in tradition does not constitute religion. This view grants orthodoxy a monopoly over religious matters in the life of the society. One expression of this monopoly has been the institutional exclusion of the Conservative and Reform movements, even though their approaches have been very significant with regard to American Judaism. The notion of Jews being divided into ideological (and political) groups, on the basis of individual piety was also foreign to many of the new immigrants from the Middle East. However, given the economic and political dependence, which characterized their initial meeting with Israeli society, they have not formulated competing religious/ideological postions to this view, which was part of the Jewish experience in Europe (see Deshen 1978). Only time will tell whether the recent electoral successes of Middle Eastern ethnic political parties, raising the banner of tradition or Torah, portend new religious developments.

The major religious and nationalist orientations outlined thus far still characterize Israeli society, close to forty years after its political independence, but there have been major shifts in their relative strength and salience. The pioneering cum socialist ethic now exists as a symbol of heroic values, with restricted institutional expression, having had to make way for commitments parallel to those found in other industrialized socieities with a significant middle class. Many of the immigrants (and those in the second generation) from Middle Eastern countries have joined the middle class, and the last two decades have witnessed the flourishing of a variety of forms of cultural expression representing the interaction of their traditions with patterns characterizing the society in general. The paper by Bilu gives one example of such expression (which perhaps is subtly influenced by popular Hasidic culture) developing among the more traditional, and older, North Africans, but touching the lives of many of their children as well.

Even though the proportion of Israelis identifying themselves as dati has declined (Goldscheider and Friedlander 1983), religion has grown in prominence in recent years, as witnessed by the move of some secular Israelis to various forms of orthodoxy (Aviad 1983), and a movement of many dati Zionists toward ultraorthodoxy. Both the importance of Middle Eastern Jewish cultural expression and the strengthening of ultraorthodoxy have a demographic base: most Israelis today are of Middle Eastern parentage, and the high birth rate of the ultraorthodox has been reinforced by immigration from abroad. In addition, the prominence of Middle Easterners reinforces the general identification of the state with Judaism, because few of them came from backgrounds in which there were militant antireligious ideologies.

The growing Jewishness of Israeli society has been commented on by various observers (see, for example, Liebman and Don-Yehiya 1983), and, as indicated, the mass immigration of traditional Middle Eastern Jews is normally mentioned as an important factor in this development. This background factor, in turn, is often cited when discussing the emergence of an extreme orthodoxy linked to activist nationalist politics, such as in the Gush Emunim movement (for a case study concerning Gush Emunim see Aran and Feige 1987). It should be noted, however, that this movement has few adherents with a Middle Eastern background. It is further noteworthy that, to date, no Moroccan saint, like the one analyzed in Bilu's paper, has relocated in the West Bank area.

The three papers in this part illustrate various facets of religious life in Israel, and each exemplifies, in its own way, complex links between text and performance in social action. The ultraorthodox, or *ḥaredim*, discussed by Friedman, probably constitute an extreme case of the written word being viewed as a blueprint for action. While presenting themselves as observers of the Torah in the manner that it has been always observed, the ultraorthodox are in fact ultrainnovators. Their consistent choice of the more severe option, when the law offers alternatives, reflects a focus on the written word that ignores the more flexible oral tradition. Overlooking the tradition of one's fathers also stems from social factors, notably the break-up of the traditional community, a process brought to its quintessence by the Nazi Holocaust and the movement of survivors to America, Israel, and elsewhere (Gutwirth 1970; Shaffir 1974). Even the realm of material culture undergoes alteration in line with the revised understandings of the written law.

Doleve-Gandelman's study, focusing on a symbolic dimension of a complex social movement, examines the expression of the classic Zionist ethos through the topic of kindergarten celebrations. Zionism stressed the return of the Jews to a natural existence in their land, as both a culmination and negation of Jewish history. In her view, the child born in Eretz Yisrael, and called after one of its characteristic plants (the *sabra*), may be seen as a symbolic shifter, both representing Zionist ideology and pointing to a concrete relationship with the soil. The focus on the child seems to generate a spate of writing on a topic that is not usually the subject of systematic attention. The attempt to return to nature, however, yields its own emergent history. Each new settlement, each tract of land redeemed, becomes part of a saga with modern and ancient textual referents and inscribes history on the landscape.

In creating texts for the celebrations, the shapers of this new tradition both consciously and unconsciously refer back to older texts of the Jewish tradition. The Jewish National Fund, which had an important role in molding the new school festivities, presents itself as based on the principles of equality enshrined in the sabbatical and jubilee year laws. The mutual blessings in the birthday parties, in which children bless the fund and the fund blesses the children, are reminiscent of the special occasion on which the children called to the Torah on Simḥat Torah recite a blessing, and are then blessed, in return (see the papers by Zohar and Goldberg, part one). In attempting to secularize Jewish tradition, these modern educators become a link in the chain of never-ending interpretations of symbols which seem to have a pervasiveness and perdurance beyond the intentions of those who seek to use them.

Bilu's paper, showing the growing importance of pilgrimages to saints' tombs among North African Jews, illustrates the development of an elaborate symbolic system bearing significance at both the personal and social levels. The veneration of saints was a key cultural symbol in traditional Moroccan life, and is in the process of being revived in present-day Israel. It is symptomatic of cultural practices which social scientists a generation ago had assumed would disappear as Middle Eastern Jews became absorbed into Israeli society, but which have become imbued with significance in the contemporary situation and reemerged with vigor. Dreams, culturally patterned in their content and modes of interpretation, are the major mechanisms by which importation and revival are carried out.

Dreams of saints take on active importance in the life of the individual, and are culturally legitimated by a community of like-minded believers. Ostensibly, this personal dominance of saints, mediated through dreams, appears to be a form of authority diametrically opposed to legitimacy based on texts. Closer scrutiny, however, reveals that dreaming, too, partakes of textual authority in the context of Jewish tradition.

Dreams appear in the Bible as mechanisms of divine communication to human beings, and the Talmud relates to them seriously as well.[1] As pointed out by Bilu, images in some dreams can best be understood against the background of biblical referents. In addition, the visitational dreams, which led to the establishment of the shrine of Rabbi David u-Moshe, were written down and publicized in printed form, utilizing forms of communication associated with sacred texts. The room in Safed, where the sainted rabbi has chosen to make his abode, is replete with symbols of the scriptural-based religion. In various ways, then, this popular form of religiosity, available to adherents with a minimum literate education (or none at all, in the case of many women), is combined with strands of staid religious tradition and woven into an intricate cultural tapestry.

Together, the three papers relate to very different sectors of Israeli society, but it would be a mistake to assume that they exist in total isolation from one another. The book maintains its importance in all three of the settings described. There are those who feel closest to it when guided by saintly intermediaries, those who seek to modernize it, and those who seek exclusive right to the furtherance of its interpretation. All these modes of relating to classic texts exist side-by-side, often in vigorous competition. In pressing the claims for their own readings, they perpetuate the texts, while influencing, subtly or otherwise, one another's interpretations.

Harvey E. Goldberg

Note

1. The relationship between dreaming and text in the Bible should perhaps be seen as complementary, rather than as oppositional. It is interesting to compare the Book of Esther and the story of Joseph, to which it bears thematic similarity and literary links. In Genesis, which reflects a preliterary milieu, God appears to Pharoah in a dream, and this is the beginning of Joseph's personal redemption and the salvation of the Israelites. Rabbinic tradition places the beginning of the miracle in the Book of Esther in chapter 6, when Ahasuerus cannot sleep. The nocturnal revelation, which elevates Mordecai in the eyes of the king, is read to him from a book.

References Cited

Aran, G., and M. Feige. (1987). "The Movement to Stop the Withdrawal from Sinai." In E. Cohen, ed. *The Price of Peace: The Removal of Israeli Settlements in Sinai.* Special issue of *The Journal of Applied Behavioral Science* (in press).

Aviad, J. (1983). *Return to Judaism.* Chicago: University of Chicago Press.

Deshen, S. (1978). "Israeli Judaism: Introduction to the Major Patterns." *International Journal of Middle East Studies* 9:141–69.

Dubnow, S. (1967–1973 [orig. 1936–1939]). *History of the Jews.* 10 vols. Translated from the Russian by M. Spiegel. London: Thomas Yosellof.

Friedman, M. (1978). *Society and Religion: The non-Zionist Orthodoxy in Eretz Israel, 1918–1939.* Jerusalem: Yad Itzhak Ben Zvi. Hebrew, English summary.

Goldscheider, C., and D. Freidlander. (1983). "Religiosity Patterns in Israel." *American Jewish Yearbook,* 83:3–40.

Gutwirth, J. (1970). *Vie juive traditionelle: ethnolgie d'une* communauté hassidique. Paris: Les editions de Minuit.

Hess, M. (1945 [orig. 1862]). Rome and Jerusalem: A Study in Jewish Nationalism. Translated and edited by M. Waxman. New York: Bloch.

Liebman, C., and E. Don-Yehiya (1983). *Civil Religion in Israel: Traditional Judaism and Political Culture in the Jewish State.* Berkeley: University of California Press.

Shaffir, W. (1974). *Life in a Religious Community, The Lubavitcher Chassidim in Montreal.* Toronto: Holt, Rinehart & Winston of Canada.

Shmeruk, Ch. (1971). "Yiddish Literature," *Encyclopedia Judaica.* Jerusalem: Keter, 16:807–15.

CHAPTER 7

Life Tradition and Book Tradition in the Development of Ultraorthodox Judaism*

MENACHEM FRIEDMAN

R abbbi Simha Elberg is the editor of *Ha-Pardes*, the oldest es- tablished orthodox rabbinic journal in America. In the course of the mid-1960s, Rabbi Elberg twice called to his readers' attention a new religious phenomenon which he at first called *Bnei Braqism*.[1] The initial discussion appeared in a 1963 issue of *Ha-Pardes;* the second was in a 1965 issue of *Digleinu*,[2] the organ of the ultraorthodox Ze'irei (Young) Agudat Israel. He defined the phenomenon of Bnei Braqism as "the world of *ḥumrot*," that is, stringent interpretations.

"The Bnei Braq concept," wrote Rabbi Elberg, "embodies a *major revolution* (emphasis added) in the very structure of religious life. Bnei Braq is looking for increased rather than decreased stringency. Gener- ally speaking, everyone, even within the religious world, is leaning toward greater permissiveness and lesser restrictivenes ... not so Bnei Braq. A young yeshiva student under the spiritual influence of the Hazon Ish will, when approaching the Shulḥan Arukh [Caro's code of *halakhah*], search out that opinion which forbids, which restricts, which is more stringent. He will not look for the phrase, 'and there are those who are more lenient' nor will he abide by that sort of decision, but will be on the watch for the words: 'there are those who are stricter.'"

Elberg, a very perceptive observer, thus graphically describes the new religious type who makes an all-out effort to discover whether one of the commentators tends toward greater stringency, and when he succeeds in finding one who does, it fills his being with delight (*mehayeh et nafsho*). He then adopts this stringent interpretation, putting it into practice in his home and in his daily life. This testimony fits in well with other evidence attesting to a major revolution in the total system of religious life. What characterizes this revolution is the readiness of the young to criticize the standards generally accepted within the religious community, in the realms of both custom and halakhah, and to institutionalize within their own lives precisely those alternatives which reflect a more stringent approach.

Elberg attributes this phenomenon specifically to those *avreikhim* (young yeshiva students) who live "under the spiritual influence of the Hazon Ish,"[3] Rabbi Avraham Yeshayahu Karlitz, who had died approximately ten years earlier (1953)—a designation which, as shall be shown, is essentially correct. Elberg's description of the strictness-oriented *avreikh* (sing.), as one who "makes an all-out effort toward stringency," is undoubtedly highly ironic, especially when he says that "[the student's] very soul is refreshed" when he succeeds in finding a new *humrah* (sing.). Elberg, whose mother tongue is Yiddish, makes use here of a familiar expression taken from the folk idiom, *"er iz zekh mekhaye neifesh,"* (he refreshes his own soul). The use of this phrase, normally appropriate to physical satisfaction (for example, after a hungry person has been satiated) is not only ironic but also suggestive of an amused bystander. It is clear that Elberg could allow himself to relate to the world of humrot in this manner as it was then only in the first stages of its development. Since then, however, it has become one of the foremost phenomena at work in shaping the life style of all of orthodox Jewry. The tendency to criticize accepted halakhic standards and to prefer, for the most part, the more stringent alternatives is not limited to the modern religious camp. This development within the *haredi* camp, however, arouses special interest from the sociological point of view.

Later on in this paper *haredi* will be defined, but it is clear that one of the outstanding characteristics of that society is its greater commitment to the traditional, Eastern European Jewish way of life. This being the case, it would seem that significant self-conscious changes in halakhah and tradition, even if in the direction of greater stringency, would create tension, since such changes must in some way reflect a certain criticism of the religious leadership of one's forebears.[4] The rhetorical question: "Should we find fault with our predecessors?"[5] is typically used by the watchdogs of the tradition when faced with change and innovation, even when it is in the direction of greater stringency. But this protest is not being voiced as the world of humrot, with its far-reaching changes in central areas of life, expands and conquers by the establishment of halakhic norms consciously different from those prevalent within the homes and the communal world of the previous generation.

Elberg believes that this is due to the influence of the Hazon Ish, and there is much truth in this assertion. As a case study, one halakhic area has been chosen for study—the shi'urim (standard measurements minimally required in the performance of a religious commandment)— in which the Hazon Ish developed norms which, while distinctly different from those generally accepted in the traditional camp, have nonetheless been adopted by almost all sectors of the haredi community in a relatively short time. Briefly, a number of the halakhot (pl.) involve size, weight, volume, and the like. The most obvious example relates to the consumption of matzah (unleavened bread) at the Passover seder meal. Halakhically speaking, at the seder, one must eat a quantity of matzah at least "equivalent to an olive" in order to have fulfilled the religious obligation of eating matzah on Passover. But what is the exact size of an olive, technically speaking? According to the Shulhan Arukh, an olive is slightly less than half an egg.[6] At first glance, these are two measurable items, the average size of which is unmistakable, being as they are both things found in nature. However, as early as the eighteenth century, one of the foremost halakhic sages, Rabbi Ezekiel ben Judah Landau, raises the possibility that "the nature of things has changed" (nishtanu ha-teva'im) that is, the sizes of olives eggs have actually changed over the centuries and are not the same today as they had been in the past.[7] When these ideas were first put forth, these legalistic ruminations had virtually no practical impact on the Jewish community.[8] However, once the possibility of natural things changing was raised and granted legitimacy, it created a potential for change. The Hazon Ish utilized this concept as a basis for a reevaluation of the major shi'urim in the halakhah,[9] and his conclusions represent a revolution in certain basic areas of religious life. He concluded, for example, that the present-day olive and egg are in fact significantly smaller in size than their counterparts in the mishnaic and talmudic periods. Therefore, in order to fulfill the commandment (mitzvah) of eating an olive's worth of matzah at the seder, one must actually eat significantly more than the generally accepted amount.[10] The fact is that the shi'urim of the Hazon Ish have become an accepted halakhic concept, these new measurements having become normative for a large segment of the ḥaredi community.

This particular example has been chosen because it has more critical religious-halakhic significance than the ordinary humrot, for two reasons:

1. The change is a conspicuous one, relating to visible and enduring objects in ceremonies which are central to Jewish life. The strict interpretation generally requires the replacement of a ceremonial object (the *kiddush* cup, that is, the wine goblet used in inaugurating the Sabbath or festivals), or ceremonial clothing (*tallit qatan*),[11] in order to meet the new standards of the shi'urim.

2. The change is not seen in the framework of a preferred alternative, in which the previously accepted norm retains its legitimacy, but as an absolute norm implying negation of other alternatives.

It is not normally expected that such a change would take place within the framework of a conservative society in which the living tradition, including ceremonial objects, is passed on from father to son in an orderly fashion. The fact that the shi'urim of the Hazon Ish became the established norm within such a short period, and with regard to such a broad segment of the ḥaredi community, shows that the latter is indeed different in a number of respects from the traditional religious community as it had developed in Eastern Europe up until the late eighteenth and early nineteenth centuries.

The Concept of Haredi (Ultraorthodox)

The term *haredi* Jewry denotes a Jewish religious community with certain defining characteristics. It has occasionally been described as "traditionalist," committed to halakhah in its traditional interpretation, and also committed to a living, vital tradition (specifically that of Eastern Europe), expressed in dress, language, and the like.[12] This definition is only partially satisfactory because the Eastern European commitment is not equally strong in all areas, nor on the part of all segments of the community. For example, even the most casual observation will reveal, that in those circles known as "Lithuanian" and connected with the *yeshivot gedolot* (advanced yeshivot), there is relatively greater flexibility with regard to the commitment to traditional garb and external appearance. In fact, it could well be argued that within these circles there is a conspicuous, self-conscious trend toward adopting Western European dress and outer appearance. Even if these differences are ignored, however, describing ḥaredi Jewry solely in terms of its traditionalism is inadequate because it overlooks the dynamic element of ongoing change so characteristic of this particular society in the last generation.

A statement, made in the name of Rabbi Israel Meir Ha-Cohen (the Hafetz Haim), provides a starting point for the understanding of the ḥaredi approach: "'Happy is the man who fears the Lord, who delights greatly in his commandments. His seed shall be mighty upon earth: the generation of the upright shall be blessed' (Ps. 112:1–2). The man who truly and completely fears God and greatly desires his 'mitzvot' *does not look for ways to free himself from the mitzvot nor does he seek out* 'qulot' [leniencies, the opposite of humrot] and 'heteirim' [relaxations of restrictions], *but rather fulfills the halakhah as it is, without consideration,* and because of this he is assured that his seed shall be mighty upon earth."[13] This statement must be viewed against the reality of Jewish life in Eastern Europe from the second half of the nineteeth century onward. It was characterized by (1) the increasing erosion of religion and tradition which in turn created a rift between the religious and those who no longer considered themselves bound by religious law (secularists); and (2) a schism within the very community desirous of remaining faithful to halakhah, which developed against a background of growing modernization and secularization, leading to a gradual disintegration of traditional religiosity.

The situation can be described generally, if somewhat simplistically, where, on the one hand, there is a group which consciously aspires to adapt itself in one way or another to the technical, social, and political changes taking place around it (within the context of an overall process of secularization and modernization), while maintaining an essential loyalty to halakhah. This results in tension between the accepted halakhic norms and traditional practices, and the changing social, political, and technological reality; this tension is frequently resolved by means of a compromise granting legitimacy to the modern, up to the limits of halakhic possibility. Concurrently, a second group develops which denies the legitimacy of this trend, not only because it deviates by definition from the established norms, but also because the very capitulation to changing reality, regardless of its formal legitimacy from the halakhic point of view, is seen as a first step in the erosion process which will undoubtedly end (so it is claimed) in the complete abandonment of halakhah as an obligatory norm.

It is in this context that we must relate to the words of the Hafetz Haim, one of the protagonists of the latter group, who accuses the opposite camp of looking for gimmicks by which to free itself from the mitzvot and for *qulot* and *heteirim.* His group is seen as aspiring to fulfill the halakhah as it stands, without consideration, that is, without taking the changing reality into consideration. By definition, this is a select group, an elite, whose heroic ideal is to carry out the mitzvot without consideration. It is paradoxical indeed that this ultraorthodox trend is able to develop and to establish itself precisely against the background of the disintegration of the traditional community as an organic society, bound together by a life style based on halakhah and the traditional practices of the community.

As a community which considers itself responsible for the provision of religious leadership to its members, seeing in this the primary expression of its independent identity, traditional society finds it difficult to cope with uncontrolled organization on the basis of the institutionalization of more stringent halakhic norms, as such organization is a threat to its own cohesion.[14] The formation of an elite based on the delegitimization of those who seek qulot and heteirim on the one hand, and the aspiration to fulfill the halakhah without consideration, on the other hand, leads to the creation of a new religious framework, which may be described as a "voluntary community," insofar as it cannot indiscriminately encompass within its bounds everyone living within a defined geographic area as does the traditional community.

Let us return to the statement of the Hafetz Haim. The religious type described as "one who fears God truly and completely" stands above the usual commonplace religious type. The term *yare'* (fearing), when used to denote this special religious type, is synonymous with the more widespread current term—*haredi*, implying "precision without compromise."[15] The concept of haredi is in fact a dynamic rather than a static one; it also has a psychological dimension, for it is precisely within these religious circles that emphasis is laid on the basic weaknesses of man as a human creature in constant struggle with his basic inclinations, a struggle which only ends with death. Thus, fulfilling the halakhah without considerations should be understood as a goal to which one constantly aspires, but whose attainment on a day-to-day basis is extremely difficult. Nevertheless, it is the obligation of the ḥaredi Jew to view this ultimate goal as the legitimate expression of Judaism in its entirety and to attempt to put it into practice.

Having said this, it must also be noted that ḥaredi Jewry considers itself by definition as bound to tradition. This means that there is an inherent tension between the obligatory attachment to tradition and its own inherent dynamism that encourages the breaching of the framework of tradition in the name of fulfillment of the halakhah without considerations and without qulot and heteirim.

Traditionalism in Eastern Europe, as carried within the family and the community, did not disappear but rather disintegrated, more quickly in the cities and less quickly in the small towns where change was relatively gradual. The living tradition, expressed in relationships and common memories extending back for several generations, and embodied in (1) the lives of individuals whose very existence testified to the validity of that tradition; (2) written testimony; and (3) the actual objects (both apparel and ritual artifacts), which were passed on from generation to generation, inhibited the dynamic potential for religious change inherent in the ḥaredi approach. However, against a background of the erosion of traditional life and of existential crisis within part of the Jewish community, ḥaredi organizational frameworks did develop in Eastern Europe, especially in Poland/Lithuania. These then formed the base for the future development of haredi Judaism.

The Yeshiva Gedolah

The yeshiva gedolah of the kind typified by the Volozhin Yeshiva,[16] has long been recognized as one of the most important internal developments to take place within the traditional Jewish framework. From the standpoint of the present discussion, this organizational/ cultural structure provides the type of voluntary community ideally suited to the needs of ultraorthodoxy. Organizationally speaking, this type of yeshiva incorporates two innovations relative to the traditional Ashkenazi yeshivot:

1. It is not an institution of the community, but rather an economically independent organization supported by the contributions of individuals from many regions.

2. The vast majority of the yeshiva students are not from the community but come from near and far for the purpose of studying there.

This has two further implications.

1. The yeshiva is a total-like institution whose students are, for the most part, alienated from their surroundings and cut off from their families for most of the year, as a result of which they are united amongst themselves, especially around the figure of the rosh yeshiva (head of the yeshiva) and his family. (It is not surprising that the relationships created within this framework are often quasifamiliar.)[17]

2. The students are for the most part young bachelors, economically marginal, who devote most of their time to the study of Torah.

In this sense, the yeshiva is a moratorium institution, and can be defined as a quasimonastic community. Its members are, as has been noted, young men cut off from their families and from direct contact with the halakhic norms and customs which crystallized and became formalized within the local, familial tradition. They spend most of their time in the study of halakhic texts and codes.[18] The system of study employed in the yeshiva tends to develop the students' critical sense; the customs and traditions which they bring with them from home are also exposed to criticism. The seclusion of the yeshiva and the religious tension fostered within it combine to create a situation conducive to the systematic re-examination of family and community traditions through a confrontation with what might be referred to as the "tradition as it finds expression in the codes." The clash between the latter and the tradition anchored in the daily life of a traditional community is, as has been noted, a recognized phenomenon in Jewish history.[19] At times the rabbis succeeded in rooting out a practice which they considered to be misguided; at other times, they were forced to give in to reality and to sanctify that very practice.

Within the quasimonastic community, however, the confrontation was a totally different one. From the outset, the tradition embodied in the codes had the advantage: in the face of the truth emanating from the codes, there was simply no social framework that could be marshalled to come to the support of the ancestral tradition. In the traditional community, if a young man reached the conclusion that this custom or that halakhic norm did not measure up to the standard set by the codes, or if he wished to adopt the more stringent alternative, he would have immediately found himself in conflict with other members of his family and with his surroundings. Within the confines of the yeshiva, however, both the familial framework and the community experience became insignificant and unreal. The yeshiva, as a quasimonastic community alienated from its environment and from economic and social reality, knowingly nurtured the ongoing reexamination of behavior on the basis of a confrontation with the codes and supported the choice of the more stringent alternative.

As has been said, ḥaredi Judaism is consciously committed to the formulation of an elitist self-image. It is relatively simple to develop such an image within the closed groups of students devoted to the study of Torah. Indeed, one of the blatant characteristics of the world of the yeshiva students immersed in Torah learning is the image which they have of themselves as an elite with respect to everyone else, the masses, the *balebatim.*[20] A clear example of this is the saying that "the opinion of the *balebatim* is the reverse of the opinion of the Torah,"[21] which reflects an intellectually elitist self-image, contemptuous of all who are not a part of it. This is also the source of the inverted conception of *merkaz* (center) and *s'vivah* (surroundings, or periphery), which places the yeshivot at the *merkaz*, the true center of existence, in contrast to everything else, which is seen as simply the *s'vivah* in which everything is imaginary, and whose sole raison d'etre is to make possible the existence of the center.[22] The refrain of a Yiddish song,[23] popular among yeshiva students, expresses this clearly and unequivocally:

When the world will be
full of yeshivot
Many centers
and few peripheries
They will learn Torah then
without limit.
Lord of the Universe, when will it be granted to us?

In such an atmosphere, no importance is assigned to practices and traditions that are seen to oppose the halakhic norms of the learned elite. The haredi ideal of "fearing God truly and completely, without searching for gimmicks by which to avoid fulfilling the mitzvot," thus finds a fertile soil, well suited to its development, in the quasimonastic community exemplified by the Volozhin-type yeshiva.

Within the Jewish world of Eastern Europe, faced with extreme economic hardship, and with the very basis of Jewish existence being challenged and the erosion of religion and tradition on the increase, the world of the yeshivot was in a defensive position. Whereas such yeshivot had been open to general currents within the Jewish world at the beginning of the nineteenth century, by the end of the century they had become strongholds of the haredi outlook, reinforced by the Musar movement.[24] Haredism was concentrated in one part of the Jewish world (the Lithuanian/Polish sector), alongside the traditional community found in Hasidic Poland and in other areas with heavy Jewish populations. Paradoxically, it was the destruction of Eastern European Jewry in the twentieth century that created the conditions which enabled the spread of ultraorthodoxy.

New Social Bases of the Growth of Ultraorthodoxy

World War II and the Holocaust created new conditions conducive to the further development of the haredi ideal. First was the changing geographic base or the transition to the West. World War II was the tragic climax to the process of migration, which had already started in the 1880s, in which the center of life and creative religious Judaism was transferred from Eastern Europe to the metropolitan centers of the West. This process, which enhanced the erosion of traditional society, eventually created a situation which was conducive as well to the development of haredi society.

The geographic change caused a break in the direct personal relationships which had characterized the traditional community. In the western countries to which the migrants came, voluntary communities developed. The conditions for membership in voluntary communities are determined by the members themselves, thus replacing the traditional, geographically determined community.[25] The process of migration to the West, at least until World War II, was accompanied by secularization and the weakening of tradition, which naturally had an affect on the character of the vast majority of voluntary communities, including those which consider themselves Orthodox. The latter have been pressured to adopt an attitude of tolerance toward deviation from religion and tradition, and even to find halakhic legitmacy for these trends. They aspired to create a harmonious relationship between halakhah and the values and norms of modern western society, and to minimize the points of conflict between them, based on the assumption that there is no essential contradiction between halakhah and modernity. At the same time, a similar process was under way in Eretz Yisrael; the development of the Zionist Yishuv (community) was also affected by the processes of modernization and secularization. Religious Zionism was also involved in this process, not only in that it had to grant legitimacy to the actions and omissions of militantly secular groups, but primarily in creating experimental social frameworks within which they sought to harmonize, in some way, halakhah and modernity. This experiment entailed what can only be called "concessions" relative to various elements of both tradition and halakhah. This author has previously defined this religious approach as "diminished religiosity" (Friedman 1984). Due to the fact that the process was realized within the framework of the creation of a new Zionist Jewish society in Eretz Yisrael, and in conjunction with the autonomous community groupings of the Yishuv under the authority of a local chief rabbinate, it led to an identification and overlapping between this diminished religiosity and religious Zionism.

Paradoxically, these very same processes formed the background for the development of stringency, that is, haredism. Migration broke the direct connection with the traditional community and this was followed by the Holocaust which involved tremendous human loss and the destruction of the sociocultural milieu in which traditional religion had developed. Practically speaking, it also entailed a loss of household items and religious artifacts that had been passed down through the generations, and in which tradition and custom were embodied. When the tradition-minded groups who had survived the Holocaust came together in the sociocultural reality of the West and of Eretz Yisrael, they found that the living tradition, which they had cherished, had been totally broken; their aim was therefore to rebuild the society which had been and to enlist new members, given the existence of a diminished orthodox Jewish community in the background. Three main factors determined the direction which the renewal was to take:

1. The rupture of the living tradition, which had been transmitted directly from generation to generation, naturally created a sense of a lack of confidence, the remedy for which was found in the strengthening of the attachment to the tradition of the book, written halakhah.

2. With the disappearance of the traditional Jewish world of Eastern Europe in the smoke of the concentration camp furnaces, there developed within the general Jewish world a romantic nostalgic attitude toward the culture which had been. Within the confines of the Jewish society which remained faithful to halakhah, and especially among those elements desirous of reconstructing that which had been, this expressed itself in a clearcut tendency to see the society that was as having been composed of righteous people, a society in which daily life and the tradition of the book were in full harmony with each other.

3. The experience of diminished religiosity constituted a negative reference norm to those attempting to reconstruct the society that had been. The primary basis for the delegitimization of diminished religiosity was its deviation from the norms of halakhah and tradition as found in halakhic literature, based on an unequivocal commitment to the latter as the determinant of life's norms.[26]

These developments found expression within the framework of the voluntary community, an associational framework based on individual choice and not related in any essential way to a geographic determinant. The voluntary community reflects what Berger (1969, 137-49) calls "the market situation," which is characterized by the believer who is free to choose for himself the form of ritual to espouse within a community of believers that he chooses to join. Clearly, in a market situation, great importance is attached to the recruitment of new members to a given community, both for ideological and for straightforward economic reasons. It is this need to grow numerically that underlies the relative pluralism within the Jewish community, even that part of the community which considers itself bound to halakhah in its traditional sense (orthodoxy), and accepts the establishment of communities on the basis of the lowest common denominator in respect to halakhic obligation. At the same time, this situation also allows for the creation of an exclusive voluntary community, based on an elite which tries to fufill the halakhah by choosing the more stringent alternatives. Moreover, the existence of diminished communities, characterized among other things by deviation from tradition and organized on a voluntary basis, frees the more strictly oriented community from its obligation to those who do not want, or are not able, to meet the criteria of a stringent ḥaredi religious approach.

It can therefore be said that it is precisely against the background of the disintegration of the traditional geographically defined community, and the development of voluntary communities, that the way was opened for an institutionalized expression of stringency as reflected in halakhic and Musar literature. Actually, this opened the way for individuals and groups to compete, as it were, among themselves on the degree of stringency and intransigency, within the range of alternatives found in the halakhic literature.

The stringent voluntary communities are in fact selective communities reflecting an elitist approach and are reminiscent of the quasimonastic communities described; the development of the former (ḥaredi) is surely related to the renewal and development of the quasimonastic yeshivot in the West.

The history of the yeshivot gedolot in the West and in Eretz Yisrael is both interesting and important, but cannot be discussed here. Briefly, it should be noted that, until World War II, these institutions were part of the Jewish religious culture of Poland/Lithuania, and, to some extent, of Hungary as well. In the West, they were seen as an essential antidote to the life style of the lands of immigration. A few attempts were made to establish institutions of this sort in Germany and Eretz Yisrael but their influence was at first marginal in the extreme. It was only after World War II that Volozhin-type yeshivot began to flourish there.

Several reasons can be given for this development. Among these are the development of the modern welfare state, economic growth, and the adaptation of traditional religious Judaism to the contemporary metropolis, allowing the recruitment of young people to the yeshivot communities for the entire period of socialization, until marriage and even afterward (in *kollel*-s).[27] Whatever the reasons for the growth of the Volozhin-type yeshiva in the West after World War II, there is no doubt that this development signals one of the most decisive changes within orthodox Jewry in the West and in Eretz Yisrael. The fact that, since the second half of the 1950s, the vast majority of the young men

who identify with the haredi camp spent the most important part of
their formative years—as human beings and as Jews—in a total-like institution has decisive implications for the image of present-day
haredi society.

A number of the relevant consequences of experiencing life within
these quasimonastic communities have been discussed. To summarize,
the removal of young people from their family circle during a period so
crucial to the formation of their world view, and their placement in a
totalizing framework in which they come face-to-face with the rich
book tradition of the Jewish people, coupled with the crystallization of
an elitist self-image and the concept of a center, are experiences which
must lead to criticism of the parental religious tradition.

The fact that, beginning with the 1950s, the vast majority of haredi
young men spent all their time learning Torah within a Volozhin-type
yeshiva (the dominant prototype today among Hasidic groups as well),
reflects a most significant social change. The voluntary communities
established by the graduates of these yeshivot, or in which they are the
dominant element, are known as kehillot lomdim (communities of
scholars). They are communities whose members are able to come to
grips with halakhic questions by means of direct confrontation with
the multifaceted legal literature of the codes, whether they continue to
immerse themselves in the study of Torah or whether they direct their
energies toward making a living. In the majority of cases the level of
Torah knowledge of these young men is much greater that that of their
parents.[28] This situation lays the foundation for the delegitimization of
the traditions and practices of the families from which they came, the
latter generally being put in the category of 'amei ha-aretz (ignoramuses
of the Torah).[29] If that same family is in any way identified with
diminished religiosity, then the process of family rejection is greatly enhanced, since the only basis on which to recreate a completely religious/
halakhic world is the corpus of legal decisions embodied in the
codes.

Legal literature, like the rest of halakhic literature, is to be found
throughout the haredi community. There is hardly a haredi family
today that does not possess an extensive Torah halakhah library. This is
particularly true of the middle generation which was educated in the
yeshivot. In addition to the classics, one also finds more recent sum-
maries of the codes, adapted to the strict approach. These are composed
by talmidei hakhamim (scholars), primarily from the kollels; they relate
to actual issues, are understood easily, and can be put into practice

directly. Most instructive is the fact that, prior to every holiday or out-of-the-ordinary halakhic/religious event, the book market is flooded with legal-type literature intended to guide the reader through the thicket of halakhot related specifically to the festival or event. The streets of ultraorthodox neighborhoods, such as Me'a She'arim in Jerusalem, or Bnei Braq, are covered with posters advertising the availability of this literature. Under these circumstances, the triumph of the legal tradition over the life tradition, as represented by the natural families, is assured.

One must not disassociate these changes from the reality of economics and technology. The rise in the standard of living of haredi families living in the metropolitan centers of the West and of Eretz Yisrael, makes possible, for the first time in Jewish history, a Jewish existence in which one can live by the Torah and carry out the mitzvot in comfort; it is now economically feasible to meet the demands imposed by the stricter interpretation. The increased standard of living, combined with the modern welfare state, allows the vast majority of young men growing up in the haredi community to achieve an advanced halakhic education. Technological changes also create new realities which make it possible to choose a stringent alternative, without that choice creating insurmountable difficulties. All of this undoubtedly influences the world of humrot.

Summary

This analysis has emphasized the background processes of secularization and modernization on the one hand, and the uprooting of Eastern European Jewry and its migration to the West on the other. The disintegration of the traditional Jewish community, the rise of the monastic community and a voluntarily based haredi society are the factors which make the dialectic process of rebellion and continuity—as represented in the world of humrot—possible.

The importance of these factors in preparing the ground for the growth of ultraorthodoxy is highlighted by reference to the shi'urim of the Hazon Ish. The ability of Rabbi Karlitz to institutionalize these significant changes in ritual expresses, more than anything else, the rupture within the living tradition. Is it conceivable that within a geographically and historically continuous society, characterized by direct contacts between several generations, in which ritual objects are handed down from generation to generation, that one person (as great a scholar as he might be) could arise and state that the accepted practices, relating to central ceremonies, must be significantly changed, without causing a reaction that would rock the society? The establishment of revised norms can only be understood against the background of a breakdown in tradition, on the one hand, and the emergence of a new generation, educated in total-like institutions and directly involved with halakhic literature, on the other. This almost complete commitment to halakhic literature, as the sole foundation for a fully religious way of life, makes it possible to create a religious experience and a new reality linked to past generations not through direct contact with their life style but through their books.

Notes

*This is part of a book-length study on "Traditional Orthodox Judaism: Continuity and Change," which will be published under the auspices of the Jerusalem Center for Israel Studies.

1. Bnei Braq is a city near Tel Aviv in which there is a concentration of ultraorthodox groups.

2. *Ha-Pardes* (The Orchard), Kislev 5724 (New York), and *Digleinu* (Our Banner), Kislev-Tevet 5725 (Tel Aviv).

3. It is common practice to refer to famous rabbis by the name of one of their major works. The Hazon Ish immigrated to Palestine from Vilna, settling in Bnei Braq in 1935.

4. This problem has dogged traditional halakhic literature whenever halakhists have attempted to question a local custom which, while having been in practice for generations, has appeared to go against the halakhah. The technical phrase used by those who try to protect the tradition against the innovators is that the change would imply *la'az al ha-'avot* (slander of the progenitors). One well-known example took place in Perpignan, in the Provence, as the result of the arrival of disciples of Nachmanides, from Gerona, in the middle of the thirteenth century, and their questioning of local practice. In his treatise, *Magen Aboth* (1909), R. Menahem Meiri strongly resisted this attack, attempting to protect the honor and religious status of previous generations which had been indirectly undermined by the disciples of Nachmanides: "It behooves all those who would challenge, to consider the fact that the practices of our ancient forebears and the early sages, whose fingernails were superior to our bellies, were not devoid of reason. It is preferable to attribute it to one's own lack of knowledge than to the lack of knowledge on the part of our forefathers and the ancient sages."

5. This phrase is taken from a letter written in 1784 by R. Abraham Katzenelbogen to R. Isaac Levi of Berdichev in which he speaks out against changes in the ancestral tradition introduced by the Hasidim, changes expressing a pietistic trend toward greater stringency (see Dubnow 1962, 31).

6. *Shulhan Arukh, Orah Haim,* cap. 486. Another example is that of the size of the *revi'it* which, in regard to the wine drunk for *kiddush* (the blessing sanctifying the Sabbath) on Friday night, is "an egg and a half."

7. This has been discussed in the book on Tractate *Pesahim* by R. Y. Landau (1876, 109). The concept that "nature has changed" since talmudic times is already found in early halakhic literature. In every case, the concept is used to explain away contradictions between medical remedies or physiological knowledge in the Talmud, and the practical, everyday experience of the halakhists of a later period. For example: (a) The Talmud (BT *'Avodah Zarah* 24b) states that a cow less than three years of age is incapable of calving, which contradicted the experience of the Tosafists (twelfth to fourteenth centuries) who knew that a two-year-old cow could already do so. Therefore, the latter determined that "it is certain that the time period is different now from what it was in former times;" and (b) The Talmud (BT *Mo'ed Qatan* 11a) recommends the eating of fish close to the time when it begins to stink. To this the Tosafists commented that "in our time, those who [go to] the [fish] barrel near the time when it begins to stink are in danger." They explain away the contradiction between that which was medically accepted in their time and in talmudic times with the possibility that "it may have changed, like the medical remedies found in the Mishnah which are not appropriate to our time." However, the comments of R. Landau are essentially different as the reference is not to a contradiction between daily experience and the early sources, but to a new idea relating to central areas of religious life.

8. This arises out of the text itself which is exegetical rather than legal, as well as from the words of R. Landau's most distinguished disciple, R. Eleazer Flekeles (1809, *Yoreh De'ah,* cap. 324).

9. See *Kuntras ha-Shi'urim* in the commentary of the Hazon Ish on the *Shulhan Arukh, Orah Haim, Hilkhot Shabbat* (Bnei Braq, 1957). R. Karlitz was indeed preceded in this respect by the *Hafetz Haim,* R. Yisrael Meir Ha-Cohen (1896–197, *Hilkhot Shabbat,* cap. 271c), but he does not reach a definitive decision (like Karlitz), and his opinion is only a matter of good advice. See Ha-Cohen's commentary *Be'ur Halakhah,* there, to sub-cap. 13.

10. From the very beginning, the conclusions drawn by the Hazon Ish created a halakhic controversy. See Avraham Hai Noeh (1943) and Yaakov Kanevsky (1948). Kanevsky (Steipler), who was the brother-in-law of the Hazon Ish, attempts to come to grips with two issues: (1) the problem of changing that which had been accepted in the past; and (2) the extent to which the acceptance of the basic principle that the measures set by the Torah are relative rather than absolute ("when the shi'urim were given at Sinai, they were given in approximation"), would adversely affect the structure of traditional orthodox society.

This notwithstanding, he claims, it does not reflect any attempt to ascribe either truth or error to the views of various authorities. The legal decisions of the great sages of the generation, such as R. Landau, and those who came after him, are binding on all because these sages have been given the right to determine halakhah. See Kanevsky (1966, 15–17).

11. Many orthodox Jews of Eastern Europe provenance will wear a garment (usually between their undergarments and outer clothing), with ritual fringes attached. This is considered a fuller observance of the law (Num. 15:38) than just wearing the prayer shawl (talllit) during morning prayers. This special garment is known as the tallit qatan.

12. In my opinion the Eastern European, Ashkenazi character of haredi Jewry remains unquestionable to this day. There are recent signs of similar developments within some segments of Middle Eastern Jewry but this is largely a self-conscious imitation of the haredi (Ashkenazi) structure. The vast majority of the Middle Eastern haredi Jews have studied either in Ashkenazi haredi institutions or in those modeled after them.

13. Meir Hai Yoshor (1959, 2:481n). See also "Hafetz Haim" (1838–1933), in EJ, 9:1068–70.

14. A good example of this is the incident cited by R. Jacob Reischer (1719, Yoreh De'ah, cap. 58). In one of the communities, the rabbis ruled that meat brought from the smaller communities of the surrounding villages was not kosher because the slaughterers in those places were thought not to know enough and/or not to be careful enough, by the stricter standards of the Jewish community in the large city. R. Reischer unequivocally rejects this approach, but not because he considered those slaughterers to be outstanding scholars. He admits that his position might be considered "lenient," but he defends it on the basis of the principle of the cohesion of the traditionally religious community, which might be adversely affected by the disqualification of village slaughterers. "It is proper for all Israel to be as one man in matters of eating and drinking, and not to distinguish, as Israel is distinguished from them (the nations); we should not multiply separate groups." There is no doubt that R. Reischer's approach represents a deeply rooted Jewish tradition.

15. See Avraham Wolf, one of the major ideologists of haredi Jewry in the present generation, in the local periodical Le-Hoshvei Shemo (Bnei Braq), Tammuz 1979,21), wherein he describes the haredi woman as "one who does not eat anything regarding which a scholar has made a ruling," that is, she is stricter for herself even with regard to something which a rabbi ruled as permissible for consumption because some doubt had been raised concerning it.

16. Volozhin, a town in Lithuania, was the site of a major yeshiva, founded at the beginning of the nineteenth century, which attracted students from many countries. Like other yeshivot gedolot, it emphasized the study of Talmud. See Stampfer (1981).

17. Almost every description of the rosh yeshiva (head of the yeshiva) by students emphasizes the fatherly image and the fact that his relations with them were oftentimes at the expense of his family. See, for example, Rabiner (1968, 37, 55).

18. Rabbinic literature which codified the halakhah in a brief, understandable, fashion, as opposed to the literature which discussed the various sides of halakhic questions.

19. See above, note 4.

20. Literally: home-owners. Those who (successfully) spend their time making a living rather than studying Torah.

21. See Meir Hai Yoshor (1958, 1:165n). Another example comes from the exegetic commentary of R. Elhanan Wasserman, one of the outstanding personalities of haredi Jewry of the generation preceding World War II, on Hosea 4:12: "Anyone who rules (leniently) receives the support of the masses." See Aharon Sorsky (1970, 300n). This approach is the keystone of the overall attitude of the Hazon Ish and his disciples. Another example: "Most of the masses follow their base desires and, in any case, we know that the truth is the opposite of what is believed by the masses." See Shlomo Cohen (1966-1973, part 4, 242).

22. Moshe Sheinfeld, an outstanding ideologist of haredi Jewry, wrote in the name of the Hazon Ish: "The Maharam from Lublin [sixteenth century] uses the expression the world asks very frequently and yet, if we go out into the streets of the city we will discover that 'the world' does not ask such questions at all. But we should learn from this that only those who are deeply engrossed in the questions and problems of the Holy Torah are called "the *true* world." See A. Rater (1978).

In haredi legends, the following story, which also reflects this attitude, is told in the name of R. Yehezkiel Loewenstein. "The Soviet authorities laid a long rail line in a remote district which was not economically viable (the Trans-Siberian Railroad), and no one could explain why the line had been laid and why it continued to operate. Only during World War II, when the line was used for the transfer of the Yeshiva of Mir from Lithuania to Japan, thus saving its students from annihilation, did the matter become clear. The railroad had been built and operated in order that, when the time came, it could be used to save the yeshiva." See *Kol be-Ramah*, local newspaper of the Ramat Aharon neighborhood of Bnei Braq, no 49, 1984.

23. Based on a song I learned in my youth as a yeshiva student. Its authenticity is vouched for by the rhyming which accords with Lithuanian Yiddish pronunciation.

24. The Musar movement developed in the latter part of the nineteenth century and stressed moral self-criticism. Musar literature became influential in yeshiva circles after it was viewed as a defense against secular influence.

25. Certain aspects of this process have been dealt with in Friedman (1982).

26. The following description of the changes which took place within the community of Gur Hasidim under the influence of R. Yisrael Alter, when their center moved from Poland to Jerusalem, is a typical reflection of this process: "On new/old foundations did R. Alter build his new house, the Building of the old House of Gur . . . to adapt the ways of Hasidism to the halakhah and to every letter in the halakhah" (Levine 1977, 150).

27. An institution of advanced talmudic study in which married men spend their time when not engaged in making a livelihood. The Kollel in late nineteenth century Eastern Europe was associated with the Musar movement (note 24).

28. Moshe Sheinfeld attempts to explain this change as follows: "Only in the environment of the Jewish villages [in Europe], which was steeped in Torah and the fear of God, could one find simple Jewish folk who, despite their ignorance, were respectful of their rabbis and truly believed in God and in his Torah. Within the secular environment of the Yishuv [in Israel] there is no possibility of an exception to the rule: 'an ignorant person is not fearful of sin.'" Digleinu, Iyyar 5715 (1955).

29. This reality often creates tension within haredi society. For example, the American R. Haim Poupko has stated: "Those who continue the tradition of their ancestors, and live by the rules of halakhah and behave according to what they have seen at home, are not sufficiently haredi; there are even those who are ashamed of the splendid past of their forebears," Tsohar (Jerusalem), Nisan 1983. A graphic reflection of this situation can be found in the following vignette which appeared in Ha-Modi'a, January 29, 1982, the newspaper of Agudat Yisrael, the main haredi political party. A group of haredi children, whose appearance testified to this fact (clothing, sidelocks, and the like) is deep in argument. Suddenly, one of the debaters turns to another and says something which is obviously intended to decide the argument: "My grandmother saw it on TV." His companions are silent for a moment and then one says in amazement: "What! Your grandmother looks at TV?" (There is a generally accepted prohibition on watching TV among haredi Jews.) The first child is confused for a minute but quickly composes himself and says: "My grandmother is from the previous generation."

References Cited

Berger, P. (1969). The Social Reality of Religion. London: Faber.

Cohen, S. (1966-1973). Peer ha-Dor (on Rabbi A. Y. Karlitz). 4 vols. Bnei Braq. Nezah.

Dubnow, S. (1962). *Chassidiana* (Oppositional Writings to Hasidism). Jerusalem: Akademon, Hebrew University of Jerusalem (in Hebrew).

Flekeles, E. (1809). *Teshuva me-Ahavah*. Prague: Franz Gommer.

Friedman, M. (1982). "The Changing Role of the Community Rabbinate." *The Jerusalem Quarterly* 25:79-99.

———. (1984). "The NRP in Transition-Behind the Party's Electoral Decline." In D. Caspi, A. Diskin, E. Gutman, eds. *The Roots of Begin's Success*. London: Croom Helm, 141-68.

Ha-Cohen, Y. M. (1896-1907). *Mishnah Berurah*. Warsaw.

Kanevsky, Y. (1948). *Shi'urim de-Oraytah*. Bnei Braq.

———. (1966). *Yesodot Ne'emanim*. Bnei Braq.

Landau, Y. (1876). *Ziyyun le-Nefesh Hayyah*. Lemberg.

Levine, Y.L. (1977). *The Admors of Gur*. Jerusalem. Hebrew.

Meiri, M. (1909). *Magen Aboth*. I. Last, ed. London: I. Narodiczky (in Hebrew).

Noeh, A. H. (1943). *Shi'urei Torah*. Jerusalem.

Rabiner, A. Z. (1968). *Ha-Gaon Rabbi Eliezer Gordon...* Tel Aviv (in Hebrew).

Rater, A. (1978). *Hashqafatenu* (Bnei Braq) 2:95.

Reischer, J. (1719). *Shevut Ya'aqov*. Halle: Bar Avraham.

Stampfer, S. (1981). *Three Lithuanian Yeshivot in the Nineteenth Century*. Ph.D. diss. Hebrew University of Jerusalem (in Hebrew, English summary).

Sorsky, A. (1970). *Ahiezer, A Collection of Letters: Selected Memoirs* (on Rabbi Hayyim Ozer Grodzinski). vol. 1. Bnei Braq: Nezah (in Hebrew).

Yoshor, M. H. (1958 - 1961). *The Hafetz Haim: His Life and Work*. 3 vols. Tel Aviv: Nezah (in Hebrew).

CHAPTER 8

The Symbolic Inscription of Zionist Ideology in the Space of Eretz Yisrael: Why the Native Israeli is called *Tsabar**

TSILI DOLEVE-GANDELMAN

Introduction

In contemporary Hebrew the term *tsabar,*[1] or cactus, has come to mean a child born in Eretz Yisrael[2] at the time of the Yishuv,[3] or thereafter. Popular etymology sees it as an affectionate nickname appropriate to the native Israeli who appears to be rough and prickly on the outside, but warm and kindhearted inside (Eben Shoshan 1980, 5:2198). In this paper, it will be shown that the notion of tsabar acts as a symbolic "shifter,"[4] or passage-operating agent, between history and nature, and that this is the basis of its symbolic efficacy.

The Jewish, Hebrew-speaking child, by virtue of his being called a tsabar, may be viewed as a linguistic shifter. The child is both an index (pointing to an existential relationship with its land of birth in which he/she is "rooted"), and a symbol (tsabar also belongs to the specific code of Zionist ideology). Similarly, the tsabar child is a shifter between time and space—or, in other words, between history and the actual land of the Jewish people. Here, history means symbols, myth, and a code-ruled relatedness; land, in its concreteness, means contact as well as an existential relatedness and an existential pointing. It is primarily through the concept of tsabar that Zionist ideology, growing out of Jewish history, was symbolically inscribed in the space of Eretz Yisrael.

257

Unraveling this web of meaning requires the consideration of several topics: (1) the conceptual connection between Zionism and Zion (Eretz Yisrael) as a circumscribed space; (2) the role of the Jewish National Fund or the *Keren Kayemet le-Israel* (KKL) in the concrete realization of this connection; and (3) the function of the preschool system in its symbolic implementation and the part played by the KKL within this preschool system.

The connection between Zionist ideology, the Jewish people, and the land of Israel was accomplished constitutionally as well as symbolically by the KKL. At the time of the Yishuv, the existing autonomous system of education was one of the main channels for the transmission of Zionist ideology. Although this paper relates exclusively to the preschool system, involving children from three to six years of age, the symbolic function of the tsabar is not limited only to this age category. However, it is during the kindergarten years that the ceremonies and rituals expressing the ultimate values of the ideology under examination are the most frequent. Thus, the links between the Hebrew kindergarten in Eretz Yisrael and Zionist ideology can be best observed at this level. It is also at this level that the functioning of the KKL, as the embodiment of the connection of the people with the land (and with the nature of Eretz Yisrael), can best be described.

This study thus attempts to demonstrate that the tsabar acts as a symbolic shifter from history to nature, from linear time to cyclical time (that is nature time). In order to illustrate this, symbolic events, such as the birthday ceremony, shall be referred to: first, as it was performed in the kindergarten (a ritual which to some extent was appropriated by the KKL); and second, as it was performed under the aegis of the KKL as the birthday ceremony of that organization. Also dealt with will be a second metaphorical use of the ceremony (the actual birthday of the child being the only celebration which is nonmetaphorical)—the so-called birthday of the almond tree—the harbinger of spring. It is the symbolic network of relationships between all of these elements which will eventually support the view of the tsabar as an agent shifting history into nature.

The Beginnings of Zionism and the Links with the Land

Zionism, like its predecessor, the *Hibbat Zion*[5] movement, derives its name from Zion. In the Bible, Zion, the old name for the "City of

David" (II Sam. 5:7), came to designate Jerusalem and the whole kingdom of Judah (Is. 1:27). It also referred to the people of Israel (Is. 51:16) and sometimes to Eretz Yisrael, "The Land of Israel," as in "The ways of Zion do mourn" (Lam. 1:4). Moreover, Zion expresses the particular connection between exile (the first Babylonian Exile) and Eretz Yisrael, as in the Psalm "By the rivers of Babylon, there we sat and wept when we remembered Zion" (Ps. 173:1).

In the twelfth century, the poet Judah Halevi, whose sacred poetry is centered on Eretz Yisrael and especially on the intimate relationship between the God of Israel, the people of Israel, and Eretz Yisrael, also used the term *Zion* in a similar sense (see *Eben Shoshan* 1980, 5:2221). Halevi, who attempted a pilgrimage to Zion during the insecure time of the Crusades, wrote a famous "Ode to Zion" beginning with the lines: "Zion! Wilt thou not ask if peace be with thy captives?"(Halevi 1924, 3–7).

At the end of the nineteenth century, N. H. Imber, who lived in Eretz Yisrael, wrote the poem *Ha-Tikvah*, "Hope," which became the hymn of the Zionist movement and later the national anthem of the State of Israel. In this hymn, Zion expresses the links between the people of Israel and Eretz Yisrael, and also the longing for the land (see EJ, 7:1471).

The modern term *Zionism* was actually coined by Nathan Birnbaum in 1890 in the journal he edited, *Selbstemanzipation* (Self Emancipation). This term was subsequently adopted by Herzl, who used it at the First Zionist Congress. Zionism, therefore, was defined as the movement whose goal was the return of the Jewish people to Eretz Yisrael.

Among all the organs of the Zionist movement, it was the KKL that put into concrete form the connection between this ideology and Eretz Yisrael. Its function was the purchasing and amelioration of the land in Zion, that is, the region in the Ottoman Empire known as Palestine and Syria and, later, under the British Mandate, as Palestine.

It was explicitly stated that the land was to remain in public ownership, as formulated during the fifth Zionist Congress (in 1901) which created the KKL: "The KKL shall be the eternal possession of the Jewish people." The KKL was the Zionist version of an agrarian reform (though, in this particular case the reform preceded the purchasing of the land). It was important to centralize the purchasing of land in order to minimize speculation in a region that was in its first phase of settlement and development (Orni 1980).

Though the idea of the KKL was a revolutionary one, it shared several reference points with Jewish tradition. Hermann Shapira, who first proposed the idea of the KKL, based his conception on the biblical institution of the jubilee year as it is expressed in Leviticus (25:33): "The land shall not be sold for ever." The very name "Keren Kayemet le-Israel" is also part of Jewish tradition since it is derived from the talmudic dictum about good deeds: "The fruit of which a man enjoys in this world, while the capital abides [*keren kayemet*] for him in the world to come" (Mishnah *Pe'ah* 1, 1). The good deed, the financing of the KKL, was to be drawn from a wide strata of the Jewish people. The KKL created a worldwide organization for fundraising by means of special stamps, inscriptions in a Golden Book (*Sefer ha-Zahav*), contributions for the planting of trees and reforestation and, above all, via the blue box.

At the beginning of the century, this tin box, designed like a charity box, was in more than one hundred thousand Jewish homes (Laqueur 1972). The KKL was felt to be the property of the entire Jewish people. For all its revolutionary character, the blue box was, nevertheless, the successor of other tin boxes with charity purposes. As the poet Tchernichovsky wrote:

My grandfather had the Meir Ba'al ha-Ness tin box
I have in my room the blue box of KKL
My rabbi is Ussishkin.[6]

The box of Rabbi Meir Ba'al ha-Ness was also widely used in Jewish homes. It was intended to collect money for the support of Jews who lived in the four holy cities in Eretz Yisrael.

The originality of the KKL is, on the one hand, its concretization of the goal of Zionism, that is, the *redemption of the land* and its dialectical counterpart, the *redemption of the people*. On the other hand, it maintained points of reference derived from Jewish tradition. In a sense, it united the temporal depth (the Jewish tradition) with the spatial extension (the worldwide distribution) of the Jewish people. These two aspects of the KKL made it the dominant symbol of Zionist ideology, especially within the educational system. The KKL was not a mere purchaser of land but also the permanent creator and generator of symbols aimed at proclaiming the rights of the Jews to Eretz Yisrael—a right which was based on an historic pact but which now derived its meaning from the concept of the redemption of the land.

J. Weitz (1936), who was the KKL official in charge of the afforesta-
tion, and one of its chief ideologues, wrote in the first volume of
Shorashim ("Roots"), the journal of teachers employed by the KKL in
Eretz Yisrael (23–24):

> The forest was the glory of Nature. . . . In the days of yore, Israel had
> been covered with forests[7]. . . . Yet, in the course of our Exile it was con-
> tinually the object of conquest, wars and depredation for conquering
> peoples who succeeded in denuding her and left her deserted and naked,
> arid and sterile as she today appears under our gaze. . . . And when the
> sons of Israel returned to their land at the beginning of the *Hibbat Zion*
> movement and they saw there were no longer trees in the land, they
> began to plant anew as though from the very beginning (*mibereshit*).

The establishment of a connection with the land for redemption of
the Jewish people was not the exclusive idea of the KKL. It was also present in a variety of ideological trends, such as the idea of the produc-
tivization of the Jewish people and the socialist ideas as interpreted and
propagated by the labor movement in Eretz Yisrael (*tenu'at ha-'avodah*).
Above all, it was A. D. Gordon, influenced by Tolstoyan ideas and the
Russian *Narodnicki*, who gave the cosmic dimension to working the
land of Eretz Yisrael. Gordon insisted that the only means of redemption for the Jewish people was through the creation of a new intimate
link with nature (see Laqueur 1972, 285ff.).

Hebrew Preschool Education and the Zionist Vision
in Eretz Yisrael

The beginnings of the Hebrew kindergarten and its development
are inseparable from the history and the struggles of the Zionist movement. The new educational tradition was, in fact, the result of permanant interaction between various pedagogical doctrines of European
and American derivation, on the one hand, and the ideological objectives of a society in the process of self-constitution, on the other. These
objectives were the creation of a new form of existence, of a new
cultural tradition. In this context, the kindergarten teachers saw the integration of the newly acquired professional doctrines with the wider
objectives set by society as their chief task. The more remarkable
among them were members of the Second Aliyah.[8]

The society of the Yishuv, with its futuristic orientation (Eisen-stadt 1967), was naturally interested in the young generation. The autonomous Jewish network of schools, which grew rapidly under the British Mandate (Minkovitch 1972), is witness to this attitude. The young generation was seen as the carrier of changes within the family during the school and preschool years, and also as young adults-to-be. It was the child who embodied the message of a new culture via a new language which was to be introduced into the home. Thus, through the educational system, the sociocultural vision, which was the heritage of the elite, was to be transmitted to the new generation, and to their parents. Hence, the paramount importance of creating and acquiring dominant symbols and values for this educational system.

The kindergarten therefore became the focus of considerable efforts aimed at inducing the children, and also their parents, to adopt an emotional attitude toward the new symbols and values. The holidays which express the return of a people to its own land played a vital role in the kindergarten.

Three phases characterize the development of the kindergarten during the period of the Yishuv. The first Hebrew-speaking kindergarten was created by Esther Schapira of Rishon-le-Zion in 1898, but was the brainchild of David Yudelevitch, the local school teacher.

In Rishon-le-Zion, as in other localities, the schools were financed by Baron Edmond de Rothschild. Yudelevitch, however, was a disciple of Ben Yehudah, prophet of the revival of the Hebrew language and creator and propagator of the Hebrew through Hebrew method in language teaching. For Yudelevitch, the main function of the Hebrew kindergarten was to prepare the children for the acquisition of the Hebrew language in their later school years.

The second phase in the development of the Hebrew kindergarten in Eretz Yisrael began with the arrival of the first professional teachers from the Froebel-Pestalozzi Haus in Berlin. It was thanks to them that the kindergarten succeeded in freeing itself from the constraints that had hindered its development enabling it to become a true kindergarten (Fayens-Glick 1956). The strength of this group of teachers stemmed, first of all, from their professionalism; secondly, from their missionary drive; and thirdly, from the power delegated to them by the *Hilfsverein*[9] to open a teachers' college for kindergarten teachers in Jerusalem.[10]

The British Mandate (1920–1948) was the beginning of a third phase. It was a new period for the Yishuv—a period of autonomous development in many fields, especially in education. Ideologically, the same basic images and symbols which had been prevalent during the Second Aliyah went on functioning until the creation of the State of Israel and for some time after this, although in many cases this meant losing touch with new social realities.

As early as 1918, under British rule, a Commission for Education, endowed with legislative power, was created by the Representative Committee elected by the Yishuv. A Department of Education, responsible for the implementation of the commission's policy, was also created. This department took charge of the direction and control of kindergarten education, as well as the financial aid allocated for this purpose.

During this period (about 1929), in spite of a grave economic crisis, there were 37 kindergartens attended by 5,525 children. However, budgetary restrictions hit the educational system and the Commission for Education had to withdraw its financial support from many kindergartens. In 1931, it totally ceased its aid to the nursery schools but kept its control over education. As a result, the burden of the kindergarten was distributed among various public institutions.

The Creation of the New Zionist Cultural Tradition in the Kindergarten

The educational system, and especially the kindergarten, translated the abstract ideology of Zionism into symbols, ceremonies, and festivals necessary for the child's social identity and the perpetuation of an engagement in a society, which until 1948, was founded on a basis of volunteer work.

The Zionist movement was born out of the negation of the diaspora, which, to a great extent, meant the negation of religious practice. But secularization was problematic. The absence of the festivals, which were no longer celebrated within the home, created a void which was felt deeply by the educators, since these traditions were an integral part of their youth in the Jewish shtetls of Eastern Europe. Beyond this nostalgia, the void was intolerable in a society that was intensely ideological and militant. This point is highlighted in the professional journals of the educators.

For instance, the kindergarten teacher N. Shargadovska wrote in *Netiveinu* (1931):

> Owing to the void which was felt by the sons of immigrants torn from their familiar environment, special importance must be granted to the preparation of the Holy Days. Everything must be done to ensure the celebration of the Shabbat or the festivals, for each holiday is not only an historical remembrance but must be related to the resurrection of our people on our land.

Traditional Jewish Holy Days, and especially festivals that lent themselves to transformation and reinterpretation, were part and parcel of the new tradition which was being constituted in Eretz Yisrael by the Zionist movement. This process of reinterpretation had a double effect. The elements within the tradition were silenced and the links between the people and its land, perserved and symbolized (precisely) through religion, were now emphasized. The connecting link between the Jews and the land was the key to the redemption of the uprooted Jew. In the words of the teacher Ts. Katinka (1935):

> It is through the festival that love for the heroes of his nation, for his people and his land, is born in the heart of the child and made strong— by festivals such as *Hanukkah* and *Pesah*. The child is brought into proximity with nature and is taught to give expression to the relation existing between the Jew and Nature. This relation existed yesterday as it exists today. The classic example is *Tu bi-Shvat*.

A similar anxiety is expressed by H. Wissman-Dizengoff (1937), who writes in *Hed ha-Gan:* "With the return to the land, with the movement of national revival, began the search for new festivals."

The Function of the KKL in the Kindergarten

The *Keren Kayemet le-Israel* was a central element in the new culture being created in the kindergarten. This was due, first of all, to its role as the purchaser of the land of Eretz Yisrael. The KKL defined the practical conditions for the revival of Zion; it concretized its symbolism into reality. Moreover, as mentioned, the KKL possessed a double dimension: it had, on the one hand, the spatial extent of the whole diaspora and, on the other hand, the temporal depth which belonged to the Jewish tradition. The KKL had become the main symbol of the redemption of Israel, and as such, it constantly generated more specific symbols which became widely used within the educational system.

This function of the KKL as a generator of symbols became institutionalized in 1927 through the initiative of the teachers who created the "Committee of Teachers for the KKL" (mo'etset ha-morim le-ma'an KKL). At first, the so-called work for the KKL was intended for children of ten years and over, but eventually came to be generalized at the kindergarten level where it was found to be especially successful.

The function of the work for the KKL in the educational system was conceived in the following manner:

> In the schools, the name of the KKL is nothing but the generic name of the complex one might call "Zionist education." . . . From the very day of its creation, the Committee of Teachers does not see itself as an institution which works exclusively for the KKL but as one which works for the school as a whole and as the main vector of Zionist education within the school. If it is true that the child contributes a great deal to the KKL, it is no less true that the latter reciprocates a thousandfold (Ben Yehudah 1935).

A similar opinion was voiced by Ussishkin (1941), the president of the KKL.

> The work done at school revolves around the idea of the redemption of the fatherland and its people. . . . Essentially, the work accomplished by the child is intended to accustom him to live the national reality, and to inculcate in him the idea that he has duties to his people and his land. . . . The role of the school is, above all, to breed the feeling of the sanctity of a unique task in the heart of the child: the one and only task with which our generation has been entrusted: redemption.

An examination in detail of the writings of the kindergarten teachers themselves, reveals a profusion of articles confirming the basic function of the KKL as a generator of the child's social identity, exalting the rootedness in Eretz Yisrael as the land of birth (eretz hu-ledet). The land of Israel is "fatherland" in the sense of the "land in which one is born" (eretz moledet). These children are fortunate to see around them, from the very moment of their birth, landscapes that belong to their own land. These words reflect the popular poem by the Hebrew poet Tchernichovsky (1930):[11]

> Man is nothing but a piece of the soil of a small land (eretz)/ Man is nothing but the form of the landscape of his native land (306).

Similarly, nature walks, even if short, were part of the kindergarten routine even in urban environments. Changes in the seasons (and in the flora and fauna which accompanied these) were all themes for lessons and discussions. Wild flowers gathered in the fields during the outings were put in vases in the corner of the class reserved for the KKL (Verbah 1940). The KKL corner (*pinat Keren Kayemet le-Israel*) was a set corner in all kindergartens. It also included the blue box and the national flag, which existed long before the creation of the State of Israel. The corner was decorated with green plants and there were books and pictures showing communities and localities in the Yishuv, which the teacher changed occasionally. The children would often come to look at these pictures.

In order to strengthen the link between the child and the land, the kindergarten possessed a real garden, which was cultivated by the teacher and children. The professional journals of the kindergarten teachers featured many articles devoted to gardening activity, which was considered to be an important educational theme, and was also associated with the KKL. For instance, during the Shavuot festival, at the beginning of summer, first fruits (*bikkurim*) picked from the garden were symbolically offered to the KKL, as had been done in the days of the Jerusalem Temple. Even in everyday life, every fruit gathered by the children from the garden was, first of all, exhibited in the KKL corner.

The blue box was part of all the ceremonies performed in the kindergarten. Every Friday, during the *kabbalat shabbat*[12] ceremony, as with the celebration of other festivals not directly linked with the KKL, the children would put symbolic contributions into the blue box.

To conclude this section, a quotation from a speech by S. Fayens-Glick (1942), a kindergarten inspector, will provide an insight into how the teachers themselves saw the presentation of the KKL in their nursery schools:

> The very fact of having made the KKL the base of kindergarten education implies a further extension of the idea it represents and its transformation into a symbol; a symbol—as Bialik said—of all the great and profound values of the Hebrew people: that is to say, on the material plane, a symbol of the tie with the land which is "mother of all life," and on the spiritual plane: a bind with the great tradition of our people.... The symbolic way toward the idea of the KKL passes, in the education of the child, through the contributions and presents which are offered to the KKL.

The Birthday Ceremony in the Kindergarten and the KKL

As the medium of Zionist education, the KKL was the creator of specific symbols. Kindergarten teachers, and those responsible for their creation, were well aware of the function of these symbols, centered around the concept of redemption, namely, the concrete redemption of the land and through it, of the people. However, this is only the explicit level. It would seem that there is another metaphorical level, which is implicit or hidden. Here the special relationship between the kindergarten child and the land and nature of Eretz Yisrael takes on its full meaning. In this metaphorical relationship, the child born in Eretz Yisrael (the tsabar) can be said to be functioning as a symbolic shifter, that is, as an operator of passage. This shifting, and the passage achieved, is from the time axis, emphasizing history (Jewish ritual has been described as "architecture in time," Heschel 1951), to the space axis, stressing land and nature, namely the specific nature of Eretz Yisrael.

From the data on the functioning of the KKL within the preschool system, it appears that this shifting action can best be observed in two types of ceremonies performed in the kindergarten. The first, non-metaphorical, ceremony is the birthday celebration of individual children. The second type is metaphorical: it includes the so-called birthday of the KKL, and the birthday of the almond tree celebrated during the Tu bi-Shvat festival, also known as "the New Year of the Trees." A detailed description of certain aspects of these ceremonies will bring to the fore the shifter character of the child. First, a brief discussion of (the lack of) birthday celebrations in Jewish tradition is warranted.

The celebration of birthdays is not part of Jewish tradition (EJ, 4:1054–5), yet such celebrations became common practice in the kindergartens. According to the testimony of Z. Katborsky (1965), a kindergarten teacher, the first individual birthday in the Yishuv was celebrated spontaneously for the child Yigael Yadin, at the age of four years, in a Jerusalem kindergarten in 1921. From that date onward, individual birthday ceremonies came to be celebrated more and more frequently until they became part of the kindergarten ceremonial repertoire.

As the birthday ceremony was not part of the Jewish tradition it was like an empty vessel with a potential to express the new ideology— much more so than other festivals in the kindergarten which, despite all the changes made to adjust them to the new Zionist spirit, remained essentially traditional.

Thus, the birthday ceremony of the child was to a large extent appropriated by the KKL. There was another reason for this. A birthday is generally part of an individual calendar, it is in many ways a celebration of the notion of "person" in its specific sense of autonomy and individuality (Dumont 1965). In this engaged society (as Zionist society was at its beginnings), autonomy and individuality appeared problematic, if not dangerous (Doleve-Gandelman 1982). Therefore, the very acceptance of the glorification of the person necessitated the intervention of the KKL as a mediator.

The Birthday Ceremony of the Child

During the birthday ceremony the KKL was present in two ways: first, through its contribution box, and second, through the greeting card sent to the child.

The blue box was set on the ceremonial table with the other objects used during the ceremony (Haskina 1940). During the celebration, when the child had become the focus of attention of the whole gathering, he inserted into the box a number of coins corresponding to his age. As Fayens-Glick expressed it:

> The symbolic way toward the idea of the KKL passes through the contributions and presents offered to the KKL during the child's birthday, when he has become the focus of attention, and all eyes are staring at him while he lets fall, one by one, his handful of coins corresponding to his age into the box of the KKL. How many invisible threads are weaving an invisible network between his soul and the box? How many rays are emanating from it and caress his soul? How deep is this experience? When the child grows older and understands the link which exists between the tilling of the soil and the redemption of the land, the symbol, and the thing it symbolizes, will be fused together to express one single idea: the man who resurrects his land and brings about its redemption also resurrects his own self and achieves his own redemption (Fayens-Glick 1942).

When the child received the *brakhot*, the verbal blessings of his peers and the customary small gifts (an album made up of drawings by the other children, a book of drawings to color, and color pencils), the KKL joined in through the intermediacy of a birthday card in the form of a calendar.[13]

This picture card consists of a blessing that is surrounded by twelve squares bearing the Hebrew names of the months, so that the whole card looks like a Hebrew calendar. In each square, two elements of the nature of the designated months are represented as part of the flora and fauna of Eretz Yisrael. The fauna belong to primeval nature in the sense that they represent nondomesticated animals, mainly birds. The represented flora, too, are wild flora. The only two elements representing cultivated plants are the pomegranate and the vine, characteristic of the Israel of biblical times, and they are represented in the squares of the summer months, when wild flowers are rare.

Thus, most of the elements belong to wild nature. Similarly, the background of their representation is wild: the sea, a barren land, or the sky. Yet, the separation between each square is a frieze of cypresses, trees which signal field limits or borders in Mediterranean lands. This surrounding area is constituted by time, which is represented both by a cultural aspect of twelve months and by a natural aspect, which is cyclical and belongs to wild primeval nature.

Culture and nature are woven into the picture. Even in the central part showing cultivated fields and distant villages, one observes nature in its primeval sense: wild flowers, two enormous trees, flights of birds passing through the sky.

It is in this wild part of the central landscape that four parts of a printed text are found (read from right to left, as in Hebrew writing). The first and second part describe the child, or rather, since they are written in the first person singular, it is the child himself who presents his person. One can read:

I just reached_____years
Day_____Month_____Year_____
My name is_____My family name_____
My father's name is_____My mother's_____
We live in_____I study at_____

A square is reserved for a picture of the child. The third and the fourth part of the text describe the relationship between the child—the individual—and the collective. The third part is a quotation from the famous blessing by Bialik,[14] the national poet, dedicated to the children of Israel:

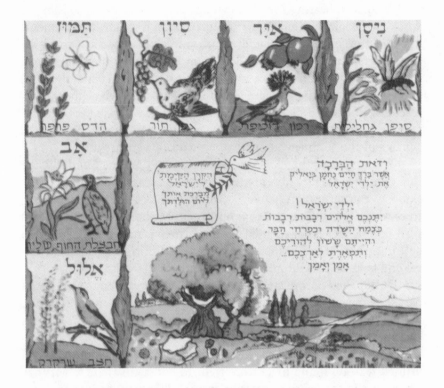

Here is the benediction
which Chaim Nachman Bialik
sends the children of Israel:

Let God multiply you from ten thousand to
ten thousand
like the plants in the fields
and the wild flowers.
May you be the joy of your parents
and the glory of your land of birth [eretz moledet]
Amen and again amen.

In the fourth part, the KKL addresses the child directly, as if in its
own voice: "The KKL sends you its blessing for your birthday." The
blessing itself is written on what looks like a scroll of parchment carried
by a dove with an olive branch in its beak.

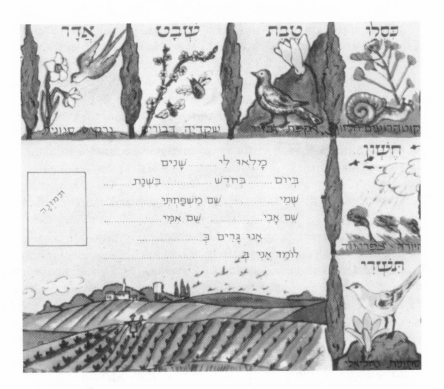

In summary, the KKL is represented in three aspects: as an institution, it is the box that unites the whole Jewish people; as the nature and culture of Eretz Yisrael, it is the "agri"-culture of the land, but the land also produces wild nature. The land is both Eretz Yisrael and *eretz moledet*, that is, the fatherland. In a song written by the poet Nathan Alterman, sung during the birthday, the fatherland is as exceptional and unique as is the birthday among the other days of the year. A refrain of the songs reads thus (1946):

> Among all the days of the year/One only is the day of birth [*yom huledet*]/Among all the lands in the world/One only is the fatherland [*moledet*]

Thus, through the *huledet/moledet* rhyming, there takes place an assimilation between the child and the land.

The Birthday Ceremony of the KKL

There are several words in Hebrew to designate anniversary. Yet it is the term *yom huledet* (birthday) which is always used when the anniversary is that of the KKL. In that sense, the phrase has already been metaphorically transposed. Thus, the professional journal of the kindergarten teacher often speaks of the birthday of the KKL.

In fact, the metaphorical usage of birthday, extended to the KKL, is also celebrated in the kindergarten. One finds documentation concerning two categories of such birthday celebrations. The first is more intimate, and takes place in the kindergarten, while the second is a central and more public celebration. The first will be referred to only briefly, but the second will be the subject of a longer and more detailed description.

The intimate ceremony of the KKL birthday continued to be performed in the kindergarten even after the creation of the State of Israel. The kindergarten teacher, Zbodanski-Rodanski (1947), tells about a celebration which took place the year before the establishment of the state: "It consisted of a theatrical performance reproducing the establishment and settlement of eleven kibbutzim, in the Negev desert." In this celebration, the KKL was presented mainly in its cultural aspect and emphasis was laid on the men who redeemed the earth from its desolate state and transformed the desert landscape and the primeval nature into culture. The second part of the ceremony concerned the blue box. Here, elements overtly taken from the birthday of the child came into play. Birthday songs were sung, contributions in coins were made, as in the case of the birthday of the child, but here the number of coins was not associated with the number of years of the KKL.

However, the large public celebration which took place in the KKL house in Tel Aviv, was not continued after the creation of the state.

The following is a very detailed description of this festival written by T. Katsiri (1939), a kindergarten teacher:

> For the first time, the children celebrate the day of the founding of the KKL. In the language of the children it is the "birthday of the KKL" ... all the kindergarten children make their way toward the House of the KKL with gifts for the KKL in their hands, with songs and blessings in their mouths. ... As they reach the threshold, the children start singing a song which celebrates the redemption of the land and of the people, thanks to the KKL and its blue box.

There, on the threshold, the reception of the children takes place. . . . From all sides can be seen the box beloved by everyone, and on a well-decorated table are the gifts of the children. In two corners of the hall are exhibitions of the fruits of the land, a present from Tnuva.[15] The children enter the hall and the ceremony begins. First, there is a blessing from the KKL. In their turn, the children answer by a blessing:

Let the KKL buy a lot of land
Let a lot of Jews come and settle in Eretz Yisrael
Let the children come to Israel and let them not be
killed over there . . . Shalom, shalom and blessings:

Each class presents a box full of coins and its presents for the KKL. Even the land offers its own blessings in the form of its crops. The cauliflower and the cabbage, the beetroot and the tomato, the carrot and the radish thank the KKL for their redemption from the arid earth and its transformation into fertile soil.

The KKL answers the blessing of the children with another; a small box, a gift for the dollhouse of each class, is offered together with a present from the earth, a banana for each child . . . The feast ends with the hymn *Ha-Tikvah.*

Here again, as during the individual birthday of the child, a veritable duet of blessings between the KKL and the child took place. The blessings were copied from the kindergarten celebration as was the central placement of the blue box during the festivities. Yet, unlike the anniversary of the individual child, the ceremony did not mark linear time,[16] which is the time marked by birthdays. The age of the KKL was never mentioned.

The KKL was presented as the institution which creates the link between the Jewish people and the land. It is the KKL that made the land fertile and brought her redemption. Thus, symbolically, by way of this circularity, a certain identification between KKL and land occurs—the latter fertilized by the former. Consequently, the KKL gives each child a gift from the land, usually a fruit.

This relationship between the land and the KKL is to be found in other texts which celebrate the interchangeability between mother and land. For instance, in one issue of *Hed ha-Gan* (1942), this "Song for the KKL" by A. Glazer is found:

I made for myself a small garden/Mother gave me a spade/But when I shall be grown up/Who shall give me the land?/Know this:/There is a good mother/who cares for you/She is my mother/and thine:/It is the KKL/On the map there are dots/and empty spaces/The dots are villages./ How can they be multiplied?/If you do not know how/Make a gift/to the KKL/Thus by thy hand/thou hast drawn/on the arid land/a new village.

As in the birthday ceremony, the KKL is described as intimately related to the land while, at the same time, being separate from it. It is both "my" and "thy" mother. The interdependence between the child and the metaphorical mother, the KKL, is repeatedly emphasized. The link is even more bilateral since the KKL relies on the child's contribution to his box in order to achieve their common aim.

To summarize the findings concerning the KKL birthday, it is observed that, despite the identification of the KKL with the land, in which it is primarily "mother" through the medium of the birthday, the KKL also presents itself as a child. There is, however, an important difference: the child's birthday (or his age) is inscribed in linear time; while the KKL birthday never relates to its age or to the number of years. The KKL is thus predominantly mother but simultaneously child.

The Birthday Story of the Almond Tree

The second metaphorical birthday which has been observed, is the so-called birthday of the almond tree, the tree which is the harbinger of spring. First among the trees with deciduous leaves, the almond tree grows a flowery bloom in springtime. Even more remarkable is the fact that it grows blossoms *before* its leaves appear.

In the tradition created in the Eretz Yisrael kindergarten, the celebration of the almond tree is associated with Tu bi-Shvat, a quasi-festival belonging to the religious tradition marking the new year of the trees. Originally, this feast was associated with the biblical custom of the tithe, the offering of one tenth of all crops to God in the Temple. In the sixteenth century, the kabbalists in Safed developed a new ritual modeled on the Passover seder. It consisted of the symbolic eating of the fruits of Eretz Yisrael. This Tu bi-Shvat festival, completely reinterpreted and controlled by the KKL, became not only the feast of the trees but also the celebration of afforestation.

Although the almond tree does not actually belong to the seven species, which characterize Eretz Yisrael (Deut. 8:7–8), it used to grow in Israel in biblical times (see Gen. 43:11; Jer. 1:11). At the turn of the present century almond trees were extensively cultivated in Eretz Yisrael. Yet, later on, almost all were destroyed by pest. The almond trees exist in two species; the cultivated one producing sweet almonds (*amygdalus communis var. dulcis*), and the wild species in the mountains, with its white blossoms and bitter fruit (*amygdalus communis ver. amara*) (see EJ, 2:665–66). During the British Mandate, the almond tree was mostly represented by the wild species, that is, the natural, noncultivated type.

In the course of time, the perception of the almond tree and its presentation in the kindergarden underwent an interesting transformation, which is very apparent in the work of L. Kipnis (1919), a foremost creator of Hebrew children stories in Eretz Yisrael. The almond tree first appears in his work as an adult religious Jew. In a well-known story published in 1919 to 1920, and entitled "Happy New Year," one reads that "the almond trees prayed to God that He should preserve them from the bad winds . . . and all the prayers were metamorphosed into blossoms." The dominant metaphor is clearly the image of the religious Jew praying during the holidays of the Jewish New Year and Yom Kippur. It is during the New Year season that the destiny of people is decided. It is also a time of forgiveness or absolution, a sign of which is the white clothes religious Jews put on—just as the almond tree puts on its white blossoms.

As time went by, Kipnis changed his symbols. The image of the tree as an adult "judaized" entity (in the traditional religious meaning of the term), existing in linear time, disappeared. It was replaced by a child almond tree denoting the cosmic elements in nature and announcing the spring revival. As such it came to be inscribed in a time that was preeminently cyclical. However, this was not a radical substitution and the old model survives as a faded watermark behind the new one.

In 1930, Kipnis published a text, entitled "The almond-tree birthday" in the journal *Gilyonot*:[17]

> Once upon a time, in the orchard surrounding the house, there was a young almond tree. Even before the end of summer the tree lost all its leaves and remained "naked." She [the author uses the feminine form *shekedia*, and not *shaked*, to designate the tree] felt cold and was very sad. And it so happened that on a cold winter day a light spring breeze visited the garden: it blew upon the trees and murmured its secret to them: "Tomorrow is the birthday of the almond tree." And immediately, the trees started shaking their branches and whispered to one another:

"Tomorrow is the birthday of the almond tree!" (A bird and a bee also heard the news and propagated it among their friends) . . . and even little Noam drew near the tree and shouted: "Tomorrow is Tu bi-Shvat: Tomorrow is your birthday: Tomorrow I shall have all my friends come to offer you their birthday blessings." Yet the almond tree, while listening to all these speeches . . . only thought to herself: "Tomorrow is my birthday, many people will come to see me—and I am stark naked; How can I receive them?" She brooded and brooded all day and all night. All the other trees went to sleep but she could not sleep.

But lo: in the middle of the night the Queen of trees appeared to her . . . : "Good evening almond tree: Why are you so worried and do not sleep?" The almond tree answered: "How can I sleep and not worry? Tomorrow is my birthday, a lot of people will come to see me and here I am stark naked." The Queen caressed her and said: "Do not worry at all, before the rise of the day you will receive a marvellous birthday robe." "Really?" asked the tree. "Yes, yes," the Queen answered. "All almond trees, whoever they be, receive a white robe for their birthday. And now go to sleep so you can be rested and gay in the morning." And the Queen caressed the almond tree until it went to sleep. And when it was asleep, she gave her kisses on her branches. And at every spot which her lips kissed sprung a delicate white, rosy blossom. . . .

In the morning, when the almond tree woke up she could hardly recognize herself; she was completely dressed up in magnificent white blossoms. And all the surrounding trees gazed at her and started blessing her. One shouted "Good morning!" Another one said: "Happy New Year!" And all exclaimed: "What a beautiful dress!" ("Let your dress bear you luck.") Many birds alighted on her branches and started singing the birthday song. (Similarly, the bees came and sang.) And Noam came with his friends, they made a circle around the tree and sang her "Happy New Year almond tree! Happy New Year!"

This story was subsequently rewritten by Goytin (1943) with musical accompaniment, and published in Hed ha-Gan. In this latter version the last lines emphasize the resurrection of spring: "All the guests shout: Good day! Good day! Long live thy new dress, almond tree!/How beautiful is thy white dress/Thou art the harbinger of spring/ and for this, beautiful tree, receive our thanks and blessings."

In the two versions, it has been seen that the almond tree is unmistakenly represented as a child. The Queen caresses her into sleep and she receives, as a feasted child does, a new and beautiful dress. Yet there is a difference in the identification: the child is inscribed in the linear time of history, whereas the almond tree is inscribed in cyclical time; her birthday is placed under the aegis of the spring revival. The anxiety of the almond tree relates to its annual capacity for self-reproduction. In a way, it can be said that its yearly blossoming annihilates linear time and substitutes cyclical time for it.

At the same time, if the almond tree is mostly perceived as a child, it is also perceived as a mother: it produces blossoms which in their turn shall produce fruit. Observe the parallelism with the KKL, which is now a mother, and now a child.

The Kindergarten Child as a Symbolic Shifter

A series of identifications have been seen: the almond tree is identified with the child, but he, in his turn, is identified with the world of plants. This has already been seen in the blessing sent by the KKL to the kindergarten for each child's birthday. Those kindergarten children are not any children: they were born in Eretz Yisrael and by virtue of this fact, are interchangeable with its nature. The children born in the land of Israel are nicknamed *tsabarim* (pl.), that is the fruit of the cactus. This cactus grows in Eretz Yisrael either as a wild plant or as a semi-cultivated one, just as the almond tree.

Thus, the child is identified with an herb of the field, with a wild flower, and, finally, with the tsabar fruit, while the KKL is related to the earth, to the land, that is, to the mother. The birthday is both a celebration and the commemoration of a separation: the birth, the separation from the mother, which introduces linear time, that is, the historical person, or, in other words, the age of the child. Yet, in the metaphorical context of the birthday, it is also the nonseparation from the mother, a nonseparation rooted in cyclical time. This is the parallelism of the nonseparation between an almond tree-tsabar-child and earth-mother-KKL, which operates a change on linear time, bringing it back to a cyclical dimension, that of the spring renaissance. Within this context cyclical time also indicates the spring renaissance of the people of Israel coming back to its land, a process most concretely expressed in the tsabar. The tsabar is an integral part of the land and, rooted in its soil, cannot be separated from it. It is the children who, since a new group of them appears year after year, embody the miracle of the spring renaissance. The child, the tsabar, has been taken away from the linear current of history and implanted in nature.

With the realization of the meaning of the Holocaust during World War II, and the necessity of creating a state for the survivors, and with the subsequent creation of the State of Israel (Laqueur 1972), the ideology of the Yishuv underwent a change. It reinscribed itself symbolically into linear time, that is, historical time, the time of Jewish history. Yet, this description clearly demonstrates that the tsabar was conceived as a creature which cannot be separated from the soil, from the land, and, by virtue of this character, became a shifter which could symbolically transform historical, linear time into spatial, cyclical time. This can be illustrated in Figure 2.

Figure 2

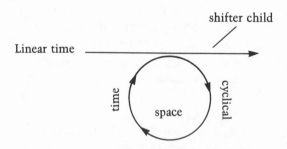

The Eretz Yisrael born child acts as a temporal shifter converting time into space: the space of *the land of* Israel.

This can be expressed in another way as shown in Figure 3. In this schema, the tsabar-child is at the crossroads between the symbolic and indexic, as befits a shifter in the Jakobson definition (see note 4). In the symbolic direction, he points to the KKL, the purchaser and redeemer of the land, to the national land of Eretz Yisrael, and to the mother-land from which he cannot be separated. In the indexic direction, the tsabar-child refers us to his indexical contacts with existential, concrete space and with the existing children of the soil: namely, the almond tree, the wild plants of the fields, and the tsabar as the actual fruit of the cactus. Thus, the shifting alternately links time and space, and also links the symbolic (history), which belongs to time, and the indexic (the soil, the actual fruit of the land), which belongs to space.

It is this shifting which permits a state of metaphorical nonseparation to exist between the tsabar and the land of Eretz Yisrael (a state
which aims at obliterating the flux of linear time, not only for the individual but also for the people). Furthermore, the shifting permits the
functioning of several nonseparation metaphors. Thus, the KKL is
assimilated to the mother through its relationship to the land, but it is
also identified with the child through the child's birthday. Similarly,
the almond tree is related to the child, but it is also mother by virtue of
its capacity to produce fruit and as a harbinger of spring.

It is interesting to observe that the KKL has been the generator of a
number of rituals. This is because it is a symbol of continuity—be it fic-
titious continuity—between a people and its land. It is precisely
because of the semi-fictitious character of this continuity that the KKL
has always been obliged to create and recreate the image of nonseparation between a people and its land through the connection it made between children and the wild nature of the land. Therein lies its symbolic
function and symbolic efficacy.

Thus, there is a perpetual interplay between the individual and the
collective, between linear time and cyclical time, in a person's life, rep-

Figure 3

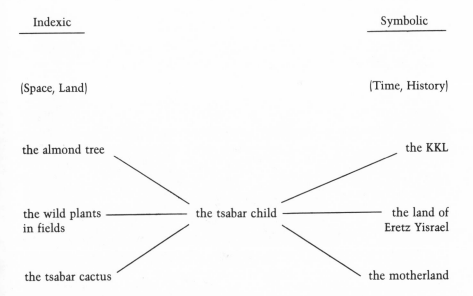

resenting both the time of history and the time of a people's renaissance—an interplay which is not arbitrary, but is part of the symbolic work of ideology.

The objective of this study has been to show the striving of a society intending to go back into the flux of history. It actually did so, not through the upholding of traditional religious practice (this was the time-honored role of the diaspora), but through the creation of shifting interchangeability between tsabar and land.

Conclusion

This study has attempted to show how in the time of the Yishuv, the symbolic inscription of Zionist ideology in the space of Eretz Yisrael was achieved by using the tsabar as a symbolic shifter from linear time and history to space and nature. This demonstration rested on two elements: (a) on the particular role played by the KKL as redeemer of the land of Eretz Yisrael (and its special function as a generator of symbols for the educational system); and (b) on the network of assimilation which made the child born in the land of Eretz Yisrael a symbolic shifter from time to space.

With the realization of the meaning of the Holocaust and the subsequent creation of the State of Israel, the ideology of the Yishuv underwent a change and reinscribed itself symbolically into the linear time of Jewish History. Consequently, the KKL, which continued to function as an organization, and also as a locus for symbolic creation, even after the creation of the state, lost its hidden symbolic function and therefore its symbolic efficacy. It was the hidden symbolic functioning that had permitted the tsabar to operate as a shifter between history and space. Its loss explains the very sharp reduction in the activities of the KKL within the preschool and the educational system in general.

As for the tsabar which, as has been seen, was primarily a symbol and an index (actually a shifter between symbol and index), it currently appears as the third mode of signification in the Peircian trilogy: as an *icon.* The term *tsabar* now evokes only the iconic image of the cactus fruit, as a psychological portrait of the native Israeli personality.

Notes

*The research for this paper was partially supported by the Fund for Basic Research of the Israel Academy of Sciences and Humanities.

1. The *tsabar* is the cactus of the *opuntia ficus indica* species. Its origin is in Central America, and it is usually used as a fence. Its fruit is sweet inside, yet protected by a thorny bark on the outside. The Arabic form of the word, *sabre*, is also commonly used in everyday speech.

2. This name designates the land which, according to the Bible, was promised to the tribes of Israel (EJ, 9:108).

3. The Jewish community in Palestine before the creation of the State of Israel from 1882 to 1948.

4. The term *shifter*, originally coined by the linguist Jespersen, came into wide use after Roman Jakobson's first article published on the subject (1962). The semiotic nature of shifters is grounded in the well-known Peircian classification of sign-objects into icon, index, and symbols. According to Peirce (1931–1958), a symbol (such as the English word blue) is associated with the represented object through a conventional rule which, itself, belongs to the set of symbolic rules, namely the code which constitutes the English language. An *index* (for example, the act of pointing with the hand or the finger) is in an existential relation with the object it represents, and implies an *existential contact* with the designated object. Shifters combine both functions and belong therefore to the class of indexical symbols.

Jakobson cites the personal pronoun as an illustration of the shifter category: "*I* means the person uttering *I*. Thus on the one hand, the sign *I* cannot represent its object without being associated with the latter "by a conventional rule," and in different codes the same meaning is assigned to different sequences such as *I*, *,ego, ich, ja* and so on; consequently *I* is a symbol. On the other hand, the sign *I* cannot represent its object without "being in existential relation" with this object: the word *I* designating the utterer is existentially related to his utterance and hence functions as an index (see Benveniste 1966).

5. The Lovers of Zion association, founded in Russia during the years 1881 to 1882, aimed to promote Jewish emigration to Eretz Yisrael.

6. See note 11. Menahem M. Ussishkin was the president of the KKL from 1922 until his death in 1941. The poet is referring to his presidential capacity. Rabbi Meir Ba'al ha-Ness is a sainted figure whose putative tomb is found in Tiberias, one of the four holy cities. Contributions for religious institutions in that city were collected in his name throughout the Jewish world.

7. It is clear that the passage refers to a symbolic manipulation and not to an actual historical process (see Felix 1966).

8. The wave of immigration to Eretz Yisrael between 1904 and 1914.

9. The *Hilfsverein der Deutschen Juden* was a German-Jewish organization, founded in 1901, which sponsored several educational institutions in Eretz Yisrael.

10. This institution actually came into existence in 1911, and its first headmistress was Hassia Feinsod-Sukenik.

11. Born in the Crimean peninsula (1875), Shaul Tchernichovsky immigrated to Eretz Yisrael in 1931 and died in 1943. One of the national Hebrew poets, his work is still studied in Israeli schools.

12. The origin of the *kabbalat shabbat* custom (the reception of Sabbath) is to be found in the kabbalistic revival which took place in the sixteenth century in the town of Safed, when Isaac Luria and his disciples went out of the town confines on Friday afternoons in order to receive the Shabbat. A kabbalat shabbat ceremony is normally celebrated in Israeli kindergartens on Friday mornings.

13. From a personal interview with Mr. Z. Poaran of the Education Department of the KKL in January 1984, it appears that the KKL first published an illustrative greeting card in the early 1930s. This card is almost identical to the one presented on p. 270 with the difference being that the earlier version was printed on both sides of the paper. In the 1940s, due to the initiative of Mr. Poaran, both sides of the card were printed on one single sheet so that it might be hung on a wall. From then on, the KKL has supplied this card to kindergartens when requested by the teachers. It should be noted that during the period of the Yishuv, every child was given this card on his birthday, whereas today, although the KKL goes on producing the card, it is only rarely given to a child in the course of birthday ceremonies.

14. Born in the Ukraine in 1873, Chaim Nachman Bialik immigrated to Israel in 1924 and died in 1934. He was involved in the educational efforts of the KKL.

15. The cooperative marketing association, founded in the 1920s, to distribute Hebrew agricultural products.

16. I am using "linear time" and "cyclical time" as it is, for instance, used by Goody (1968). To be more specific, linear time is continuous, irreversible time, the time of history, whereas cyclical time is the time of nonseparation of the Eliadean eternal return, which is the time of space and nature.

17. It was in this journal, intended for kindergarten teachers, that the new songs and stories of the developing Hebrew culture were published.

References

Alterman, N. (1946). "Yom Huledet" (Birthday). In Y. Gurevitch, ed. *Ma Asaper la-Yeled?* (What shall I tell the child?) Tel Aviv.

Benveniste, E. (1966). *Problèmes de linguistique general.* Paris: Edition Minuit.

Ben Yehudah, B. (1935). "Ha-Keren ha-Kayemet be-Gan ha-Yeladim" (KKL in the Kindergarten). *Hed ha-Gan* 1:37–40.

Doleve-Gandelman, Ts. (1982). *Identité Sociale et Ceremonie d'Anniversaire dans les Jardins d'enfants Israeliens.* Ph.D. diss. Paris: Ecole des Hautes Etudes en Science Sociales.

Dumont, L. (1965). "The Modern Conception of the Individual: Notes on its genesis and that of concomitant institutions." *Contributions to Indian Sociology* 8:13–61.

Eisenstadt, S. N. (1967). *Israeli Society: Background, development, problems.* New York: Basic Books.

Eben Shoshan, A. (1980). *The New Dictionary* (Hebrew). 8 vols. Jerusalem: Kiryat Sefer.

Fayens-Glick, S. (1942). "Kenes Gananot: KKL be-Gan ha-Yeladim" (Congress of Kindergarten Teachers: the KKL in the Kindergarten). *Hed ha-Gan* 9:11–17.

_____.(1956). "Hitpathut Ganei ha-Yeladim be-Eretz Yisrael" (The Development of Kindergartens in Eretz Yisrael). In *The Jubilee Book of the Teacher's Syndicate.* Tel Aviv: Publishing House of the Teachers' Union.

Felix, Y. (1966). "The Tree and the Forest in the Ancient Landscape of Eretz Israel," *Teva' va-Arets* 8:71–74. Hebrew.

Glazer, A. (1942). "Shir la-KKL" (Song for the KKL). *Hed ha-Gan* 7:57.

Goody, J. (1968). "Time: Social Organization." In *International Encyclopedia of the Social Sciences.* New York: Macmillan, 16:30–42.

Goytin, L. (1943). "Yom Huledet shel ha-Shkediah" (The Almond Tree's Birthday). *Hed ha-Gan* 9:69–71.

Halevi, J. (1924). *Selected Poems of Jehuhah Halevi.* Edited by H. Brody. Philadelphia: The Jewish Publication Society.

Haskina, T. (1940). "Yom-Huledet ba-Gan" (Birthday Party in the Kindergarten). *Hed ha-Gan* 5:34–37.

Heschel, A. J. (1951). *The Sabbath: Its Meaning for Modern Man.* New York: Farrar, Straus and Young.

Jakobson, R. (1962). *Selected Writings.* The Hague/Paris: Mouton.

Katborsky, Ts. (1965). *Bi-netivot ha-Gan* (Along the Paths of the Kindergarten). Tel Aviv: Publishing House of the Teachers' Union.

Katinka, Ts. (1935). "Ha-Hagiga ba-Gan" (Festivals in the Kindergarten). *Hed ha-Gan* 1:39–41.

Katsiri, Ts. (1939). "Yom Huledet la-KKL be-Tel Aviv" (The Birthday of the KKL in Tel Aviv). *Hed ha-Gan* 5:49.

Kipnis, L. (1919). "Loven ba-'Etz" (Whiteness of the Trees). In *In Honour of the Tu bi-Shvat Holiday.* Jaffa.

———. (1930). "Yom Huledet shel ha-Shkediah" (The Almond Tree's Birthday). *Gilyonot* 1:25–27.

Laqueur, W. (1972). *A History of Zionism.* London: Weidenfeld and Nicolson.

Minkovitch, A. (1972). "Early Childhood Education in Israel" In S. J. Braun and E. P. Edwards, eds. *History and Theory of Early Childhood Education.* Worthington, Ohio: C. A. Jones, 132–45.

Orni, E. (1980). *Admat Israel* (The Soil of Israel). Jerusalem: KKL Publishing House.

Peirce, C. S. (1931–1958). *Collected Papers.* Cambridge, Ma.: Harvard University Press.

Shargadovska, N. (1931). "Al 'Erech Ganei ha-Yeladim" (The Value of the Kindergarten). *Netiveinu* 1:24–27.

Tchernichovsky, Sh. (1930). "'Al Kupat Meir ba'al ha-Ness" (The Meir Ba'al ha-Hess Charity Box). In *Kinus Kofsa'ot ha-KKL.* Varsovie: KKL Edition.

Ussishkin, M. (1941). "Raq Ra'ayon ha-Geula" (Only the Idea of Redemption). *Hed ha-Gan* 6:2.

Verbah, H. (1940). "Ra'ayon ha-Geula be-Gan ha-Yeladim" (The Idea of Redemption in the Kindergarten). *Hed ha-Gan* 5:42–45.

Weitz, J. (1936). "Anu Not'im" (We plant). *Shorashim* 1:22–28.

Wissman-Dizengoff, H. (1937). "Hagigat Hag ha-Hanukkah ba-Gan" (The Hanukkah Festival in the Kindergarten). *Hed ha-Gan* 2:42–44.

Zbodanski-Rodanski, Sh. (1947). "Yovel KKL ba-Gan" (The KKL Jubilee in the Kindergarten). *Hed ha-Gan* 13:41–42.

CHAPTER 9

Dreams and the Wishes of the Saint*

YORAM BILU

I. Folk Veneration of Saints Among Moroccan Jews

The veneration of saints (hagiolatry) played a major role in the lives of many Jews in Morocco and constituted a basic component of their ethnic identity (Ben Ami 1984). In form, style, and prevalence, the patterning of this cultural phenomenon clearly bears the hallmarks of indigenous maraboutism, perhaps the most significant feature of Moroccan Islam (Eickelman 1967; Geertz 1968; Gellner 1969). At the same time, however, it was also reinforced by the deep-seated conception of the *tzaddik* (pious, holy man) in classical Jewish tradition (Stillman 1982). The saints were charismatic rabbis, distinguished by their erudition and piety, who were believed to possess a special spiritual force, the manifestations of which are similar to those of the Moroccan Muslim *baraka* (see Rabinow 1975, 17–30; Westermarck 1926, I:35–261). This force, which does not fade away after the holy man's death, may be utilized for the benefit of their adherents. Most of the Jewish Moroccan *tzaddikim* (pl.) were acknowledged as possessing saintly attributes only after their death (Stillman 1982); therefore their miraculous feats were usually associated with their tombs, scattered all over Morocco but most heavily concentrated in the southern, mountainous regions.

On the basis of recent studies (Ben Ami 1984; Goldberg 1983), it seems safe to conclude that virtually every Moroccan Jewish community had its own patron saint. While the reputation of most of these saints was quite circumscribed, some of them acquired popularity and followings which transcended regional boundaries. Sainted figures like Rabbi Ya'akov Abu-Hatsera, Rabbi Amram Ben-Diwan, and Rabbi David u-Moshe, were venerated by large segments of Jews in various areas of the country. Some of the saints were well-known historical figures, at times founders or descendants of veritable dynasties of tzaddikim (such as the Abu-Hatsera and Pinto families), while others, of unclear historical identification, seemed to be legendary figures. The stereotypical stories of the latter, nonhistorical, tzaddikim depicted them as rabbis from the Holy Land who had been sent to the Jewish communities in the Moroccan diaspora to collect funds and met their death on the road. In coming from the land of Israel and in striving to return there but failing to do so, the life stories of the legendary tzaddikim seem to have encapsulated and reflected major themes in the collective Jewish experience in exile. The Israeli origin of many popular tzaddikim seems conducive to current attempts, represented by the case study that ensues, to symbolically transfer saints from Morocco to Israel. For it is only natural that these cultural identities will ultimately return to the place where they originally belonged, all the more so after their adherents have done so.

Certainly the main event in the veneration of each saint was the collective pilgrimage to his tomb on the anniversary of his death and the *hillulah* (celebration) there. In the case of the more renowned saints many thousands of pilgrims from various regions would flock around the tomb in a formidable spectacle during which they feasted on slaughtered cattle, drank arak (*mahia*), danced and chanted, prayed and lit candles. All these activities, combining marked spirituality and high ecstasy with flesh and blood concerns, in a relaxed, at times frivolous, picnic-like atmosphere, were conducted in honor of the tzaddik. These *hillulot* (pl.) constituted cultural patterns which highlighted and reinforced Jewish solidarity and fraternity as manifested in the spirit of *communitas* (Turner 1969) which prevailed in most (though not in all) aspects of the celebration.

In addition to collective pilgrimages, visits to saints' sanctuaries were made on an individual basis in times of plight. The problems which saints were considered capable of solving included the whole range of human afflictions. Although pilgrimages were the core of Jewish Moroccan hagiolatry, they did not exhaust the vast array of beliefs and practices involved in it. The presence of the saint was also strongly felt in daily routine as people would utter his name and dream about him whenever facing a problem. At homes, candles were lit and festive meals were organized in his name. By and large the saint was a basic given in the culturally constituted reality of traditional Moroccan Jews, a central idiom for articulating a wide range of experiences. In many cases the enduring and pervasive nature of the relationship with the saint has amounted to a symbiotic association spanning the entire life course of the devotee.

In the densely populated Jewish Moroccan pantheon of saints, Rabbi David u-Moshe stands out as one of the small, select group of tzaddikim whose following was hardly bounded by regional geography. Buried in the western High Atlas near the village of Agouim, his hillulah on the new moon of *Heshvan* (the second month in the Jewish calendar) drew thousands of devotees from all over Morocco. In accordance with the stereotypical life story of legendary tzaddikim, he has been portrayed as an emissary from Jerusalem who died on the road while collecting donations from the Jewish communities in the High Atlas regions. Some accounts depicted the discovery of his tomb as precipitated by a dream in which he had disclosed his burial site to a Muslim villager (Ben Ami 1981, 287). The role of visitational dreams in identifying heretofore unknown saints, and in maintaining and reinforcing the linkage to known ones has been emphasized in both Jewish and Muslim hagiolatric traditions (Ben Ami 1984; Crapanzano 1975, 198; Westermarck 1926). However the fact that dreams were involved in the original discovery of Rabbi David u-Moshe's original site in Morocco bears special significance given the centrality of dreams in his second coming, which is the focus of this paper.

Since the personal identities of Jewish Moroccan saints and the notion of specific areas of specialization have not been well developed, Rabbi David u-Moshe can hardly be differentiated from other popular tzaddikim in terms of miraculous feats or worship patterns. More than with other saints, however, his hillulah has been associated with a strong sense of communality and equality. Thus, each of the participants in the hillulah at Agouim was allotted an equal share of the ritual meal irrespective of his status and his contribution to the tzaddik (Ben Ami 1981).

As with other tzaddikim, pilgrimages to Rabbi David u-Moshe's tomb, particularly during the time of the hillulah, constituted the focus of a rich complex of hagiolatric practices related to him. It was in his holy precinct that most of Rabbi David u-Moshe's miraculous interventions are said to have occurred. His sanctuary has been the natural habitat, so to speak, for experiencing his presence through visions, dreams, and other indirect signs, and for establishing rapport with him. Though not entirely locus bound, hagiolatric practices seemed to have been reenacted and revitalized by the pilgrimages to the miracle-saturated sanctuary. Consequently, the mass-immigration of Moroccan Jews to Israel during the 1950s and 1960s confronted the newcomers with a major challenge of maintaining their linkage to the saint (as well as to other tzaddikim), despite the fact that they had been separated from his tomb. This separation was clearly apparent in the general diminution and decentralization that Jewish Moroccan hagiolatry underwent in the first harsh years after aliyah (immigration). The idiom of the saint was too central and viable to entirely disappear, but the hillulot, including Rabbi David u-Moshe's, were celebrated in small numbers on a domestic level, such as in the neighborhood synagogues (Ben Ami 1981, 303). Once the predicaments of homecoming were mitigated, however, Moroccan Jews responded to their separation from the saints by reviving hagiolatric practices using various compensatory substitutes for the tombs that had been left behind. Most accessible among these alternatives were the tombs of local tzaddikim, mainly from the Talmudic era, which had been cherished as pilgrimage centers as early as the Middle Ages. Indeed, the Moroccanization of these pilgrimages has been systematically growing in recent years, particularly in the case of Rabbi Shim'on Bar-Yohai, the alleged author of the mystical Zohar (The Book of Splendor), who had been highly venerated by the masses in Morocco.

Aside from annexing old-time native pilgrimage sites, new centers have been established around the tombs of contemporary rabbis who were allotted saintly attributes in their lifetimes or, more often, posthumously. The most impressive example in this category is the mass pilgrimage to the tomb of Rabbi Haim Houri, a Tunisian rabbi who died in 1957, located in the municipal cemetery of Beersheba (Weingrod n.d.). Other minor, local-bound hillulot following this pattern take place in various communities in Israel.

While the Moroccanization of local hillulot and the creation of new saints have contributed to the preservation of hagiolatric practices under changing circumstances, their function should be seen as conpensatory rather than restorative. Through these patterns some local tombs, old as well as new, have become the focus of mass celebrations; but the Jewish saints of Morocco still withstood a potential devaluation as their sanctuaries have remained inaccessible since aliyah. In order to preserve the *content*, rather than merely the *form* of Jewish Moroccan hagiolatry, a third, more direct and daring accommodation had to be called for, namely, the symbolic transfer of saints from Morocco to Israel and their reinstallation in the new country. Among the Maghrebi tzaddikim who have thus been Israelized, Rabbi David u-Moshe's assumes a central position. Given his immense popularity in Morocco, it is not surprising that several attempts have been made to establish a new residence for him in various parts of the country. The most successful of these attempts is The House of Rabbi David u-Moshe in Safed which, for most of the saint's adherents, constitutes a legitimate substitute for the original burial site in Morocco. In fact, there is no doubt that in recent years the hillulah in Safed has outgrown its Moroccan counterpart in number of participants.

Before discussing its development, the hillulah in Safed will be described in some detail.

II. The Hillulah of Rabbi David u-Moshe in Safed

The House of Rabbi David u-Moshe in Safed is located in Shikun Canaan, an inconspicuous working-class neighborhood built in the mid-fifties for the newcomers of that era, mostly North Africans. In 1973 a forty-year-old man named Avraham dedicated a small room in his modest appartment to Rabbi David u-Moshe, following a dream-series in which the saint had appeared to him and indicated his wish to reside with him. In so doing Avraham claimed to have transferred the saint from the Atlas mountains to Israel.

Inside the room of the tzaddik, adjacent to the wall facing the entrance, a marble tablet, on which the saint's name and distinguished titles are inscribed, appears as a substitute for the missing gravestone. Underneath the tablet a donation box is located, surrounded by various ritual objects (for example, big candles, prayer shawls, miniature Torah scrolls in embellished cases, books of prayer). The furniture in the room consists of a decorated bookcase designed as a Holy Ark, an ornamented Chair of Elijah (traditionally used in circumcision rituals), and a narrow bench for praying. They are placed against a colorfully rich, eye-dazzling background of carpets, tapestries, and amulets which cover all the walls of the narrow room and invest it with an aura of ceremoniality.

On the day of the hillulah the tiny room becomes the focus of a mass celebration in which some 15,000 to 20,000 people take part.

Although the inhabitants of Safed and its hinterland are overrepresented among the celebrants, many pilgrims come from all over the country, using public transportation, hired buses, or private vehicles. The hillulah is conducted along clear-cut ethnic lines as most of the participants are of Moroccan extraction. In recent years groups of Libyan and Tunisian Jews have participated in the celebration, but non-Maghrebi celebrants are virtually nonexistent.

The pilgrimage to Rabbi David u-Moshe's House is essentially a one-day journey. As early as the late morning of the day preceding the new moon of Heshvan people begin to flock to the site, but the zenith of the hillulah, in terms of numbers, is in the early evening. The pilgrims' goal is located in Avraham's standard, unattractive house, entirely indistinguishable from other houses in the neighborhood. On their way to the site the visitors, clustered in groups of relatives, neighbors, and friends, are pressed into a narrow, ascending alley, on both sides of which a small but variegated market spontaneously emerges at the time of the hillulah. On low improvised platforms, commodities are sold that comprise the peculiar mixture of the sacred and the secular typical of the pilgrimage spirit. Holy books, prayer artifacts, oil and candles, and popular portraits of renowned tzaddikim are offered alongside a variety of edibles, garments, and ornaments. Beggars and sellers of blessings, an indispensable part of the pilgrimage setting, are grouped at the end of the trail, near the entrance to the apartment, where the front yard of the home has been enlarged and reshaped into a smooth plateau to absorb the pilgrims. However, since this area is too small to contain them all, most of the celebrants locate themselves wherever they find an empty space, be it a yard of a neighboring house or a nearby sidewalk. The distribution of pilgrims in the densely built neighborhood, which appears so unfitting to serve as an arena for mass gatherings, is marked by spontaneity and lacks any centrally based organization. They sit in groups in the open air or in tents, and indulge themselves in a traditional meal in which large quantities of meat (barbecued on the spot), and spirits are consumed. The feast is punctuated by songs of praise addressed to the tzaddik and by stories of his miraculous feats.

In the absence of a formally imposed ritual structure, the only act deemed compulsory during the hillulah is a visit to the saint's room. From the early hours of the evening until late at night a long line is formed opposite the entrance to the apartment. Some sturdy men, recruited from a group of relatives, neighbors, and friends who voluntarily participate in the organization of the hillulah, regulate the massive flow of traffic. During these busy hours they try to maintain a strict separation between the sexes by alternately allowing unmixed groups of men and women into the room. When the pressure in the shrine is alleviated, men and women freely and carelessly intermingle as they do elsewhere in the rapidly expanding picnic area, in a manner which very orthodox Ashkenazi Jews would never approve.

Inside the tzaddik's room an atmosphere of fervor and ecstasy prevails. The devotees, particularly women, enter the room displaying gestures of submission. They kiss the marble tablet and the carpeted walls and utter their prayers and wishes with great excitement. Before exiting they leave generous sums of money in the donation box. Bottles of water and oil may be left in the room for a while to absorb the saint's sanctity. Later on, the liquids in these bottles will be drunk or smeared on ailing organs for healing purposes. On their way out, the visitors have ample opportunity to survey the rest of the apartment, the modesty of which stands in sharp contrast to the grandeur of the tzaddik's richly decorated room. Although the very act of participation in the hillulah indicates a firm belief in the authenticity of the place, new visitors sometimes appear to be puzzled by the unfitting scenery in which the saint chose to relocate himself.

Most of the celebrants conclude their visit to the saints' room by lighting candles in his honor. In other pilgrimages, where the tombs are located in the open, candles are lit very close to the grave. In Rabbi David u-Moshe's House, a special covered compartment on the far side of the front yard is used for this purpose. Pilgrims throw candles inside the compartment which soon becomes a fiery furnace, and is the focus of much excited praying and crying. Other spots of attraction are three small booths adjacent to the house where teams of volunteers deliver food for free to the celebrants. One of the teams serves hot dishes, including meat, while the others offer hot and cold drinks. The food is prepared during the week preceding the hillulah day by a group of female relatives and neighbors supervised by Avraham's wife. The purchase of products is a complicated project, ranging over most of the year, and a very expensive one too, since huge quantities of food must be bought to satisfy the appetites of thousands of visitors. Indeed, the lion's share of the donated money in the tzaddik's room is dedicated to this end.

Another booth in the open space serves as an abattoir. Some pilgrims bring sheep with them while others prefer to buy an animal from Avraham, who raises a few sheep on the other side of the house.

The ritual slaughterer and his aides also belong to the ring of neighbors and friends on whose shoulders rest the organization and smooth functioning of the hillulah.

Toward the late evening the hillulah becomes a formidable spectacle of mass celebration. The streets near the house are jammed with parking vehicles as visitors continue to flow toward the house, pushing their way to the tzaddik's room. Policemen from the nearby station are called to control the heavy traffic. The crowded front yard becomes the scene of varied social activities as groups from places throughout the country intermingle, old acquaintances meet again, and new associations are formed. Women whose vows have been granted offer trays of sweets to the people around; popular singers attract the celebrants with traditional songs in praise of Rabbi David u-Moshe; and local political figures appear and congratulate the pilgrims. Rhythmic chanting and dancing erupt spontaneously from time to time and are welcomed by traditional ululations of the women. The overall atmosphere conveys a true sense of communality and fraternity, overriding differences in rank and status.

The shift from this climax of mass celebration to the ending of the hillulah is quite abrupt. At midnight the plateau in front of the house appears vacant as most of the visitors have already left for their homes. Only a handful of families stay in their tents overnight. As noted, the pilgrimage area does not constitute a convenient setting for a long stay. Most of the people to be found around the site in the morning following the hillulah belong to the hard core of relatives and friends who help Avraham's family in putting the stage back into its original, ordinary state. Soon the neighborhood resumes its shabby provincial contenance. An accidental visitor would hardly believe that only a few hours ago it drew thousands of celebrants from all over the country.

III. The Role of Dreams in Building
Rabbi David u-Moshe's House

Rabbi David u-Moshe's House, together with other pilgrimage centers, provides a cultural resource through which the group consciousness of traditional Moroccan Jews, presently the largest Jewish ethnic community in Israel, is heightened and their distincitve ethnic identity reconsolidated. As such, the hillulah in Safed may be conceived of as an ethnic renewal ceremony (Gluckman 1963; Weingrod n.d.), which reflects the growing confidence of an emigré in being part of the contemporary Israeli scene while, at the same time, indicating a strong sense of ethnic distinctiveness. Given this social significance, the most striking feature of Rabbi David u-Moshe's House is that it was erected through the spontaneous initiative of one person whose background and education clearly place him among the rank and file. In building the site, Avraham was inspired by dream messages delivered to him by Rabbi David u-Moshe. His success in reviving a pilgrimage tradition, in which thousands of people participate, should be attributed primarily to the impact that these dreams had on his fellow Moroccans. The oneiric encounters with Rabbi David u-Moshe, which continue up to today, constitute for Avraham confirmational evidence that his liaison with the saint is permanent and inseparable. For him the dreams are a constant reminder urging him to pursue his calling with the same dedication and stamina that were characteristic of his first steps on the site. Before sketching the development of Rabbi David u-Moshe's House, through Avraham's dreams, the cultural traditions from which these dreams have emerged should be briefly reviewed.

The idea that dreams have mantic properties with direct consequences to waking life is taken for granted in the Bible, in which the dreams of people of prominence, like Jacob, Joseph, Pharaoh, and Nebuchadnezzar, are taken to be messages from God (Spero 1980). The Talmud, a compilation of numerous rabbinical teachings, contains different, at times opposing, views concerning dreams (Bakan 1958; Bilu 1979; Lorand 1957).[1] While some of these conceptualizations insightfully anticipated modern psychological dream approaches (for example, "nothing is shown [in a dream], but the thoughts of one's heart"), the idea that dreams are heavenly messages, "one-sixtieth of prophecy," represents a dominant approach there as well (Spero 1980). This approach was maintained in sources as distinct as Maimonides and the Zohar, both of which contend that, since traditional means for prophecy are no longer available, dreams may be the contemporary vehicle for divine inspiration.

While Jewish Moroccan dream conceptions were undoubtedly influenced by these classical sources, they were also shaped by indigenous Moroccan culture, where dreams are accorded an important role (Kilborne 1978; 1981; Westermarck 1926). This influence is particularly manifested in dreams associated with folk veneration of saints. In both Muslim and Jewish hagiolatries, a special genre of visitational dreams has prevailed focusing on the potentially rewarding encounter with the saint (Bilu and Abramovitch 1985; Crapanzano 1975). The fact that in both groups these dreams have often been associated with the saints' tombs make them quite akin to the widespread phenomenon of temple sleep or incubation (Dodds 1958; Edelstein and Edelstein 1945). This prevalent dream pattern is explicated as reflecting universal human needs to perceive healers in dreams (O'Nell 1976, 65). While Jewish Moroccan visitational dreams do not necessarily involve ailing patients with medically defined symptoms, they exist against a background of specific life predicaments of which the saint is expected to relieve the dreamer, his devotee (Bilu and Abramovitch 1985).

As visitational dreams, Avraham's oneiric encounters with Rabbi David u-Moshe seem to emanate from a solid, well-defined cultural tradition. In his case, however, the dreams served to create a uniquely enduring alliance with the saint that brought forth a dramatic transformation in his life and had a considerable impact on the Moroccan community at large.

Prior to the first revelation of Rabbi David u-Moshe in 1973, Avraham's life had been comprised of two distinct periods, separated by the aliyah to Israel in 1954. All his years in Morocco had been spent in the village of Imi-n-Tanout, southwest of Marrakesh. Avraham views those years with nostalgic affection, stressing the harmonious relations within the Jewish community and between Jews and Muslims, as well as the spirituality and strict observance of the laws that marked the Jewish life style there. His linkage to the saints, which was established at an early age, was fed by two sources: first, like many other inhabitants of southern Morocco, his infantile recollections were vividly embedded with visits to the local saints of his village. Second, and more important, some of Avraham's own forefathers were considered tzaddikim by their fellow Jews. The fact that those admired nobles and sages were all on his maternal, less cardinal, side may have created a motivational background conducive to Avraham's future initiative, for his claim to having a share in their zekhut (virtue, blessedness), heretofore far from guaranteed, now could be forcefully asserted. Avraham was particularly attached to the later exponent of this familial thread of piety, his maternal grandfather, Rabbi Shlomo, who was venerated by the Jews of Imi-n-Tanout in his lifetime. His death in the town of Essaouira (Mogador), where he had been receiving medical treatment, constituted a traumatic experience of loss and privation for Avraham. These feelings were exacerbated by the fact that the Jews of that coastal town, well aware of the late rabbi's virtue, hastened to bury him in their cemetery. It might be suggested that in building Rabbi David u-Moshe's House, Avraham has unconsciously compensated for the vacuum created by his grandfather's disappearance. The original situation, in which the family tzaddik was appropriated by others, to be buried afar, has been reversed by bringing a tzaddik from afar into the house.

Another familial tradition related to tzaddikim might have served as a model for Avraham's later project. According to this tradition, the tomb of a second sainted figure of his maternal ancestors, originally located at Marrakesh, miraculously reappeared in the cemetery of the Mount of Olives in Jerusalem.

Like all the Jewish boys in his native village, Avraham acquired his Jewish education in the community synagogue (sla), under the strict discipline of the local rabbi. He quit his studies in early adolescence and became a shoemaker, following his father. He pursued this occupation until his immigration to Israel at the age of twenty-four. At that time Avraham was already married and father to a six-month-old daughter.

Ever since his aliyah, thirty years ago, Avraham has lived in Shikun Canaan in Safed. Since his parents and most of his siblings were settled in the same neighborhood, the extended family has managed to preserve a sense of union and togetherness supported by growing feelings of patriotic pride and rootedness in their place of living. Like many of his fellow newcomers, Avraham had to give up his former occupation and earn his living as a forest worker. Unlike most of them, however, he has stayed in this job until this day, clearly one of the lowest in prestige and salary on the vocational echelon. During the first harsh years after the aliyah, the rapidly growing family faced considerable economic difficulties. Nevertheless, Avraham was more than content to live in Safed, a town imbued with a special mystical atmosphere and surrounded by many saints' tombs. Some of these tombs are located on the surrounding hillsides where Avraham spends most of his working time and it is possible that some of his inspiration was acquired there.

While the local tzaddikim constituted natural foci for resuming hagiolatric practices in the new country, Avraham was still attached to the saints of Imi-n-Tanout, and, most of all, to his pious grandfather, Rabbi Shlomo. The painful separation from the latter was particularly felt during the first year after their aliyah in which the economic situation of the family was quite shaky. It is not surprising, therefore, that during that year Avraham had a couple of dreams in which he was visited and encouraged by Rabbi Shlomo. The last of his dreams bears special significance in light of the ambiguity in saints' allegiances instigated by the transfer from Morocco to Israel. It was dreamed on a Saturday night, after Avraham had found a large sum of money that helped him celebrate the Sabbath in abundance.

> On that night I see the tzaddik, Rabbi Shlomo, in a dream. He says to me: "Listen, look who is standing next to you." I turned my face and I saw Rabbi Shim'on Bar-Yohai. He [Rabbi Shlomo] said to me: "Here he is, [standing] next to you. If you need something, you just come to him. He will give you." Rabbi Shim'on took a loaf of bread, handed it to me, and said: "Go, make your Sabbath, from now on you won't be lacking anything."

The message of the dream is quite explicit: while in Morocco Rabbi Shlomo had been the patron of his grandson, in Israel he transferred him to the custody of Rabbi Shim'on, a most potent saint who resides in the vicinity of Safed. Thus the transition from Morocco to Israel was completed through a symbolic reorganization of saints' allegiances. Two points are worth mentioning in this regard. First, this dream marked the termination of Avraham's repeated oneiric encounters with Rabbi Shlomo. Second, when Avraham established a liaison with Rabbi David u-Moshe eighteen years later, Rabbi Shim'on was present in some of his dreams, just as Rabbi Shlomo before him.

Avraham's growing attachment to the local tzaddikim was expressed in the names he gave to his two oldest sons. (All in all, he has ten children, six of whom are boys.) His first Israeli-born son, whose birth date coincided with the dream episode discussed, was accordingly named Shim'on, while the second bears the name of Rabbi Meir. The burial sites of these two sages, located at Meron and Tiberias respectively, are by far the largest pilgrimage centers in Israel. Avraham's third son was given the name of his venerated grandfather, Shlomo.

The neighborhood synagogue at Shikun Canaan was another area in which Avraham's religious faith and dedication to the saints could be expressed. He was one of the founders of the synagogue, and soon became its *gabbai*, an administrative role which constituted excellent preparation for the organizational task of running his later enterprise. In this job he participated in organizing the hillulah of Rabbi Ya'akov Abu-Hatsera, the most popular tzaddik among the historical sainted figures of Moroccan Jewry, which, in the synagogue context, took the form of a communal meal (*se'udah*). In 1971 a dispute among the worshippers made it impossible to conduct the se'udah in the synagogue. Avraham, infuriated by the participants' lack of readiness to relinquish their quarrel for such sublime an end, publicly announced that he would arrange the meal for Rabbi Ya'akov at his place, using his own modest means.

This commitment, in which a personal initiative replaced an institutionalized pattern in maintaining hagiolatric practices, may be conceived as a significant anticipation of Avraham's later project. The model for admitting a saint into one's own house had thus been established on a modest ground. (The synagogue se'udah involved no more than a few dozen celebrants.) Unsurprisingly, it was supported by a dream encounter with the tzaddik involved:

> I saw myself walking on a plateau [full] of sand, and it was terribly hot there. Then I was running together with all those people [of the synagogue]. I was so thirsty that I almost fainted. I began to tremble all over my body. Suddenly I saw a mountain on which a rabbi was seated holding a big book in his hand. All the grass around him was made of big snakes. He looked around and said: Woe to the one who enters this place, I'll send the snakes against him! I stood up and he said: "No, you can come; you shouldn't be afraid, come on, hold this stick!" All the snakes lowered their heads, and I entered. He filled a glass of water for me and I drank it. He said: "Do you know who I am!" I said: "No." [He said:] "I am Rabbi Ya'akov Abu-Hatsera." Then he said: "You should proceed [in your way]. You won't be lacking anything."

The plot of this dream, which depicts the dreamer's singular success in achieving contact with the tzaddik despite hindrances and predicaments, conveys the sense of Avraham's calling precipitated by his public commitment to Rabbi Ya'akov. The saint's grace is bestowed on him alone, while all other synagogue attendants fail to gain access to the tzaddik. Variations on this theme recur in his later dreams relating to Rabbi David u-Moshe. The dream is replete with biblical associations. The metaphor of water relieving the thirsty supplicant brings to mind similar images depicting contact with the divine in Psalms (and blessing, uttered over water, has long been Abu-Hatsera's peculiar method of choice in healing), and the juxtaposition of the stick to the snakes in a competitive context seems to allude to the contest between Moses and Pharaoh's royal magicians. (If correctly deciphered, this association may indicate the dreamer's deep-seated messianic fervor.) It should be noted that the latter episode took place in Egypt, where Rabbi Ya'akov's burial site is located. The dream setting (sand, extreme heat) seems to be adapted to the desert ecology of that country as probably perceived by the dreamer.

Notwithstanding these biblical associations, a more recent, personally based episode seems to have participated in the construction of this dream. During the summertime Avraham and some of his fellow workers used to take refuge from the heat in an ancient burial cave near Safed, ascribed to two Talmudic sages, Abbaye and Rava. On Fridays they stored, in the chilly cave, bottles of wine with which they celebrated the approaching Sabbath. On one Friday afternoon a worker, who had been sent to bring the wine, returned in panic after he had seen a snake at the entrance. Other companions tried to force their way in but they were also deterred by the reptile. Avraham alone was able to enter the cave and to retrieve the wine safely. Since he had met no snake on his way he interpreted the episode as a divine message indicating his virtue as against his companions. The impact of this occurrence seems to have been reflected in the dream of Rabbi Ya'akov. The transfer might also have been facilitated by the fact that the two groups, Avraham's coworkers and his fellow attendants, greatly overlap. It should be noted that the dream ends with the same reassuring message that sealed the oneiric encounter with Rabbi Shim'on: in both cases nurturance is guaranteed to the loyal supplicant.

These two dreams were selected from a larger collection of visitational dreams, all of which belong, insofar as Rabbi David u-Moshe is concerned, to the prerevelation period. Hence the idea that the latter tzaddik's apparition was an unexpected act of sudden inspiration cannot be maintained. More correctly, it appears as the product of a persistent process of active search in the course of which a veteran member of the cult of the saints gradually shifts saint allegiances until he finds his own patron-tzaddik. Rabbi Shlomo, a natural object of veneration, is rightly his own, but his reputation among the Moroccan emigrés is meager. Rabbi Shim'on is the most reputed saint in Israel, a core symbol of mysticism and piety, but his tradition is well established and cannot be appropriated by any single devotee, dutiful and resourceful as he may be. This also holds true for Rabbi Ya'akov whose living descendants' claim to be his legitimate heirs cannot easily be challenged. Rabbi David u-Moshe, a tzaddik whom Avraham claims not to have known in Morocco, seemed to be a cultural figure ready to be enshrined. Well known and highly venerated by many southern Moroccan Jews, the hagiolatric practices related to him lacked focus and coherence since his sanctuary had been left far behind.

In explicating the timing of Rabbi David u-Moshe's apparition, Avraham's stage in his life cycle seems significant. Approaching midlife, the growth of his family has been attenuated. His last son was born a few months after the visitation of Rabbi David u-Moshe in 1973. He was given, of course, one of the tzaddik's names, Moshe. The appearance of the saint thus marked the termination of the fertile phase of family expansion followed by a shift toward spiritual concerns, more appropriate to midlife.

In 1972, Avraham's dearest brother and neighbor was killed in a ridiculously minor car accident in which neither the car nor the other passengers was hurt. Avraham, basically optimistic and complacent, became despondent and melancholic and could not find consolation. To his ninth child, who was born a few months later, he gave the name of his beloved brother. The loss created in Avraham a state of emotional turmoil which constituted a fertile matrix for the appearance of the tzadddik. As will be shown, it was Rabbi David u-Moshe, in one of his first oneiric apparitions, who put an end to Avraham's prolonged distress.

The event which immediately precipitated Rabbi David u-Moshe's first visitation was Avraham's firm intention to move from his apartment to a bigger, more comfortable place in another neighborhood. The change was prevented at the last moment by the saint's announcement that he desires the old apartment as his permanent abode. As a result, Avraham and his family were tied to their original place of residence by inextricable bonds. It should be noted that the same sequence of events—an intention to leave followed by a renewed commitment to one's place of residence—has underlain the erection of other sacred sites in Israel. It also has found varied expressions in other dreams which will be discussed.

The revelation of Rabbi David u-Moshe in 1973 marked a dramatic transformation in Avraham's life. From then on the saint's oneiric messages became his sole guidelines for action. One of these first messages was to write down his dreams and to distribute them in all the Moroccan communities in Israel. In complying with the tzaddik's command, Avraham dramatically and sweepingly transformed his private vision into a public affair, shared and supported by many. The announcement to the public, includes Avraham's first initiation dreams. The ornate style of rendering, which stands in sharp contrast with Avraham's plain oral recounting of his dreams, betrays the fact that he was helped by the local rabbi in formulating the announcement. Nevertheless, he insisted that the written report constitutes a veracious representation of the saint's messages. In fact, when the scribe dared to deviate somewhat from the original version, an acute attack of dizziness, allegedly brought on by the tzaddik, forced him to reword the text as presented to him by Avraham.

Announcement to the Public

I, Avraham Ben Hayim, who live in Canaan, Building 172, in Safed, the Holy City, have been privileged by the Lord to see wonders. And as I was ordered, I make known to you a message from our master the tzaddik, Rabbi David u-Moshe, may the memory of the tzaddik be for a blessing, who has revealed himself to me many times.

In my first dream I looked, and lo! There stood before me a man dressed in white, and the radiance of his face was like an angel's. He approached me, seized my hand, and led me to high hills. And among their huge boulders, I saw a white stretch of land. When we came to this clearing, he sat on the ground and said to me: "See, only ten people celebrate and mark my hillula day. And I ask you: Why have those who left Morocco forsaken me and deserted me? Where are all the thousands—my followers and believers?" I replied to him: "Do you really want them to return to Morocco from Israel to perform the hillula?" The man took me again by the hand, turned me around, and asked: "What place is this?" I answered him: "This is my house." The tzaddik continued: "In this place I want you to observe my hillula day, from year to year." I asked him: "What does my lord want?" And he answered me: "I am the man who revealed himself to those who loved me in Morocco. I am Rabbi David u-Moshe!!! I am he, the man who makes supplication and prays before God everyday to preserve the soldiers of Israel, on the borders of the land! If so, why have they deserted me, those who left Morocco? Now here I am in the Holy Land, and my request is that they renew the marking of my hillula."

Two days later, he returned and revealed himself to me in a dream, at a time when I was tossing in my bed between sleep and wakefulness. He woke me up and said to me: "My son, you made a mistake when you told people you saw me in a dream. You shoud have said to them that you saw me eye to eye. But never mind, I forgive you for this. And now hear my words: I left Morocco and came here, because this place is holy, and I chose you to be my servant in this holy work. And now, you will do this:

1. Establish a place for yourself where candles will be burned in my memory and whoever comes to pray and to make supplication for his soul will light me a candle!

2. Beside the place of the candles, set a collection box, and each will donate according to his desire and his means!

3. Whoever approaches the place of the candles will do so with awe, love, and wholeheartedly!

4. He who enters this place must be clean, in his body and his deeds!

5. It is forbidden to deal in and sell these candles or these memorial cups. Whoever wishes will light a candle, on condition that he be clean, as stated above!

6. The place will be open to the public night and day!

7. In the feast of my hillula, there will be no distinction between big and small or between rich and poor, but all will be equal.

8. My hillula will be held on the eve of the new moon of Heshvan. If the new moon of Heshvan falls on Friday, the hillula will take place on the preceding Thursday!

9. Warn your wife and the members of your household, not to allow entry to a man or a woman who is unclean!

10. With the contributions that will accumulate in the collection box, enlarge the place, so that it will be able to contain the thousands of people who will come here to celebrate and to pray!

After three days the tzaddik again revealed himself to me in a dream in the night, and this time he was accompanied by two men. He turned to me and asked: "Do you recognize these?" I answered: "One I saw with you in the second dream, and the second one I recognize from a different dream." The tzaddik continued: "Do you know who they are?" I answered him: "The first is Elijah the Prophet, remembered for the good, and the second is Rabbi Ya'akov Abu-Hatsera, may the memory of the tzaddik be for a blessing." The tzaddik nodded to signal agreement, and he concluded his words as follows: that I have to be strict and to let into this place only people who are clean in body and soul.

As the tzaddik has requested, we shall hold the hillula. God willing, on the night of the new moon of Heshvan, this year and every year, at my house as mentioned above.

May the Lord help us for the sake of His honor and His great name.

Come one and all, and may the blessing be with us and with you!!!

In the first dream the tzaddik's transition from Morocco to Israel and his selection of Avraham's house as his new sanctuary are straightforwardly portrayed. The dreamer's underlying wish seems to have been externalized and displaced onto the saint as it is he, rather than the dreamer, who initiated his move to Safed. The latter is described as a passive object on whom the tzaddik's grace impinges. The written version of the dream somewhat blurs the fact that Avraham did not identify the saint on his first apparition. While this ignorance is typical of visitational dreams in general (see Bilu and Abramovitch 1985), in this case it was congruent with Avraham's own claim not to have known the saint before the revelation. Long after the tzaddik's first visitation, however, Avraham retrieved a long-forgotten childhood memory which may have contributed to his selection. The fact that Avraham altogether forgot that episode, which concerned gathering contributions for the saint's box, may have found expression in the tzaddik's allegations in their first oneiric meeting: "Why have those who left Morocco forsaken me and deserted me?" Avraham's covert sense of guilt, indicated by the deserted saint's reproach, may have reflected a collective mood of many exdevotees who had also been dissociated from their once-cherished saint on immigrating to Israel. Unlike them, the saint appears attuned to the prevailing sentiments in contemporary Israel and prays for the soldiers on the borders.

The second dream in the announcement, in which the saint paradoxically denies the oneiric nature of his first apparition (thus enhancing its credibility), includes ten precepts (echoing the ten commandments) which establish the rules of conduct in the reconstituted site of the tzaddik. While most of these requirements reflect the traditional pattern of saint's veneration, they also convey Avraham's vision and confidence in the prospects of the place as a major pilgrimage center.

In the third dream, the tzaddik is accompanied by Elijah the Prophet and Rabbi Ya'akov Abu-Hatsera, two eminent figures whose appearance grants more credence to the messages in the former dreams. Although Avraham's initiative is oriented toward one particular tzaddik, his project is supported by other saints as well. As will be shown, some of these saints claimed their share in the new site.

The second announcement to the public (which is too lengthy to present here) reflects Avraham's growing assertiveness and sense of confidence in his calling following the recurrent visits of the saint and the positive response of the community. It includes one detailed dream account in which the encounter with Rabbi David u-Moshe is created along lines inversely related to the first version. The dreamer, determined and tenacious, heads for the tzaddik's place in Morocco. After overcoming many obstacles on the way, he reaches the cave in which Rabbi David u-Moshe is studying Torah with other sages. He takes the saint on his shoulders and brings him to his home in Safed. The former pattern of an active, initiating saint vis-à-vis a passive adherent is thus reversed. The second announcement ends with the same injunctions as the first one, but their tone is more commanding and assertive. In addition, the tzaddik explicitly condemns any attempt to celebrate his hillulah outside his chosen abode in Shikun Canaan which he designates as his permanent home.

The third announcement, which was published around 1975, departs sharply in content and style from the two earlier publications. Designated "a call for the purity of the family," this is essentially a moral comment in which different misfortunes and adversities, from car accidents to terrorist attacks, are attributed to negligence in maintaining purity laws related to the ritual bath. While this information was disclosed to Avraham through his dream encounters with the tzaddik, no mention is made of the new site, the legitimacy of which seems to have been already secured. This was the last announcement Avraham dispatched to the public. The sweepingly growing recognition of his place over the country has made the dissemination of further announcements superfluous.

Before publicizing his newly erected site as a healing shrine, Avraham had to come to terms with a personal predicament which haunted him for a long time, namely, his brother's untimely, futile death. As noted, this event might have urged him to seek the protection of an omnipotent patron in the first place. As might be expected, the tzaddik soon intervened in order to terminate his devotee's prolonged distress. In one of his first oneiric apparitions he took Avraham to a magnificent garden and picked one of the most beautiful roses that grew there, explaining that in the same way God selects the best people to reside with him. Under his explicit demand Avraham stopped his mourning and complaints. The significance of the saint as an indispensable resource at times of personal crisis was thus well established.

Following the apparition of Rabbi David u-Moshe, Avraham's life has been drastically reconstituted. As the saint's emissary he has dedicated all his free time and energy to the shrine he has founded, fluctuating between inspiring moments of spiritual exaltation invoked by his intimate contacts with the holy and long hours of routine work in maintaining the site, to serve the perennial flow of supplicants, and

to prepare for the next hillulah. In one of his first postrevelation dreams
this drastic transformation was expressed through the theme of death
and rebirth, a common metaphor for articulating abrupt and profound
changes in life:

> I am asleep and suddenly I see that someone is coming. A man, he
> brought a kind of notebook. He said to me, "Do you know from whence
> I bring this?" I said, "From whence?" He said, "From a celestial court. I
> have brought it." I said, "How come? Is this a law court?" "Yes, this is a
> kind of law court." I said, "What is it for?" He said, "Do you know, up to
> this hour—this is your life. That's it. Finished." I see myself as if I am
> dead. I hear people talking. This man, with his lies, talks of the tzaddik.
> Everyone says something. All this in a dream. While I am like this, all of
> a sudden I see that someone arrives. He passed his hand over me and
> said, "Get up!" He said, "Do you know who I am?" I said, "Yes," He said,
> "I am Elijah the Prophet." I said, "What's here?" He said, "True, your life
> was finished but do you see this one with the fringed garment praying
> for your sake?" I said, "I see two." He said, "Who are they?" I said, "Rabbi
> Ya'akov Abu-Hatsera and Rabbi David u-Moshe." He said," I see only
> one! Do you know what he says?" "What says Rabbi David u-Moshe?" I
> said, "What does he say?" "Listen well. He says that your years will be
> renewed, since no one has been born yet who does what you do and
> takes care of what you take care of." I asked him, "And what will be the
> end of the matter?" He said to me, "Do you know how much [time] is
> left until the hillula?" I said, "No." He said. "There remains seventy-six
> days, by calculation. Take out six days, there will remain seventy [days]
> exactly." He said, "After this hillula, in another seventy days, you will
> have about seventy years. Now you are here. You must hold seventy
> hillulot." I said to him, "How have I merited this?" "You have merited it,
> because [in] everything you do for the tzaddik, you do not consult with
> anybody." And then he turned around and addressed Rabbi David u-
> Moshe and said "No! I have added two more years to you. Seventy-two.
> And after seventy-two years, the Lord will have mercy." He added: "Do
> you see all these people who are talking? Their time has yet to come. But
> slowly, slowly!" And he pulled out a sort of paper from his pocket and
> spread it out like a map. He said, "Do you see this plan and these
> buildings? You will yet make them from this collection box. All this will
> be executed. Only patience. As for the people who are holding hillulot
> [elsewhere], I will bring them here. Till they assemble here." And then
> he was gone.

Avraham's premature death would have put an end to his initiative
and therefore altogether discredit it, as indicated in the dream by the
denigrating response of the people around his dead body. To forestall
this, the same triad of saints that appeared in the first announcement

(Rabbi David u-Moshe, Elijah the Prophet, and Rabbi Ya'akov Abu-Hatsera) grant Avraham seventy-two more years. Since during his rebirth Avraham was in his forties, this increment would draw him near the ripe old age of one hundred and twenty, the ideal life span according to Jewish tradition, usually reserved for the righteous. The quota of years added to Avraham's life follows a peculiar sequence of permutations which seems to be based on mystical traditions. According to a midrash,[2] Adam yielded seventy years from his life span to King David. According to the kabbalistic doctrine, seventy-two is a number impregnated with holiness since it contains one of God's most enigmatic and potent appellations.

The temporal contingency between this dream and the preceding one does not seem haphazard as both of them deal with death. It might be conjectured that Avraham, taken aback by his brother's untimely end, feared a similar fate. The brothers, apart from being inseparably attached to each other, were close in age and their life courses were quite similar. Avraham was spared his brother's destiny, however, due to the protective cover of the saint, which his brother had lacked.

Following Avraham's rebirth each of his site-related activities has been initiated and monitored by the tzaddik, as clearly indicated in the epilogue of the dream. Rabbi David u-Moshe appears as the architect of his own shrine. He also takes it upon himself to castigate Avraham's opponents and to bring his devotees to his place. The fact that these adherents were described as holding hillulot elsewhere is significant since, in order to turn his newly erected site into a widely attended pilgrimage center, Avraham had to abrogate those domestic hillulot which symbolized the decentralized nature of hagiolatry in the early postimmigration era. Indeed, the centripetal emphasis has become a recurrent theme in the saint's oneiric instructions to Avraham. When he himself lit a candle for the tzaddik in his brother-in-law's apartment in Tiberias he was immediately informed by Rabbi David u-Moshe of the inappropriateness and futility of his act: "I have put out the candle ... [since] I do not want the candle here! Only in the place where I dwell." The saint also appeared determined in regard to collection boxes: "Whoever comes [asking] for a collection box, do not give it to him! Whoever wants something, let him come and put it here in the box." On another nightly visit he reprimanded Avraham for allowing a supplicant to take a portion of the sacrificial meal back to his home. When Avraham questioned this prohibition, the saint explained that, "if one takes [the portion] and gives it to other people, they *won't come*;

but if they all come here, they'll eat and be satisfied" (emphasis added).

Following the charismatic phase of the early postrevelation era, in which Rabbi David u-Moshe's House emerged as the saint's chosen abode, there came a long period of strenuous efforts aimed at developing the site, securing the economic basis of the hillulah, and crystallizing its patterns. In pursuing these goals, Avraham could not rely on his own resources alone but had to gain the cooperation of many artisans and the acquiescence of various civil servants. Since the latter were quite often hostile to his demands, the saint's support became all the more important during that period of institutionalization. Two episodes clearly demonstrate the indispensable role played by the tzaddik during that time:

> The tzaddik came and said to me: "Listen, if you have money you can build. Build, by force. if they want to take you to court, go to court. If they say to you: Destroy this place, you say to them: I built, you destroy, and in that hour they'll see who is sitting in this place."

> A contractor came and I asked him to finish a room or two for me. He didn't want to. He couldn't care less. I sought out the tzaddik and said to him: "You dwell here now: Go to the contractor and talk to him." He went. For two days he [the contractor] and his wife could not sleep. On Friday he came to me and said: "In the name of the Lord, ask the tzaddik to let me be." He [the tzaddik] came to him [the contractor] in a dream . . . He said to him: "Either you finish the place or I'll finish you." He came and asked him forgiveness.

The first dream deals with the most pressing problem which Avraham has had to face up to now, the granting of permits from various municipal and governmental agencies for enlarging the site and installing facilities (such as bathrooms, an abbatoir). While in this dream the tzaddik merely encourages Avraham to pursue his goal despite the officials' opposition, in the second episode his intervention is more strongly felt as he forces a recalcitrant contractor to keep a commitment heretofore abrogated. What is witnessed here for the first time is an oneiric apparition of Rabbi David u-Moshe which involves other people than Avraham. Such dream messages have allegedly compelled many of Avraham's antagonists, from a jealous old neighbor to the mayor of Safed, to acquiesce to many of Avraham's initiatives which they had formerly resisted.

IV. Epilogue: The Community of Dreamers and the
Holy Calendar

The rapid development of Rabbi David u-Moshe's House cannot be accounted for only by the impact Avraham's dreams have had on his fellow Moroccan Jews. The dynamics underlying its emergence as a major pilgrimage center involved an ongoing dialogue between the initiator and the community based on dreams. Since the announcements to the public were not idiosyncratically construed but were rather mediated by a cultural figure, with whom many Jews from Morocco had been eager to resume their relationships, there emerged a community of dreamers through which Avraham's initiative was consensually validated. Even the very first visitation of the tzaddik in Avraham's flat, a private event reflected in a dream, was later corroborated by a female neighbor who dreamed that an old bearded man, dressed in white, passed by her house. She invited him to her place but he refused, explaining that his goal was her neighbor's (Avraham's) flat.

Rabbi David u-Moshe's most incumbent mission in the community was to draw supplicants to his new place. In light of the potential rivalry between Shikun Canaan and other places where the tzaddik's hillulot had been conducted, his burial site at Agouim in particular, dreams that diverted pilgrims from other sites to Safed acquired a special significance. The following is a typical example dreamed by a barren woman living in France who vowed to make a pilgrimage to Agouim:

> The saint came to her and said: "Madame, I heard that you are coming to me, that you want to be a guest in my house." She said, "Yes, at once!" Then he said: "But I am not in Agouim any more; I am among the Jews in Safed. Here, take this address!" She woke up and wrote down the address of this place (Rabbi David u-Moshe's House). She came here indeed and later on gave birth to a male child.

Once his potential clientele had been secured, Rabbi David u-Moshe's traditional role as an intermediary between the people in need and God could be forcefully enacted. Since the first hillulah coincided with the Yom Kippur (Day of Atonement) War (1973) many of his early oneiric interventions dealt with the aftermath of that event (for example, curing the wounded soldiers). Later on they have been extended to other public events, from earthquakes to terrorist attacks and to political upheavals, moralizing and rendering them meaningful. However, the lion's share of his oneiric apparitions in the community since 1973 has been activated by personal concerns. A wide array of human afflictions, including physical and mental ailments, pregnancy and birth problems, interpersonal disputes and economic downfalls, were all assuaged and cared for in dreams of the tzaddik. Although older people who had known the tzaddik in Morocco had occasionally dreamed about him before his transfer to Safed, it was Avraham's initiative that precipitated most of the dreams.

Inspired by the positive response of the public to his dream-based project, Avraham on his part sought to maximize its potentialities by absorbing other tzaddikim into it. While Rabbi David u-Moshe, Avraham's patron saint, has indisputably remained the dominant figure in the site, in recent years the house bearing his name has become a pantheon of saints, as six other tzaddikim successively appeared in Avraham's dreams and expressed their wish to have their hillulot celebrated in his place. This expansionist trend has clearly capitalized on Avraham's initial success with Rabbi David u-Moshe since, according to a folk tradition represented in Avraham's own dreams, tzaddikim tend to assemble and study Torah together. It should be emphasized that as against Rabbi David u-Moshe's alleged permanent residence in the site, the presence of other tzaddikim is said to be limited to their death anniversaries. Moreover, their hillulot are clearly domestic occurrences which take the form of a communal meal (se'udah). As mentioned, the hillulah of one of these saints, Rabbi Ya'akov Abu-Hatsera, had preceded, in fact, that of Rabbi David u-Moshe.

The first hillulot to be celebrated in Rabbi David u-Moshe's House were those of Rabbi Meir Ba'al ha-Ness and Rabbi Shim'on Bar Yohai, the most venerated native saints, whose death anniversaries fall on the thirtieth and thirty-third days after Passover, respectively. Their absorption into the new site has been quite a daring act since both saints' burial sites, located not far from Safed, have been old pilgrimage centers with international reputations. The same allegations which Avraham raised against those who insisted on celebrating Rabbi David u-Moshe's hillulah separately, on a local level, could be leveled against him. In this delicate situation the fact that Avraham was motivated by explicit dream messages is of particular significance. A dream excerpt portrays Rabbi Shim'on's apparition in Avraham's site:

On Lag ba-'Omer (the feast of Rabbi Shim'on) we never used to prepare. But last week he himself, peace upon him, Rabbi Shim'on stood before me and said to me in a dream: "Listen! You know that this place doesn't belong just to Rabbi David u-Moshe? I have a portion here. And now take heed!" And Rabbi David u-Moshe was sitting nearby and laughing. And Rabbi Shim'on was outside. Rabbi Shim'on speaks in Hebrew with me and Rabbi David u-Moshe speaks to me in Moroccan Arabic.... He said to me: "Take heed, I order you that on the eve of the hillulah you are not to let anyone enter this place, from evening until seven in the morning. Draw the curtain, and don't let anyone enter, because we want to sit here." I answered him: "How can this be? On that very evening of the hillulah thousands of Jews come to prostrate themselves on your grave. And how did you choose to come to this place?" He replied: 'Here I know that this is a holy place.'

This dream seems to have been produced by the potential rivalry between Meron and Shikun Canaan, two pilgrimage centers which are territorially adjacent. The divergent cultural traditions underlying these sites is reflected in the fact that Rabbi Shim'on and Rabbi David u-Moshe communicate with Avraham in Hebrew and in Moroccan Arabic, respectively. Avraham's ambivalence toward the native saint, formerly a nurturing patron, but now an impending menace to the success of his initiative, is implied in Rabbi David u-Moshe's laughing reception of Rabbi Shim'on and the fact that the latter stayed outside. The tension is resolved, however, through an unexpectedly ambitious maneuver: although Meron is by far the most popular site in the country, Rabbi Shim'on finds it appropriate to spend the night of his own hillulah in Rabbi David u-Moshe's House. The tacit dissatisfaction of Rabbi Shim'on with his own sanctuary, left unstated here, was openly expressed in another dream, in which the impious actions of some of the numerous celebrants there (such as gambling, courting) were condemned. Retrospectively, the new site has benefited rather than been damaged by the geographical proximity to Meron, since it has been frequented by many pilgrims on their way to Rabbi Shim'on's sanctuary.

The fifth tzaddik to be incorporated into Avraham's house was Rabbi David m-Barukh,[3] a renowned Jewish Moroccan saint buried in Oulad Brakhil near Taroudant in southern Morocco. Since his hillulah had been conducted in Shikun Canaan by a family from that village long before Rabbi David u-Moshe's House was erected, Avraham was quite reluctant to appear as a usurper and declined the saint's oneiric request to arrange a se'udah for him. Rabbi David's response was fast and harsh; in a subsequent dream he tied Avraham's ten children together and threatened to kill them unless his demand is met. Fearing for his children's lives, Avraham has made it his custom to slaughter sheep on the third day of Tevet (the fourth month in the Jewish calendar), the death anniversary of the tzaddik, from which a communal meal is prepared in his honor.

This episode constitutes another example of the effectiveness of dreams as a flexible cultural resource in cases of potential, territorially based conflicts. The fact that the adoption of Rabbi David m-Barukh by Avraham deprived a neighboring family of their long-standing tradition was mitigated by the compulsory nature of the saint's threatening dream message.

The sixth tzaddik to be introduced to Avraham's site is another well-known Jewish Moroccan saint, Rabbi Daniel Hashomer Ashkenazi, whose burial site is located near Marrakesh. In this case the initiatory dream message was accepted immediately as Avraham has been entreated for a long time by a close friend of his, a veteran adherent of that saint, to arrange a se'udah for the latter. Rabbi Daniel's hillulah is celebrated on the first day of Elul (the twelfth month in the Jewish calendar).

The seventh se'udah honors the death anniversary of Ahiyah Ha-Shiloni, a biblical prophet of minor importance who was imbued with a special aura of holiness in Jewish mystical sources. As in the former cases, it was initiated by a dream in which Avraham found himself in his own apartment, encircled by many tzaddikim who were celebrating the hillulah of Ahiyah. As the householder, they granted him the honor of commencing the se'udah by reciting the blessing on the food. Ahiyah himself beseeched Avraham to follow the model set by the tzaddikim and to celebrate his hillulah "in the same way the hillulot of the other tzaddikim are conducted." Since this dream was dreamed on the fifteenth day of Tammuz (the tenth month in the Jewish calendar), the hillulah was set up for that date.

Two related points are worth mentioning regarding the incorporation of Ahiyah Ha-Shiloni to the site. First, it demonstrates Avraham's growing creativeness and urge for innovation in expanding his project. Unlike the other cultural identities he relocated in his site, Ahiyah has never been a saint in the ordinary sense within Jewish lore; therefore no pilgrimage tradition has hitherto been associated with his name. In this case, then, Avraham appears truly as a cultural innovator. Second, the dream amply conveys the sense of confidence and assertiveness that Avraham has gained in the course of the successful development of his project. In this regard, the contrast with the dream of the first tzaddik to be taken in, Rabbi Ya'akov Abu-Hatsera seems illuminating. While in that dream Avraham had to prove himself as a worthy host of the saint by persevering hardships and predicaments in the desert, far away from his home, now he is located quite comfortably in his own house, surrounded by many tzaddikim, his tenants, who acknowledge his importance as their benefactor. This comparison strikingly shows that Avraham and his site have come of age.

Well dispersed over the whole year, the seven hillulot have strengthened Avraham's web of associations with the saints. By erecting Rabbi David u-Moshe's House, he delineated a sacred space and a sacred time (Eliade 1954)—the hillulah day of the tzaddik. Since then he has expanded the temporal dimension of this self-generated holiness by creating a sacred annual calendar, embedded with spiritual markers—the seven hillulot—which punctuate his entire life course and regulate its rhythm. With Rabbi David u-Moshe as its overarching symbol, Avraham's site now maintains a neat balance between Jewish Moroccan and native Israeli hagiolatric practices; both of them are represented by three tzaddikim each.

Does this closure set limits on Avraham's initiative? Judging from the dynamic development of Rabbi David u-Moshe's House during the last decade and its absorptive nature it seems that its growth potentialities have not been exhausted. Having dreamed recently of Rabbi Israel Ba'al Shem-Tov (Besht), the eighteenth century founder of the Hasidic movement in Eastern Europe, it is not impossible that Avraham's next initiative will cross the ethnic boundaries toward adopting Ashkenazi tzaddikim to his site.

The important role of dreams in sustaining cultural traditions and in facilitating cultural innovations has been discerned in many societies (Bourguignon 1972; O'Nell 1976; Stephen 1979). Lanternari (1975), who designates dreams underlying the rise of new religious movements "charismatic significants," emphasizes the transformation that the dreamer may undergo following the encounter with the supernatural beings and forces of his cultural tradition: "When, through the dream experience, the dreamer comes into contact with these typically creative, sacred forces he acquires a creative, sacred power. Thus, from his dream, the individual draws the certainty of a favorable fate, a reason for self-confidence, inspiration for his decisions and actions and, therefore, his self-identification" (322–23). While all of these changes hold true for Avraham, his major significance lies in his contributions to the Jewish Moroccan community in Israel. By furnishing members of this community with a viable idiom to articulate their experiences in the contemporary Israeli scene, Avraham's project, a healing shrine and a community center, has become a cultural resource of considerable importance.

Notes

*I wish to express my appreciation to I. Ben Ami for permission to quote excerpts from his article (1981), concerning the dreams.

1. See BT *Berakhot* 55a–57b.

2. See the Zohar on Genesis 5:1, English translation by H. Sperling, M. Simon, and P. Levertoff (London: Soncino, 1933).

3. The *m*, like the *u* in Rabbi David u-Moshe, is a Berber linguistic form.

References

Bakan, D. (1958). *Sigmund Freud and the Jewish Mystical Tradition*. Princeton, N.J.: D. Van Nostrand Co.

Ben Ami, I. (1981). "The Folk-Veneration of Saints among Moroccan Jews; Traditions: Continuity and Change. The Case of the Holy Man, Rabbi David u-Moshe." In *Studies in Judaism and Islam*. S. Morag, I. Ben Ami, and N. Stillman, eds. Jerusalem: Magnes Press, 283–345.

Ben Ami, I. (1984). "Saint Veneration among the Jews in Morocco." *Folklore Research Center Studies* vol. 8 Jerusalem: Magnes Press. Hebrew.

Bilu, Y. (1979). "Sigmund Freud and Rabbi Yehudah: On a Jewish Mystical Tradition of 'Psychoanalytic' Dream Interpretation." *The Journal of Psychological Anthropology* 2:443–63.

Bilu, Y. and H. Abramovitch (1985). "In Search of the Saddiq: Visitational Dreams among Moroccan Jews in Israel." *Psychiatry* 48:83–92.

Bourguignon, E. (1972). "Dreams and Altered States of Consciousness in Anthropological Research." In *Psychological Anthropology*, F. L. K. Hsu, ed. Cambridge, Ma.: Schenkman Publications, 403–434.

Crapanzano, V. (1975). "Saints, Jnun and Dreams: An Essay in Moroccan Ethnopsychiatry." *Psychiatry* 38:145–59.

Dodds, E. R. (1958).*The Greeks and the Irrational*. Berkeley: University of California Press.

Edelstein, E., and L. Edelstein. (1945). *Ascelapius: A Collection and Interpretation of the Testimonies.* Baltimore: Johns Hopkins Press.

Eickelman, D. F. (1976). *Moroccan Islam.* Austin: University of Texas Press.

Eliade, M. (1954). *The Myth of the Eternal Return.* New York: Pantheon Books.

Gellner, E. (1969). *Saints of the Atlas.* Chicago: University of Chicago Press.

Geertz, C. (1968). *Islam Observed.* New Haven: Yale University Press.

Gluckman, M. (1963). *Order and Rebellion in Tribal Africa.* London: Cohen and West.

Goldberg, H. (1983). "The Mellahs of Southern Morocco: Report of a Survey." *The Maghreb Review* 8(3–4):61–69.

Kilborne, B. (1978). *Interpretations du Rêve au Maroc.* Claix: La Pensée Sauvage.

———. (1981). "Moroccan Dream Interpretation and Culturally Constituted Defense Mechanisms." *Ethos* 9:294–312.

Lanternari, V. (1975). "Dreams as Charismatic Significants: Their Bearing on the Rise of New Religious Movements." In T. R. Williams, ed. *Psychological Anthropology.* The Hague: Mouton, 221–35.

Lorand, S. (1957). "Dream Interpretation in the Talmud." *International Journal of Psychoanalysis* 38:92–97.

O'Nell, C. W. (1976). *Dreams, Culture, and the Individual.* New York: Chandler and Sharp.

Rabinow, P. (1975). *Symbolic Domination.* Chicago: University of Chicago Press.

Spero, M. H. (1980). *Judaism and Psychology.* New York: Yeshiva University Press.

Stephen, M. (1979). "Dreams of Change: The Innovative Role of Altered States of Consciousness in Traditional Melanesian Religion." *Oceania* 50:3–22.

Stillman, N. A. (1982). "Saddiq and Marabout in Morocco." In I. Ben Ami, ed. *The Sepharadi and Oriental Jewish Heritage Studies.* Jerusalem: The Magnes Press, 489–500.

Turner, V. (1969). *The Ritual Process.* Chicago: Aldine.

Weingrod, A. (n.d.). *Rabbi Haim Houri: The Saint of Beersheva.* Typescript.

Westermarck, E. (1926). *Ritual and Belief in Morocco.* London: Macmillian and Co.

Epilogue: Text in Jewish Society and the Challenge of Comparison

HARVEY E. GOLDBERG

The nine papers presented in this volume have all pointed to the importance of texts in Jewish society and culture, both with regard to the maintenance of tradition and to the process of change. To conclude, a further elucidation of the dynamics of text in relation to social action in Jewish contexts will take place, setting the topic in comparative perspective.

A number of works have examined the impact of literacy on social and cultural life (Goody 1968; Clanchy 1979; Ong 1970; and, in particular, Demsky 1976 on the biblical period). These authors have stressed that, in traditional societies, literacy may strengthen the ability to view objectively and criticize cultural forms, given their permanence as written records. At the same time, the relegation of central cultural texts (myths) to written form, and their delegation to the hands of specialists (Demsky 1976, 1-21), may inhibit popular reflection on the ideological underpinnings of a society, restricting such scrutiny to an insulated elite. The existence of literacy in a society must be assessed, therefore, in the context of the values and social-structural features of that society which condition its impact.

Similarly, the art of writing, even if it is widespread in a society, may be practiced selectively. Jewish social history, to a large extent, is built on the study of texts, such as communal ordinances (often given the backing of rabbis), and rabbinic responsa, both of which may reveal detailed information concerning community, and even family, life. These frequently are written in such a way, however, as to mute the complex realities behind the legal decisions (Zenner 1980). The same point may apply to Prell's reference to the conventional frolicking of Simhat Torah. While jokes and antics are commonplace in the celebration of the day, the atmosphere and specific pranks have little expression in texts. Similarly, the colorful, but rabbinically dubious, practices associated with the veneration of saints among North African Jews are not infrequently referred to in traditional texts, but are not likely to be described in detail in writing, except by an ethnographer (as in the paper by Bilu). The absence of writing in a given situation, therefore, should be viewed in the context of the (nonexercised) possibility of writing, and the importance of texts considered in the context of values attached to texts in a given civilization. With these various possible implications of textual culture in mind, a review will be made of some of the aspects of literacy and writing, in relations to ritual, in Judaic contexts.

I. Mythologizing the Mundane and Domesticating the Divine

Judaic tradition, as reflected in the Pentateuch, is one which lays great emphasis on the text, its integrity and its general availability. This is made explicit in Deuteronomy (6:4–9),[1] and is implied in the exhortation, which preludes the Sinaitic revelation, to become a "kingdom of priests" (Ex. 19:6)—literacy and knowledge of the law having been linked with the priesthood in the ancient world. The emphasis on education and study of the text fits comfortably with the severe curtailment of mythology within the biblical tradition. Conversely, the luxuriance of mythical narrative may have an elective affinity to oral tradition, in which the momentary impact of an image does not have to survive the searching eye of repeated study, for such exuberance of imagery may be dampened when rendered into a standard written form widely available to a public.

Several writers have stressed that the Old Testament (the *Tanakh*) is a document that moves from myth to history, with Pitt-Rivers (1977) focusing on the Book of Genesis, and Andriolo (1981) placing this observation into the comparative context of a number of different traditions. Cassuto (1973, 7–16), too, sees the books of the Tanakh as reflecting the development of historical writing, in an independent form, but fully comparable (even though prior to), a parallel development among the Greeks. All these views characterize the tradition, beginning with the Tanakh, as one which grew out of a given mythic[2] outlook on the universe, which was later to undergo historicization while retaining the threads linking the history to its cosmological origins. Pitt-Rivers, in particular, stresses the movement of the text from a mythic perspective to the promulgation of detailed and empirically oriented rules for behavior. Thus the fabulous, while clearly belonging to the mythical past, is nevertheless brought into consciousness, by the text, within the framework of ongoing everyday history. Popular study of the text establishes this connection in daily life.

Continuing this line of thought, it may be claimed that the tension and mediation between the two, between the mundane and the cosmic, is a feature not only of the biblical text, but of Jewish practice as it has evolved in the postbiblical period. Neusner (1979) has reached a parallel conclusion, not only on the basis of the content of texts, but on consideration of the linguistic structure of the Mishnah. The Mishnah (see the introduction to part one and the paper by Zohar) is a postbiblical compilation of laws which provides succinct and detailed rules for daily behavior, both in the real present and in the ideal situation when the Temple in Jerusalem (destroyed in 70 C.E.) is standing. The Mishnah, which helped shape Jewish life for centuries thereafter (see the paper by Cooper), Neusner asserts, "talks of this-worldly things, but the things stand for and speak of another world entirely" (1979, 161). A body of legal and formulaic texts, the Mishnah was originally transmitted by oral recitation, and only later was committed to writing. Neusner suggests that the repetition and study of the Mishnah helped fill the void created by the impossibility of carrying out the rituals of the Temple cult which were the former mediators of the this-worldly and other-worldly: "it is by the formalization of speech, its limitation to a few patterns and its perfection through the patterns of relationships in particular, that the old nexus of heaven and earth, the cult, now is to be replicated in the new and complementary nexus, cultic speech about all things" (Neusner 1979, 176).

The retention, however subtle, within the same text of both the fabulous and the quotidian, may also have implications for the process of change, an issue explicitly or implicitly central to all the papers in this collection. The Mishnah is, in the first instance, a codification of rules and principles seeking to regulate behavior. It should be noted, however, that it contains diverse and even opposite legal traditions. Moreover, if it is correct that the structure of the corpus maintains the tension between the mundane laws and their ideological raison d'etre, it may provide the groundwork for change, which, though slow, is

nevertheless real and significant, even while there is continual reference back to the written and oral laws in the process of self-
modification.

It is therefore necessary to move beyond the simplified identification of writing and written codes with orthodoxy and intolerance of
change, which only finds flexibility and potentiality of innovation in
liminal settings which are spatially and temporally removed from the
centrality of the written word. An official text may serve to dampen the
creativity of liminality by imposing a regulated and rationalized order
that is cautious, if not hostile, with regard to expressions of innovation.
At the same time, the symbolic value attached to a text through its
ritualization may hold the seeds of such expression and innovation in
suspension. Even though they may not burst forth with energy and
splendor,[3] neither do they completely disappear from view. Moreover,
as shown in Friedman's paper, constant adherence to the letter of the
law can be harnessed to value systems stressing innovation, in which
the most strict alternative of the law is constantly pursued. While this
may appear as traditionality to the outsider, it in fact stems from the
break up of the traditional community, and encourages the individual
to rebel against his parents and to strive to attain perfection in the performance of the commandments.

The importance of texts and understanding in Jewish tradition, as
has been seen, is often closely bound up with ritual. The Bible and rabbinic codes prescribe rituals, but the study of texts, itself, often is part of
a ritual performance. There always exists the danger of the ritualization
of literacy, a case of which is analyzed by Deshen (1975), but even this
stereotypic behavior underlines the importance of study and preserves
the possibility of informed reading on other occasions and/or by
specific segments of the community. The study of Jewish texts, known
as *lernen* in the Ashkenazi tradition (see Heilman 1983), is neither completely intellectual in its orientation, nor completely ritualistic, and
carries within it the potentiality of reinvigorating ossified rituals
through the deepening of understanding. Schoenfeld (1984) indicates
that the attachment of North American Jews to the bar mitzvah
ceremony provides the occasion for religious leaders to demand greater
systematic familiarity with Jewish tradition.

Study as rite takes place prominently within the synagogal liturgy,
but also has pride of place in a central, and to many *the* central ritual of
the Jewish home, the Passover *seder*. The exodus from Egypt is reviewed
by reference to both symbolic act and biblical passage. Quite appro-

priately, the basic text read during the seder is known as *haggadah*, or narration. At the same time, very much in the performative spirit, the seder text tells us that "in every generation a person is required to regard himself as if he went out from Egypt" (see Bokser 1984, particularly chap. 7).

Even popular ritual gets partially pulled into the net of textual study and interpretation, as exemplified by Epstein's study of the purim-shpil. In the realm of folk narrative Noy (1971), for example, has shown that allusion to the biblical text is one of the main factors which gives a universal tale-type a specific Jewish character. Bakhtin's (1968) discussion of festival and spectacle in medieval Europe stresses that these celebrations were "sharply distinct from serious official, ecclesiastical, feudal, and political cult forms and ceremonies" (5). When, as in traditional Jewish society, religious leadership appears in many informal expressions, and any person with some learning can become a representative of the great tradition, an easy interchange between official religion and folk life becomes possible.

II. Group and Individual in Relation to Text

Within the Jewish tradition, the study of texts is eminently a social phenomenon. The text represents the communal norms, and is studied in a group framework (see Zborowski 1955). The social setting of study is taken for granted by the structure of the talmudic text, which assumes that the text will be accompanied by instruction (see Heilman 1983). This metonymic or indexical link between the written word and a committed community is a third aspect of performance (as discussed by Tambiah [1979, 156], see the introduction), which imbues the message of a text/ritual with naturalness within group life. In the words of a song often sung on the festival of Simhat Torah (see the papers by Goldberg and Prell): "Israel and the Torah are one."

At the same time, advanced study clearly moves beyond the stages of rote learning, and demands individual comprehension and judgment.[4] Greater socialization and greater individuation may thereby go hand in hand, even though in the traditional setting the accomplishments of students were not praised in terms of virtuosity of the individual. Rather, an outstanding insight received accolades because the student had divined the intentions of a renowned scholar of an earlier age. As new meanings of text and rituals are discovered, through continuous interpretation, the attitude is maintained that one is simply uncovering further depths which always had been implicit in the divinely revealed or inspired writings.

In his discussion of liminality and morality, Turner (1980) notes that the concept of the individual in the West, whose gradual development stemmed from sources of innovation in liminal moments and life-ways, "arose most explicitly in the Judeo-Christian tradition among peoples belonging to minority cultures whose strongly held world views were under constant direct and indirect assault from a vast range of powerful environing polities and belief systems." It is possible that in the case of Jewish society, whose very existence was always liminal (neither completely in nor completely out of the wider society), such growth must be understood in relationship to the importance of literacy and textual study in the religious tradition (see Goody and Watt 1968, 61–63).

The interplay between text and rite is sometimes maintained, even in contemporary practice which consciously sought to turn its back on Jewish religion. The birthday party in the modern Israeli kindergarten, analyzed by Doleve-Gandelman, shows the development of new nationalist and collective values which gave rise to an innovative (from the point of view Jewish tradition) focus on the individual. This new celebration, her paper indicates, was accompanied by a flurry of texts concerning this normally informal part of childhood. Even though an overemphasis on the individual was a potential challenge to certain aspects of the Zionist ethos, the extensive written material on the parties in the kindergartens shows an interweaving of concern for the individual in the context of powerful societal ideals.

The semiotic concept of a shifter is central to Doleve-Gandelman's analysis. Shifters, referring to a sign that simultaneously represents (symbolizes) an idea and places that idea in a compelling context, can undoubtedly be identified in many different Jewish rituals, and/or midrashim. More generally, the semiotic framework from which the term is taken might help explore further such distinctions such as the one used by Scholem (1941, 26–27) between allegory and symbol, in his contrast of medieval Jewish philosophy with mysticism. Scholem states that "philosophers wanted concepts, but the mystics wanted symbols" (1966, 430–31); and Saperstein (1980) has discussed the differences that these schools had with respect to the understanding of midrash. It should be appreciated that the *aggadah* (narrative portions of talmudic and later rabbinical literature), built up of midrashim, plays an important role in both approaches. Saperstein (20) states "how naturally the aggadah is mustered for the service of the philosophers, how pliant it becomes in the hands of the master dialectician."

Jewish scholars in the modern period debated the merits of midrash, opposing its analytic limitations, being "essentially concrete, circumscribed and episodic," to its capacity for renewal and revitalization (Schorsch 1983). Semiotic theory allows a refined view of these issues, which become topics of conscious deliberation as individuals and groups seek to establish their relationship to Jewish law and tradition. Semiotic theory also permits the appreciation that midrash can be based on analytic insight, while revealing that every conceptual system has its rhetorical, and sometimes religious, base. Thus Rotenberg (1983) has argued that a Protestant ethic informs many social science theories of deviance, and contrasts this with a perspective growing out of Hasidic philosophy concerning ego and alter.

A stark contrast between innovating and structured contexts does not appear applicable to some of the cases considered. It seems possible for individuality, and for collective self-reflection, to be expressed in highly established situations, which circumscribe liminality, for in Jewish tradition moments of liminality are well guarded by tradition. Zohar's study of the biblical sabbatical laws stresses that the expression of *communitas* is highly regulated, and given meaning in terms of the central values of the society which apply to mundane activities as well. Epstein's analysis of the Purim play among the Bobover Hasidim provides another example of the conjuction of spontaneous expression and communal surveillance. The levity and reversal exhibited there are striking, not in any absolute sense, based on a comparative view of festivities among the world's cultures, but in relation to the stringent demands for adherence to the law, and the strict communal control, which operate in everyday life. With all its colorfulness, and on the background of the black garb of the Hasidim, the purim-shpil is at first inscribed as a text, and does not in any way overstep the bounds of the law. Even in instances when men dress as women, an act which is explicitly proscribed in Deuteronomy (22:5), it is part of the law that such behavior is permitted on Purim.

The great tradition, constantly reinterpreted in terms of its sanctified writings, extends into the ceremonial and ritual realm of the liminal, giving it a particular shape and direction. The drive to perform the mitzvot precisely as they are outlined in the authoritative texts, within the flux of historical change, produces a tension that generates gloss upon gloss, interpretation upon interpretation. In this manner the daily round of prayers, the grace after meals, and the rules outlining behavior on festivals and the Sabbath, all carry elements of the liminal, or liminoid, into everyday life and serve to maintain, in changing secular conditions, "that intimate relationship between the inexhaustible Word and human society" (Goldin 1965, 278).

III. The Search for Meaningful Units of Comparison

As emphasized in Turner's (1982) notion of "comparative symbology," there is the challenge to face of appreciating the elements of pan-human experiences revealed by comparative study, while not ignoring the substance and content of particular religious traditions. Van Gennep's classical study of rites of passage (1960) showed similarities in rituals from tribal cultures all over the world. In Turner's (1980) words: "human experience . . . is ransacked for telling symbols, metaphors and images which can provide building blocks, or better, the alphabet blocks, for a liminal language." How may these similarities be taken into account at the same time that one is keenly aware of civilizational and historic differences?

It is not difficult, as has been known since Frazer's time, to demonstrate individual likenesses, and even lists of similarities, among various traditions. When social divisions are temporarily suspended, the sense of *communitas* may have emerged among the ancient Israelites, as among the Ndembu. The act of lighting candles, in addition to its official status in Jewish law, may signify entrance into paradise, as in many other settings. Dreaming in Safed may be likened to oneiric encounters in tribal cultures. Individuals from very different parts of the world may share passions and perceptions, and even "symbol" their experiences in parallel ways, but these elementary meaningful units become interlaced with the dictates of traditions which organize them into quite distinctive patterns. Thus, when Myerhoff likens the lighting of candles on the eve of the Sabbath to fire at the entrance of paradise, she subtly shifts from an idiom in which time is dominant to discourse in terms of territory. In Jewish tradition the sabbath is a taste of "the world to come," and analysis must not distort overall cultural themes while focusing on specific symbols.

In attempting to relate these two aspects of symbolic structuring, which arose from the phenomenology of everyday life and was passed on over the generations, it is possible to utilize Turner's metaphor of alphabet blocks at the level of cultural tradition as well as at the level of panhuman experience. In addition to universal alphabet blocks, may there not be such blocks specific to each tradition which become part of an individual's (and group's) inventory of reactions at an early age through exposure to language, stories, rituals, the comportment of adults, artifacts, and so forth, which are then available for use and reuse in different (and even changing) settings within the given traditions?

Such symbolic units, if identified, would be specific enough (though not necessarily unique) to be solidly placed within a given tradition, but also general enough to take on meanings appropriate to varying historical periods and social conditions. Goldberg's discussion shows, for example, that an association between Torah and people may be such an elemental unit, which does not disintegrate even in the very modern setting described in the paper by Prell. Another example is provided by Myerhoff's paper discussing the intertextuality between a protest demonstration and a group mural drawn by the elderly. Both of these events recapitulate the movement of the Passover Haggadah, whose narrative, as described by the Talmud, moves from disgrace to distinction (gnut to shevah; BT Pesahim 116a). Such a movement is clearly distinct, for example, from the model of tragedy (which aimed to have an uplifting effect on the individual), which held a central place in ancient Greek civilization. The notion that ownership of land ultimately resided in a national community with an historic purpose animated the jubilee laws of Leviticus (Zohar), and took on new symbolic force in the context of modern Zionism (Doleve-Gandelman). It may be possible to reduce such elemental cultural units to terms that admit of comparison, but it must be appreciated that, in doing so, something of the specific stands that particular cultures take on existential issues is being ignored.

The problem of comparison may be looked at in the following way. There are certain basic and perpetual issues facing all humanity, as individuals and as organized societies, but the ways in which these issues are *defined* are by no means identical from one tradition to the next. The wholeness of human experience is of necessity dissected by language and culture into units or blocks. As men go on to construct their social and cultural worlds, these blocks must be aggregated into larger meaningful patterns. Carrying out this work is surely one of the things that religion is about, and just as a given architectural creation reflects the drab, raw materials used, as well as the overall design, so different religious traditions can build on experiences common to mankind, or common within a given tradition, but erect varying structures in diverse settings and historical circumstances.

One aspect of the division of the world (and of its integration), on the part of different traditions, is reflected in the grand dichotomies (good/evil, chaos/order, and so on) with which we have become familiar through structuralist analysis. All these dichotomies, perhaps, are testimonies to the lost oneness of the world, but that does not mean that they all may legitimately be reduced to one another. Lévi-Strauss appears to have adopted different views on this point. While early in his structuralist writings nature/culture appears as a pervasive and basic opposition, he later states that he has come to view it as mainly "methodological" (1966, 247n). In his summary of *Mythologiques* (1971, 621), he states clearly that all the oppositions he has analyzed in the Amerindian myths can be reduced to a single *antimonie première*, the one expressed by Hamlet: "to be or not to be?" But what is the locus of this "to be?" Is it the individual introspection of the melancholy prince, or the collective "to be" of a people, dramatized during events such as Simḥat Torah celebrations, or the purim-shpil?

A case may be made, as is done by Cooper, that not all dichotomous oppositions are interchangeable: that some fit a given culture better than others. He finds, by the analysis of biblical laws and their rabbinic development, that the life/death opposition, in relation to the laws of mixture, is more apposite than nature/culture. His selection of the life/death pair, while growing out of the legal data analyzed, also has the advantage of conforming to other aspects of Judaic culture, such as the peroration in Deuteronomy 30:15–20 exhorting the Israelites to choose life. One may also wonder whether the octogenarians demonstrating in the community discussed by Myerhoff, who painted the placard "Life not Death in Venice," had in mind a well-known Jewish text,[5] as well as the local newspaper headlines and the work of Thomas Mann (popularized in a film).

IV. Methodological Implications

This discussion, which emphasized the openness of symbol units—how they may fit into different world views and how they may receive varying interpretations depending on circumstance—also has methodological implications. These implications point in the direction both of greater freedom of interpretation and of greater caution. It is suggested, on the one hand, that it may sometimes be useful to break the bounds imposed by the strictures of historical research, in order to understand the potentialities of a system of signification, and not only those meanings tied firmly to current social realities. For example, the highly explicit and systematized sexual symbolism in kabbalistic tradition (for example, Scholem 1965; Bilu 1979) draws on images and metaphors to be found in the Bible and Talmud. While no one would claim that the whole range of more recent kabbalistic interpretation was an ever-present and never-changing aspect of Jewish symbolism throughout the ages, it could be that this later symbolization throws light on directions and currents which were present in other times and other places, though in less dominant and explicit forms. Even the verbal abuse of the Torah in the West Coast minyan described by Prell may have a remote affinity, in connotative structure, to Shabbetai Zvi's (the seventeenth century false messiah) scandalous marriage to the Torah (Scholem 1973, 159–60, 400–401). (The gestures she describes are not so much unthinkable as they are "bad to think.")

The fact that interpretive communities can greatly alter earlier readings of text, does not necessitate a sociological determinism, blind to the suggestive and perduring power of the original documents (see Goodheart 1983). In the case of Judaism, where the text and rituals are central as constitutive symbols, every community, it may be argued, is interpretive. In discussing the work of historian Neusner, who stresses the differing interpretations of biblical purity laws, Douglas makes the following observation: "What he finds to be distinctive of say the Pharisees, the Zealots, or the Rabbis, appears to this anthropologist only to be selections from what is clearly to be found in the biblical literature itself" (Douglas 1973, 140).

It appears plausible, therefore, given the historical continuity of several central texts and the observance of the same basic laws and rituals, that there exist constancies of signification which bridge different periods and social settings. This is not to say that these significations can be viewed as the frozen dogma of a given tradition, but rather should be seen as a system of signs (alphabet blocks) which may be, or even must be, elaborated on in a given historical reality. Prell's paper demonstrates how even a conditional commitment to these texts and rituals, on the part of highly self-conscious individuals, explicitly seeking forms of religious innovation, provokes innovative responses, on the one hand, while placing limits on the form and extent of innovations on the other. It is by looking at related systems of meanings in different temporal settings that the subtle interplay of continuity, innovation, and accommodation can be elucidated.

This type of analysis, on the other hand, requires an informed approach to data, which, in turn, often means a familiarity with classic textual materials. It is indeed a difficult balancing act to remove data from a specific historical context while preserving its integrity to the extent that it can be compared with other cases within and without a given tradition. There is much room for debate as to whether a certain set of facts can be comprehended within a general theory, or whether the application of a given conceptual scheme reduces the data to a form in which it is unrecognizable by the tradition from which it was lifted. Thus Cooper finds notions such as "pollution" and "danger," developed by Douglas (1966), misleading with regard to the rationalized and legalistic rules that have developed upon the base of the biblical prohibitions. Such a problem is best faced when the same researcher (or group of researchers), who is (are) utilizing anthropological observation, participation, and general theory is (are) also capable of direct and critical evaluation of texts. Thus, the greater interpretive license encouraged must go hand in hand with greater methodological awareness when confronted with a specific corpus of data to be analyzed. It is hoped that this volume will encourage work in this dual direction.

Notes

1. This portion of Deuteronomy has become the central element of daily Jewish prayer. It is taken to refer to the Pentateuch and the broader category of Torah in general, and also provides the scriptural basis for the wearing of phylacteries.

2. Kaufmann's (1948; 1960) analysis of Israelite religion emphasizes the absence of mythology in the Bible. Here he refers to the absence of texts which portray the humanlike attributes of the gods in which they eat, sleep, feel lust, jealousy, and so on. Except for a relatively few passages in Genesis and Exodus (for example, the "sons of God" marrying the daughters of man, God's encounter with Moses at the inn), the Tanakh is strikingly devoid of such narratives. (Even these may have been included to combat widely accepted pagan mythological notions, see Cassuto [1973] on the "sons of God"). At the same time, the term *mythology* may be applied to the Genesis narrative in that it begins with a cosmological description containing fabulous elements (including, for example, the great ages of the descendants of Adam), and then moves toward the historical.

3. Goody (1968, 2) notes that in literate religions change often takes the form of sudden shifts or heresies.

4. This is expressed, among other ways, in the sociolinguistic style in which the Talmud is often taught and discussed. The text itself consists of Hebrew and Babylonian Aramaic, which is constantly cited by quoting terms and whole phrases, while the entire framework of the lesson is carried out in the vernacular, be that Yiddish, Arabic, English, or modern Hebrew. In contemporary Israel, for example, the modern Hebrew used in carrying out discussions is clearly different from the textual Hebrew-Aramaic, and the latter is often marked in the language of learning (Heilman 1983), by the Yiddish-based intonation with which concepts and phrases from the text are introduced into the discussion. The style of learning thus combines elements of rote recitation and of complex logical analysis, which is most flexibly carried out by people in their first language.

At the same time, the use of a special linguistic style in Torah study may help isolate this quasi-ritualized intellectual endeavor from the standards for argument which apply in secular rational discourse. A parallel hypothesis, reflexively, may also be applied to anthropological work. Separating the study of the formal aspects of ritual behavior from the cultural content in which it is grounded (Tambiah 1979), may relieve the social analyst from serious confrontation with the existential claims of that cultural world.

5. The reference here is to Leviticus 18:5 "You shall keep My laws and My norms, by the pursuit of which man shall live," which the Talmud interprets as intending: "by which he shall live, not die." This interpretation is offered to support the halakhah that if a person's life is threatened, he may transgress the Sabbath laws (BT *Yoma*, 85b).

References Cited

Andriolo, K. R. (1981). "Myth and History: A General Model and Its Application to the Bible." *American Anthropologist* 83:261–84.

Bakhtin, M. (1968). *Rabelais and His World*. Translated by H. Iswolsky. Cambridge, Ma.: M.I.T. Press.

Bilu, Y. (1979). "Sigmund Freud and Rabbi Yehudah: On a Jewish Mystical Tradition of 'Psychoanalytic' Dream Interpretation." *The Journal of Psychological Anthropology* 2:443–63.

Bokser, B. (1984). *The Origins of the Seder: The Passover Rite and Early Rabbinic Judaism*. Berkeley: University of California Press.

Cassuto, U. (1973). *Biblical and Oriental Studies*, vol. 1. Translated by Israel Abrahams. Jerusalem: Magnes Press.

Clanchy, M. T. (1979). *From Memory to Written Record: England 1066–1307*. London: Edward Arnold.

Demsky, A. (1976). *Literacy in Israel and Among Neighboring Peoples in the Biblical Period.* Ph.D. diss. Hebrew University of Jerusalem. Hebrew with English summary.

Deshen, S. (1975). "Ritualization of Literacy: The Works of Tunisian Scholars in Israel." *American Ethnologist* 2:251–59.

Douglas, M. (1966). *Purity and Danger: An Analysis of Concepts of Pollution and Taboo.* New York: Praeger.

_____. (1973). "Critique and Commentary." In J. Neusner, ed. *The Idea of Purity in Ancient Judaism.* Leiden: Brill, 137–42.

Goldin, J. (1965). "On Change and Adaptation in Judaism." *History of Religion* 4:269–94.

Goodheart, E. (1983). "The Text and the Interpretive Community." *Daedalus* 112:215–23.

Goody, J., ed. (1968). *Literacy in Traditional Societies.* Cambridge: Cambridge University Press.

Goody, J., and I. Watt. (1968). "The Consequences of Literacy." In J. Goody, ed. *Literacy in Traditional Societies.* Cambridge: Cambridge University Press, 27–68.

Heilman, S. (1983). *People of the Book: Drama, Fellowship and Religion.* Chicago: University of Chicago Press.

Kaufmann, Y. (1948). *The History of the Israelite Religion: From Early Times Until the End of the Second Temple Period.* 4 vols. Jerusalem and Tel Aviv: Bialik Institute and Dvir. Hebrew.

_____. (1960). *The Religion of Israel: From its Beginnings to the Babylonian Exile.* Translated and abridged by Moshe Greenberg. Chicago: University of Chicago Press.

Lévi-Strauss, C. (1966). *The Savage Mind.* Chicago: University of Chicago Press.

_____. (1971). *L'Homme Nu.* Paris: Plon.

Neusner, J. (1979). *Method and Meaning in Ancient Judaism.* Brown Judaic Studies. Missoula, Montana: Scholars Press.

Noy, D. (1971). "The Jewish Versions of the 'Animal Languages' Folktale (AT 670)." In J. Heinemann and D. Noy, eds. *Studies in Aggadah and Folk-Literature.* Scripta Hierosolymitana. Jerusalem: Magnes Press, 22:171–208.

Ong, W. (1970). *The Presence of the Word: Some Prolegemena for Cultural and Religious History.* New York: Clarion.

Pitt-Rivers, J. (1977). *The Fate of Shechem, or the Politics of Sex: Essays in the*

Anthropology of the Mediterranean. Cambridge: Cambridge University Press.

Rotenberg, M. (1983). *Dialogue with Deviance: The Hasidic Ethic and the Theory of Social Contraction.* Philadelphia: Institute for the Study of Human Issues.

Saperstein, M. (1980). *Decoding the Rabbis: A Thirteenth-Century Commentary on the Aggadah.* Cambridge, Ma: Harvard University Press.

Schoenfeld, S. (1984). "Changing Patterns of North American Bar Mitzvah: Towards a History and Sociological Analysis." (Typescript).

Scholem, G. (1941). *Major Trends in Jewish Mysticism.* New York: Schocken.

_____. (1965). On the Kabbalah and Its Symbolism. Translated by R. Mannheim. New York: Schocken Books.

_____. (1966). *Les Origines de la Kabbale.* Traduit par J. Loewenson. Paris: Aubier-Montaigne.

_____. (1973). *Sabbatai Sevi: The Mystical Messiah, 1626–1676.* Princeton: Princeton University Press.

Schorsch, I. (1983). "The Emergence of Historical Consciousness in Modern Judaism." *The Leo Baeck Institute Year Book* 28:413–37.

Tambiah, S. J. (1979). "A Performative Approach to Ritual." *Proceedings of the British Academy,* vol. 65. London: Oxford University Press.

Turner, V. (1980). "Liminality and Morality." Paper presented at the Annual Meeting of the Israel Anthropological Association, Jerusalem, April 1980.

_____. (1982). *From Ritual to Theatre: The Human Seriousness of Play.* New York: Performing Arts Journal Publications.

Van Gennep, A. (1960 [orig. 1908]). *The Rites of Passage.* Translated by M. B. Vizedom and G. L. Caffee. Chicago: University of Chicago Press.

Zborowski, M. (1955). "The Place of Book-Learning in Traditional Jewish Culture." In M. Mead and M. Wolfenstein, eds. *Childhood in Contemporary Cultures.* Chicago: University of Chicago Press, 118–41.

Zenner, W. (1980). "Censorship and Syncretism: Some Social Anthropological Approaches to the Study of Middle Eastern Jews." In F. Talmadge, ed. *Studies in Jewish Folklore.* Cambridge, Ma.: Association for Jewish Studies, 377–94.

Glossary

AGGADAH: That part of the Oral Law, made up of diverse elements such as stories, ethical and moral teachings, theological speculations, gnomic sayings, historical information, and visions of the future, which does not deal with halakhah, but which complements the latter.

ALIYAH (Heb.: ascent): Incorporated into Yiddish, the word means a ritual honor in which a man is "called up" to recite the blessings over the reading of the Torah (this honor is designated a *mitzvah* in the Sephardi tradition). In modern Hebrew, the term refers to the act of immigration to the land of Israel.

ASHKENAZ: The name of a place/people in the Bible (Gen. 10) which medieval Jews applied to the Rhineland when Jewish life began to develop there. The Yiddish language, and Ashkenazi laws and customs which developed in the region, were later carried eastward by migration so that Eastern European Jews also belong to the Ashkenazi tradition.

BAR MITZVAH: Belonging to the category upon which the observance of the mitzvot is incumbent. In Jewish law this takes place at the age of thirteen for boys and at the age of twelve for girls. Traditionally, males are called to recite the blessings at a public reading of the Torah at that age. The term has thus come to refer to this event and the accompanying celebration.

BESHT: A Hebrew acronym designating Yisrael Ba'al Shem Tov, the founder of the movement of Hasidism in the eighteenth century. Hasidic rebbes all trace a genealogy of disciplehood to the Besht.

DERASHA: A sermon or lesson with a homiletic purpose. Based on the same stem as the term *midrash*, a derasha can take place in the synagogue, at a study session, at a home memorial service, and so forth.

ELIJAH; ELIJAH'S CHAIR: The biblical prophet Elijah, appears in the book of Malachi (3:23) as the harbinger of the Messiah, and has assumed, in

331

Jewish legend, the role of a figure who miraculously comes to the aid of communities and individuals. Another reference in the same book (Mal. 3:1) establishes an association between him and the circumcision ceremony, and the custom developed of setting aside a chair during the ceremony on which Elijah, invisible but present, may sit.

GABBAI (Gabe in Bobover Yiddish; pl.: gabbaim, gabbuim): The role of organizing the people and activities associated with the reading of the Torah in the synagogue, or some other administrative role in service of a religious cause. The task often involves the collection of funds.

GENIZAH: The practice of caching worn Hebrew texts, particularly sacred texts or any document that has God's name on it, and the place, typically in a synagogue, where these texts are stored, before their ultimate burial.

HAGGADAH (Heb.: narration): The text which is used during the Passover seder containing the rituals and the narration of the exodus from Egypt.

HALAKHAH: The traditions, stemming from the time of the Talmud and onward, which deal with ritual, ethical, civil, and criminal law. Halakhic literature is noted for its inclusion of diverse interpretations and opinions, while *a* halakhah may refer to a specific authoritative ruling.

HALAV AKUM (Bobover Yiddish: Khulev akum): AKUM is a Hebrew acronym for an idol worshipper. Milk (Heb.: halav) from kosher animals is not ritually pure or impure, in itself, but a talmudic prohibition developed against using the milk of heathens, which might be adulterated with other ritually unfit substances. The trend in rabbinic literature has been to distinguish Muslims and Christians from AKUM, and many observant Jews consider the rules inapplicable today because of the health and commercial regulations under which milk is marketed. There are ultraorthodox groups, however, which persist in applying the rules of Halav AKUM to contemporary non-Jews.

HANUKKAH: A holiday taking place on the twenty-fifth day of the month of Kislev (in December), commemorating the victory of the Jews over the Syrian Greeks, and the restoration of the Temple service, under the leadership of the Maccabees, in 164 B.C.E.

HAREDIM: Ultraorthodox Jews characterized by their rejection of the values of modern society and a tendency to follow Jewish law in its most strict fashion. They also reject Zionism and the claim that the state of Israel represents the fulfillment of traditional Jewish aspirations for religious and national redemption.

HASID: In talmudic literature, the term denotes an individual of unusual piety and godliness, and while normally referring to Jews, could be applied, in a marked fashion, to Gentiles. In the medieval period in Central Europe, there developed a pietistic movement whose adherents were known as the hasidim (pl.) of Ashkenaz. In the modern period, the social and religious-mystical movement associated with Rabbi Yisrael Ba'al Shem Tov (Besht) in southern Poland (in the eighteenth century), which stressed the simple devotion of every Jew as opposed to an aristocracy of Torah scholars, became known as Hasidism. Hasidic groups, identified by their place of origin in Europe (for example, Satmar, Lubavitch), and organized around leaders known as rebbes, persist into the present, and most have become part of haredi, or ultraorthodox Judaism.

HATIKVAH (Heb.: The Hope): The Israeli national anthem.

HATAN (Heb.: bridegroom): In the context of the Simhat Torah service, several of the men who are given aliyot of special import are designated in this manner, particularly those who are called to the reading of the end of the Torah (Hatan Torah), and to the reading of its beginning (Hatan Bereshit).

HAZZAN: An official of the synagogue, whose precise duties varied in time and place. In recent Ashkenazi tradition the term has come to mean cantor.

JUBILEE YEAR: After the celebration of seven sabbatical years, the bible (Lev. 25) commands the observance of a fiftieth jubilee year. The laws of the sabbatical year apply during the jubilee, but the fiftieth year involves additional prescriptions. Important among these were the requirements that all Israelite slaves be released and that land acquired through purchase or mortgage for debt revert to its original owner.

KABBALAH: Based on a stem meaning "received" (tradition), the term came to refer to the traditions of mysticism which developed in Spain and southern France in the twelfth century and which culminated in the writing of the Zohar. In the sixteenth century, Isaac Luria of Safed, basing himself on kabbalistic theory, introduced new prayer rituals and customs and incorporated sections of the Zohar into the liturgy. More generally, the term *Kabbalah* is sometimes used as synonymous with Jewish mysticism in all periods.

KABBALAT SHABBAT (Heb.: reception of the Sabbath): The psalms and hymns preceding the Friday night prayer service ("'arvit" or "ma'ariv"). The term has come to be applied to various ceremonies signaling the approach or inauguration of the Sabbath.

KOHEN: A member of the priestly class, putatively descended patrilineally from Aaron, Moses' brother. In ancient times the kohanim (pl.) had ritual duties and rights associated with the Temple service, and they retain several ritual privileges in traditional Jewish worship.

KOLLEL (Bobover Yiddish: koilel): Originally meaning community in Hebrew, the term has also come to refer to a place where the study of Torah is carried out on a regular basis, usually by married men.

KOSHER: The term, meaning "fitting," or "permitted according to law," is used most commonly with regard to food (dietary laws are the laws of Kashrut), but can be applied to other matters governed by religious rules as well.

LAG BA'OMER: See *Rabbi Shim'on Bar Yohai.*

LEVI: A descendant of the biblical tribe of Levi. The levi'im (pl.) served as the assistants of the priests (see kohen) in the Temple service, and continue to have minor ritual duties and privileges in that regard.

MATZAH (Matze in Bobover *Yiddish: pl.:* matzot, matzos): Unleavened bread eaten on Passover.

MIDRASH: Deriving from a stem meaning to "inquire" or "investigate," the term implies the discovery of nonliteral interpretations of the Bible. There is *midrash halakhah,* which refers to inferences concerning legal matters, and *midrash aggadah,* which relates to a wide range of ethical teachings, legends, and so forth. In popular parlance, midrash is usually associated with nonlegal homiletic uses of the biblical text, reflecting the fact that the classic books of midrash are replete with aggadah.

MINYAN: A quorum of ten Jewish males which is the minimum number required to conduct public prayers. Recently, it has become common for both Reform and Conservative Jewish communities in the United States to include women in a minyan.

MISHNAH: The earliest codification of the oral law, which took its final form about 200 C.E., under the authority of Rabbi Yehudah Ha-Nasi. The Mishnah is organized into six *sedarim* (orders), with each of these consisting of seven to twelve tractates.

MITZVAH (pl. mitzvot): A commandment in the Bible. A deed of religious merit.

NEW YEAR: See Rosh Ha-Shanah.

NINTH OF AV: A fast day, the ninth of the Hebrew summer month of Av, which commemorates the destruction of the First Temple by the Babylonians and the Second Temple by the Romans. Another fast day is the Tenth of Tevet, which marks the beginning of the Babylonian siege of Jerusalem.

ORAL LAW: The traditions that have developed interpreting the biblical books which are the basis of the written law. The oral law, stemming from the interpretations of rabbis over the generations (see midrash), always attempted to demonstrate the antiquity of its authority. Despite the fact that it too eventually was committed to writing, the term *oral law* was preserved indicating its special status in relation to the canonical books.

PASSOVER (In Heb.: *Pesah*): The festival taking place (in the spring) on the fifteenth of the month of Nisan, which commemorates the exodus of the Israelites from Egypt. The biblical rule (for example Ex. 12:15) forbids the eating of leavened bread, or even the presence of leaven in the house, during the seven days of the festival. This requirement entails a full cleaning of the house before the festival, in order to rid it of all traces of leaven. There are also positive injunctions, including the requirement to eat matzah, unleavened bread, as a reminder of bondage in Egypt. This ritual, along with others, is an element of the elaborate seder on the first night of Pesah.

PHARISEES: One of the main divisions among the Jews during the Second Temple period, who differed in their religious approach from the Sadducees and the Essenes. They stressed the importance of the Oral Law as the correct body of tradition for interpreting the biblical text, and stood for the authority of scholars in interpreting the law, rather than that of the priests (kohanim). The approach of the Pharisees was continued by the sages of the Talmud, and the rabbinic scholars who followed them. The New Testament refers to the Pharisees pejoratively because of their insistence on the rigid adherence to religious law.

PURIM: The holiday commemorating the events recorded in the biblical book of Esther, in which the Jews of the Persian empire were saved from a plot, stemming from blind hatred, designed to destroy them. The celebration of Purim involves reading the Book of Esther from a scroll (megillah), and entails much gaiety including noisemaking in the synagogue, masquerading, and, in some communities, the staging of a Purim-shpil.

PURIM-SHPIL (Yid.: a play on the holiday of Purim): The tradition of having special plays during Purim is known from medieval times in Europe.

RASHI: Acronym for Rabbi Shlomoh Yitzhaqi, an eleventh-century scholar who wrote popular commentaries on the Bible and the Talmud. His commentary on the Bible became a basic work studied by young children when they first gained mastery of the sacred text. This commentary is printed in many standard editions of the Bible in Hebrew, and learning "Humash [the Pentateuch] with Rashi" was a form of study known throughout the traditional Jewish world.

RABBI (REBBE, Bobover Yiddish: rebe) (Heb.: "My master"): The term was used to refer to scholars of authority in ancient Palestine. In Babylonia, the term *Rav* was used, and these terms are the basis of titles accorded to religious scholars and leaders throughout the generations. The nature of training and ordination of rabbis varied greatly, as did their official place in the community and the definition of their duties. The term could often be applied to a scholar of the Torah who held no communal office. Rebbe is a Yiddish derivation of the term, used to refer to Hasidic leaders to whom the individual Hasid is charismatically attached.

RABBI MEIR BA'AL HA-NESS: A Rabbi, whose identity is in question, who is believed to be buried in a large mausoleum just south of the city of Tiberias. Jews throughout the traditional world contributed funds for the upkeep of this site, and believed that Rabbi Meir would intercede in helping bring answers to their prayers. The anniversary of Rabbi Meir's death is on the fifteenth of the month of Iyyar, three days before a similar anniversary of Rabbi Shim'on Bar Yohai. A combined visit to the tombs of these two Rabbis, as well as to the grave sites of other saints believed to be found in the Galilee, form part of an elaborate pilgrimage tradition among Middle Eastern Jews and Hasidim.

RABBI SHIM'ON BAR YOHAI: From the second century C.E., a tanna who, in fleeing from the Romans, is believed to have lived for many years hiding in a cave in the Galilee. The mystical book of the Zohar, which scholars agree was written in the fourteenth century, was attributed to his authorship. The putative date of his death, the eighteenth of the month of Iyyar, or Lag Ba'omer, thirty-three days after Passover, has become a minor festival, interpreted as marking the mystical union of the soul of the sainted rabbi with God. In Meron, near Safed, a large cupola-top building stands over his traditional tomb. This site is visited each year by over 100,000 pilgrims on the anniversary of his death, and many other visitors attend the site at various times throughout the year.

RESPONSA: From the end of the talmudic period onward, rabbinic scholars were sent queries (*she'elot*), often from distant communities, asking for guidance and direction with regard to the law, as new situations arose. The written responses to these questions formed part of the expanding oral law, and were consulted by authorities thereafter. Their influence is seen in codifications such as the Shulḥan Arukh, and they have proven to be of immense value in the study of social history.

ROSH HA-SHANAH: The Solemn New Year. Celebrated on the first two days of the month of Tishrei, in the autumn, this holy day inaugurates ten days of penitence which culminate on Yom Ha-Kippurim.

SABBATICAL YEAR: Known in Hebrew as the "shemittah" year or the "shevi'it" (seventh), this was a year when agricultural work was forbidden and the land was to lay fallow (Lev. 25:3ff.). Other rules pertaining to the seventh year were the releasing of slaves and the cancellation of debts (see, for example, Ex. 23:10–11). After seven sabbatical years a jubilee year was proclaimed.

SECOND TEMPLE: A designation for the period in Jewish history beginning with the rebuilding of the Temple under Persian rule in the sixth century, B.C.E., and ending with its destruction by the Romans in 70 C.E. Often the term implies a more limited period, preceding the destruction of the Temple, for which there is fuller information, based on sources such as the Talmud, Josephus, and archeological finds.

SEDER (Heb.: order): Referring to the ritual order appropriate to the evening of a festival, the seder (par excellence) means the domestic celebration which takes place on the first night of Passover in Israel and on the first two nights in the diaspora. The seder consists of reading and discussing a narration of the exodus from Egypt, the performance of related rituals, the singing of psalms and hymns, and a festive meal which is bracketed by the other parts of the ceremony. The seder is an occasion that highlights family unity, and children are given a prominent place in it.

SEFER TORAH: See *Torah*.

SEPHARAD: A biblical place name which was applied to the Iberian peninsula in medieval times. After the expulsions from Spain and Portugal at the end of the fifteenth century, Spanish Jews (Sephardim) spread to Mediterranean lands, to Northwest Europe, and even to the New World. Later, Jews who had been forced to convert to Catholicism, but maintained their Judaism secretly (Marranos), rejoined the ranks of Spanish communities. Today, Sephardi may refer, narrowly, to Jews who speak Judeo-Spanish ("Judezmo," "Landino") and/or those who are descended from the emigrés from the Iberian peninsula. More broadly, the term refers to Jews who came under the influence of these emigrés and who accepted Sephardi law, liturgy, and customs.

SHAVU'OT: The Feast of Weeks. One of the pilgrimage festivals prescribed by the Bible to take place fifty days (seven weeks plus one day) from the second day of Passover. It is associated, in Jewish tradition, with the day on which the Torah was given on Mt. Sinai.

SHE'ELOT U-TESHUVOT: See Responsa.

SHMINI ATZERET: See Sukkot.

SHOFAR: A ram's horn. Used in antiquity on a variety of occasions, such as the anointing of kings or the proclamation of the jubilee year, the sounding of shofar is an integral part of the Rosh Ha-Shanah service, and concludes the prayers of Yom Ha-Kippurim. In some traditions it is sounded throughout the period leading up to these solemn festivals.

SHTETL (Yid.: small town): A small town in the countryside in Eastern Europe in which Jews resided, while their economic activities brought them into contact with the non-Jewish peasants around them. While in all Eastern European countries the Jews had undergone extensive urbanization by the first quarter of the present century, close to one-fourth of the Jews of Poland resided in shtetl communities at that time.

SHULHAN ARUKH (Heb.: Set Table): Based on a midrash that describes God telling Moses to present the laws to the Israelites as a set table, prepared for eating, the phrase was used by Rabbi Joseph Caro to name his codification of Jewish law in the sixteenth century. This was the last great compendium of that nature. The Shulhan Arukh was intended to be a more popular version of Caro's more thorough halakhic work, the "Bet Yosef." This latter opus is based on the divisions of an earlier codification by Rabbi Jacob ben Asher (twelfth to thirteenth century), which organizes the law into four parts: (1) *Orah Hayyim*, dealing with the ritual obligations of the daily, weekly, and calendrical cycles; (2) *Yoreh De'ah*, dealing mainly with dietary and other rituals, such as mourning and menstrual restrictions, but also including laws of interest, charity, and respect for parents; (3) *Even Ha-'ezer*, on personal status (marriage, divorce, and so on); and (4) *Hoshen Ha-mishpat*, on civil law insofar as it is applicable in the diaspora. These divisions are still the framework for commentary and reference in halakhic discourse. One major commentary on the Shulhan Arukh is that of Rabbi Moshe Isserles (sixteenth century Poland), and is a basic source for Ashkenazi halakhah (Caro was Sephardi). Acceptance of the Shulhan

Arukh as authoritative in guiding life symbolizes the adherence to orthodox Judaism in the modern world.

SHUSHAN PURIM: The Purim of Susa. According to the biblical Book of Esther, the Jews of Susa were given an extra day to defend themselves against their enemies. It has therefore become the practice that communities living in ancient walled cities celebrate Purim on the fourteenth of the month of Adar, the day following its celebration in other locales.

SIMHAT TORAH: The Rejoicing of the Torah. A celebration taking place on the last of the festive days beginning with Sukkot. On this day the final portion of the Torah (the end of Deuteronomy) is read in the synagogue, and the yearly cycle begins again with a reading from the beginning of Genesis. It is a widespread custom to assign every (male) member of the community an aliyah on that day, and even to call up, as a group, the young boys who have not reached the age of bar mitzvah. Before the reading, the Torah scrolls are paraded around the synagogue amidst singing and dancing. In general, there is an atmosphere of drama mixed with levity and relaxation during the synagogue celebration.

SUKKOT: The festival of Tabernacles (booths), which takes place on the fifteenth day of the month of Tishrei, in the autumn, and continues for seven days. As in the case of other festivals, an extra eighth day is celebrated in the diaspora. Sukkot follows soon after the solemn holy days of Rosh Ha-Shanah and Yom Ha-Kippurim, and, to a limited extent, shares in their solemnity. The day immediately following Sukkot is an independent festival known as "shmini 'atzeret," which thereby forms an eight-day holiday series, or nine days in the diaspora. The ninth day has a special characteristic and customs, and is known as Simhat Torah. This Torah celebration is merged with shmini 'atzeret in Israel.

TALLIT: The Hebrew word originally referred to a wide, four cornered garment worn in talmudic times. Such a garment must be adorned with fringes, according to the law, and in contemporary Hebrew, based on the Ashkenazi usage, a fringed prayer shawl is known as tallit. In many Sephardi communities the prayer shawl is called "tzitzit" (fringe).

TALMUD: The term is most commonly used comprehensively to include both the Mishnah and the Gemara which developed in the postmishnaic period, but also can refer to the larger work alone. The scholars of the Gemara were known as "amoraim" (who succeeded and elaborated the teachings of the tannaim), and they created the Babylonian Talmud, which took its final form at about 500 c.e. and the Palestinian (Jerusalem) Talmud, which assumed its ultimate shape about a century earlier.

TANAKH: An acronym in Hebrew, referring to what is commonly known as the "Old Testament," reflecting the division of scripture into three levels of revelation-based sanctity: Torah (the Pentateuch), Nevi'im (the Prophets), and Ketuvim (the Writings).

TANNA: A scholar appearing in the Mishnah or parts of the Tosefta. Some of the tannaim (pl.) were reciters of the authoritative texts, which had not been committed to writing.

TEFILLIN (Tfiln in Bobover Yiddish): Phylacteries. Based on biblical verses (for example, Deut. 6:4–9), tefillin, in the form of black cubes made of leather with attached straps, house defined paragraphs of the Bible written on parchment, and are donned on the left arm, facing the heart, and on the forehead. They are normally worn during the morning weekday prayers, a mitzvah incumbent on males from the age of thirteen years. In some North African communities the bar mitzvah ceremony was called to "do tefillin," and the donning of phylacteries is universally recognized as a mark of attaining religious majority.

TENTH OF TEVET: See Ninth of Av.

TORAH (Heb.: teaching): The term in the Bible is one of many referring to God's laws, but in the Second Temple period came to refer to the whole tradition of teachings and laws stemming from divine relevation. Torah was thus envisioned as including the written law (Torah is often translated as "the law") and the oral law. A more restricted use of the term is in reference to the Pentateuch in contrast to the other divisions of the Tanakh. In the synagogue the Pentateuch is read from a Torah scroll, or sefer Torah which must be hand written on parchment or skin. This scroll, which has a decorative covering, is called "the Torah" in Ashkenazi tradition and "the Sefer" in Sephardi tradition.

TOSEFTA: A collection of teachings of the tannaim, which is parallel to the Mishnah. This collection, the various midrashei halakhah (pl.), and scattered tannaitic teachings in the Talmud constitute the baraita.

TU BI-SHVAT: The fifteenth day of the month of Shvat (about February). In the Mishnah this date is recognized as the new year with regard to trees, and the kabbalists of sixteenth-century Safed created an elaborate seder appropriate to the day. The holiday also has achieved prominence in Zionist tradition because of its association with the land.

TZITZIT: Ritual fringes. See Tallit.

YESHIVA: A traditional academy of higher Torah study. First known from the second century in Babylonia, yeshivot (pl.) continue to exist today. They are mostly known for the study of Talmud, but may emphasize other branches of learning as well.

YIDDISH: The Jewish language (called Judeo-German by linguists), which took form in the Rhineland about the tenth century. Its distinctiveness from the neighboring non-Jewish language was shaped by the influence of earlier Jewish languages (Judeo-Romance) and the ongoing religious life of the Jews. Like Jewish languages elsewhere, it was written in Hebrew script. Ashkenazi Jews continued to speak Yiddish when they migrated eastward, so that their language in eastern Europe was basically incomprehensible to the non-Jews surrounding them.

YISHUV: The Jewish community or population of the land of Israel. A distinction is made between the old yishuv, consisting of people living there for religious reasons only, and the new yishuv based on Zionist immigration beginning in 1882.

YOM HA-KIPPURIM (Heb.: The Day of Atonement): Falling on the tenth day of the Hebrew month of Tishrei (in the autumn), which is the seventh month according to the biblical calendar, this day is considered to be the most solemn day of the year. It culminates the central penitential period beginning with Rosh Ha-Shanah on the first of Tishrei. Based on biblical precepts (see, for example, Lev. 16, 23:26–32), it is the day on which the community of Israel, and the individuals comprising it, atone for their sins. Characterized by an elaborate sacrificial ritual in ancient times, it currently involves a day of continuous prayers, featuring penitential themes. It is prohibited to eat and drink during the period from sundown to sundown the following day (there are other restrictions as well—such as on sexual intercourse), prohibitions that are kept by many Jews who are otherwise not concerned with ritual observance. In Ashkenazi tradition it is often called "yom kippur" while the common Sephardi term is "kippur."

ZOHAR: A mystical work composed in the fourteenth century, but attributed to Rabbi Shim'on Bar Yohai, a tanna of the second century C.E. The Zohar relates the ideas of the Kabbalah systematically to the biblical text, and became the central work of that tradition.

Contributors

DR. HARVEY GOLDBERG, Associate Professor of Sociology and Social Anthropology at the Hebrew University of Jerusalem, has done work on the traditional culture of North African Jews and on ethnicity in Israeli society. His books include *Cave Dwellers and Citrus Growers, Greentown's Youth* and he has edited *The Book of Mordechai: A Study of the Jews of Libya*.

DR. YORAM BILU is a Senior Lecturer in Social Anthropology and in Psychology at the Hebrew University of Jerusalem. He has carried out field work on folk-curing among Moroccan Jews in Israel and has published psycho-cultural studies on the basis of traditional Jewish texts. Presently he is engaged in the study of pilgrimages in Israel.

DR. SAMUEL COOPER is a Lecturer in the Department of Sociology and Anthropology of Bar-Ilan University. He has done research on the second generation of immigrants in a Development Town in Israel, and has written on Jewish ethnicity, anthropology and halakhah, and mental illness. He is presently completing a study of psychiatric patients.

DR. TSILI DOLEVE-GANDELMAN is a Researcher at the NCJW Institute for Innovation in Education at the Hebrew University of Jerusalem and a Lecturer at the Technion, Israel Institute of Technology, in Haifa. Her work has concerned rituals in modern contexts, and the perception of the Land of Israel in Zionist ideology. Recently she has done field work among Ethiopian Jewish immigrants to Israel, focusing on integration into the educational structure and on the family structure.

DR. SHIFRA EPSTEIN has worked as Curator of Jewish Ethnography at the Israel Museum in Jerusalem, where she was involved in the documentation and exhibition of the material culture of traditional Jewish communities. She has published both popular and scholarly articles on the celebration of Purim and on the Hasidic Purim play. Currently she is carrying out research on Hasidic women and on Jewish pilgrimages in contemporary Israel.

DR. MENACHEM FRIEDMAN is a Senior Lecturer in the Department of Sociology and Anthropology of Bar Ilan University. His work in the sociology of religion and social history has focused on the reaction of traditional Jewish society to processes of secularization and modernization. His publications include the book *Society and Religion: Non-Zionist Orthodoxy in Eretz-Israel* (in Hebrew), and he is currently completing a study to be entitled *Growth and Segregation—The Ultra-Orthodox Community of Jerusalem: The Poster People.*

DR. BARBARA MYERHOFF was a Professor of Anthropology at the University of Southern California. Among her publications are the books *Peyote Hunt, Number Our Days,* and several co-edited volumes including *Secular Ritual. Number Our Days* was also the basis of an award winning documentary, and a second film, *In Her Own Time,* concerning her research in a Jewish community, was recently released.

DR. RIV-ELLEN PRELL is an Assistant Professor of Anthropology at the University of Minnesota who has written about contemporary American Judaism, particulary on the topics of gender and prayer. She has just completed *Recreating American Judaism: An Anthropology of Contemporary Prayer.* Her current interests focus on religion in complex society.

MR. ZVI ZOHAR directs the Center for Contemporary Halacha at the Shalom Hartman Institute and teaches at the Institute for Contemporary Jewry of the Hebrew University of Jerusalem. He has done work on modern Sephardi halakhah, on the philosophy of halakhah, and has published *Halacha and Modernization in Egypt* (in Hebrew).

Index